COMPUTER-AIDED SOFTWARE DESIGN

COMPUTER-AIDED SOFTWARE DESIGN

BUILD QUALITY SOFTWARE WITH CASE

Max Schindler

WILEY

John Wiley & Sons

New York · Chichester · Brisbane · Toronto · Singapore

Cover art courtesy of IBM, Thomas J. Watson Research Center

Library of Congress Cataloging in Publication Data:

Schindler, Max J.
    Computer-aided software design : Build quality software with CASE
  / by Max Schindler.
       p. cm.
    Includes bibliographical references.
    1. Computer-aided software engineering.   I. Title.
  QA76.758.S35   1989
  005.1 − dc20
  ISBN 0-471-50650-8   89-38138
                                                   CIP

Printed in the United States of America

10 9 8 7 6 5 4 3 2

To Norbert

Grau, teurer Freund, ist alle Theorie,
doch grün des Lebens goldner Baum.*

Goethe, *Faust I*

---

*Dear friend, all theory is gray, but green the golden tree of life.

CONTENTS

PREFACE

In barely more than a decade, computers have turned from corporate marvels into workaday tools. High school freshmen carry in their bookbags more computing power than all humanity could muster during World War II, when the "electronic brain" emerged. Yet megatons of raw computing power are no more useful to people than unmanned bulldozers are to a road crew.

We have learned to mass produce computers whose horsepower ranges from the moped to the bulldozer level, but we have failed to teach people how to "drive" them. Without software that truly matches the user's need, computers will remain somewhat hostile artifacts. Automation in office and factory won't really click until all users can also be programmers. Until then we'll feel frustrated. Remember when the telephone exchanges were automated, yet we had to wait until professionals dialed each long-distance call for us?

Writing software may never be quite as simple as calling a friend in Paris, but it need not be as mysterious as it is now. Nor can we wait until somebody invents touch-tone software. The U.S. economy so depends on computers that the nation can't compete while only a tiny elite knows how to work our most important tools. Now, finally, there's hope. With the advent of CASE (computer-aided software engineering), a new avenue has opened that may eventually bring "software to the masses."

Harnessing computers is already much simpler than when I first got involved with software. That was about 25 B.C. (before CASE), when a previous wave of software "automation" had just captured the limelight. At the time, I made a living by "training" electrons to maneuver deftly in tight beam formations, so that they could relay "The Flintstones" from a satellite to America's living rooms. Since electrons are hard to see, I needed a computer model for my act. Just then, my assembly-language programmer suffered a heart attack.

Fortunately, the lab where I worked had decided to teach engineers Fortran, the language that would "automate programming." I enrolled posthaste, but the instructor barely got through chapter 1 of the User's Manual in that first evening. At this rate I would surely miss my deadlines. So I cornered the teacher after class and explained my quandary. "Which chapters should I study," I demanded, "so I can go to work right away?" I was about to get my first vital lesson in programming.

"Have you built your model and arrived at any solutions yet?" the instructor wanted to know. I was annoyed: "If I had solutions I wouldn't need a computer." My teacher (a physicist himself) shook his head: "You're wrong. Don't even think of using a computer until you have some solutions. So go to work, and by the time you're ready the course will be over."

It took me a while to realize that he was right and that I had been very lucky to learn this lesson up front. In those days, I had to develop my model line-by-line in code, and check it out with a hand calculator—a tedious procedure. Today, CASE tools and rapid prototyping greatly simplify the process, but building and verifying a model still has to precede any "production run," regardless of whether we wish to predict the behavior of tiny electrons or giant corporations.

Since then, I've talked with many students and associates— in physics, engineering, computer science, and publishing—and found that few software novices are put on the right track so early in their pursuit of digital happiness. Often I have been asked to name some good practical texts that will get colleagues up to speed quickly, and rarely have I been able to help.

Of course, professors have produced hosts of books for computer science students. And practitioners have published oodles of articles in journals that cater to their specialties. But neither group writes the kind of book that would have helped me 25 years ago and that would help others desperately seeking software today. Worse yet, the circle of discouraged supplicants is growing by leaps and bounds.

Today, professionals of every calling need computer programs among their tools. They require software that is simple and dependable, elegant and reliable, artful and robust. To generate such tools demands several talents—artistic, scientific, and engineering. But of the three, engineering will be the most important ingredient, because in a tool reliability and dependability are more essential than beauty, elegance, or even simplicity.

Fortunately, the advent of CASE tools will help professionals to leverage their software experience, with an accent on solid engineering. Today's CASE systems, however, are still complex and rather dumb. The software they produce will fall short of expectations if the user lacks an understanding of its inner workings. This book is an attempt to put the problems, solutions and tradeoffs that prevail in the software realm into perspective—in plain English.

To provide first-hand impressions of the CASE tools that are about to mold the way software will be created, I have engaged the help of roughly a dozen CASE vendors, who provided at least partial solutions to a realistic "toy" problem. Much of the credit for this book's ability to illustrate the many choices that confront the modern programmer must go to them. But today's CASE tools don't offer "womb-to-tomb" solutions. They can only perform effectively within the framework of a suitable methodology.

Unfortunately, methodologies keep sprouting like mushrooms. This book follows the simplest one, described by His Majesty when he advised Alice in (software) Wonderland: "Start at the beginning and go on till you come to the end. Then stop." In the software culture, this approach is linked to the so-called waterfall diagram, which will guide you through most of the book's chapters.

Not all topics fit easily into the sequence "Specify, design, implement, test, deliver." Therefore, basic concepts as well as language and management issues are taken up right after the introduction, while advanced topics like standards, parallel computers, and futuristic subjects (say, artificial intelligence) follow the main discussion. Appendixes covering computer history, hardware basics, and software jargon round out the book.

Vital as computer languages are in a software book like this, an author still must rely on English as the communications medium. An extended stint in technical publishing has taught me a few tricks from which the reader should benefit. For example, typographical conventions can greatly enhance clarity and speed up reading. (Don't we all remember texts that create more puzzles than they solve?) To this end, code fragments and identifiers are printed in a monospace font to simulate computer output. Italics, as usual, denote foreign words and emphasis. Bold italics identify terms contained in the glossary and names of companies included in the vendor listing. Each chapter is followed by references, and an authors' cross-index has been added to help you find them more easily.

I wrestled, like most contemporary authors, with the problem of "gender discrimination." Most languages offer a word for "human being" that differs from the term for "male," but English does not. Although a stifled revolutionary in some ways, I decided against a radical solution (e.g., substituting "mensch" or "homo s.") and stuck with the tried and true. So, unless "man" refers to a specific male of the species, it *always* includes men and women in this book. (Myself, I've long since reprogrammed my visual cortex to substitute "person" for "man"). Similarly, "he and she" sounds awkward, except amidst the "Whereases." I personally like Eliza Doolittle's solution: "E" (as in sez I, sez U, sez E). But I'll leave it to literati of stature to spearhead the innovation— since we lack an *Académie Anglaise.*

Let's face it, in a book like this, readability must not be jeopardized. After all, what good is a reader who's fast asleep? Since this book is neither a legal contract nor a scientific treatise, we can leave the verbal stilts in the closet. Having read my share of learned texts, I side with Winston Churchill, who protested (perhaps after stumbling over a "personholecover"): "This is the kind of English up with which I will not put." Neither should you.

⅃ Acknowledgments

This is not a large book by any measure, yet without the right circumstances and the help of many it would have remained a dream. To start at the beginning, I'm greatly indebted to Stephen E. Scrupski, Editor-in-Chief, and Stephan Ohr, then Executive Editor, of Electronic Design. During 1988 they let me present the concepts espoused in the book to an audience of 150,000. The response to this (award-winning) "Software Series" was so favorable that I felt compelled to expand on its concepts. Scrupski also eased the burden of producing this book by letting me recycle much of the artwork.

However, neither the series nor the book would have been possible without the cooperation of many CASE vendors. The bulk of the illustrations in the book comes from the screens of "living" CASE tools. I'm grateful to vendors who took the time to crank a meaningful example through their tool systems. Some spent days, others weeks on this chore, and I sincerely hope the effort will pay off for them.

Like all authors (except for any surviving hermits) I appreciate the patience of my wife, Dudy. She had to bear a nearly two-year disruption of normal family life—first for the Series, then for this book. But unlike most authors I'm indebted to Dudy for much help in researching a number of topics. She is not just a librarian but a driving force in the conversion of New Jersey's school libraries to computerized information retrieval, and I greatly benefited from her labors.

Naturally, many people must contribute their expertise to the realization of a book, from editors to typesetters to reviewers. Among the latter I'm especially indebted to Gene Forte, Executive Editor of CASE Outlook. He went over the manuscript with great care and his unparalleled knowledge of the extremely diversified CASE industry led to many valuable suggestions. I only regret that I couldn't follow up on all of them.

Finally, I must acknowledge that without the help of my faithful PC and an excellent word processor this book would have taken much longer to write, and never could have been as comprehensive. I'm at a loss how people compiled technical books in the past, without the thousands of global searches and consistency checks that only automation makes possible. Now, if we could only automate the reading as well . . .

COMPUTER-AIDED
SOFTWARE DESIGN

1

SOFTWARE SINS—AND DELIVERANCE

Authority, gone to one's head, is the greatest enemy of truth.

Albert Einstein

Troubled software trade
Software mimics hardware
Design methodologies abound
Quickie tour of the bookscape

In an age when computers run nearly everything in our society, many toddlers already know what a computer is. But when it comes to defining **software**, even professionals are often at a loss for words. Of course, the term "software" has been used for a long time (even excluding the kind they once sold in general stores). Software in the technical sense, for example, took the form of wax cylinders for Edison's phonograph and of celluloid strips for movie projectors. More recently, compact discs and computer programs have joined the fray. In other words, software is whatever brings hardware to life. In fact, one popular definition has it that "hardware is the stage, and software is the play."

1

Like most analogies, this one limps a little. A few dozen playwrights can bring all the world's stages to life, but who will write the "plays" for billions of computers? In the U.S. we have about a million programmers trying to feed just the computers in data processing (DP) and management information systems (MIS). They aren't doing so well. In 1981 the average backlog ran 19 months; by 1984 it had crept up to 24 months; and today one hears estimates as high as three years.

If anything, the situation is worse in highly technical applications. For instance, in 1986 the Pentagon spent $15 billion (gigabucks, in proper lingo) on software. By 1988 the number had escalated to $20 billion, and some 1990 estimates go as high as $60 billion. The rest of the federal bureaucracy ran up even higher tabs in years past. If this trend continued, the whole GNP would be soaked up by federal software around the year 2000.

If software has grown into big business, it has also become vital business. By 1985 data processing shops had accumulated 77 billion lines of Cobol code, and expenditures for DP software and services alone had reached $164 billion—a cool 8% of the GNP. With a projected yearly growth rate of 20% to 25% for applications software (now about $8 billion), the GNP fraction might actually run into double digits when the millennium turns.

But the more pervasive and vital software becomes, the less can the troubles of the software trade be ignored. Mistakes of a single character in a large program can cost millions. In fact, the three costliest such blunders reportedly add up to $2.7 *billion*. One was a missing hyphen that destroyed a Venus probe in 1960 at a cost of $18.5 million. (The Russian Mars probe, lost in 1988 due to a single bug, is not included in the total.)

A much-quoted 1982 report from the General Accounting Office asserts that of the agency's $7 million software purchases only 2% were usable as delivered, and another 3% could be fixed up. Fully 30% were never delivered, and a stunning 47% were never used. And that at a time when the average programming backlog ran "only" 17 months. Now it's twice that. To make matters worse, the shortfall of programmers keeps rising, as the number of freshmen aspiring to programming keeps dropping (down 60% from 1984). The Pentagon projects the shortfall to reach one million within a decade unless we learn to crank out software much faster. That has not happened so far. In the three decades starting in 1955, productivity improved only by a factor of 3.6—a measly 4% per year.

It would appear that we have precious little to show for the invention of high-level languages in the 1960s, followed by the advent of "fourth-generation" languages in the 1970s. In fact, many software gurus believe there is little chance of a radical improvement. When Fred Brooks claimed in *IEEE Computer* magazine that there is "No Silver Bullet,"[1] a lively discussion ensued (see the "Letters" section of the magazine's July 1987 issue).

CASE to the rescue.   The situation remained bleak indeed until a new knight in shining armor took center stage in the mid-1980s. He rides under the *CASE* banner and packs a veritable software cornucopia. Will he awaken the sleeping Princess Productivity? She's already stirring, so stay tuned.

Keywords are defined in Appendix C

CASE stands for computer-aided software engineering. But hasn't software creation been computer-aided all along—practically by definition? It is the second half of the CASE name that promises relief. Yet, until recently, the term "software engineering" was considered by many an oxymoron, akin to military intelligence or the Long Island Expressway. After all, engineering is a very structured activity that applies the well-established laws of physics to building tangible, commercial goods. Software, on the other hand, is intangible and based more on creative impulse than on any science. Indeed, many software writers feel closer to Shakespeare or Schiller than, say, to Edison or Ohm.

That is, unless they themselves are engineers. Following the practices of their profession, engineers have looked at software design as an engineering effort all along—an effort that requires precision and careful choices among alternatives. Now this idea is finally catching on outside the technical community, helped along by the CASE buzzword. With popularity, however, comes contempt. What CASE really means—engineering via strict *methodologies*—has almost been rendered meaningless by marketing hype. (Some say the acronym stands for "Can Always Sell Everything.")

To add to the confusion, marketers now peddle more alphabet soup, including UC for "Upper CASE" (the early design phases with an emphasis on management tools) and LC for "Lower CASE" (comprising those stages where the tough work gets done, naturally). These, however, must not be confused with "front-end" and "back-end" CASE, because their bounds differ.

("Front-end" includes detail design, so that "back-end" starts with coding.)

Bewildered? The overview of CASE tools in Figure 1.1 should help maintain some perspective. However, by now there's also "integrated" I-CASE, and CISE (computer-integrated software engineering), not to mention IPSE (the European version of I-CASE). Make no mistake, cradle-to-grave CASE tool integration is essential. Actually, since most CASE tools address the conceptual part of software design, the "womb-to-tomb" designation is gaining favor.

In this book, however, the word "CASE" will be used in its original sense—that is, methodical, semiautomated software construction, using tools that emphasize graphical representations, in the best engineering tradition. What we expect from CASE is not just cheaper code, but above all better code.

Automation is nothing new.   Long before the discovery of software engineering, the concept of software automation was already playing well in America's corporate offices. In fact, the urge to automate replaced machine languages with assembly code in the early 1950s. Data processing was the dominant computer use at the time, and it gratefully embraced the new technology. But, as the statistics prove, the software crunch continued. When the first high-level languages (HLLs) bowed in the late 1950s, the marketing pitch was again automatic programming and higher software productivity. (We'll get back to that issue in Chapter 2.)

But neither the HLLs nor their supposed successors, the 4GLs (fourth-generation languages), turned into the advertised Second Coming. Not even the much-touted "structured-programming revolution" of the 1970s turned the tide. Hope and hype are just not enough. CASE has a better chance; already some recent projects (primarily in the defense industry) have proven that software productivity can indeed be raised by at least a factor of 10 through modular design, careful programming, and reusable code. Still, the CASE millennium will not arrive until software engineering has become as ubiquitous as the computer itself.

With "CASE" turning into a meaningless buzzword, some have already declared software engineering dead. "Industry is doing it, but not talking about it. Academics are talking about

Tool type	Description
UPPER CASE	Helps management interface with customer and staff
Project management	Assists in task breakdown and tracking progress. Simplifies resource allocation and monitoring.
Requirements analysis	Identifies the subject system's functions. Reports on completeness and consistency versus requirements.
Prototyping	Simulates systems based on their specifications, usually to provide early feedback (on specs) from the customer.
Configuration control	Keeps track of software versions and modules. Should also identify all modules affected by any given code change.
LOWER CASE	Helps programmers with software design and debugging
Data/control flow diagrams	Assists in the decomposition of software systems. Simplifies comparison of architecture and detail design alternatives.
Data dictionary	Compiles and cross-references data element (or object) names. Ideally it should tie together all tools in a CASE system.
Simulation	Carries prototyping concepts into the design and implementation phase. Especially vital in real-time systems.
CODE LIBRARIES	Essential for prototyping and automatic code generation. Can reduce programming efforts by orders of magnitude.

Figure 1.1 CASE tools are often grouped into major categories. Borders tend to be somewhat arbitrary, as in this upper/lower separation.

it, but aren't doing it," commented one industry pundit. But if CASE keeps its promise, it may well emerge as the new engine of progress in the developed world. Progress in our "postindustrial" age is fueled by information, just as capital fueled the industrial epoch. Information today means software, and lack of it could lead to stagnation of any high-tech economy or even to chaos. Without the proper software nothing works anymore—even the money stops flowing.

This is not idle speculation. Today about 90% of all purchases are processed by computer. The American stock markets alone transfer over a *trillion* dollars' worth of capital every *day.* We were warned how computer abuse can lead to disaster on October 19, 1987, better known as "Black Monday." But look at the bright side—the West's addiction to half-baked computer technology has probably rendered shooting wars obsolete.[2] An attack by "binary viruses" and well-disguised "Trojan horses" (to be discussed further in Chapter 4) can bring us to our knees.

Fortunately, industry may not be quite as vulnerable to software debacles as high finance, because in a pinch most engineers know how to fix their own software problems. Still, the tedious process of writing and debugging code consumes precious engineering resources that would be better spent designing advanced products and building more productive factories.

For example, over the past decade, the electronics industry had to create a huge stockpile of computer-aided engineering (CAE) software to realize advanced digital circuits in silicon. America's most creative engineers were often tied up for many months converting their ideas into machine-readable code. That slowed the all-important time to market, and our international competitors put the delays to good use.

Why can't such work be turned over to software specialists, permitting hardware designers to design more hardware? This approach has been tried since the dawn of the computer age and, in fact, was a necessity in the days of machine code. But studies have shown that the designers' domain knowledge is hard to pass on to others. So, the most talented professionals keep writing their own software rather than trying to explain their concepts to programmers.

What goes for engineering applies to other domains. Already CAE has acquired many cousins, ranging from CABS (computer-aided brain surgery, no joking!) to CAY (computer-aided yachting), a most serious matter when The Cup is at stake. As computer use spreads, legions of professionals—from brokers to toolmakers—will have to become their own programmers.

Without CASE tools, most would give up in disgust. Fortunately, tools for any taste are rapidly becoming available.[3]

An onerous reputation.   To better gauge the impact of CASE, we must first unmask the culprits responsible for the plight in which the software trade languishes today. We have already pried into the troubled evolution of data processing and engineering software. But less than a decade ago, another force burst upon the scene—a force that has already begun to dwarf both in sheer size and social impact.

We can blame the microcomputer for an entire new culture. Personal computers (PCs) caught the fancy of a whole generation of bright youngsters, and they took up the challenge of teaching these docile new animals some fancy tricks. (For good reason, one of the first personal computers was called PET.) In those days, memory was in short supply, and processors were painfully slow. As a result, the wildest shortcuts—affectionately called "hacks"— were highly prized and rewarded.

This heady atmosphere of creative improvisation has now come home to haunt us. A generation of "hackers" resists exchanging its freewheeling tradition for one of painstaking discipline. In their quest for elegant solutions, these artists of the blinking cursor are fond of citing examples of how discipline and schedules dried up the creative juices of poets and painters past. All too often, the results just reinforce the onerous reputation of software: It is never on time, and it never works properly.*

The whiz kids of the microcomputer age had to write software that was finely tuned to the hardware and not to the user. This original sin of the microcomputer era has contributed mightily to software's bad name, and for good reason. To find examples one need go no further than the package that runs

---

*If book authors were as confident in their output as software authors, each book would begin thus: "By opening this book to ANY page you accept the terms and conditions for using this product as set forth below:

1. The publisher provides no warranty, express or implied, of quality or fitness for any purpose whatsoever.

2. The user assumes full risk for content and accuracy (or lack thereof) of this publication and for any corrections deemed necessary in either syntax or semantics.

3. Under no circumstances will author or publisher be held liable for damages, including lost profits, lost savings, or consequential damages arising from the use of, or the inability to use, this publication.
So help you God."

on practically everybody's desk, and helped create these very sentences: PC-DOS. Luckily, a DOS (disk operating system) usually toils unseen, but some of its utilities are meant to interface with humans. Not that PC-DOS is any worse than other microcomputer software. Quite the contrary—after all, there may well be 20 million copies running worldwide.

One DOS utility, the simple line editor EDLIN, nicely demonstrates the hacker spirit. Assume you have a file of 200 lines and want to erase line 19. According to the manual, the command for deletion has the following form:

```
line-i,△line-j△d
```

Here i indicates where the deletion starts, and j indicates where it ends. The symbol △ signifies a space (to this day few instruction manuals bother to identify the ASCII character "space"). The comma stands for "to", as in "3 to 8 delete." But to speed up the editor, its designers provided shortcuts. For example, 3,8△d can also be typed as 3△8d. To delete line 19, you type either 19△d or 19d. But 1△9△d will erase lines 1 to 9.

Confusing? Just read on. Another feature is the "implied" line number—that is, the line that the editor last worked on. The prompt is an asterisk, which also stands for "current line." So, if the last line on the screen reads *△19d and the current line happens to be line 1, then the first 19 lines of the file vanish when you press Enter. If you tried to delete line 190 in this manner, most of your 200-line file could disappear, and you'd probably never know why. You see, EDLIN ups the ante by automatically (and invisibly) renumbering all the lines after a deletion. Suddenly, your whole program could read

```
1 END
```

Or, take the FORMAT command. If you wanted to format several disks, DOS originally asked you to insert another disk and press any key. It's very easy to hit the space bar or one of the corner keys in the process of, say, picking up the phone or rescuing the baby. (Remember the days when PCs were called home computers?) Since formatting wipes a disk squeaky clean, the results were at times distressing—especially when hard disks became popular. Fortunately, recent DOS versions dispense a dire warning before letting you format a hard disk, and you must now press "Enter" rather than just any key.

Programming for the computer rather than for the user spills over into the documentation. For example, the following "code" comes from the PC-DOS manual shipped by a very big and very reputable American company:

```
RESTORE <d:
[<d:][<path>][<filespec>][/S][/P]
[/B:<date>][p/A:<date>][/E:<time>]
[/L:<time>][/M][/N]
```

Keep in mind, this explanation of the RESTORE command is not meant for computer professionals, but for housewives, managers, and even dentists. In computer science fashion, user-selected identifiers appear within angle brackets, while square brackets indicate optional parts of the command. Never mind that angle brackets are also used in the command syntax. Furthermore, nothing tells you where a space is required (or optional). If you goof, an unfathomable error message like "No such command or file name" provides the machine with a lame excuse to decline further service. No wonder a Passaic, New Jersey man took out his .44 Desert Eagle one September day in 1987 and shot his PC to pieces. (Ironically, the man's name was Case.)

Enter computer science. The last example not only demonstrates a disregard for the user, but the haphazard evolution of PC-DOS software. To stay with *computer science* notation, the RESTORE command smacks of tacked-on <features> [/bells] [/whistles]. The use of the two bracket types in computer science classes was justifiable when instruction manuals were limited to the character set on the teletype keyboard. Today, extensive font choices have become so commonplace that the use of brackets amounts to a pretense of scientific notation where none is needed.

Such a notation, however, represents the first step into a popular concept among scholars: *abstraction*. While abstraction is essential for the analytical (deductive) reasoning of scientists, it can turn from boon to bane by excessive exposure. (Abstraction was once believed to cause "constipation of the mind." Surgeon General, take note).

Like living in space without gravity, living with abstraction can induce *homo sapiens* to lose touch. In fact, research has shown that an individual feels most comfortable at a specific level of abstraction. Going beyond it not only slows down the work, but produces errors to boot. As one researcher put it: "That is the realm where disasters dwell."

In the software world, abstraction levels tend to run unusually high. After all, the dictionary definition for the word "abstract" could almost be the definition for software: "Thoughts apart from material objects." While the physical world imposes the rigorous constraints of nature's laws, in software anything goes. That perceived freedom backfires if designers fail to impose, meticulously, the same constraints on their software models that reality will impose on the real system, in the real world. For example, aerospace designers better make sure that a fighter plane does not drop its missiles while flying upside down. (Indeed, the launch software was fixed only after some costly dented wings).

For the majority of mankind even the lowest level of software abstraction is too high. No wonder software often conforms with the dictionary's second definition for "abstract", namely, "not representing things realistically." A small minority of us—foremost mathematicians—feels at home with pure abstraction. But the number is far too small to fill the widening "programmer gap," especially if those prevail who predict that someday soon everybody will be a programmer of sorts. Half a century ago, futurists predicted that everybody would be turned into a telephone operator of sorts. How right they were!

⅃ Software Parallels Hardware

By relying on graphics, CASE tools tend to minimize abstraction. After all, the "E" stands for engineering, and engineers (like most people) rely much more on inductive than on deductive reasoning. Consequently, they have traditionally preferred the real world of hardware over the abstract and formalistic one of software. In fact, many would like to paraphrase Professor Higgins in *My Fair Lady*: "Why can't software be more like hardware?" It can, and much of this book will prove it. If we review computer history objectively, the parallels become quite obvious. Unfortunately, computer science graduates are unaware of these parallels because they tend to believe that the modern computer results from Boole's formulation of logic, Babbage's discovery of program storage, and Turing's concept of byte-serial computing.

Setting the record straight. In reality, computers have evolved on two separate but intertwined tracks: (1) as calculators and (2) as controllers. (see Appendix A). The former have only one purpose in life: producing some numerical result, which is exactly what Babbage wanted to accomplish. The latter, also known as reactive systems, control machinery like elevators or lathes, and usually get along with grade school arithmetic. Paradoxically, mathematician Boole's logic found its first practical applications in such controllers, as used in telegraphy.

Alan Turing—yet another mathematician—in reality had little impact on the evolution of today's computers outside Great Britain. Nevertheless, Turing enjoys the adulation of his disciples, as expressed in the Turing Award—the most coveted prize in computerdom. It is given out each year by the world's most prestigious computer fraternity, the ACM. This venerable society's full name, Association of Computing Machinery, betrays its age, but it still prides itself in uniting the disparate spheres of computer scientists and practitioners. It's ironic that Turing's scientific heritage has turned out to be a mixed blessing for both groups.

Turing is best known for the Turing machine. This "machine" is a purely conceptual model—what a German mathematician like David Hilbert would have called a *Gedankenexperiment* (thought experiment). The purpose of Turing's research was to disprove Hilbert's conclusions in the *Entscheidungsproblem*.[4] Turing succeeded by breaking computations down into their most elementary steps. He showed that most but not all computations can be performed with a sequence of single-character instructions.[5] This important insight has created a serious problem. Computer scientists still cling to this serial view of programming—a mindset that may well have slowed down software evolution by more years than Turing's contributions advanced it.

Computer science (or "informatics," as the Europeans call it), usually considers itself a mathematical subdiscipline. Traditionally, mathematicians have been developing formulas composed of one-dimensional symbol strings (e.g., differential equations). The step to Fortran code just substituted a new set of (English) symbols for the old (Greek) ones. Engineers, on the other hand, have been thinking in terms of two- or three-dimensional images, such as bridge elevations or flow charts. The battle between these contradictory models of reality rages to this day.

With CASE, for the first time in computer history, the visual representation appears to be winning. The credit must largely go to two groups that have taken on the symbol-string religion of computer science—AI prophets and Cobolites. (If all this sounds like a Holy War, it is.) Researchers in artificial intelligence (AI) were overjoyed when the old teletypes gave way to screens. After all, natural intelligence didn't rely on text strings either.

Mankind has always thought in terms of images—except for the brief period in man's evolution when reading and writing became (or should we say "were") essential social skills. So, the researchers at Xerox PARC and other citadels of AI kept tinkering with languages and interfaces until they had graphics, fancy fonts, windows, and icons—things we view today as integral parts of the computer culture.

Beware of linguini. The second group, commercial data processors, meanwhile got hopelessly entangled in messy patched-up *spaghetti code*. So, DP's high priests declared structured programming their golden calf. Analysts were supposed to draw diagrams that would illustrate the flow of *data*, as well as the relationships between software modules and hardware, and among data groups in databases. But not until the AI school had infiltrated the fledgling PC industry with its graphics (Xerox PARC lies in Silicon Valley, after all), did it become practical to design real-life programs in the structured paradigm. The CASE industry was off and running, and even die-hard mathematicians have had to reckon with the onslaught.

Engineers, of course, are taking to data flow diagrams like ducks to water. Like most of us, engineers were never quite at ease with endless listings of code that so frequently purport to "illustrate" software literature. Engineers prefer flowcharts by far, because they resemble schematics and show how data move through a program. Fortunately, you don't have to be an engineer to understand a simple schematic.

To demonstrate the similarity between computer hardware and software, we'll use elementary schematics, like those showing you how to hook up a stereo system or house wiring. We only need a few symbols—switches, which close one or more circuits, and relays, which throw these switches electrically rather than by hand. In both hardware and software, we'll have Boolean logic operate these switches.

Almost since Boole's time, his logic calculus served to work out the relay circuitry for telegraph systems. These circuits transmitted signals in the form of Morse code, which represents numbers or letters, just as modern computer code does. The Morse code used dots and dashes, while computer code employs zeros and ones. If you like computers and Shakespeare, you might write the Morse-code message "101 00 000 000 11 0 101 01 1 0," which really looks just like machine code. Clearly Binary data are nothing but a special kind of electrical signal.

Now let's route the signals with relay switches. A simple "single-throw" relay like the one in Figure 1.2a can only open or close one circuit and can be described in software terms with this "construct"

```
IF Current > Imin THEN OutSignal = InSignal
```

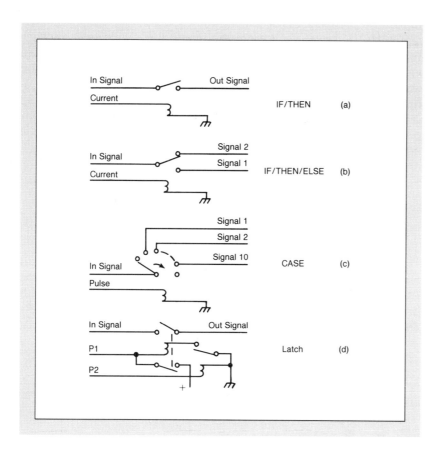

Figure 1.2 Parallels between hardware and software abound. Conditional statements may represent a single-throw (a) or double-throw (b) relay, while CASE statements resemble rotary switches (c). Some DO loops can trace their ancestry to a "latch" circuit (d).

Here, `Current` is the variable that controls the relay, and `Imin` is the current needed to make the relay close the switch. For a "double-throw" relay, which switches a signal between two circuits (as in Figure 1.2*b*), you would have to write:

```
IF Current > Imin THEN Signal_1 = InSignal
                  ELSE Signal_2 = InSignal
```

When telegraphs gave way to the telephone, the relay did not become obsolete. (Even today, relays are still a billion-dollar industry.) The telegraph circuitry simply migrated to the new technology. Instead of two-level currents, the same relays now switched the analog ones that carry speech—at least for a while. Currently, speech is being converted to digital signals again, very much like the Morse code example, only lightning fast. The phone companies apply the same technology that's used in digital audio tapes and compact discs.

With the advent of automatic telephone exchanges, another type of relay evolved—one that could drive a rotary switch (see Figure 1.2*c*). Its purpose was (and, in remote areas from the Ozarks to Timbuktu, still is) to convert the rotary dial's chopped-up currents back into rotation. Its software equivalent would resemble the following, where `PulseNum` is the number of current pulses emanating from the dial:

```
CASE PulseNum = 1: Signal_1 = InSignal
             = 2: Signal_2 = InSignal
                   :
                   :
             = 10: Signal_10 = InSignal
```

Telephone systems also need "latches," which keep a circuit closed when the switching pulses cease (see Figure 1.2*d*). Here, P1 would indicate that a signal line must be closed and that it must stay closed even after the pulse has passed. The latch lets go when another pulse, P2 appears:

```
IF P1 = true
   DO UNTIL P2 = true
       OutSignal = InSignal
       WAIT 1 ms
   END DO
END IF
```

In this code, the DO loop starts executing when the first pulse triggers it, and it keeps going until the second one stops it. Each loop takes a thousandth of a second—technically 1 ms—(plus some negligible machine time) to run. Within a very short time after P2 arrives, the connection between input and output will thus be interrupted. The latched signal can carry control as well as data. It was primarily for such control circuits that designers relied heavily on Boolean logic to minimize the number of relays needed. (You can find exercises of that ilk in old electronics texts.)

Modern computer circuits consist of transistors—which are really nothing but switches. Consequently, these circuits have both relay and software equivalents. Take an AND gate, which can be built with four or five transistors. It is used to compare two bits or to perform a control function (see Figures 1.3*a* and 1.3*b*). In software terms:

Figure 1.3 The Boolean AND was used in relay form (*a*) long before it became a "logic gate" (*b*). Compiled into object code, an AND statement could appear as three bytes, one for the instruction and the others for the operands (*c*). Compiled into silicon, a transistorized version of the AND circuit results (*d*).

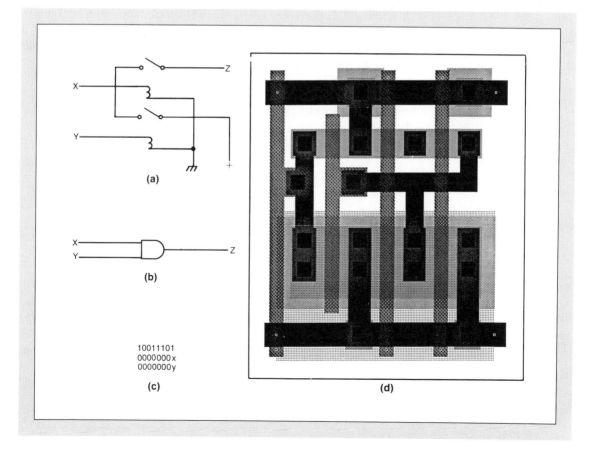

```
10011101
0000000x
0000000y
```

(a)

(b)

(c)

(d)

```
IF X=1 AND Y=1 THEN Z=1
```

Before the hardware can execute this "sentence," a compiler must convert it to object code—that is, the strings of zeros and ones the computer can understand (see Figure 1.3c). Feed the same equation to a silicon compiler (which compiles into integrated circuits instead of object code), and the result will be a pattern of transistors and interconnections (see Figure 1.3d). But both the object code and the transistor circuit perform exactly the same function.

Instead of representing software with switches and relays, let's introduce a universal symbol for software constructs. We'll call it IP (integrated procedure), corresponding to a hardware's IC (integrated circuit). We'll use a rectangular box into which signals flow at the top and from which they leave at the bottom. Controls enter from the side; for the time being they'll just indicate whether a condition (e.g., an IF) is true. The simple IF construct of Figure 1.2a will take the form of Figure 1.4a.

To indicate that only either Signal_1 or Signal_2 can enter into (or emerge from) an IP, these two signals are joined at the box's top (or bottom). The IF/THEN/ELSE circuit of Figure 1.2b thus assumes the IP form of Figure 1.4b. We'll expand on the IP concept in Chapter 6, after which you won't be able to escape the nifty boxes for long.

Hardware spaghetti.   If you have ever seen the innards of a pre-IC computer (or for that matter, an old-fashioned telephone

Figure 1.4 Software can be expressed in these graphs called "IPs," corresponding to hardware "ICs." The two shown here correspond to Figures 1.2a and 1.2b.

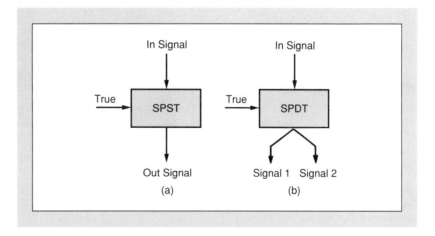

exchange), you know that all those interconnected components create quite a rat's nest of color-coded wires. Suppose a relay had burned out and the telephone mechanic must replace it. How could he make sure that he did not get the wires carrying the control pulses mixed up with those carrying the speech signal (i.e., the data)?

Simple. Touching a wire with his earphone jack, he hears either clicks or talk. Although he may not know it, he performs "type checking." In our software description, any mixup can be simply prevented by adding two lines at the beginning of the "latch" code:

```
DECLARE P1, P2: TYPE Control
DECLARE InSignal, OutSignal: TYPE Signal
```

The importance of type checking becomes more apparent if we assume that the mechanic fixes a numerically controlled lathe, where the "signal" carries 110 or 220 volts AC. Touching the signal wires with an earphone jack could have rather dire consequences for the mechanic. He could rely on the wires' color code, but would probably prefer some stronger type identification—say much heavier wires for the power lines. In software, declarations resembling the two above prevent any mixup and are known under the heavy-handed term "strong *typing*."

A method that's even safer for the mechanic comes to mind right away: put the relay (in this case, called a circuit breaker) in a box with two outlets—one for the power line with an AC socket, the other for the control line with a modular telephone jack. The serviceman no longer has to know what's inside the box; the interface only accepts two types of standards, power and control. In electrical wiring, such standardized interfaces are not only commonplace, the force of law usually stands behind them.

Modularity über alles.   In software we are still rather careless. Only the defense community adheres to any kind of software "building code." It didn't go into effect until 1987, in the form of a Pentagon edict that requires vendors to deliver Ada code (more about that in Chapter 2), which means you must encapsulate your code modules and define their interfaces—or you won't get paid. Computer science labels such encapsulation with the rather bizarre term *information hiding*. This formulation, in turn, led to the programmer's Golden Rule: "Disclose as little as possible." So much for *glasnost* in software. (To help you get past the jargon Appendix C, the "Jargonauts' Catechism," craves to come to your assistance.)

The box-like IP we introduced earlier provides a perfect vehicle for encapsulation. To be perfectly honest, that's the IP's primary *raison d'être*. Encapsulation (or modularization) is nothing new. At least in the early design stages, both hardware and software engineers have always applied it, sketching the main components of a system as interconnected boxes (as you'll see in Chapter 6). In fact, to decide how a design can be subdivided into simpler **tasks** is often as hard as it is vital. Once again, hardware and software are treated very much alike, with one difference: hardware designers don't talk about levels of abstraction or information hiding.

When laying out a hardware system, it is usually helpful to have a fabrication method in mind. Which parts of the system will be built from standard components, and which will be implemented as custom, or application-specific, ICs (also called ASICs)? How many circuit boards will be needed? What kind of bus will be best?

Software is no different. Trying to design a software system without understanding the "production" method—how and where the software will execute—is a somewhat academic exercise. True to their faith in abstraction, academics (especially AI scholars) insist that software must be conceived without any regard to the hardware. Tell that to designers of embedded systems, where software and hardware are so intimately intertwined that any "abstraction" must apply to the whole system. (More about this in Chapter 9.)

In fact, some of the CASE methods we shall discuss later start off developing a system's hardware and software as a single entity. However, sooner or later tradeoffs between hardware and software must be made. Experience suggests that sooner is better, lest tradeoffs in the software part turn into ugly fixes. All too often the resulting jumble of patches all but obscures the code's original function, while inviting future disasters to boot. Sadly, the number of programmers trying to unravel exactly this kind of mess in Cobol programs worldwide probably exceeds a million gifted professionals. What a waste.

⅃ Methodologies Galore

In the preceding paragraphs we have subscribed (albeit implicitly) to the favored design methodology for hardware as well as software—top-down decomposition. It is a well-proven approach, but it must not be taken to extremes. For example, it makes no sense to decompose a major design problem in any engineering discipline without first understanding how it can be solved (in software, choosing the main algorithms); what building blocks already exist (reusable code); and in what environment the solution will be placed (human and machine interfaces).

Assume for a moment you are roughing it at your remote cabin on the Alaskan Peninsula. Your radio went on the fritz,* and you missed warnings about a neighboring volcano threatening to erupt. When you hear ominous rumblings, you hike to a neighbor's house, but she's gone. From her cabin you call the general store in King Cove, but no one answers. Now you feel the same urgency that grips many a programmer in the defense industry. You both need vital results in a hurry. Would you construct a speedboat from scratch (top-down) in the King Cove boatyard?

Bottoms up.   Such scenarios are grist for the mills of the bottom-up school. Its disciples insist that software should be built from tinkertoys, which is probably the way you would want to improvise a motorboat—from existing components. (Hopefully, you'll find them in the abandoned King Cove marina). Not only will you reach your goal much faster, but you can be fairly certain that an existing outboard engine will really work (albeit after a little tinkering).

In software, too, a part that has already been tested and proven in actual use will likely get you to the finish line faster than a new solution, no matter how ingenious. Especially for software with a great deal of hardware interfaces (e.g., an operating system), the bottom-up approach seems to work best.

More often than not, however, good software results from the "sandwich" (or layer cake) method, a hybrid of top-down and bottom-up design. You will certainly have an "architectural" concept in mind before you rig up your evacuation vessel. There is a price to pay: sandwich aficionados must watch out for frayed edges in the middle, where the two approaches meet. If you only find an inboard hull without the engine and an outboard engine without a prop, you're in trouble. The more sophisticated your

---

*Rumor has it the original Fritz was a Radio Mechanic Third Class.

software project is and the more it relies on prepackaged method-ologies, the more elusive a smoothly structured hybrid design will be. Just polishing the interfaces of "reusable" software boosts their cost by 20% to 40%.

Many experienced programmers never choose a design methodology consciously. They often have the whole "script" clearly in their heads before they touch a keyboard; then they just start writing code, as Mozart did. This approach may work well for a genius or for PC-type programs that don't exceed 1000 lines (or about 20 pages). Only rarely do several programmers cooperate closely on such programs. At least not for long—reports about lasting friendships between hackers appear to be greatly exaggerated.[6]

Software for a telephone system or an airplane is a different matter. For example, the space shuttle's flight software exceeds half a million bytes in object code. Designers of the ATF (advanced tactical fighter) even project a million lines of source code in the cockpit (four times as much as the F16) and 10 million on the ground. Obviously, such a system requires the teamwork of a whole orchestra of designers. Just as obviously, their program-ming style must be much more formalized than that of a soloist or a trio.

Indeed, programmers who are used to PC-level software devel-opment have a great deal of trouble with the concept of "indus-trial-strength" software. In a 1987 interview, software genius and Borland founder Phillipe Kahn asserted: "Programming is a labor-intensive activity, suited to a small group of the most talented professionals working in a given area—not an army of **software engineers**, each of whom can only address a small piece of the puzzle."[7] Well, in a classified project programmers aren't even *per-mitted* to know more than a very small piece of the puzzle.

Some readers who practice "in-the-small" programming undoubtedly will regard some of the techniques discussed in this book as extreme. At the same time, "in-the-large" programmers may consider some discussions too superficial. Hopefully, they will immerse themselves in the literature that follows each chapter. The references serve only to lead the reader to additional information—not to prove a point, or to scratch a colleague's back.

Certainly some will feel that their favorite methodology has been given short shrift, and they will be right. This book addresses the problems of software design from a CASE perspective, and since nearly all commercial CASE products follow the top-down **paradigm**, this method will dominate.

However, the following brief overview of alternative methodologies should help to restore some balance to the discussion.

Tool baskets.   First, a disclaimer: in software parlance, a methodology is not a study or classification of methods, as the dictionary would have it. Rather, a methodology constitutes a basket of design tools, chosen and interconnected in such a way that between them they can cover a substantial part of the design process. One could almost say that a methodology is a software development paradigm, were it not for the fact that the dictionary defines a paradigm as an example or epitome. Software people use the word "paradigm" more in the sense of a plan or a general concept—a *Weltanschauung.*

Methodologies range from the hacker's view of "inspiration plus some debugging tools" to the rigid "analyst and coding sheet" approach still popular among many data processing professionals. As we have seen, the failure of this primeval DP method gave rise to the first viable methodology—namely, structured design. Advocated by computer science sage Edsger Dijkstra and his colleagues, the methodology initially was known as "GOTO-less programming." After a decade of seminars and hype, *structured* came to mean simply "with it." So, structured software development was joined by structured review (or walkthrough), structured management, and even structured cooking.

What the apostles of structuring really meant was systematic, data-oriented design, as advocated by Tom DeMarco and Edward Yourdon. Indeed, structured design is still widely known as the Yourdon-DeMarco methodology. Its trademarks are data flow diagrams (or bubble charts), which will become your constant companions throughout this book. For data processing, competing (or, more accurately, complementary) systems evolved, such as the Chen methodology, which relies on entity relationships, or the Jackson methodology, where data structures play a dominant role. In fact, too many methodology variants developed in the DP community to mention them all.[8-10]

Perhaps some later DP solutions to the software dilemma should also be called methodologies. As mentioned earlier, the still controversial 4GL subculture burst on the scene just as structuring ran out of steam. It hopes to boost software productivity by means of fourth-generation languages, which are also (perhaps more properly) known as database languages. Born on mainframes, they are running even on PCs today. Thus, 4GLs form a vital part of what we might call the spreadsheet programming paradigm, which is very effective in its narrow niche.

Billions and billions.   Data processing, with its voracious appetite for software (purchases plus in-house development probably exceed $200 billion a year), still represents the biggest chunk of the software industry. No wonder that it also lures CASE vendors irresistably into its orbit. In 1988 U.S. firms spent about $5 billion on DP–related CASE hardware and software, which by 1992 will double to $10 billion. (Hardware generally outruns software by at least 2:1.) According to the same study, the majority of users expect to recover their investment in two to four years.[11]

At a projected growth rate of 15% to 18% per year, Japan's software industry may soon overtake ours in terms of sheer financial muscle. It has chosen a somewhat peculiar approach with its *software factories*. There, CASE methodologies *do* play an important role, but they are proprietary and, consequently, little known. Although more responsive to individual users today than they used to be, the factories nevertheless accentuate software reuse and standard packages. But then, as the legendary success of the Lotus 1-2-3 spreadsheet implies, custom-made software is often no more essential than custom-made gloves.

While in software one size may not fit all, how many accounts receivable programs does the world really need? The software factories' dedication to quality and reliability is far more important than humoring every customer's whim. However, let us beware. Once Japan's software houses have zeroed in on a versatile CASE methodology, they will pose a formidable threat to America's software primacy.

A standard methodology must, however, be powerful enough to accommodate more than DP or MIS (management information systems) software. It must take the growing importance of embedded software into account as well. No fewer than half the processor chips sold today wind up in embedded applications, which range from toasters to ocean liners.

We observed earlier how such software applications have grown, not only in number but also in complexity. No wonder that an exploding number of CASE vendors lusts after the spoils, which are expected to reach a billion dollars by 1992—about one-third of it software. But there is a small problem: conventional structured methodologies can't handle the time-sensitive nature of embedded software.[12]

Shuttle bugs.　You may recall the many delays in the launch of the space shuttle Columbia. Real-time software carries its share of the blame. During launch tests, for example, synchronization errors led to some hasty patches, one of which could have spelled disaster during the actual launch. A few seconds before liftoff of Columbia's maiden voyage the launch was aborted due to—as the bulletin had it—computer failure. The story behind that story illustrates the intractability of real-time bugs.

For safety's sake, the shuttle's avionics software runs on two redundant pairs of computers. But the many problems encountered during system tests raised this issue: "What if a bug remains in one of the vital routines? We can't safeguard against it because both computer pairs execute identical programs." Late in the game though it was, a fifth computer was added to execute functionally identical but totally rewritten backup flight software. If the two systems disagreed, the launch was to be aborted.

All worked well during tests; however, just before the launch, the backup computer found that no sensor data were being passed within the control hardware, and the launch was promptly scrubbed. The cause was faulty synchronization. The data were moving correctly, but whenever the main computers talked, the backup wasn't listening. It took some time to nail the bug because the faulty subroutine had worked well in an earlier application. Someone had just forgotten to reset a constant.

How do you guard against such surprises? Traditional data flow diagrams of the Yourdon-DeMarco variety were never meant to handle timing problems. To penetrate the aerospace business, CASE vendors patched in real-time methodologies, such as the Ward-Mellor or the Hatley-Pirbhal (also known as Boeing-Hatley) methods, which add control flow to the data flow diagram. You will get to know them quite well in Chapter 9, when we solve a real-time problem of our own.

⌐ Express Tour of the Bookscape

If you followed the preceding discussion closely, you may have gleaned the basic organization of the book from scattered references to other chapters. Actually, the book's layout is quite simple. After this introduction there follows a chapter on software history, aimed at dispelling some widely held misconceptions and charting the evolution of today's procedural languages.

A growing number of CASE systems provide automatic code generation, at least to the level of language-specific templates. But you still must select the language(s) best suited to the job at hand. The language comparison in Chapter 3 quickly reveals that some of today's leading computer tongues are definitely more equal than others. For manual coding (which will stay with us for some time), the choice of a common "mother tongue" heavily impacts programming style and communications within the design group. Since language idiosyncracies can affect the whole software life cycle, it is best to tackle language choice early on.

This selection is, in fact, one of the dominant management concerns—issues that are scrutinized in the final introductory section, Chapter 4. After all, cost estimates must be prepared by the project manager regardless of methodologies and CASE tools used. Furthermore, project plans need to be drawn up to include not only budgeting concerns but quality control and security measures as well.

Code is to a software system what schematics are to hardware, and it should be treated with the same care and circumspection. Version control is as essential to an industrial CASE system as it has always been to any sizeable engineering organization. This is one management function that software groups all too often brush aside—at their own peril.

Journey down the waterfall.   After the introductory chapters, the book follows what's known in the software trade as the *waterfall* diagram; a glance at Figure 1.5 amply explains how it got its name. Although much maligned of late, the waterfall model still remains valid. Like any other product, commercial software starts with a requirements specification (Chapter 5). The "spec" could simply state, "Build a spreadsheet optimized for software designers," or it could comprise 50 pages. (If it's for the government, make that 50,000 pages. Even the "civilian" spec for the Boeing 747 flight management software took up 15 volumes at up to 900 pages apiece.)

As an alternative, buyer and seller can settle on a program definition via prototyping. Next the chief designer (who goes by many pseudonyms) must find one or more ways to approach the task and work out how to break it down at the architectural level (this will be discussed further in Chapter 6). Both the techni-

Figure 1.5 Software design differs little from the design of physical products. This "waterfall" diagram represents traditional development phases.

cal (or formal) specification and the architectural design remain closely linked with project management. After all, until you know what pieces you have to build, it's hard to hang price tags on them.

In Chapter 7 we'll apply the methods developed in the previous chapter to a design example called G-Train. This permits us to probe the architectural design alternatives in more detail and to develop a realistic rapport with available techniques. The G-Train also provides continuity when we explore a variety of CASE systems in later chapters. Since the example does not represent a step in the waterfall diagram, you might regard this chapter as an appendix to Chapter 6, dictated more by pragmatism than logic.

Usually, architectural design with CASE tools leads directly to detail (or algorithm) design (Chapter 8). CASE tools can assure that the software modules into which a system has been divided fit together properly, without any clashes between data structures or types. Some examples, including the one from Chapter 7, serve to clarify algorithmic concepts.

From here on, many of the solutions are played out on different CASE systems. Partial implementations of the G-Train subsystems take up Chapters 8 to 11, sometimes including code generation and simulation. But especially for the latter, an alternative to conventional software design has lately been catching on, flying the flag of object-oriented programming. Since different CASE systems emphasize different aspects of the software life cycle, the orientation chart of Figure 1.6 should prove helpful.

Chapter 12 is dedicated to a tour of "descriptive" languages, which also drive the brilliant (and sometimes whacky) world of artificial intelligence. If procedural languages tend to encourage chauvinism, descriptive ones may invite religious strife. In fact, object-oriented programming (OOP) has been labeled both cureall and snake oil. We shall treat OOP as just another tool and remember that a fool with a tool still remains a fool.

Nevertheless, Chapters 13 and 14 will demonstrate that alternate approaches enrich the software design process. In

Figure 1.6 The chapters dealing with specific design phases are summarized in this chart. Full-white boxes indicate primary and half-white boxes secondary emphasis. Chapter 7 introduces the "G-Train" example.

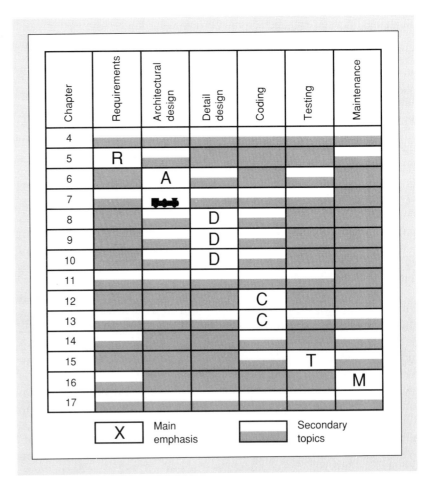

Chapter 13 the G-Train takes flight on the wings of OOP, while Chapter 14 presents a solution that mixes AI concepts with "software math." The latter approach comes as close to a "provably correct" implementation as today's technology can provide.

No matter how the working code—a software project's "product"—comes about, tests must be performed on individual components, subassemblies, and the complete system. Test procedures differ from hardware primarily by the absence of "environmental tests"—that is, cooking, freezing, and shaking the product until it comes apart. But software also works within an environment, and failure to test for its impact has led to many a software disaster. As Chapter 15 reveals, CASE tools can help with component testing and system integration as well, even making the latter one fairly automatic.

In fact, some CASE disciples maintain that software tests eventually will become superfluous because code "never touched by human hands" will be true by axiom. But even if CASE tools eventually produce error-free code, a commercial customer will no more accept a software product sight unseen than, say, a drill press. At the very least, tests must ensure the code's compliance with the spec, as well as its correctness. Such tests are formally known as validation and verification (or V&V) and they tend to be contractually required for industrial-strength software. Only after thorough testing is a software package ready for "production."

Along a different track.   At this point, the construction of abstract (software) products begins to diverge from that of concrete (hardware) products—not because software is more complex than hardware, but because software corresponds only to hardware's blueprints. The "production" step actually takes place inside the customer's computer, especially if the deliverable program consists of human-readable source code that the user's compiler transforms into machine-readable *object code*.

Only when the latter is executed does any production (namely, of output data structures) take place. Here, standards (to be discussed in Chapter 18) become vital since they can eliminate the hardware-dependent compilation step—for example in the case of the standardized PC-DOS interface. Such software can undergo meaningful evaluation without much concern about the customer's computer.

The waterfall model's last phase, usually called "maintenance," must deal with another difference between software and hardware: software does not wear out (even though it sometimes self-destructs*). The bottom basin deserves a better moniker that does not blend so many ingredients. The biggest concern of maintenance is the correction of undiscovered errors that surface during operation. More often than not, these "bugs," however, turn out to be misinterpretations of the spec rather than coding mistakes. In fact, once the CASE millennium has arrived, all errors will be either such misunderstandings or those ghastly algorithmic blunders that probably account for most software mayhem even now. Imagine an F16 test pilot, waiting for takeoff clearance. He passes the time by checking out various functions of the on-board computers. When he presses the button that raises the plane's landing gear, the computer faithfully obliges. Ridiculous? A maintenance mechanic actually experienced such a rather disheartening—and costly—"letdown."

The most common "maintenance" function, however, is really the addition of enhancements (also known as "creeping featurism"). Obviously, the only safeguard against this curse is strict adherence to the requirements specification (provided it doesn't promise the impossible). Reverse engineering tools should lighten this burden because they will permit the reconstruction of requirements from the end product. Maintenance issues will be discussed in Chapter 16.

At this point we'll have examined the capabilities of nearly a dozen representative CASE systems. Chapter 17 provides us with an opportunity to summarize our observations and draw some conclusions about the strengths and weaknesses of the discussed systems and about the status of the whole CASE culture. Checklists will help you to choose those CASE tools that best suit your specific applications.

Chapter 18, which deals with present and coming standards, will explore by what means tools from different vendors are (or will be) able to communicate. CASE tools impose tough requirements on the underlying system software, rather more subtle than the demands of PCs and local area networks. A number of groups, representing vendors, users, and government agencies (the biggest user of them all), are hard at work defining

---

*Even before viruses began to contaminate the realm of computers, code degradation affected performance. While I evaluated a "loaner" PC equipped with a hard disk, the resident word processor mysteriously slowed down after some use, and then lost feature after feature. In the end I resorted to a floppy to finish the assignment. The most likely cause: bugs in the package that affected memory pointers as I "stress-tested" the system.

the required interfaces, data structures, and even terminology. For good measure, standards developed by professional societies such as the IEEE will also be discussed.

The final two chapters deal more with the future than with the present. Chapter 19 scrutinizes software design for tomorrow's computers. The rapid emergence of multiprocessor systems will saddle users with the problem of finding the sources of errors when dozens—or perhaps even thousands—of program segments execute simultaneously. Of course, even more helpful will be measures that avoid these nasty problems from the start. There is no time to be lost; multiprocessor machines are already fighting over the most lucrative turf.

Chapter 20 looks at the more remote future—primarily at work still brewing in university and industry labs. AI often sets the pace in this research, but other voices must also be heard. New miracle cures for software ills surface regularly, and some are gaining ground. Even if they have proven their value only in academe on small and specialized tasks, missionaries stand ready to convert you. To be prepared, you should know as much about them as possible. Understanding the difference between salvation and snake oil in the software realm can be quite a challenge.

Beyond the waterfall.   By following the waterfall model we can explore most software topics in a logical sequence. But critics like to emphasize the model's shortcomings, sometimes in efforts to advance less-proven schemes. However, no model can hope to fit all occasions.

In real life the unexpected has a way of messing up man's best-laid plans. If, for example, a problem with timing pops up halfway into the architectural design phase, the project returns to the requirement phase. More often still, bugs can force a project back to square one when they creep out of the woodwork during testing or worse yet, in the field. One company had installed dozens of systems when one crashed repeatedly and fatally: all tape drives rewound simultaneously. After much fruitless digging in the operating system, the culprit was found outside the computer. Whenever one bright light was switched on, it triggered all the end-of-file sensors! It's doubtful that any amount of forethought could have prevented this fiasco—the tape drives were from a reputable company.

To account for all eventualities, the waterfall diagram is often adorned with many a feedback path—until it resembles a

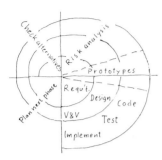

baroque facade more than a waterfall. Some sages have simply declared the whole waterfall model obsolete, replacing it with more complex ones. Best known perhaps is Barry Boehm's spiral model.[13] It breaks down each of the waterfall basins into a number of phases: determine objectives; assess risks; prototype the concept; implement the concept; and verify the implementation. So the model wanders around in a spiral until it winds up at maintenance. We prefer the simple waterfall, because it provides a straightforward road map. If you get lost, just return to the previous box.

Commitment to the waterfall does not mean that other routes will be ignored in this book. Because unambiguous specifications are so hard to accomplish, a technique called "rapid prototyping" is gaining favor. You will find it discussed in Chapter 5, which treats the requirements phase, and in Chapter 16, which discusses reuse. Prototyping has been incorporated in commercial CASE systems and easily meshes with graphic design methods. After all, prototyping should primarily serve as a vendor-user interface; efficient production code still must be generated and tested in the traditional way.

Some take an opposite approach to the requirements problem. They favor "executable specifications," a way to convert the requirements automatically into machine code. If the program does not work as it should, you fix the spec, not the program. Someday this idea may work, as one of the solutions (in Chapter 14) illustrates.

Still, for the next 50 years or so, corrections after software delivery will remain a fact of life. But that's no reason to relax on the quality front. Software vendors should study the automobile industry. It used to be understood that you took a new car back to the dealer until everything worked. Only when imports had eaten into their markets did domestic car makers find ways to fix bugs *before* shipping the product.

The European Economic Community (EEC) has been pouring untold millions into software tools, which are known there as software design automation (SDA) or integrated project support environment (IPSE). The essential attribute of an IPSE is a common database for all tools—not yet a common trait among CASE systems. In addition, five EEC countries have embarked on an ambitious 2500 man-year project to develop the "Eureka Software Factory" within 10 years. Germany has also launched a program for software quality certification (see p. 31), following the pattern set by Japan's mighty MITI (Ministry for International Trade and Industry).

But competition is gearing up everywhere, from huge countries like China and India, to tiny ones like Hungary, Ireland, and Singapore. So far the impact is small, but it won't be for long if India's 40% annual growth rate persists. Let's hope U.S. software firms wake up before they become one more endangered American industry.

SOFTWARE

Gütezeichen RAL

⅃ References

1. Frederick P. Brooks, "No silver bullet: essence and accidents of software engineering." *IEEE Computer*, April 1987, p. 10.

2. Thierry Breton and Denis Beneich, *Software*, Holt, Rinehart, and Winston, New York, 1985.

3. Gene Forte, Ed., *1988 CASE Industry Directory*, CASE Consulting Group, Portland, OR, 1988.

4. Alan Turing, "On computable numbers, with an application to the *Entscheidungsproblem*," *Proceedings of the London Mathematical Society*, 1936.

5. Robert Slater, *Portraits in Silicon*, MIT Press, Cambridge, MA, 1987.

6. Susan Lammers, *Programmers at Work*, Microsoft Press, Redmond WA, 1986.

7. Max Schindler, "Coding languages to change little as libraries offer reusable code," *Electronic Design*, January 7, 1988, p. 96.

8. Alan S. Fisher, *CASE: Using Software Development Tools*, Wiley, New York, 1988.

9. E. J. Chikofsky, Ed., *Computer-Aided Software Engineering (CASE)*, IEEE Computer Society Press, Washington, DC, 1988.

10. Albert F. Case Jr., *Information Systems Development*, Prentice-Hall, Englewood Cliffs, NJ, 1986.

11. Victoria Hinder, Ed., *Software Development Automation: 1987. Vol. 1: Analysis*, The Technology Research Group, Boston, 1988.

12. C. R. Vick and C. V. Ramamoorthy, Eds., *Handbook of Software Engineering*, Van Nostrand Reinhold, New York, 1984.

13. Barry Boehm, "A spiral model of software development enhancement," *ACM Sigsoft, Software Engineering Notes*, August 1986, p. 14.

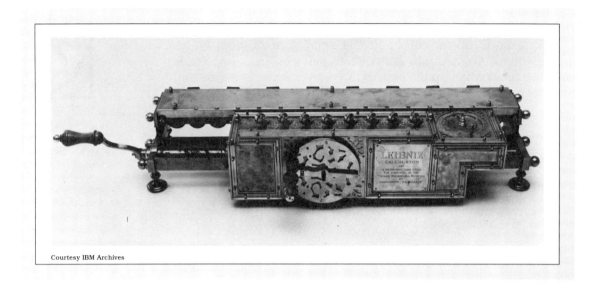

Courtesy IBM Archives

In 1694, Leibniz built this remarkable machine, which performed not only the four basic arithmetic functions, but also took square roots.

2

COMPUTER LANGUAGES— ORIGIN OF THE SPECIES

More than iron, more than lead, more than gold I need electricity . . . I need it for my dreams.

Racter (A computer program)

Early software counts on holes
Evolution speeds after Eniac
Languages for the PC era

In a domain as huge as that of computing we must know where we come from to understand where we are going. We study history not just for entertainment, but to avoid repeating past blunders. If you know software history well enough, you may wish just to scan this chapter swiftly. [1]

But you should still peruse Appendix A, "A Stereoscopic View of Computer History." It sets the record straight on pioneers from Atanasoff to Zuse, and it shatters the revolutionary picture of the computer's development that historians have painted. The computer was not propelled forward in big leaps by wizards like

Boole, Babbage, and Turing; rather, computers evolved slowly over the centuries. More importantly, they evolved on two distinct tracks: calculation and control.

On the calculation side, most of us are familiar with Blaise Pascal and his mechanical reckoner built in 1642 (see Figure 2.1). But the computer's unfamiliar controller ancestry, dating back even further, had a much deeper impact on present software than anything Pascal did. Actually, the only software he ever produced was created with pen and paper, purely for human consumption. And it set the direction of French literature for a century.

However, when evangelist John asserted "In the beginning was the word," he was not talking about the genesis of computer software. In *its* beginning were punched holes—long before IBM cards and the punched film strips Zuse used for programming his computers as far back as 1936. We are not even talking about the punched cards Babbage would have used had he ever finished his Analytical Engine. The holes we are referring to were punched nearly two centuries ago by French prodigy Jean Marie Jacquard.

If that surprises you, you're not alone. Most computer historians have ignored the fact that Jacquard invented the first programming language. It had the form of "microcode" and ran

Figure 2.1. Pascal's 1642 calculator, widely acclaimed as the first computer, only performed additions. The mechanism resembles that of today's odometers.

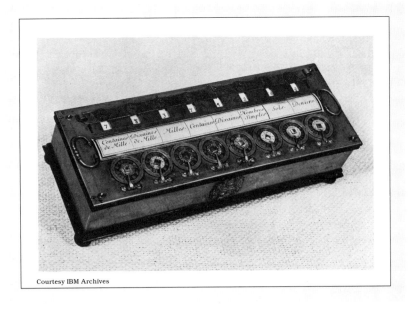

Courtesy IBM Archives

a computer that automated weaving looms resembling the one in Figure 2.2 (for more detail see Appendix A). But Jacquard's machine could crank out only patterned fabrics and tapestries, not numbers. His was a control computer, which doesn't count for much among mathophilic computer scientists—even though they lay claim to automata theory. What Jacquard had built certainly qualifies as an automaton with finite states.

Automata were indeed popular long before Jacquard (or even Pascal), but his was the first one to use binary programming technology. Considering that it produced patterns, Jacquard's loom controller could even be called the first binary graphics system—centuries before an unknown AI researcher built the second one. The concepts are alike except that Jacquard's punched cards instructed a *mechanical* processor to produce green, weave white, make stripes, alternate red and blue. A Jacquard card might contain this instruction: make herringbone with 200-thread repeat, 100-thread taper. That's essentially the kind of information punched into an IBM card with the following Fortran command:

```
PRINT ((I(M,N)M=1,100),N=1,200)
```

Jacquard's programs were large by any standard. Indeed, it would take 150 years before program decks with 25,000 cards would be amassed once more.

The only other early "computer" to use any kind of programming would have been Babbage's Analytical Engine, had it ever gotten that far. Babbage's "programs" should perhaps rightly be called algorithmic macros. For example, c (a + b) would be broken down as follows:

$$V1 + V2 = V4$$

$$V3 \cdot V4 = V5$$

where V1, V2, and V3 represent the starting variables a, b, and c, V4 is an intermediate variable, and V5 is the result.

Another first programmer. Babbage's alleged software assistant, Countess Ada of Lovelace, was awarded the title of "world's first programmer" by the Department of Defense (DoD)

Figure 2.2. The eighteenth-century control computer built by Jacquard fits today's French term "ordinateur" (*a*). Its programs closely resemble recent IBM decks (*b*). Each of these holes causes a group of threads to be raised, resulting in bit-mapped "cloth graphics" from table linens to tapestries. (*Part (a) courtesy of IBM Archives.*)

in 1979. (A new DoD language would be named after her, which we'll examine a little later.) Anyway, Ada died in 1852, when only the processing "mill" of the Analytical Engine existed. The only person other than Babbage who could actually have programmed the machine was his oldest son, Herschel. (Thank DoD for not saddling us with a language called Herschel.)

Ada was familiar enough with the design to develop a "program," but no evidence exists that she ever did more than explain to Babbage's friends how the problem of calculating Bernoulli's numbers would be solved (see Figure 2.3). Even this simple feat amazed many, because back then abstraction was believed to be too strenuous for a woman.

So who was this *wunderkind* Ada? None other than the only daughter born to Lord Byron and his wife, née Annabella Milbanke, on December 10, 1815. (Not by coincidence, MIL-STD 1815, which defines the Ada language, was released on her birthday 165 years later.) When Ada was just a few months old, her poet father took refuge on the continent, never to see his Ada again. Her mother (whose mathematical inclinations Ada inherited) brought her up to despise her father, and only in her last year did Ada get to know his poetry ("Ada, sole daughter of my house and heart . . . .").

Lady Byron's household must have been a cheerless one. Ada was unable to walk from age 14 to 17 (apparently for psychosomatic reasons), while she studied math, languages, and music, becoming an accomplished violinist. At age 20, she married Lord King, the later Earl of Lovelace. Widower Babbage, whose acquaintance she had made during her studies, was a frequent guest at the King estate. Ada was about the age Babbage's daughter Georgianna would have been had she lived. It stands to reason that Babbage readily accepted the father figure role Ada apparently bestowed on him, probably reinforcing their ties of common intellectual interests.

In the beginning Ada, by all accounts, greatly admired and respected the inventor and academician. She grew bolder after she had established herself as a kind of public relations agent for him. She documented his work, studied the literature for him, and in 1842 translated and annotated an article about the Analytical Engine by Italian mathematician Menabrea. (As is so often true, the prophet was recognized abroad earlier than at home.) However, Ada's interest in Babbage's work may not have been of a purely scientific bent.

After her third child was born in 1844 Ada suffered a nervous breakdown that led to an escalating dependence on drugs and

Number	Operation	Input Variables	Output Variables	Change in Variables' Values	Results	Data				
						$^1V_1$	$^1V_2$	$^1V_3$	$^0V_4$	$^0V_5$
						$\boxed{1}$	$\boxed{2}$	$\boxed{n}$	$\square$	$\square$
1	$\times$	$^1V_2 \times {}^1V_3$	$^1V_4, {}^1V_5, {}^1V_6$	$\left\{\begin{matrix}^1V_2 = {}^1V_2 \\ {}^1V_3 = {}^1V_3\end{matrix}\right\}$	$= 2n$	. . .	2	n	$2n$	$2n$
2	$-$	$^1V_4 - {}^1V_1$	$^2V_4\ldots$	$\left\{\begin{matrix}^1V_4 = {}^2V_4 \\ {}^1V_1 = {}^1V_1\end{matrix}\right\}$	$= 2n-1$	1	. . .	. . .	$2n-1$	. . .
3	$+$	$^1V_5 + {}^1V_1$	$^2V_5\ldots$	$\left\{\begin{matrix}^1V_5 = {}^2V_5 \\ {}^1V_1 = {}^1V_1\end{matrix}\right\}$	$= 2n+1$	1	. . .	. . .	. . .	$2n+1$
4	$\div$	$^2V_5 \div {}^3V_4$	$^1V_{11}\ldots$	$\left\{\begin{matrix}^2V_5 = {}^0V_5 \\ {}^3V_4 = {}^0V_4\end{matrix}\right\}$	$= \dfrac{2n-1}{2n+1}$	. . .	. . .	. . .	0	0
5	$\div$	$^1V_{11} \div {}^1V_2$	$^2V_{11}\ldots$	$\left\{\begin{matrix}^1V_{11} = {}^2V_{11} \\ {}^1V_2 = {}^1V_2\end{matrix}\right\}$	$= \dfrac{1}{2}\cdot\dfrac{2n-1}{2n+1}$	. . .	2	. . .	. . .	. . .
6	$-$	$^0V_{12} - {}^2V_{11}$	$^1V_{12}\ldots$	$\left\{\begin{matrix}^2V_{11} = {}^0V_{11} \\ {}^0V_{13} = {}^0V_{13}\end{matrix}\right\}$	$= -\dfrac{1}{2}\cdot\dfrac{2n-1}{2n+1} = A_0$.	. . .	. . .	. . .	. . .	. . .
7	$-$	$^1V_3 - {}^1V_1$	$^1V_{10}\ldots$	$\left\{\begin{matrix}^1V_3 = {}^1V_3 \\ {}^1V_1 = {}^1V_1\end{matrix}\right\}$	$= n-1(=3)$	1	. . .	n	. . .	. . .
8	$+$	$^1V_2 + {}^0V_7$	$^1V_7\ldots$	$\left\{\begin{matrix}^1V_2 = {}^1V_2 \\ {}^0V_7 = {}^1V_7\end{matrix}\right\}$	$= 2+0 = 2$	. . .	2	. . .	. . .	. . .
9	$\div$	$^1V_6 \div {}^1V_7$	$^3V_{11}\ldots$	$\left\{\begin{matrix}^1V_6 = {}^1V_6 \\ {}^0V_{11} = {}^3V_{11}\end{matrix}\right\}$	$= \dfrac{2n}{2} = A_1$	. . .	. . .	. . .	. . .	. . .
10	$\times$	$^1V_{21} \times {}^3V_{11}$	$^1V_{12}\ldots$	$\left\{\begin{matrix}^1V_{21} = {}^1V_{21} \\ {}^3V_{11} = {}^3V_{11}\end{matrix}\right\}$	$= B_1\cdot\dfrac{2n}{2} = B_1A_1$ . . .	. . .	. . .	. . .	. . .	. . .
11	$+$	$^1V_{12} + {}^1V_{13}$	$^2V_{13}\ldots$	$\left\{\begin{matrix}^1V_{12} = {}^0V_{12} \\ {}^1V_{13} = {}^2V_{13}\end{matrix}\right\}$	$= -\dfrac{1}{2}\cdot\dfrac{2n-1}{2n+1} + B_1\cdot\dfrac{2n}{2}$	. . .	. . .	. . .	. . .	. . .
12	$-$	$^1V_{10} - {}^1V_1$	$^2V_{10}\ldots$	$\left\{\begin{matrix}^1V_{10} = {}^2V_{10} \\ {}^1V_1 = {}^1V_1\end{matrix}\right\}$	$= n-2(=2)$	1	. . .	. . .	. . .	. . .

Figure 2.3. Countess Ada of Lovelace has been hailed as the world's first programmer. However, this partial "program" for Bernoulli numbers hardly resembles computer code. (See Ref. 1, Appendix A.)

alcohol. A genuine Victorian melodrama ensued. Ada suggested that Babbage cooperate with her and the Earl to develop a system to beat the odds at horse races. (She may have been the first "programmer" with such ambitions, but she certainly was not the last.)

Gambling got out of hand, and twice Ada pawned the family jewels. Perhaps the cervical cancer that eventually was to claim her life had already sunk its claws into Ada. Only opium could control the escalating pain she suffered for at least two years, and toward the end her own mother deprived her even of that comfort. She died a few days shy of her thirty-seventh birthday.

Enter the logician.   Babbage apparently missed Ada more than her own family did. He turned increasingly irascible and solitary. For 70 years Babbage was known in his country only as the instigator of the "Babbage law," a product of his eternal warfare against street musicians. It's too bad that Babbage's temperament prevented him from emulating another computer idol, George Boole, who endured a much harder life with magnificent grace.

Born in 1815 as a shoemaker's son, he had to hustle throughout his youth but always retained high spirits. At the age of 20 he opened a school, while still filling big gaps in his own education. Math became his great passion—practically an adjunct to his religion. By 1840 he published his first paper (on analytical transformations), and eight years later defined his *Mathematical Theory of Logic*. The work was so original and convincing that the largely self-educated Boole was appointed professor of mathematics at Queens College in Cork, Ireland.

There he met Mary Everest, niece of Sir George of Mt. Everest fame. She was also mathematically inclined and actually had hoped to go to Cambridge to meet the high priest of math, Charles Babbage. It was not to be, but she enrolled with Boole and married her teacher just after he had published *The Laws of Thought* in 1854. (When Bertrand Russell later read it, he declared "Pure mathematics was discovered by Boole.") So absorbed was Boole in his cogitation that once he ignored his students for a whole hour and later told his wife: "A most extraordinary thing happened today. None of my students showed up." Just imagine that many students remaining that quiet that long nowadays!

Logic for engineers.   Almost exactly a century went by before Boolean logic was to be applied to computing. Electrical engineers, however, had utilized it almost since Boole's day to design telegraph exchanges. The first to use Boolean logic for a working computer was Konrad Zuse (for a discussion of his hardware, see Appendix A). He developed a computer language he called *Plankalkül* (plan calculus) for his relay computer. Published in 1948, the language influences European informatics to this day.[2]

The language's name is somewhat misleading: *Plan* was an abbreviation of *Rechenplan* (calculation plan), which is synonymous with "program." So, what Zuse really devised at his rustic alpine refuge was programming calculus—a formal computer logic not limited to calculation. In fact, Zuse provides an example from chess. The following expresses the statement "White king can move without being checkmated." This assertion is broken down into several subprograms, the one defining that squares V0 and V1 are adjacent reads:

```
  | R17 (V,   V)
V |    0    1
S |   12   12
```

Figure 2.4. For his relay computer, Konrad Zuse developed a logic-based programming language called *Plankalkül*. One procedure from a chess program is shown here. *(Source: Communications ACM, 15(7), July 1972, p. 684.)*

The first line simply defines this routine as R17 (*Rechnung* 17), which deals with two variables. S is predefined in the third line as consisting of two values indicating the coordinates. The whole "plan," P148, consists of defining (1) that a square x exists that is adjacent to the king's square, Z0, and contains either no chess piece or a black one; and (2) that no black chessman can be moved to square x. As Figure 2.4 shows, Zuse's formulation of the program strongly resembles the formal definitions in today's software calculus, which will be discussed in Chapter 14.

$$
\begin{array}{c|cc}
P148 & R(V) & \Rightarrow R148 \\
\hline
V & 0 & 0 \\
A & 5 & 0
\end{array}
$$

$$
\begin{array}{c|c|cc|c}
 & \acute{x} & (x \in V) & \wedge & (x = \text{L0}) & \Rightarrow Z \\
\hline
V & & 0 & & & 0 \\
K & & & & 1 & \\
A & 4 & 5 & & 3 & 4
\end{array}
$$

$$
\begin{array}{c|c|cccc}
 & (Ex) & (x \in V) & \wedge & R17\ (Z,x) & \wedge\ (x = 0) & \vee\ x \\
\hline
V & & 0 & & 0 & & \\
K & & & & 0\,0 & 1 & 1.3 \\
A & 4 & 4\ \ 5 & & 2\,2 & 3 & 0
\end{array}
$$

$$
\begin{array}{c|c|ccc}
 & \wedge \overline{Ey} & (y \in V) & \wedge\ y & \wedge\ R128\ (v,y,x) \\
\hline
V & & 0 & & 0 \\
K & & & 1.3 & 0\,0 \\
A & & 4 & 5 & 0 & 5\,2\,2
\end{array}
$$

⅃ **Programming After Eniac**

The mainstream of computing was not ready for formal logic quite yet. In fact, when fancy calculators finally metamorphosed into electronic computers, such as the Eckert-Mauchley Eniac, they were at first programmed with patchcords. Even when computers turned into commercial tools, they could only understand ones and zeros—just like Jacquard's loom 150 years earlier. So their programmers had to formulate instructions (e.g., "add" or "shift right") laboriously in binary code, which had to be translated (by hand, of course) into toggle switch positions and later into punched cards.

In fact, programmers were called "coders" until headhunters needed a catchier term for the new profession. Soon coders replaced binary with octal code and became quite proficient in adding octal addresses for machines such as the Binac, which was built for the Air Force's Snark Missile in 1949 (see Appendix A). Unfortunately, the skill backfired when some tried to balance their checkbooks using octal arithmetic. Then the first language finally arrived—assembly code. Even after nearly 40 years assembly's mnemonics remain as useful as ever. Although not strictly a language, we are justified in defining assembly code as the trunk of the language tree in Figure 2.5. The tree's procedural branch will be explored in the next chapter and the declarative branch in Chapter 12.

Finally, a language.   Of course, mnemonics are not really words; clearly, they were meant for a machine. Indeed, purists would soon take issue with the whole "computer language" concept, because computers are still too dumb to understand a real language. They have a point. After all, real human languages aren't able to express ideas unambiguously, or we wouldn't need a lawyer for every 360 Americans. Still, well-chosen subsets of English have provided us with the best means yet for communicating with computers, so why not call them languages?

However, it was tough to make these languages meaningful to humans as well as to machines, at a time when a computer with 1000 words of memory was considered big. Fortunately, most early computing dealt with scientific and engineering problems, so the sometimes cryptic terseness of early languages posed no conflict. (Zuse's *Plankalkül*, based on logic, never spread beyond its native valley.) And Turing had recognized important

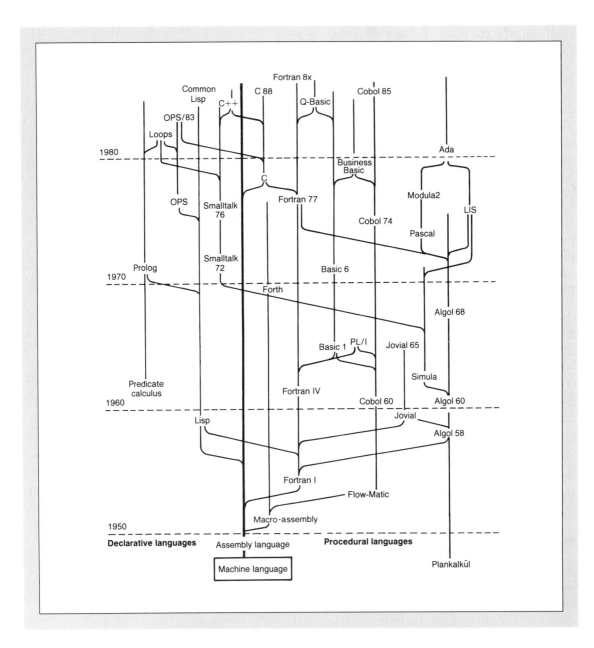

Figure 2.5. The evolution of today's computer languages has taken many wondrous paths, as shown by this language tree. Scrutinize it again when you read Chapters 3 and 12.

software properties, but only a few mathematicians ever heard about them. In the mainstream of computing, language evolution proceeded by trial and error, when low-level assembly languages finally gave way to high-level languages (HLLs), grown in American soil.

The first HLL to meet with success was called Fortran (Formula translator), and was developed by John Backus and his group. It was meant to run on IBM's latest model, the 704, which was due out in 1956. As the first production computer with a floating-point processor, it would run 10 times faster than its predecessor and provide a perfect platform for the new language. At the time, other numerical languages were evolving in several research labs, but none had even remotely the impact on the evolution of today's language species as IBM's Fortran. In fact, it will remain *numero uno* with scientists well into the next century.

The first report on the language was out by the end of 1954. The essential features were in place, except for input and output (I/O). It proved auspicious that John Backus and his colleagues did not rush that part of the language, because the powerful format declarations would soon give the language a long leg up on the competition. In fact, during the next three decades, several languages (including Algol and PL/I) would have to capitulate before Fortran's I/O power.

Only one language feature eventually drew fire. By defining blanks as meaningless (rather than as delimiters), Fortran was born with a time bomb. It went off during the Mariner 1 launch in July 1962, when a programmer substituted a period for a comma in the statement DO 100 I=1,10. Because Fortran does not require explicit type definitions, the computer parsed DO100I = 1.10, making up the strange but perfectly legal variable DO100I, which it set to 1.10. In retrospect, the "no blanks" rule may seem silly, but there had been a good reason for it at the time. Keypunch operators tended to either ignore or insert blanks, causing a good deal of needless debugging. Attempts to use deltas (or triangles) for spaces also backfired when keypunchers turned them into 4s. (None of this can serve as an excuse to leave *mandatory* blanks unidentified to this day.)

The official *Programmers Reference Manual* was dated October 15, 1956, and its cover proclaimed proudly:

Fortran
Automatic Coding System
for the IBM 704

Today this phrase may smell of·hype, but the documented 80% to 90% time savings over assembly programming justified the claim as a legitimate marketing tool. The whole manual filled 51 pages, of which 30 dealt with machine-specific features. Compare that with the nearly 400 pages in the Ada manual, and you can measure software "progress." In due course Fortran IV followed— the version most engineers and scientists of the fledgling computer era encountered first. Fortran IV was released in 1962 for the IBM 7090 and was standardized four years later—the first language ever to attain the exalted position of an ANSI standard.

Compiler efficiency crucial.   Actually, the original language design proved much easier than the next step—building a compiler. When the job was finished in 1957, 30 staff years had been invested. However, the effort was worth the toil because the Fortran I compiler produced very efficient code. Not until optimizing compilers became available in the 1960s did it lose its luster. Fortran IV ran much less efficiently; it succumbed to "creeping featurism" in the form of debugging aids. Back then, storage was still so precious that the compiler designers decided to make compromises between efficiency and user friendliness (still undiscovered at the time), rather than design two separate compilers. We live and learn.

While Fortran immediately swept scientific programming, assembly still ruled the burgeoning data processing (DP) "shops," both in industry and in the Pentagon. The Navy was the first service branch to grasp the need for automation in procurement and warehousing. And among Navy personnel nobody was more enthusiastic than Grace Hopper, known to generations of programmers as "Amazing Grace." After graduating from Vassar in 1928, Dr. Hopper taught math there, and in 1943, she joined the Navy to help win the war. A scant 43 years later, she retired (like her grandfather) as a rear admiral—only to sign up as a consultant with Digital Equipment Corporation. As they say, old soldiers never die.

Hopper's first assignment as a lieutenant had been with Aiken's Mark I at Harvard; she also worked with Eckert and Mauchley on the Binac. Hopper has indeed graced the computer scene from the start. In fact, she built Univac's first compiler, the A-0, in 1952. Faced with the necessity to implement forward jumps, she set up a "neutral corner" in high memory—inspired by women's basketball rules. Later, Hopper used the B-0 (renamed

Flow-Matic) language to plant the seeds for Cobol (COmmon Business-Oriented Language).

Today it is hard to imagine what it was like when main memory was limited to 1 kword. Under such constraints, how does one design a language so English-like that even bank managers would understand it? Hopper's "Protocobol" compiler accomplished the feat by looking only at the first and third letter in each command "verb"; the concept of keeping these two letters unique persisted in Cobol until 1977.

The new business language was defined in a meeting at the University of Pennsylvania in April 1959 and was to be completed by year's end. (Clearly wishful thinking when both the Pentagon and IBM were involved.) The meetings of the group, known as CODASYL, dragged on and on. In fact, the RCA representative was so frustrated that in 1960 he mailed a child's tombstone with the inscription "COBOL" to the Pentagon—COD. As behooves a tame black hole, that subtle reminder just vanished in the Pentagon's gravity vortex.

Eventually, the language's first version emerged. It comprised 23 verbs, fortunately including one supporting abbreviations:

```
DEFINE SSN = SOCIAL-SECURITY-NUMBER
```

Scarce memory resources had imposed this compromise on the spell-it-all-out language philosophy. The language was formally christened Cobol in September 1959, but a compiler did not become available until December 1960. In fact, a compiler from RCA and one from Univac came in neck and neck, and when the Navy ran the same program on both, the results were (almost) identical. Cobol had chalked up its first victory.

Cobol was no work of art, even as early languages went. Two major causes for this clumsiness stand out: (1) the decision to stick with the standard typewriter character set and (2) Cobol's obsession with an English-like appearance. To make the language acceptable to DP management, Cobol's verbs included ADD, SUBTRACT, MULTIPLY, and so on. The rationale throws a dim light on the people who manage our bank accounts and pension plans: "We don't want to use formulas" was the nearly unanimous verdict. American math education was in trouble even then.

No wonder the emerging computer science clan sneered at Cobol's patent lack of elegance. Cobolites, however, point out that in reality DP poses a much greater challenge to man and machine than scientific computing. Fortran's six-character variables certainly were easier to implement than the variable-length labels needed in Cobol. More importantly, DP requires far more complex filing capabilities than the Fortran team ever imagined. In fact, to this day the technical community suffers from inferior data management, compared with DP. Quibbling aside, Cobol met its objectives, but although promoted jointly by IBM and the Pentagon for nearly three decades, it still has not quite dislodged the much faster assembly code from DP shops. (In fact, many are now switching to C, bypassing Cobol altogether.)

A plethora of languages.   After the language shakeout of the 1970s, it's hard to imagine that languages once popped up like mushrooms. There was JOSS (Johnniac Open Shop System), GPSS (General-Purpose Simulation System)—an ancestor of Simscript—CORC (Cornell Compiler), and SNOBOL, whose full name lampooned contrived acronyms: StriNg Oriented symBOlic Language.[1] Some of the 1960s languages are still hanging on. For example, IBM's APL (A Programming Language) is very effective if you use it daily, because its huge function set and interactive execution make short work of matrix manipulations.[3,4] However, occasional users soon found out that writing a few lines of Fortran was less troublesome than going through the APL manual to find the proper canned function. APL's weird character set, adorned with greek letters and overstrike symbols, did not exactly marshal converts either.

Meanwhile, across the Atlantic, the quest for more elegant solutions to programming got underway. (This although some gurus had pointed out that few users want—or even recognize—elegance, but all howl when the bugs bite.) At first, the effort to develop an algorithmic language to replace Fortran was an international effort. It began with a petition by user groups to the ACM in May 1957. Fortran was unacceptable as the *lingua franca* of all programmers, because it was an IBM product, and it lacked the grace computer scientists desired. Besides, Fortran's insistence on a decimal point had upset comma-happy Europeans from the start.

The new language was to be called IAL, (International Algorithmic Language). That pompous name gave way to ***Algol*** (algorithmic language) during the first session of the language committee in May 1958 at the prestigious ***ETH*** (Swiss Technical

University) in Zurich. A second meeting in Paris the following year settled many of the hotly debated issues, including the comma/period controversy.*

When the dust settled and Algol 60 finally emerged from the turmoil, one American committee member declared it "an object of stunning beauty." This was a chivalrous act, because American contributions and concerns had impacted the language far less than those from the Europeans. The introduction of blocks, name properties, and a coherent concept of *abstract data types* turned language evolution in a new direction.

Algol underwent further revisions in 1968, but it never really succeeded as a language.† The main reason was probably its lack of ready-made I/O—quite a disadvantage in the competition with the two established, I/O-rich languages of Fortran and Cobol. Still, the academic bickering from which Algol emerged clarified many basic concepts, and consequently impacted future languages, all the way to Ada. Algol also demonstrated that in the description of algorithms, a computer language could indeed facilitate communications not only between man and machine, but between humans as well.

Another fringe benefit emerged: the modification and general acceptance of a type of syntax definition first applied by Fortran developer Backus. The notation is known as BNF, short for Backus Normal Form or Backus-Naur Form, after the Algol "keeper of the grail" who introduced the present standard. For example,

```
<basic statement> ::=
      <unlabeled statement> |
      <label> : <statement>
```

means that a basic statement's format can either be an unlabeled statement or a label followed by a colon followed by a statement.[5]

---

*At one point, a European participant banged the table, shouting "No, I will never use a period instead of a comma as the decimal point."

†Some European academics tend to blame the commercial failure of Algol on industry hostility. Let us remember that from Galileo to Einstein scientists were victimized more by their own colleagues than by the powers that be.

Jules's own language.   Among the languages inspired by Algol, three achieved prominence on their own: Jovial, Pascal, and Ada. Just as the IAL group met in Zurich (and changed its name), the Air Force laid out plans to replace its SAGE real-time hardware (see Appendix A). A language had to be developed, because the new system was to run on the byte-oriented AN/FSQ-31, after development on the (totally incompatible) IBM 709. Lightheartedly, the design team called their language "our version of IAL," or Ovial for short. During a presentation by design team leader Jules Schwartz, somebody called the language "Jules's own version of IAL," and the acronym Jovial stuck.

A brief sample demonstrates the influence of Algol on the new language:

```
FOR I=0$
BEGIN X1.
IF A1($I$)=3$ D1($I$)=5$
I=I+A1($I$) $
IF A1($I$)=0$ STOP
GOTO X1$
END
```

The many dollar signs may seem appropriate for a DoD language, but they only served as delimiters and were replaced in later versions. The 50,000-line Jovial compiler took eight hours to compile itself on a 709. Its official successor, a typical Ada compiler, weighs in at 10 times the number of lines and (if written in Ada) at least 20 times the number of bytes.

Jovial left an impact on other languages, including Neliac (from the Naval Electronics Lab), Coral (the British defense language), and PL/I (which stands modestly for programming language I). Internally known at IBM first as Fortran 6 and later as NPL (the new programming language), PL/I was meant to replace all other high-level languages. Trying to construct a superset of Fortran and Cobol, with all the features of Algol thrown in for good measure, was a pretty ambitious undertaking. In fact, when NPL was first presented in 1964 to IBM's powerful Share user group, one wise guy asked, "Why did you omit the kitchen sink?" He was even wiser than he thought.

PL/I did break some new ground. Implied typing by context was implemented to provide type checking because DP users were deemed incapable or unwilling to embrace an explicit form of type declaration. More importantly, the language includes a statement ON CONDITION, which serves well as an exception handler (Applesoft Basic modified it to ONERR GOTO). So why did PL/I fail to garner a following? For one thing, no "universal" anything is likely to succeed, because it tends to collapse under the weight of its built-in compromises. For another, languages designed by committee act like camels, not like racehorses, no matter how elegant they may appear to their creators.

↳ Language Genealogy for the PC Era

Pascal was devised at the same ETH lab in Zurich where Algol was born. Designed by one man, Niklaus Wirth, Pascal succeeded where Algol had failed, not because it's so different—in fact, one might almost call it Algol 74. Pascal thrived because it was designed as a teaching language for *informatics* students, and in this role it spread all over the world. But when it comes to practical applications, pure ISO Pascal has been less fortunate. The reasons were spelled out in an April Fool "interview" with Wirth.[6] There the professor declares Pascal a practical joke and remarks "When some people added features to the language that would make it truly useful, I got the last laugh. I had the original version standardized [by the International Standards Organization]."

Like Algol, Pascal is short on I/O. You can read and write a line without too much trouble, but that's not enough. A scientist must be able to print a table, and a DP programmer must be able to read a database. An engineer often has to access hardware, but ISO Pascal won't let you peek into memory. However, when Professor Ken Bowles at the San Diego campus of the University of California popularized "UCSD Pascal" in the mid-1970s, Silicon Valley techies fell in love with the language. By the time the former students uncovered the shortcomings of microcomputer Pascal, they were too committed to abandon it.

The result has been a jumble of *dialects*, each tuned for a different application. In contrast, Fortran remains a very portable language, and is consequently regaining lost ground. Pascal's lack of extended precision, variable initialization, complex arithmetic, easy array passing, and especially its defiance of separate compilation are giving Fortran an edge—even more so once the next standard, Fortran 8x, incorporates most of Pascal's goodies. Pascal is still hanging in there (propped up primarily by commercial Turbo Pascal), but the bloom is off the rose.

Basic's basics.   Another teaching language, Basic (Beginners' All-purpose Symbolic Instruction Code, believe it or not) had similar problems. Invented by John Kemeny and Thomas Kurtz, two professors at Dartmouth College, it really spread like wildfire in spite of its contrived name. Asked why Basic has turned into the true *lingua franca* of microcomputing, Kurtz answered "Because there are far more people than programmers in the world." This sentence should give the computer science establishment some food for thought.

Basic was indeed meant to serve the 75% of Dartmouth students who neither knew nor cared to know about math, science, or engineering. Nevertheless, it was clear in 1957 that these future decision makers in government and business could not function effectively without any first-hand knowledge of computers. At that time, Kurtz had to design some statistics programs, for which he used assembly language. After wasting much time—and precious CPU hours—he was upset enough to try the as yet unproven Fortran. Lo and behold, the Fortran version ran after only five minutes' CPU time for debugging on the school's IBM 704!

Kurtz realized that such a Fortran-like language would stand a much better chance with his students than formalistic Cobol. But even Fortran was too complex for them. The students he had in mind could not distinguish between integers and real numbers, nor could they be expected to start each statement in the sixth column. (This Fortran quirk allowed users to insert five-digit statement numbers without upsetting the compiler.) In the mid-1950s timesharing technology made it possible to hook up dozens of terminals to a computer and even to write programs interactively. But Kemehy and Kurtz decided that interactive debugging would be too distracting, so Basic was to be compiled.

Keeping Basic small was easy—the barely born language took its first hesitating steps on a computer with 4 Kwords of memory. (Remember the resurrection of 4-K Basic when the PC emerged?) Each statement would begin with a verb (good training for Cobol), and there would be only 10 functions, each three characters long. But as Basic 1 took hold in 1964, additional demands cropped up. The second edition added arrays, and the third one even offered matrix arithmetic.

After its first decade, Basic had become an overwhelming success, not only at Dartmouth (where 85% of the students have used it), but worldwide. As Basic turned into a workhorse, its original simplicity eroded. One of the most recent entries,

Microsoft's Q-Basic, has shed line numbers and the LET verb and has added symbolic labels and separately compilable modules. In other words, it looks and feels more like Fortran IV than Dartmouth Basic. So far, several hundred Basic dialects have emerged, many of which are machine specific. So, while Basic did become the *lingua franca* for the PC era, portable it's not.

Take the C train. By the time the Basic 6 manuals came off the press at Dartmouth in 1971, Dennis Richie was developing a new language at Bell Labs that was to impact technical programming as much as Basic has impacted popular programming. AT&T wanted to set up a timesharing network and needed a suitable operating system for the PDP-6 and PDP-11 computers. That operating system turned out to be Unix, and the language in which it was written was called C.

Refreshingly, C stands for nothing; it is simply the language that followed B. Academics don't approve of C, because it sacrifices too many of computer science's sacred cows. But by now most system software is being written in C for two important reasons: (1) it can easily get at the hardware, and (2) it produces tight code. The second point may not seem too important in the era of megabyte memories, but true to Parkinson's law, software packages always outgrow available memory.

The only viable competitor for C in system programming is Ada, which provides hardware access more reluctantly and produces voluminous source code. It is now catching on not so much because programmers or computer scientists love it, but because the Pentagon imposes it. The Ada language gives the DoD some hope to bring software spending under control. For one thing, Ada comes close to being a superset of the 400 languages now used in military software; for another, Ada includes most of the known safeguards against coding errors. After nearly a decade of evolution, the language became an ANSI standard in 1983, and in 1987 obtained the ISO seal of good codekeeping as well. To nip in the bud any sprouting dialects, the DoD copyrighted the Ada name, but has finally decided such "protection" was no longer needed.

Will AI divert the software tide? Let us hope that the Ada language will lead a longer and happier life than Lady Ada. You'll get to know the language fairly well in this book, because it incorporates many features essential to creating tough software. Still, though Ada may provide a durable plateau in procedural languages, outside that realm language evolution is very much in flux. New languages keep sprouting from the second-oldest language around—Lisp. It was born when MIT researchers needed a declarative language to facilitate symbolic (in contrast with numeric) computing in their pursuit of artificial intelligence.

CASE tools owe a huge debt to AI and Lisp, because CASE's visual approach to programming evolved in the AI community—even though this book deals primarily with the still dominant software category known as procedural programming. However, AI-inspired object-oriented concepts (explored in Chapter 13) are starting to trickle down and to spread the AI gospel. In fact, most Ada advocates are promoting their darling as an **object-oriented** language these days.

Considering that Lisp emerged even before Cobol and that no powerful organization stood behind it, the language has proven amazingly tenacious. The reason lies in its expandability. Anybody can (and most do) build specialized languages atop a Lisp infrastructure—a tremendous boon to designers of such AI products as **expert systems**. As with Basic, the worldwide, uncontrolled diffusion of Lisp has naturally resulted in a cornucopia of dialects. The embarrassment of riches became so intolerable that even Lisp hackers—who rarely see eye to eye with the Pentagon—by and large appreciate DoD's enforcement of the Common Lisp standard.

Lisp may have been the first nonprocedural language, but it's certainly no longer the only one. In addition to specialized languages, some general ones have sprouted from Lisp's "heap." You'll find a discussion of their evolution and abilities in Chapter 12, where both object-oriented and logic languages get their due.

This brief historic overview could only touch the surface of software's tortuous journey through time. But it did show how software sprang from the same roots as hardware, going back almost 200 years. Hopefully we have shed new light on some computer prophets—though not as effectively as the play "Breaking the Code" (which deals with Turing's work). How appropriate to end this review with a piece of "software" that has now played on the "hardware" of London's West End and New York's Broadway. Its run, alas, was brief. What we really need is a musical starring the Countess of Lovelace—say, "The Sound of Logic."

⸎ References

1. Richard L. Wexelblat, Ed., *History of Programming Languages*, Academic Press, New York, 1981.

2. Konrad Zuse, *Der Computer, Mein Lebenswerk*, Springer-Verlag, Heidelberg, 1984.

3. Leonard Gilman and Allen Rose, *APL: An Interactive Approach*, Wiley, New York, 1976.

4. Allen Rose and Barbara Schick, *APL in Practice*, Wiley, New York, 1980.

5. Frank G. Pagan, *Formal Specification of Programming Languages*, Prentice-Hall, Englewood Cliffs, NJ, 1981.

6. Bruce Tonkin, "Niklaus Wirth reveals Pascal," *Computer Language*, April 1986, p. 97.

For more language references see Chapters 3 and 12.

Jean Marie Jacquard, inventor of the first industrial controller and the punched card, remains a familiar figure among all the world's textile workers.

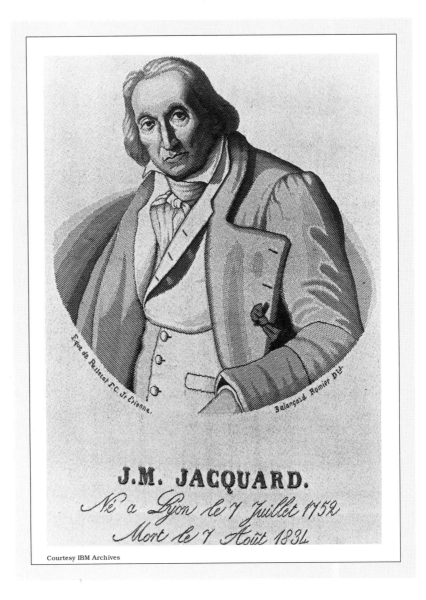

J.M. JACQUARD.

Né a Lyon le 7 Juillet 1752
Mort le 7 Août 1834

Courtesy IBM Archives

3

LET THE LANGUAGE SUIT THE JOB

Come let us go down and confuse their language that they may not understand each other's speech.

Genesis 11:7

Similarities and differences
Let there be typing
Oddballs still effective

Whether you design your software with a CASE system or not, in the end you have to deliver code. Eventually, all CASE systems may produce flawless code automatically, but for now most require your intervention at the coding stage. Furthermore, all major customers will still demand to see source code for the foreseeable future—even if they never inspect it. Big organizations (very lucrative customers, judging by Microsoft's success) just won't change their rules very easily.

You might be able to choose the source language, though, at least within broad groups. As CASE tools become commonplace and produce correct code in all the major languages, it will matter less and less to the executing computer which source language you choose. But Voltaire's quip that "language was given to man to hide his thoughts" remains valid for the human code reader. So you might as well pick the language you find most readable, as long as it is fairly writable too. But readability weighs more heavily.

If you work with supercomputers, the chosen language will most likely be Fortran; if you're involved in education, Pascal might be your choice; as a budding captain of industry, you'll probably go with Basic; as a "hip" programmer, you're sure to pick C; if you're in it for the money, you'll like Ada. According to one recent survey the primary languages for VAX computers (which dominate the "mini" field) stack up as follows:

Fortran	46%
C	13%
Basic	12%
Pascal	6%
Ada	3%
Assembly	3%

For definitions of *key terms* see Appendix C

Although Ada and **assembly code** share the bottom rung, Ada is quickly gaining (its use doubled between mid-1987 and mid-1988). These six languages are procedural languages—the only kind to be discussed in this chapter.

Some might ask, "Where is Cobol?" Indeed, it's not in the list, nor will it appear in this chapter. And for good reasons. While it's true that of all languages Cobol can still boast the biggest accumulation of code, relatively few programmers write *new* Cobol code. Those who do either need no help or can't be helped. Even the stuffiest DP shops are forced to switch to other languages because the labor pool for Cobol is drying up, thank heaven. Therefore, most Cobol work deals with maintenance, and a whole Cobol circumvention industry stands ready to help those mired in old Cobol to "reverse engineer" their programs.

Why does an even more ancient language, Fortran, head the list? For one thing, VAX machines have always been popular with engineers and scientists. For another, supercomputers from Alliant to Cray use special Fortran compilers that parallelize the code for swift execution. The programs they run are often so huge and complex they may run forever. Besides, they contain such clever programming tricks! Take this example:

```
    DO 10 I=1,N
    DO 10 J=1,N
    X(I,J)=(I/J)*(J/I)
10 CONTINUE
```

What an "elegant" (and absolutely *verboten*) way to create an N-by-N array in which the diagonal (where I = J) is populated with ones and all other places with zeros. (If you don't know Fortran, this example will become clearer later in this chapter.) The point is that no re-engineering tool can automatically convert such enigmas.

CASE spotlights the essence.   Enough digression. You may or may not find a CASE tool that produces source code automatically. Many, however, provide flowcharts or templates, so that you need no longer be concerned about language syntax. You can concentrate on the actual transformations, which are described primarily by assignment statements. (They account for 34% of the average program.) With CASE, you'll worry much less about IF statements (which contribute 14%) or DO loops (a mere 4%). Conditionals like the IF appear to be the most troublesome. According to an MIT study, a full third of all coding errors stem from missing or malformed "guards" (essentially, conditions).

Whether you can enlist CASE assistance or not, it's worthwhile to examine the syntax of popular languages and see how they fit in with your programming style. Take a very trivial example: a variable I always has a value of 1 or 2. If it is 1, change it to 2; if it is 2, change it to 1. This task requires only the two most frequently used software *constructs*—assignment and conditional jumps.*

If you're mathematically inclined, you might come up with an elegant one-liner:

```
I := 3 - I
```

This statement looks strange, but it really works—provided that I is either 1 or 2, as advertised. No CASE system will ever come up with such an ingenious solution, though, because it can't

---

*To be consistent, reserved words or keywords are written in upper case; all other labels are written in a mix of upper and lower case, regardless of the language under discussion.

be obtained by a transformation of the problem statement. And that is just as well, because *elegant* shortcuts often backfire eventually. For example, such a shortcut led to Gemini-5's splash-down 100 miles off target. If a maintenance programmer ever got stuck with this code (and no explanation), he'd rack his brain over its intent.

A software novice, in contrast, might write

```
IF I=1 THEN I := 2;
IF I=2 THEN I := 1;
```

This code's intent is probably clear, but it will not work because the second statement negates the first one. In a language without an ELSE clause, you would have to insert a GOTO between the two statements, which is cumbersome to say the least. (Actually, *every* IF has its ELSE, namely "else execute the next line.") Most modern languages, however, permit you to write

```
IF I=1 THEN I := 2
        ELSE I := 1;
```

As long as I really sticks to the designated values, that's a good solution. But by building in an exception handler, you no longer have to rely on the premise that I (or U, for that matter) will never go astray:

```
IF I=1 THEN I := 2
        ELSE IF I=2 THEN I := 1
                ELSE Exception;
```

Not all languages permit this type of construct, so the choice of language is still important. To compare all currently popular languages would take a book, but we should at least be on nodding terms with the most important ones. Naturally, there has been a great deal of cross-pollination between these species. A mini-course in their etymology remains helpful to understanding the main thrust of the major high-level languages (see Chapter 2).

Pseudocode no redeemer.   Let's assume for a moment that your CASE system can derive actual source code from pseudocode. Why not let the CASE computer figure out the best implementation? For one thing, when you use pseudocode in a

CASE environment, you must still abide by that code's syntax rules and provide all the information the system needs. If you leave anything out, the system will come back and ask you questions. Although this is indeed a great advance over the glib "syntax error" messages of the past (which have contributed mightily to the present *average* price tag of $100 per line of code), playing 20 questions with your workstation can be more time consuming than writing correct code to begin with. While it is true that most current procedural languages include the same basic conditional and looping constructs, the internal implementations of specific languages can still lead you astray and add the insult of inefficient execution to the injury of breeding bugs.

Before deciding on a language, try some relevant test cases to stave off surprises. For example, Fortran updates its counter at the end of the loop, while other languages do it at the beginning. In fact, to provide a way for jumping to the end of a loop without skipping the index counter, Fortran originally had to introduce the CONTINUE statement. But if you work with certain supercomputers or need complex numbers (often indispensable for engineers), you may be stuck with Fortran.[1,2] There are also differences between languages in the way the IF/THEN/ELSE concept is implemented. The original "arithmetic" Fortran IF was a three-way switch, closer to the Lisp COND statement than to Algol's IF/THEN/ELSE.[3]

Differences between languages escalate for more complex constructs—say, CASE or DO. In fact, if you use Fortran IV, you must mimic CASE with strings of IFs. In C's CASE equivalent, if you don't specify `break` after executable instructions, the rest of the cases will be evaluated as well. In most other languages, the choices are mutually exclusive. The CASE construct has been a topic of heated debate for years—especially the question of an ELSE clause. Some languages have it, others will get it, still others won't. Only the Shadow knows.

Finding a common denominator. For some strange reason, languages (computer or natural) tend to bring out the chauvinist in us—if not the missionary zealot. So, let's get on neutral ground with yet another language, KISS (use your favorite interpretation).[4] It will help us impartially compare the constructs used in several popular languages. The instruction manual is brief:

Pseudocode	KISS
Begin..End	(..) or [..] or {..}
IF (True) S1..Sn	?[True: S1..Sn]
FOR n=1 TO 5 STEP 2	![n=1,3..5: ...
DO WHEN (True)....	![True: .....

where True is short for condition = true. That's it, except for the special symbol @, a wildcard representing any permissible value.

Let's try some simple constructs:

    IF (a>b) THEN x := r

In KISS this would be written as

    ?[a>b: x := r]

Now for a two-way switch in pseudocode:

    IF (a>b) THEN x := r
             ELSE x := s

In KISS this becomes

    ?[a>b: x := r
        @: x := s]

Getting bolder, we'll try a three-way switch:

    ?[a<b: x := r
       a=b: x := s
       a>b: x := t]

If you're inclined toward C, you may prefer to see it written this way:

    ?{
        a<b: x := r
        a=b: x := s
        a>b: x := t
    }

In Fortran IV, you could implement the three-way switch with the arithmetic IF. Depending on whether E is negative, zero, or positive, execution jumps to one of three alternatives:

```
        E = a-b
        IF (E) 10,20,30
10      x = r
        GO TO 40
20      x = s
        GO TO 40
30      x = t
40      ...
```

To accomplish the same effect in Pascal you write:

```
IF a<b THEN x := r
        ELSE IF a=b THEN x := s
            ELSE x := t;
```

In Ada, the code would look the same except that you replace ELSE IF with ELSIF. That saves two characters, at the expense of yet another keyword. But then, in Ada, who's counting?

Vive la difference. There is, however, a subtle difference between the KISS and Fortran version on one hand, and the Pascal and Ada code on the other hand.[5] The former duo uses a three-way switch in which all alternatives are hierarchically "flat." The latter two implementations apply two two-way switches in series (which is also apparent from the indentations). Shown as **IPs** (properly defined in Chapter 6) the three-way switch neatly separates "control" from "signal" (see Figure 3.1*a*), while in a cascaded IF each one must produce the switch control as one of its outputs (see Figure 3.1*b*).

If you want to use the value of a-b to drive a four-way (or more-way) switch, KISS will give you no problem:

```
?[ (a-b) <0: x := r
          <10: x := s
            :
            :
          @: x := z]
```

The last line would take care of all conditions not specifically listed, similar to an ELSE. In Ada, you could use a CASE construct, or you could create a string of IF statements if some conditions are conceptually subordinated to others.

In the original (Wirth) Pascal, however, you run into trouble because its CASE lacks an ELSE (or OTHERWISE) clause. (**Borland**'s Turbo Pascal, however, includes this feature, as does Modula-2, which can be regarded as Wirth's own successor to Pascal.[6]) Ada provides the WHEN OTHERS clause; capriciously, Ada's CASE insists on the keyword WHEN and an arrow in all its CASE cases:

For addresses of highlighted *companies* see Appendix D

```
CASE a-b IS
        WHEN <0      => x := r
        WHEN <10     => x := s
                :
                :
        WHEN OTHERS => x := z
```

Finally, let's consider the C version of CASE. Like other relatively new languages, C uses the seven-bit ASCII character set, which includes upper and lower case. Unlike others, however, C is case sensitive,[7] so watch out if you want to try this upper-case CASE:

```
SWITCH (a-b) {
CASE <0   x = r; BREAK;
             :
             :
DEFAULT: x = z; BREAK;
}
```

By now you should begin to like KISS. Too bad we have to carry all this syntactic luggage around when a simple question mark could do the trick.

Looping the loop.   Important as conditional statements are, their value pales against that of DO loops. After all, it is repetitious work that makes computers really shine. Loop constructs, however, can get quite acrobatic. In fact, if two languages look alike otherwise, you can usually tell them apart by their loops. Fortran planted the DO jungle's first tree with this syntax:

```
DO label i = n1, n2, [n3]
```

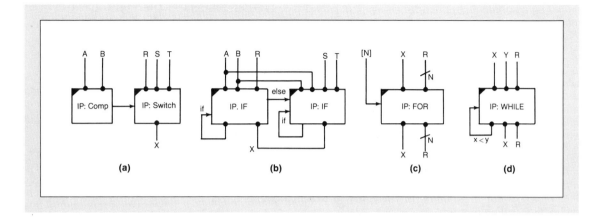

where the label identifies the last statement to be included, and the three integers following the line counter i are its starting and final value and, optionally, the step size. Algol follows the same pattern with

```
FOR i FROM n1 TO n2 BY n3 DO
   ...
OD
```

Algol also adds another kind of loop:

```
WHILE condition DO ...
```

which executes when the condition is met upon entering the loop. Basic, too, follows this pattern:[8]

```
FOR i = n1 TO n2
LET x = r(i)
   ...
NEXT i
```

and (in most dialects),

```
WHILE x<y
LET x = r
   ...
ENDLOOP
```

C also offers FOR and WHILE loops, but you must increment the loop variables explicitly. That gives you more control, but also

Figure 3.1 When a three-way switch is represented in IP form, IP.Comp assumes control functions (*a*). Two cascaded IFs lead to a much more complex structure (*b*). Similarly, a FOR loop (*c*) shows much cleaner control flow than a WHILE loop (*d*).

more opportunities for mistakes.[9] Purists, therefore, deny C the predicate "HOLy" (nothing sacred—just higher-order language). Pascal's WHILE . . . DO follows in Algol's footsteps, but the language adds REPEAT . . . UNTIL, which evaluates the loop condition at the *end* of the loop. Similarly, the FOR construct gives you a choice for the loop counter: TO for counting up and DOWNTO for counting down.

Is it not amazing what a jungle of alternatives computer science had to create, all under the motto of "abstraction"? Again, it remains for KISS to find a common denominator. Essentially, there are two kinds of DO loops: one that is governed by a counter, and one that evaluates a condition. The former requires a beginning and an ending value, as well as a step size. So, why not specify the counter values simply by listing them: I = 1, 2 ..10 or I = 11, 8 ..−6? This approach still needs three numbers to define a loop, but you don't have to remember any keywords at all. Of course, it's not very scientific to tick three numbers off.

As long as the loop counter values are True, the KISS loop executes—in the first case obviously 10 times, and in the second case six times, for the counter values 11, 8, 5, 2, −1, and −4. In the general case, we can simply write

```
![i=n_1, n_2..n_max:
     ...              ]
```

Furthermore, there is no need to contrive yet another syntax for WHILE loops. We just write:

```
![condition:
     ...    ]
```

If the condition is True, the loop executes, as in an IF statement. Next, the question arises whether it's worthwhile to add an UNTIL construct. Probably not, because you can always use an endless loop and a line that tests the controlling variable, Var, and tells the compiler whether to exit. To eliminate the test at the loop entrance, we use @, which always evaluates to True:

```
![ @:
   :
 ? Var>Limit ->]
```

Here, the closing bracket sits right next to the exit arrow, but if that offends you, put it on a line by itself. KISS is a very accommodating language (until you need a compiler).

When using WHILE and UNTIL loops, we must realize that they really violate the concept of separating signal from control variables. During the formative years of Algol, this question did, in fact, lead to some lively debates. Similar to the distinction between straight and arithmetic IFs, the FOR loop has a clear control input (see Figure 3.1c), whereas the WHILE loop (in the case of the Basic example above) must manufacture its own controls (see Figure 3.1d). Undeniably, though, computed conditionals in CASE or WHILE constructs simplify the designer's life. In the end, that's all that really counts.

Unless you want to build a KISS compiler, you must pick your favorite flavor from among the already implemented languages. But even so, working out an algorithm in IPs and KISS could help you clarify your thinking. Of course, before you settle on a language, things other than IF statements and DO loops must be considered as well. For example, how much (or little) type checking do you feel comfortable with? As Figure 3.2 proves, languages still vary widely in this respect.

Figure 3.2 Among today's popular languages only Ada flaunts as many data types at 25-year-old PL/I. Some ideas must simmer for a long time.

Type	Ada	Basic	C	Fortran	Pascal	PL/1
Aligned bit				X	X	X
Array	X	X		X	X	X
Bit	X					X
Boolean	X			X	X	X
Character	X	X	X	X	X	X
Complex				X		X
Enumeration	X		X		X	X
Fixed-point binary	X	X	X	X	X	X
Floating-point binary	X		X	X	X	X
Generic	X					
Label	X		X		X	X
Pointer	X		X		X	X
Private	X				X	
Unsigned integer	X		X		X	X

⌐ Not All Types Are Created Equal

Types were originally introduced for very mundane reasons. Whatever you store in a computer memory winds up there as a bit string. Now, if we stick with ASCII code, the bit string 01001110 could stand for N or for 78, and we must tell the computer which it is to be. Also, a large number could be stored either as an integer or as a real number. Again, the computer must be told that, for the latter, the final byte or so represents the exponent. (Sometimes it is also convenient to convert numbers from one type to another, as with the Fortran EQUIVALENCE statement.)

But when computer scientists talk about types, they want to go beyond such basic types, and rightly so. As we discussed in Chapter 1, getting your signals mixed up can be dangerous to your health. Few people would feel comfortable in their homes if they had a boardful of banana jacks in each room, with labels reading:

Blue: Telephone	Green: Cable TV
Yellow: Antenna	Red: 120V AC

For an adventurous soul with a roof garden it might be very handy to patch the power line into the antenna leads to fire up a barbecue on the roof. A lightly typed language such as C will permit you to do that sort of thing—and eventually you'll get zapped. To think that airplanes (and missiles) fly by software written not only in weakly typed C but even in typeless assembly code can make one shudder.

Unfortunately, C has become so popular precisely because of its weak typing. Together with C's *pointers*, sloppy type checking makes hardware access much easier. You get the storage location of an integer Count with the statement

```
pc = &Count;
```

Then you can assign the contents of this location to another integer, New, by writing

```
New = *pc;
```

Such machinations are especially handy for dealing with arrays, but they produce fragile code. By mingling Boolean and integer types, the language compounds such problems.

C's designers should have studied the protocols of the Algol committee. As it worked out its new language, one of the major issues was that of typing. The sages were distressed because Fortran commanded only three basic types, which, by computer science standards, existed for the wrong reason—namely, properties of the underlying hardware. Scientifically, other type distinctions are just as important. To name a few such "functional" types, consider arrays, Boolean variables, or types that are specific to the user's application—for example, the following enumeration types:

```
type Banana_plug: blue, yellow, green;
type Power_jack: red;
```

This is no substitute for a proper "building code," but in the software world it keeps you from getting zapped. In fact, the second line prevents you from even *touching* the power jack with a banana plug.

The Pentagon shows the way.   While few people use the Algol language for which the committee labored so hard, its typing studies later benefited Pascal and Ada as well. In fact, under Jean Ichbiah's guidance, Ada's designers have tried hard to incorporate a safe "software building code" into their language. Indeed, Ada has been endowed with a wealth of types worthy of the Countess of Lovelace. Declarations and types take up 44 pages in the Ada manual, and that's just for starters. First, there are the predefined types: Boolean, character, count, duration, float, integer, long float, long integer, priority, short float, short integer, string, time, universal integer, and universal real.

For good measure, you get predefined subtypes, generic types, and private types; most come in several flavors, such as constrained or unconstrained, and limited or unlimited. Henry Ledgard, whose book combines a tutorial with the official DoD manual, calls Ada's type facilities "intimidating but very powerful."[10] (If you like the "railroad" type of syntax definitions, you should consider I. C. Pyle's Ada text.[11])

Naturally, when it comes to private (and enumeration) types, you can make up pretty much any flavor your heart desires. But there lurks danger in Ada's wealth. The language does not clearly distinguish between hardware-imposed and functional types. The former, usually called "base types," include the customary integer, Boolean, and so on; the latter might be exemplified by an enumeration type similar to the color-coded banana jacks, or by the type Day, which includes Monday through Sunday. You can thus create a functional type Volt, with a given range, and a subtype Low_Volt, with a smaller range. But such a type packs no more power than a subtype Low_Real, which is simply a subset of all real numbers. We'll see in Chapter 6 why these foibles limit code *robustness*.

To snare followers of the object-oriented creed, Ada also offers derived types, which belong to the same "class" of types as a parent type. *Inheritance*—the *sine qua non* of object-oriented programming—gets its (meager) due in the form of a type's attributes, which a derived type acquires from the parent. As to the inheritance of procedures, the manual is vague: "Certain subprograms applicable to the parent type . . . are derived by the derived type. These derived subprograms are implicitly declared at the place of the derived type definition."[12] English is a good vehicle for information hiding.

To illustrate the derived type quandary, imagine you have a type Money. Two derived types could be Dollar and D_Mark. You could set their permissible range (formally, constraints) to different values—say, your expense account can be authorized for $2000 or for DM3000. But there is no easy way to specify an attribute such as "subunit" and give it the name "cents" for one currency and "Pfennig" for the other. No wonder most true AI disciples exclude Ada from the realm of True Objects.

If you wish to model a real-world system, such as San Francisco's BART trains, Ada's types and constraints provide you with a suitable toolkit. (Chances are that, for example, the infamous "ghost trains" that blocked traffic for hours in 1983 could have been busted by Ada.) To keep tight reigns on your variables, Ada provides you with range declarations. So, to return to our roof garden, even when you forego subtypes and only declare one type Voltage, you can still make sure that the power lines (RANGE -300..300) don't get into the antenna leads (RANGE 0..0.1). As mentioned before, Ada's exception handler adds the "circuit breakers" that can help you determine where the lines got crossed.

Building complex rule checking into a language has its drawbacks. Because checking must take place every time a value is assigned, execution can become painfully slow. To let you run Ada without switching to a Cray (or to take very long lunch breaks), the language permits you to turn off various checks— even for type violations. To dodge any charges of "being soft on typing," Ada relegates these overrides to hardware-sensitive instructions called "pragmas."

Functions and procedures.   Never did the Algol committee dream that its work on type definitions would be carried to such extremes as in Ada. Nor could the scholars foresee the tenacity of such tainted practices as Fortran's "schizophrenic" distinction between functions and procedures. The former—say, sin(x)—are generally taken from a library, while programmers often provide the latter themselves. Functions are usually "called by value" (or argument), as in sin(60), while procedures are "called by name." (or reference), as in PROCEDURE Speed (Time, Distance). Pascal permits you to choose the calling mechanism. While in the default mode, all variables are passed by argument; you can impose passing by reference with the declaration VAR.

Ada lumps functions and procedures together as "subprograms," but it retains a different syntax for each. (Ada code samples in this book deviate from the Ada convention, which prescribes bold lower case for keywords and upper case for user names. We have chosen instead to stay consistent throughout all code samples.) For example, a function that provides the dot (scalar) product of two vectors, A and B, could be called within an assignment as follows:

```
Z := 2*pi + Dot_product(A,B)
```

Naturally, we must assume that you have defined such a function, as shown in Figure 3.3a.

A procedure is called, as in Pascal, by simply citing it. To push element E on a stack S, you would first write the procedure, as in Figure 3.3b, and then call it wherever needed by writing:

```
PROCEDURE Push(E,S)
```

These two subprograms also provide a glimpse of Ada's meticulous (some say pedantic) attention to detail. RAISE, by the way, invokes the exception handler.

Figure 3.3 In Ada the structure of a function (*a*) closely resembles that of a procedure (*b*). The former implements a vector product; the latter a stack.

```
FUNCTION Dot_product(A,B: vector) RETURN real IS
        Sum: Real :=0.0;
BEGIN
        Check(A'first = B'first AND A'last = B'last);
        FOR j IN A'range LOOP
                Sum := Sum + A(j)*B(j);
        END LOOP;
        RETURN Sum;
END Dot_product;
```

(a)

```
PROCEDURE Push(E: IN element_type; S: IN OUT stack IS
BEGIN
        IF S.index = S.size THEN
                RAISE Stack_overflow;
        ELSE
                S.index := S.index + 1;
                S.space(S.index) := E;
        END IF;
END Push
```

(b)

During the (not so immaculate) conception of Algol, the question of "scoping" also had to be thrashed out. Again, Ada has pursued Algol's concerns to the bitter end. The scope of a variable (e.g., Mobile) defines the section of a program where that name is valid—let's say, the package La_Scala. Step outside the scope, and the compiler will deny ever having met Donna Mobile. In essence, the scope is defined by the variable's declaration, but it extends beyond this "immediate" scope for a number of specific declarations (e.g., a block, package, or task). Otherwise, visibility rules govern the scope.*

Ada basically controls scope via the keyword WITH, followed by the names of packages to be imported from a library. If the name of a subprogram is mentioned within a compilation unit, it can be called within that unit. But beyond the direct visibility of identifiers (in plain English, names), Ada provides the USE clause. For example, if you write,

WITH La_Scala; USE La_Scala;

---

*If you don't mind digging your way through three tightly packed pages of software legalese, Chapter 8.3 of the Ada manual stands ready to explain where Ms. Mobile is visible and where she is hidden.

you don't have to address *la donna* as La_Scala.Mobile, just plain Mobile will do. However, distinguished Ada proponent and teacher Grady Booch prefers not to use USE because "it can cause loss of clarity and could introduce a name clash."[13]

This potential trouble is related to yet another Ada feature, called (in exemplary computer-science style) **overloading**. Near the end of the previous paragraph, the word "use" was—like so many English words—overloaded, because it meant two different things: (1) "to apply," and (2) a string of ASCII symbols with a special meaning for an Ada compiler. A Fortran statement provides another example:

AVGE = ((M+N)*A + (I+J)*B)/2†

According to Fortran rules, the variables I, J, M, and N are integers, while A, B, and AVGE are real numbers. So what could be overloaded? The symbol "+" is because first it means "add to the binary number in storage location M the number in location N," while the second time it means "equalize the exponents of the two products and then perform integer addition on the resulting mantissas."

If we had declared A and B complex numbers, "+" would assume yet another meaning. Ada lacks complex numbers, but it permits the addition of arrays, where "+" again means something totally different. Fortunately, Ada insists on spelling out the Boolean operators (and, or, xor, not), or "+" could have yet another meaning, namely "or" (depending on whose notation you follow). Clearly, overloading the same symbol to all generally accepted forms of addition makes sense; conscripting it for, say, string concatenation or logic is questionable; declaring it the operator for matrix dot products would be absurd.

So, will Ada really replace all other procedural (and some declarative) languages? Hardly, but since Ada includes nearly all the features of all procedural languages, it's possible to translate most such languages into Ada. By and large, though, we must expect software to remain a multilingual territory. Once "baptized," programmers tend to cling to their chosen language's features.

This is not all bad; a moderate amount of chaos keeps the imagination fertile. Perhaps here lies the true meaning of the divine intervention at the original Tower of Babel: "Come let us go

---

† Judging by recent court claims, "/2" may now be a trademark of IBM.

down and confuse their language that they may not understand each other's speech." The implication must have been: "For that will keep them on their toes."

In pursuit of side effects.   Much as the Founding Fathers of Algol might be pleased with adolescent Ada, the popularity of C would probably make them wonder whether they had wasted their time after all. They would shudder not only on account of its cavalier typing, but also for its indulgence in *side effects*. For example, strictly speaking, the C function `printf(control,arg1,arg2)` does nothing with the arguments, but its side effect provides formatted output.

Perhaps one could argue whether this really constitutes a side effect. Even in everyday usage, the "side effect" label depends on your viewpoint. If you drink Napoleon brandy to get drunk, then its superb flavor is a (rather pleasant) side effect; if you drink Zeller Schwarze Katz to award a gold medal for the richest bouquet, then getting drunk would be a rather embarrassing side effect. More serious examples of side effects abound in the world of medicine. You'll probably recall the Jarvik heart, which promised transplant candidates an end to their dependence on human donors. A side effect—due to inadequate computer modeling—may have killed not just a patient, but the whole idea. (Minute eddies in the *ersatz* heart caused blood to clot, leading to numerous strokes.)

In software, side effects can be just as deadly—for example, when a function call messes up the called function during a missile launch. Formally a side effect is defined as the modification of a data object bound to a nonlocal variable.[14] In other words, inadequate type checking and scope control can play havoc with a program.

True to the hacker spirit, C addicts see side effects more as opportunities than threats. For example, they may call a function merely to pass parameters (call them "functions traveling under assumed names") without ever using the value it returns. Pity the programmer who has to debug someone else's side effects. But what triggered the whole issue in the hallowed halls of the Algol committee was unrelated to C—which had not yet been conceived. Rather, the fire was kindled by the desire of some members to mimic the conditional statement in Lisp, which was just catching on in academia. We'll return to Lisp and its progeny (which includes the C derivative C++) in Chapter 12.

⌙ Hungarian and Other Alternatives

In spite of all engineering and academic misgivings, you can write fairly reliable code even in a freewheeling language like C. Whatever controls are lacking in the language can be built into the design environment. In fact, such a solution may eventually prevail because it satisfies the rule-checking needs without burdening the language itself. But even without such an environment, much can be done to make programming safer. For example, you can impose some discipline on C programming—by learning Hungarian.

There's some confusion about the origin of the term "Hungarian," but not about the originator of the technique. He is Charles Simonyi of Microsoft (and long before that, of Hungary).[15] It seems that one of Simonyi's early disciples commented: "Looks Hungarian to me," and the name stuck. Hungarian is essentially a naming convention that tags variable or procedure names in such a way that the name conveys a great deal of information to other programmers. To the computer, Hungarian C looks exactly like plain Kernighan C. (Any other language that does not restrict word length unduly can also benefit from Hungarian.)

Under the convention, variable names consist of prefixes (also called "constructors"), base types, and qualifiers. Constructors help describe the variable's type; for example, p identifies a pointer, and i an index into an array. The base types include such mnemonics as f for flag, b for byte, ch for character, or v for a "void" (a lucid C term for an unspecified type). Thus, "pch" identifies a pointer to a character, and "ib" an index for a byte array. But such type descriptions are not necessarily unique. For example, "hrgch" could be a huge (32-bit) pointer to an array of characters, or it could be a handle (a pointer to a pointer) to a character array; it is definitely not a Hungarian first name.

Qualifiers are capitalized and include such Ada-like terms as "First" and "Last" (element in a set), and "Src" and "Dest" (the source and destination in a transfer operation). Functions or procedures are also capitalized and should disclose their purpose. For example, a function that calculates centimeters from inches could be called CmFromIn(in), where (in) identifies the input type. (No information hiding in this function's name!) Although C-Hungarian (like real Hungarian) takes some getting used to, converts swear by it. Figure 3.4 offers a choice morsel to whet your appetite.

```
        /* excerpts from a program that handles cursor movement */
                yw = YwFromYp(noldr, idr, edl.ypTop);
                if (!vfLastCursor)
                        {
                        FormatLineDr(wwCur, cpFirst, pdr);
                        vxwCursor = XwFromXp(hpldr, idr,
                                XpFromDco(0, (uns)(cp - vfli.cpMin),
                                    &xpDummy, &ichDummy));
                        }
                xw = vxwCursor;
                if (yw + edl.dyo >= ywMin && yw < ywMac)
                        {
/* cursor is visible before the move */
                        if (sty == styLine)
                                {
                                if ((fUp && (--yw) < ywMin) ||
                                    (!fUp && (yw += edl.dyp) >= ywMac))
/* cursor not visible after the move */
                                        yw = YwScrollForCursor(sty, fUp, hpldr, idr);
                                else
                                        fAlreadyChanged = fFalse;
                                }
                        }
                else
                        goto LNotVisible;
                }
        else
                {
LNotVisible:
/* routine gets cursor invisible before, visible after move */
```

Figure 3.4 "Hungarian" notation offers (manual) type control for weakly typed languages, such as C. A segment from a cursor control routine is shown here.

In a way, Simonyi's conventions provide a kind of design rule checker for programmers rather than for computers. The statement

```
if(co==coRed)
    *mpcopx[coBlue] += dx;
```

passes scrutiny for proper typing, because in the condition a co is compared with another co, and in the assignment statement one ..x is added to another ..x. If the (dereferencing) asterisk were missing, the line would be in error because you would add a pointer to a value (px signifies a pointer, dx the difference between two instances). That would amount to adding, say, a minute to a meter—something a rule checker would never allow.

How to venture Forth. And now, as Monty Python's flying acrobats used to say, something completely different. So far, we've talked about mainstream languages that could be more or less translated into each other (***Rapitech***'s Conversionware, for example, includes translators between Fortran, Cobol, Pascal, Ada, and C). We've discussed these languages in the framework of CASE-driven top-down design. But bottom-up design also merits its place in the sun because it promotes the reuse of existing building blocks.

Now we'll pay homage to the brotherhood of the True Bottoms-Uppers, who believe in design from scratch. Programmers who must interact with hardware, as in operating systems or device drivers, mostly rely on C today (or on assembly language when speed is of the essence). However, there is an intermediate language waiting in the wings that—according to partisans of a small but hardy clan—combines the power of high-level languages with the speed of assembly code. In fact, zealots insist that Forth is faster than assembly code and is higher-level than high-level languages.

Forth was invented about two decades ago by Charles Moore to squeeze more real-time juice from anemic 1960s-style minicomputers. He found his lingo so powerful that he defined it as a fourth-generation language. But his computer would accept five-letter words at most, so he dropped the "u" from "fourth," and the "small is beautiful" deluge was on its way. (Nuff sed?) The power of the Forth clan (which by now includes polyForth, Multi-Forth, MacForth, and even Fifth) stems from expandability. You can define "words" (basically, instructions) to your heart's content. Forth also creates dense code, so a normal routine plus the Forth kernel fit into most microcomputers' on-board ROM (where they are immune to virus infections).

Like every remedy, Forth's compactness has its price. Terse C has been called a write-only language, because it's hard for anyone other than the writer to understand.[16] In fact, one of the motives of Hungarian C was to adapt programming in C to teamwork. Well, Forth (according to many of its users) is a ***write-only*** language even for the author. So why should we bother with it at all? Because, unlike assembly, Forth lets you construct routines so easily that some programmers use it to write and debug assembly code.[17] Forth's multitasking capability furnishes system hackers with another inducement.

Not only can Forth speed up development of embedded systems as much as tenfold, you can also use it to write your own system software—for example, a KISS compiler. Furthermore, Forth helps software people understand how stack-oriented hardware works. Forth's built-in interpreter is so fast because it pops values as well as instructions off a stack. (It can, however, not be faster than a well-written assembly program for the same task.) That's also the reason why Forth must use reverse Polish notation, best known to users of ***Hewlett-Packard*** calculators.[18] Instead of (2+3)*5, in Forth you write 5 2 3 + * , so that the interpreter finds numbers in the stack that it can work on. But how can you do that if one number appears twice, as in a*(a+b)? You need the operator DUP, which copies its operand: a DUP b + *. Some love Forth's stickshift-like control, but does anybody really appreciate double clutching?

Things get even more perplexing when you write an IF/THEN/ELSE construct in Forth. Take the statement

IF count<10 THEN Forward ELSE Back

where Forward and Back are procedures. In Forth you write:

10 < IF Forward ELSE Back THEN ;

Of course, you must be sure that count is indeed the variable currently on top of the stack. (Perhaps Forth will someday be discovered for memory proficiency exercises.)

This is not the place for a Forth tutorial,[19] so we'll just take a brief look at a small Forth program and then move on.

```
HEX 27A0 CONSTANT 'OVEN
7 CONSTANT TIME (minutes)
0 CONSTANT ON
1 CONSTANT OFF
: OVEN 'OVEN !; (store definition)
: COOK 0 DO 60270 MS LOOP;
: DINNER ON OVEN TIME COOK OFF OVEN;
```

The first line identifies the output port for a microwave oven; the next three lines define the program's constants; and the remaining lines form new "words" (procedures). Because one loop execution takes about a millisecond, we need quite a big loop to get a one-minute time interval. The last line is actually the main program, feeding first a "1" (defined as "on") to the oven port, and after the delay COOK a "0" (defined as "off"). Now you simply type DINNER, followed by its variables, and after seven minutes dinner will be ready. (Provided you first put a tray in the oven. Even Forth has its limits.)

Simulation beats perspiration. As we have just seen, Forth makes for quite a neat simulation language. Although unconventional, it is strictly a procedural language, down to the byte level. At a time when computers control the whole industrial world, simulation is indeed essential to our survival. Training airline pilots on real 747s or astronauts on real spaceships is a bit expensive, to wit:

During tests of the Columbia space shuttle, a bug prevented firing of the solid-fuel boosters. Why? Because the hydrogen pumps in the shuttle weren't quite ready when the model predicted they should be. Draining and refueling the shuttle costs approximately $200,000. Or you may recall the crash of an F-14, caught in an uncontrollable spin. A bad code patch was at fault, and simulation did not uncover it. The same fate awaited the twelfth F-18 prototype, dispatching additional millions. A few sloppy models like that, and you'll notice the side effects on your 1040 form.

Inadequate modeling also brought down United's flight 310 to Denver in 1983. The control computer, programmed to optimize for fuel efficiency, ran the 767's engines so slowly during the landing approach that ice formed, causing the engines to overheat and lose power altogether. This possibility had escaped the model builders or overwhelmed their computers (designed by simulation, naturally). We could go on and on; such events should convince everybody that simulation software is just as critical as operational software.

A number of specialty languages have indeed emerged in different fields (e.g., Chill for telephone and Ada-like VHDL for computer system designers). But as an example for a procedural simulation language, we'll examine a more general-purpose one, Simscript. Marketed by *CACI Inc.*, the rather Basic-like language enjoys a large following both in technical and management applications. A typical Simscript program has the following form:[20]

```
Main
    CALL Read.Data
    CALL Initialize
    START SIMULATION
    Define output
END Main
```

Actually, most procedural programs would sport a similar outline. Data files may not have to be read explicitly, but initialization nearly always precedes the main algorithms. A brief example should convey the flavor of Simscript.[21] It endeavors to determine the most efficient staffing of a gas station, and is shown in Figure 3.5. The program's preamble describes the model adequately. Note that neither input data nor initialization require separate program units. Lines 6 and 7 of the main program define the output; the format description follows the keyword THUS. For the first run, it produces this output:

```
Simple Gas Station Model with 2 attendants
Average customer queue length is      7.809
Maximum customer queue length is     21
The attendants were busy  98.64 percent of the time.
```

Figure 3.5 A specialized simulation language like Simscript can express the operation of a filling station much more concisely than a general-purpose language.

What makes the model realistic is the random arrival of customers. It is determined by the function call UNIFORM, which assumes a normal random distribution within prescribed limits. Thanks to its wide choice of event distribution functions, Sim-

```
1   PREAMBLE
2       Processes include Generator and Customer
3       Resources include Attendant
4       Accumulate Avg.Queue.Length as the Average and
5          Max.Queue.Length as Maximum of N.Q.Attendant
6       Accumulate utilization as the Average of N.X.Attendant
7   END

1   MAIN
2       CREATE EVERY Attendant(I)
3       LET U.Attendant(I) = 2
4       ACTIVATE Generator NOW
5       START SIMULATION
6       PRINT 4 LINES WITH Avg.Queue.Length(I), Max.Queue.Length(I),
7          AND Utilization(I)  * 100. / 2 THUS
Simple Gas Station Model with 2 attendants
        Average customer queue length is      *.***
        Maximum customer queue length is      *
        The attendants were busy  **.** percent of the time.
8   END

1   PROCESS GENERATOR
2       FOR I = 1 TO 1000,
3       DO
4          ACTIVATE Customer NOW
5          WAIT UNIFORM.F(2.0,8.0,1) Minutes
6       LOOP
7   END

1   PROCESS CUSTOMER
2       REQUEST 1 Attendant(I)
3       WORK UNIFORM.F(5.0,15.0,2) Minutes
4       RELINQUISH 1 Attendant(I)
5   END
```

script adapts well to most modeling needs. This rich library will prove extremely beneficial if you ever want to develop a large simulation routine with the help of CASE tools. It's unlikely you'll ever find any Simscript code generators to ease the chore, but you can see from the example that Simscript constructs closely follow those of mainstream programs.

In contrast, descriptive simulation languages derived from Simula tend to lack such convenience. We'll get back to them when we peruse the descriptive lifestyle in Chapter 12. This still leaves one group of languages out in the cold—specialized (or, as Kernighan calls them, "little") languages like those used in database interfaces. Because their application spectrum must necessarily be quite narrow, they do not fit within the scope of this book.

⊓ **References**

1. Elliot B. Koffman and Frank L. Friedman, *Problem Solving and Structured Programming in Fortran 77*, 3rd Ed., Addison Wesley, Reading, MA, 1987.

2. J. W. Perry Cole, *ANSI Foertran IV with Fortran 77 Extensions*, 2nd Ed., Wm. C. Brown Publishers, Dubuque, IA, 1983.

3. William J. Birnes, Ed., *Personal Computer Programming Encyclopedia*, 2nd Ed., McGraw-Hill, New York, 1985.

4. Max Schindler, "KISS: Keep it simple . . ." *Computer Language*, January 1986, p. 69.

5. Niklaus Wirth and Kathleen Jensen, *Pascal User Manual and Report*, Springer-Verlag, Heidelberg/New York, 1974.

6. Niklaus Wirth, *Programming in Modula-2*, Springer Verlag, Berlin/New York, 1982.

7. Brian W. Kernighan and Dennis M. Ritchie, *The C Programming Language*, 2nd Ed., Prentice-Hall, Englewood Cliffs, NJ, 1988.

8. Dale E. Nelson, et al., *BASIC: A Simplified Structured Approach*, Reston Publishing (Prentice-Hall), Reston, VA, 1981.

9. Brian Kernighan and P. J. Plauger, *The Elements of Programming Style*, McGraw-Hill, New York, 1974.

10. Henry Ledgard, *ADA: An Introduction*, Springer-Verlag, New York, 1981.

11. I. C. Pyle, *The Ada Programming Language*, Prentice-Hall, London, 1981.

12. Department of Defense, *Reference Manual for the Ada Programming Language ANSI/MIL Std. 1815A* OUSDRE(R&AT), Government Printing Office, Washington, DC, 1983.*

13. Grady Booch, *Software Engineering with Ada*, Benjamin Cummings Publishing, Menlo Park, CA, 1983.

14. Carlo Ghezzi and Mehdi Jazayeri, *Programming Language Concepts*, 2nd Ed. Wiley, New York, 1987.

15. Charles Simonyi, "Metaprogramming, a Software Production Method" Xerox PARC Report, CSL 76-2, 1976.

16. Greg Comeau, "A guide to understanding even the most complex C declarations," *Microsoft Systems Journal*, September 1988, p. 10.

17. W. H. Payne, "Combine Forth with other tools for rapid software developmment," *Electronic Design*, January 2, 1988, p. 103.

18. Leo Brodie, *Starting Forth*, Prentice-Hall, Englewood Cliffs, NJ, 1981.

19. A. J. Reynolds, *Advanced Forth*, Wiley, New York, 1986.

20. Averill M. Law and Christopher Larmey, *An Introduction to Simulation Using Simscript II.5*, CACI Inc., Los Angeles, 1984.

21. Edward C. Russell, *Building Simulation Models with Simscript II.5*, CACI Inc., Los Angeles, 1983.

---

*See Appendix D

4

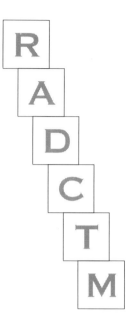

MANAGING SOFTWARE—NO BED OF ROSES

Why software projects flounder
The productivity bugaboo
Spreading the allowance
To tend a software flock

Now that the background wisdom is out of the way we should be ready to embark on our journey along the software waterfall. However, the diagram never mentions **management**. We could relegate that subject to an appendix, but much of it impacts the whole development cycle. Some issues, in fact, must be considered before a project can begin. Alas, we can't avoid bringing up technical issues that will be discussed more fully in later chapters. If you are on the way up the management ladder, you may just want to return to this chapter after you've finished the rest of the book.

Managing a software engineering project isn't all that different from managing a mechanical engineering job (except you won't ever get grease on your fingers). Hopefully you have studied some of the numerous American books that deal with management issues. Judging by a lifetime of experience, however, very few managers seem to pay them any heed—except in Japan. One explanation for this paradox might be that "over there" engineering projects are managed by experienced senior engineers, while on the home turf of "scientific" management, M.B.A. graduates often get the job. That's not necessarily bad, as long as they know their limitations. Sadly, few do.

Nothing can bring home the pitfalls of a casual approach to software management better than the study of a mismanaged project.[1] A few years ago, the New Jersey Division of Motor Vehicles (DMV) had outgrown its computer system, and in November 1983 it awarded a $6.5 million contract to New York–based Price Waterhouse & Company, one of the Big Eight accounting firms. The company had just finished another (much smaller) project using a new fourth generation (database) language, ominously named Ideal. DMV awarded a fixed-price contract with stiff penalties for missing the election-sensitive deadline of July 1985. The contractor had already provided the system specification and, in view of the tight schedule, the DMV felt that Price Waterhouse already knew what was needed and had a better chance than DMV's in-house Systems and Communications Group to finish on time.

The system was installed in stages between January and July of 1985, and New Jersey motorists were still feeling the results three years later. Under real-life conditions log-on sometimes took an hour. Response times, expected to run under five seconds, could reach several minutes. Nightly batch updates took several days, quickly building up a backlog of 1.4 million transactions. For a year the Garden State was peppered with involuntary lawbreakers, as drivers' licenses failed to arrive. (Interestingly, the fee collection part of the software never missed a beat.)

In addition to this license chaos, New Jersey police forces were thrown back into the dark ages. They either couldn't get drivers' records at all, or they got outdated ones, which is even worse. To add insult to injury, a new telephone system was unable to handle 10,000 desperate calls a day, sending out busy signals even when 100 operators were free.

In other words, it was a doozy. But what indeed had gone so terribly wrong?

The decision to let the contractor be his own project administrator could have done any pre-*glasnost* commissar proud. (*Moral*: No matter how tight the deadline and how inept in-house management, you never put the safecracker in charge of the data bank). Like all software projects, this one ran late—a fact already known at halftime. Someone at DMV had done a very simplistic benchmark on Ideal and found the language to be three times slower than Cobol. Slowness may be a new unit of measurement, but with these two languages it's more appropriate than speed. (*Moral*: Don't bet your livelihood on a dark horse, especially if it already limps on the way to the starting gate.)

Nevertheless, the beast blundered on, until installation began and the deficiencies could no longer be hidden even from Price Waterhouse brass. They faced a tough decision: Should the techies be permitted to start over (remember the penalty clause!), or was the better choice "Full steam ahead, and never mind the torpedoes."? The beancounters won, naturally. (*Moral*: If your boss's edict flies in the face of nature's laws, update your résumé.)

In the end, the vendor paid the penalty anyhow (around $6 million), because only reworking the massive updates from supposedly mercuric Ideal into plodding Cobol could get New Jersey moving again. (*Moral*: Never hitch race horses to a beer wagon.) In addition, the vendor deepened his pit by throwing $1000-a-day "experts" into the fray. (*Moral*: Adding people to a late project makes it later. Thus spoke Fred Brooks in 1975, and his computer career dates back to Harvard's Mark III.[2])

Unfortunately, the case of the conned Garden State is more the rule than the exception in the software trade. Hardly a day goes by without a story of million-dollar awards for grave injury—either to corporate or personal well-being. One company, for example, just couldn't figure out its bottom line for six years, even with help from the IRS. And a hospital was sued for $400 million when scores of patients received bills in the amount of $3500 each—for an $18 test.

In fact, software houses could soon face higher malpractice premiums than heart surgeons, lest they mend their ways. The good news is that most of the disasters can be averted with prudent management. The bad news is that good software managers are rarer than Cray computers. Even small software projects can indeed be harder to manage than big factories because only a knowledgeable software designer can tell progress from procrastination. Trouble is, good software designers would much rather go on designing good software.

What will it cost you?   Let us not emulate untold scores of management texts and belabor the obvious. If you have been put in charge of a software project, the first thing you are faced with is already impossible: estimate the project's cost in terms of time and money. Unless you can draw on experience with a similar project, you must (by tomorrow) divine the problem's solution and even assay the worth of the still undiscovered data lode.

Chances are you'll need to consult references before putting down cost numbers, but in the software arena you'll uncover few factual data. It's a rare software company that publicizes its financial track record, especially when the output included *vaporware* (which regrettably can't be converted to natural gas).

Look up *key terms* in Appendix C and *organizations* in Appendix D.

To make matters worse, nearly a decade passes before performance data can be collected and published, even when an agency (e.g., *DACS*) is already in place for that purpose. By the time the information is available in the form of cost estimation tools, more years pass by. Your best proposition is to find some estimating tool that's based on projects similar to yours. It will at least point you in the right direction and let you adjust the results according to your locus on the learning curve. Cocomo, developed by Barry Boehm[3] and based on TRW's experiences, at present enjoys the trust of many software managers even outside the technical sector. But to use it, you must first predict the size of your project's programs.

How to measure software "size" has been a bone of contention between academics and practitioners for decades. Counting lines of source code admittedly can be misleading, dependent as it is on language, application, and programmer skills.[4,5] But so far all attempts to find a better metric (e.g., by program functionality based on a specification) have found little support since they often seem arbitrary and far-fetched. Inherent complexity based on level of abstraction or control flow is less intimidating and can prove helpful if you find a tool to gauge it automatically.

One such metric, developed by Maurice Halstead, is known as Software Science; another devised by Tom McCabe, is based on control flow and has been dubbed "cyclomatic complexity." Both measures can be determined automatically (and inexpensively) by the package PC-Metric from *SET Laboratories*. The popular Cocomo, available from *Softstar*, provides estimates for a number of software categories, including application, utility, and system software.

Cocomo graphs plot cost (in man-months) as a function of line count and indicate that the cost rises faster as the program gets larger. Not all experts agree. Several databases show a fairly linear cost increase, and some even exhibit a drop due to "efficiency of scale." But the used data often scatter so widely (±50% or more) that deriving a mean value is about as meaningful as finding the center of gravity for a cumulus cloud.

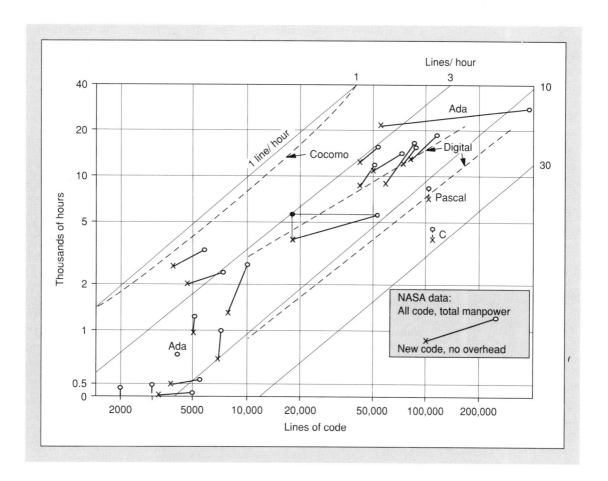

Figure 4.1 summarizes some estimates of programmer productivity. They have all been converted to lines per hour, from person-years, staff-days, and the ubiquitous man-month. (A work year comprises 2000 work hours, a month 167.) In most cases the data reflect productivity for a complete project, rather than just for coding and unit tests. The difference can approach an order of magnitude, which might explain some of the tremendous variations between otherwise similar programs. Reused code provides another stumbling block. However, unless you can borrow at least one-third of the needed KLOCs of code, interface tailoring eats up most of the profit (and then some, in many cases—see Chapter 16.)

A KLOC stands for 1000 lines of code, but as a *softworker* you probably realize it's not that simple. What is a "line"? Usually

Figure 4.1 After converting data from many sources to the same metric, programmer productivity turns out to range from 2 to 25 lines per hour. Ada grants an experienced programmer 3 to 10 lines per hour, and C programmers can attain over 20 lines in an hour's work.

it is not what looks like a line on the printout. For one thing, comments are rarely counted (but sometimes they are). Multiple statements per line (common with assembly code) usually count as separate lines (but sometimes they don't). Ada statements that can run into three or even five lines usually count as one line but . . . (You guessed it.)

In the light of such uncertainties, it would seem best to postpone the language decision as long as possible. In fact, some languages (Lisp or Smalltalk, to name two) work well in the architectural design phase; others (procedural languages like Ada) function best in detail design. Lest you think we have uncovered the rare case where procrastination can be condoned, keep in mind that software languages must also facilitate communications among a software shop's personnel. If one language dominates among them, your choice is made.

You also have to pick one language, if only temporarily, to finish your cost estimate. Fortunately, some authors present productivity data not in KLOCs but in KLEACs (which count lines of equivalent assembly code). After probing your reference with magnifier and scalpel you may know which language a given report is talking about. If so, a translation between KLEACs and KLOCs should not prove too difficult. You can find a fairly extensive table in Jones,[6] but the following short form (revised with more recent data) might suffice:

Language	Multiplier
Assembly	1
C	2
Cobol	3
Fortran	3
Basic	4
Ada	5
Objective C	15*
Typical 4GL	20

* Assumes availability of a prepacked "Software IC" that suits your application. Otherwise use 2.5.

⅃ Shooting for Five Lines per Hour

Now all you still need for a cost estimate is the productivity of an average design team for a given language. Believe it or not, when all is said and done, a line is a line is a line (sorry, Ms. Stein). Ada is the one exception, unless your toolkit automatically fills in all the verbiage. You can figure a surcharge of 50% for experienced and 100% for novice Adaphiles. (Yes, some people *do* love Ada.) But you can get your money back if you recycle any of your Ada code, because you'll have much less hassle with the interfaces.

Another possible exception should be mentioned, although few would miss it: APL programs tend to be more tedious to write than normal languages. But then, each line of APL is worth five lines of C, they say. (However, debugging APL code is nothing for the fainthearted.) Some have proposed to use APL as a "second language" in so-called n-version coding. The idea is to have the same requirement spec resolved independently in several languages to see if they produce identical results. Unfortunately, the concept has not kept its promise in practice—the majority of errors occur at the design phase, not the coding phase.

Reused (soon to be known as "preowned") code will further diminish the impact of coding errors and boost productivity. Hughes Aircraft, for example, reused 70% of the code of one air defense package in the next one, saving a cool 50%. Raytheon's Missile Division earned a 50% productivity bonus by reusing, on average, 60% of existing Cobol code. Hartford Insurance reports that 30% to 40% of new system code now comes from the reusable library, and one of Toshiba's **software factories** averages 10 lines per hour, thanks largely to reused code.[7]

If you develop technical programs, however, keep in mind that their higher diversity makes it much tougher to reach the reusability levels of MIS code, except if you profit from a CASE system specifically designed for such applications. In Chapter 13 we'll look into such a system that demonstrated a speedup of between one and two orders of magnitude over conventional programming on a benchmark example.

When you compare productivity data from different sources, you will also have to make some adjustment for "software deflation." As Figure 4.1 demonstrates, the "one-line-an-hour" rule that held 10 years ago is probably passé. Better tools (and perhaps experience) are improving the output by 10% per year, give or take 3%. That's progress compared with the 4% improvement in the 1950s ane 1960s, but it's nothing compared with the gains well above 20% that some gurus predict for the near future—and not all of them are CASE vendors.

Which language you want to use in your project should not be based on productivity calculations, though. Yes, you get much more bang for the buck from Ideal (now that it's ripe) than from Ada, but you won't win any 110-KLOC dash with it. Even more important than execution speed should be the language's relability record, usually expressed in faults per KLOC. In this race Ada *is* winning medals. Naturally, reliability carries a price tag, even though it has generally been overestimated. Actual data suggest that designing high-quality software imposes at most a 40% "penalty."

The proverbial exception that confirms this rule could be classified as "far out" in more ways than one. Software for the space shuttle is reportedly running at $1000 per line—pretty stiff even though that price tag delivers (as contractor IBM asserts) the best software money can buy. The big difference between the cost of life-supporting software versus normal (e.g., accounting) software lies in the required testing and documentation, not in the choice of language or methodology.

Let experience speak.   General Electric[8] has pegged the productivity for mission-critical or life-supporting real-time software at about $100 per line. Assuming a rate of $50 per hour, this amounts to one-half line per hour. By comparison, other software categories come in at the following levels, all in lines of code per programmer-hour:

Type of software	Simple	Average	Complex
Real-time	2–4	1–2.5	0.7–2
Other	6–10	2–7	1.2–3.3

These estimates should also help you interpret the productivity ranges given in Cocomo curves and in Figure 4.1.

This figure may appear somewhat crowded, but it does pack a lot of information. The base data stem from NASA and involve programs written in Fortran with some assembly language mixed in—not uncommon for older aerospace projects. The smaller programs (under roughly 10,000 lines) were neither real-time nor mission-critical, while over half of the larger ones served at least real-time functions. For each program (or project), Figure 4.1 contains one line. The left end, marked with an X, indicates new lines of code versus the effort required to design and debug that code (net productivity). The right end, marked with a circle, includes reused code and all project overhead such as management, documentation, and so forth (gross productivity).

In one case, a triangle has been constructed atop this line. Its apex marks the point where the circle would lie if you neglected the old code altogether. Thus, the vertical side of the triangle directly measures the project's overhead, including the cost of integration with the old code. If little modification or retesting was necessary, this apex point could be more meaningful than the one marked with the circle. You can, naturally, construct such triangles for all the programs shown as solid lines. Just by looking at the lines, though, it is obvious that both reused code and overhead varied over wide ranges. That's to be expected, but we'll never know how much of the spread simply stems from sloppy data.

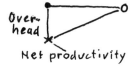

Interestingly, net productivity for nearly all the projects lies close to 3 lines of code per hour (L/h). Only one reaches the Cocomo estimate (on page 67 of Fairley[9]) for system software—about 1 L/h. Even the Cocomo curve labeled "utilities" (at about 2.5 L/h) seems quite conservative. The General Electric estimates[8] appear to be more realistic, especially when you recall that the NASA data stem from the late 1970s.

Two entries marked "Pascal" and "C" fall into the 10 to 30 L/h range. Both projects stem from 1980; the former reflects a collection of programs written in Pascal and Fortran, the latter a compiler written in C. The Pascal project dealt with electronic design automation—specifically the layout of custom integrated circuits. At the time when the company reported this productivity, the system had been released, but maintenance was yet to come. The same goes for the C project, whose remarkable productivity can be attributed to two factors: (1) development under the Unix Programmer's Workbench and (2) the composition of the group—all hand-picked graduate students.

The illustration also contains two broken lines marked Digital. They were gleaned from programs written over an eight-year period at **Digital Equipment** in the proprietary Bliss language. The top line summarizes projects between 1980 and 1985, the bottom line averages results from then until 1988, after productivity tools such as VAXset had been adopted by the group. Although these entries can't be compared with others in the chart because they include comment lines, they do make a powerful statement for software automation. Perhaps even more interesting is the comparison of error reports from the field: It tumbled from an average of about 1 error per KLOC to under 0.07.[10] (The national average hovers around 10.)

Ada stacks up well.   Two chart entries are marked Ada, one near the top, and the other near the left edge. Both stem from an Ada project realized during 1985 at Concurrent Computer Corporation in Tinton Falls, New Jersey. The company developed an Ada compiler for its line of multiprocessor machines. Luckily it was able to buy the front-end of an already validated compiler, so that only 50,000 of the 400,000 lines (5 to 10 times the size of most other compilers) had to be developed. Judging by the graph, the productivity appears disappointing at first glance. However, data collected from four large Ada users by *Reifer Consultants* (which offers the cost estimation tool Softcost-Ada) puts the average during *development* at 1.9 L/h for Ada, compared with an aerospace industry average of 1.2 L/h.

The Ada results earn more respect when you convert the count into equivalent assembly lines (which carries its own risks, as we'll see in a moment). From 11 benchmarks, we can conclude that one Ada line can supplant between 1.5 and 8.5 assembly line instructions. For a program that employs 75% Ada-specific constructs, the average comes out to a factor of 6. To be on the safe side, we'll assume a multiplier of 2.5 against NASA's Fortran/assembly programs. That brings the Concurrent compiler project right in line with the NASA cluster.

This still may leave you underwhelmed unless you take two other factors into account. First, only half the compiler team was experienced in Ada, and it took much longer to get the hang of it than originally anticipated (well over a year is needed to become proficient). Second, an Ada compiler must undergo extensive validation tests—close to 1900 at last count. The resulting code is just about as perfect as we know how to make it.

The single point marked "Ada" at the bottome left of Figure 4.1 may provide a value more typical of normal Ada projects. It represents the code generator of the compiler, whose 4183 lines include 87 procedures. Based on previous experience, a code production rate of 1.5 L/h had been anticipated, but actual productivity was nearly four times that. After converting to equivalent assembly lines, the productivity corresponds to about 15 lines of C code per hour, which is nothing to sneeze at.

To conclude the discussion on programming productivity, a word of caution when you normalize to assembly line equivalents. Data from previously mentioned *DACS* imply a strong dependence of such an equivalence ratio on program size. As Figure 4.2 reveals, productivity with Fortran on the surveyed projects rose slightly from 2 L/h on very small projects to

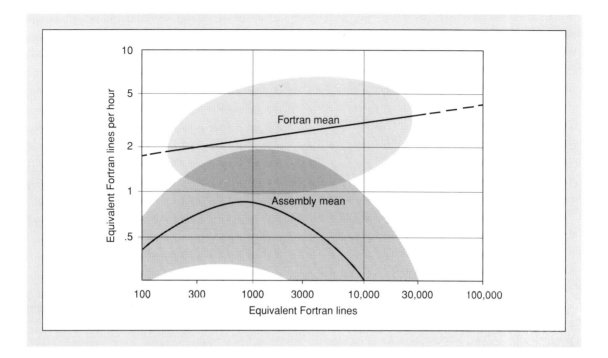

about 3 L/h on moderately large ones. In contrast, assembly code productivity—when plotted in Fortran equivalent units—peaks at around 1000 lines, dropping sharply for larger programs. Although the data scattered widely, the trend is manifest.

⌐ When You Spend Affects How Much You Spend

Steady staffing levels throughout a project's duration can reduce costs substantially. In fact, attaining this goal is a primary objective of the CASE movement—and of Ada. As we'll soon see, both shift manpower needs toward the front of the project—more time is spent on design and less on testing. However, reliable data on the distribution of effort for the waterfall model are hard to come by, because no two project managers ever define the phases in the same way. Still, by compiling existing data from the literature we can come up with a reasonable approximation.

In Figure 4.3*a*, the solid line represents the present situation: as a project progresses, the manpower requirements

Figure 4.2 Converting the code harvest in diverse languages into equivalent lines of assembly code can be misleading: Compared with a high-level language like Fortran, assembly programming becomes very inefficient as program size grows.

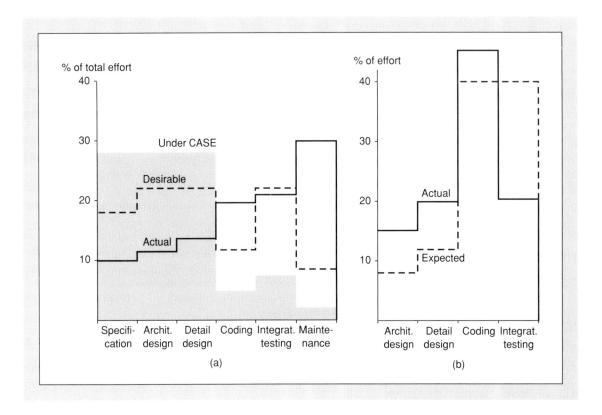

Figure 4.3 Present software development is shown (*a*) to deviate from a desirable load (broken line) by bunching manpower demands toward the end of the life cycle (solid line). Under CASE, this trend should be reversed (overlay). An Ada project (*b*) implies that this language by itself shifts the emphasis toward design (solid line) compared with past experience (broken line).

increase. (Keep in mind that the horizontal axis does not represent time, but only the sequence of life cycle phases.) Maintenance presently consumes more than any other phase for two reasons: (1) it lasts nearly forever and (2) bugs uncovered in the field cost up to 1000 times as much to fix as bugs in the early design stages. As one consultant put it, software problems are like cancer; it pays to get them under control early.

Actually, the figure may understate the cost of maintenance. Ten years ago Sperry-Univac reported that 50% of a software product's cost ensues after the first release. (We'll get back to that in Figure 5.1.) Revisions, documentation, and other support go on for years. Here too the old 80/20 rule holds. As software guru Boehm explains, 80% of the rework typically results from 20% of unresolved errors.

The broken line in the figure stems from data obtained by *The Technology Research Group* and reflects the wishes of software professionals for embedded systems, adjusted for our waterfall model. More effort should go into the design phase, they say, and less into coding and maintenance. Of the surveyed programmers 43% believe that analysis and simulation tools will indeed cut software cost. With the help of CASE tools, correct design and automatic coding should therefore reduce the maintenance problem dramatically.

We have added an overlay to Figure 4.3a that expresses the dreams of CASE proponents. In their scenario, coding is reduced to fine-tuning the output of the code generator, and testing turns into a mere formality that customers (irrationally) cling to. Maintenance becomes obsolete because changes will be made to the requirement specification, and the CASE system will automatically revise the software accordingly. Time will tell.

Actually, there never has been any software "maintenance"—code does not wear out. Perhaps we should dub this activity "sustaining the code," to imply adaptations rather than repairs. Anyway, in avionics software, this function tends to consume 60% of the total *project* cost. Under a third of this (18%) went for corrections, while a whopping 42% of the project cost went for modifications. We should keep this number in mind when debating formal software specifications.

Figure 4.3b can shed some light on the impact Ada will have on software production. It reflects the Concurrent project whose nature demanded no resources for requirement or maintenance efforts. For an Ada compiler, a detailed specification exists; besides, the compiler's front-end was purchased fully validated. Maintenance should be minimal, once testing satisfies the official validation suite. The broken line represents the resources allocated in the project plan; the solid line shows actual costs.

As it turns out, Ada did require considerably more design effort than experience with prior projects suggested—certainly a step in the right direction. Integration testing also followed the CASE script and dropped 19%. However, the coding effort sharply exceeded estimates, because Ada proved to be rather capricious. Then again, once code generation is automated, the unexpected hump in the curve will turn into a dale.

As for testing, the old saw still rings true: Quality can't be tested into a product once it's finished. Software producers serious about quality must record every bug trapped and rubbed out from day one. You have a leg up with Ada: in one comparison there were 70% more errors in Fortran than in comparable Ada programs. Still, testing will remain an integral part of your plan, because even automatically generated software must undergo at least a formal acceptance test. In the long run we can expect testing tools like those discussed in Chapter 15 to be integrated with CASE systems.

Let's remember, though, that programmer productivity is only one facet of project planning; code robustness and quality figure just as prominently. According to an AT&T study, half of all errors are made in the specification phase, 30% during design, and 20% in coding (which pretty much confirms the numbers given previously). Add to that the fact that fixing an error after the coding phase can cost hundreds (if not thousands) of dollars per error, and an ancient cigarette ad acquires new meaning— "It's what's up front that counts."

Nothing eclipses quality. We keep coming back to code quality, since all bets on project costs are off when quality lags. The price of exterminating bugs depends on many variables, but we gain some insight from the NASA programs used in Figure 4.1. Between 1 and 14% (on average, 2% for small and 1% for large projects) of the new lines of code contained errors at the end of the coding phase. Over half the total stemmed from just two causes of about equal magnitude: typos, and design (or algorithmic) errors. To *find* the bugs took under one hour for 58% of them, up to eight hours for 32%, while the balance consumed more than a day. To *fix* the bugs was tougher: 44% took less than an hour, 32% less than a day, 16% up to three days, and the rest took even longer.

Thus, about 150 hours were needed to fix 20 bugs in every 1,000 lines of code. With an average production rate of five lines per hour, 75% of the programming effort thus goes into fixing bugs. Today, language-sensitive editors wipe out most typos, but the algorithmic errors still consume the same time, unless they can be prevented to begin with—which makes an excellent case for CASE. As to the C and Pascal projects in Figure 4.1, no error figures are available, but we know that the Ada compiler project generated 389 problem reports for 50,000 lines, primarily during integration testing. That amounts to 7.8 faults per 1000 lines— three times better than the NASA code. In fact, Concurrent had expected 800 mistakes based on prior experience, the same rate as for NASA programs of the same size a decade earlier. Designing with Ada[11] appears to be a sound choice.

Let's say you have made your language decision and established overall manpower needs for each design phase. Now these must be scaled to meet the customer's delivery goal. Let's assume that the project requires 20 staff-years, but the customer wants the product in 12 months. Needless to say, putting 20 programmers with a mix of experience on the job won't do. If you had a sadistic math teacher in high school, you may remember this type of problem: "If it takes 4 cows 9 months to bear 3 calves, how long will it take 40 cows to produce 12?" Software, too, can't be rushed.

Barry Boehm of Cocomo fame put together a chart comparing three companies' experience regarding "time compression" with the Cocomo recommendations.[12] The best anybody ever did with a 3500-man-month project was an elapsed time to delivery of 27 months. Boehm gives an "impossible region," defined by $1.875 \sqrt[3]{\text{man-months}}$. In other words, if the project requires 1000 man-months, then it can't be completed in less than 18.75 months, which works out to an average crew size of 53 people. More realistically, Boehm's graph suggests a factor of about 2.5 rather than 1.9. But whatever factor you pick, remember that only rarely has a group larger than 50 programmers delivered anything.

These numbers apply to "average programmers" who, alas, are not for hire. As with almost all professions, the 80/20 rule applies in the software field: 20% of programmers produce 80% of the code. Actually, this rule isn't quite accurate—it implies a productivity spread of 16:1. Actual observations run as high as 25:1 for coding and 28:1 for debugging. Because teams larger than 30 aren't practical for, say, a 250,000-line program, you'll obviously want to hire the most productive staff you can get.

This poses an interesting challenge, because the super-programmers you want are generally known as hackers. While formerly denoting compulsive programmers, the word has by now assumed the connotation of software safecrackers, responsible for billions of dollars of damage a year. The fine line between challenging a computer system and vandalizing it, unfortunately, is poorly defined at best.

Swan song for the happy hacker.   In any case, neither kind of hacker takes easily to the discipline of software engineering. This is not to say that hackers can't write reliable programs—Pac-man never seems to break down. Somehow, it just doesn't feel comfortable to hire the designer of the Amiga virus,* even though "it takes one to catch one."[13,14] Having a computer immunologist aboard may offer some comfort nowadays. This is especially true if yours is the typical contemporary programming environment with networked workstations, since their hard disks and communications links provide ideal breeding grounds for electronic locusts.

Just make sure your resident exterminator clears all ideas with the boss. One hacker—with the best of intentions, said he—built a time bomb into a customer's software to make sure his employer would get a contract for fixing it. Then there was the programmer who hoped to please the boss by creating a ghost warehouse for the South California Rapid Transit System. Labeled "Storage Depot 14," it soon built a reputation as the place where missing parts went—a small black hole. "Get it from SD14" came to mean "why don't you call Santa Claus."

Viruses truly "arrived" when they made the evening news in November 1988, after hacker Robert T. Morris had managed to infect over 6000 Unix systems worldwide. (Technically the culprit was actually a "worm" because it did not multiply inside the host "tissue"). Although the German Chaos Computer Club's Steffen Wernery had pulled a similar stunt by invading NASA's VAXes via a "trap door" in the VMS operating system, nobody had taken any precautions—in spite of the fact that Unix was known to be more vulnerable than VMS.

In self-defense, DoD has since cut links to its ARPAnet, and the government is setting up SWAT teams—even though the designer of the Unix worm claimed that an experiment had gone awry. We had heard that before, when a Texas A&M student "researched" the sex life of viruses on his Apple II. Occasionally he took a break to play a game of Congo, the story goes. A friend copied the game, and soon Apples were rotting all over the country.

Assertions by the "Milwaukee 414 Gang" to the contrary, software corruption is rarely well intentioned. In the fall of 1987

---

*The Amiga virus, typical of many, breeds in floppy disks' 1024-byte boot block, from where it spreads into other disks. Because the DO-I/O vector points to this virus, it has a chance to multiply with each warm boot. Countermeasures include "cold" (hardware) rebooting, keeping all system software write-protected (better yet, in ROM), and disabling hard disks before loading any unknown software. Eliminating "holes" between code blocks also deprives the pests of breeding grounds. Inexpensive antidotes are available, but the "Tylenol effect" (which doomed *all* drug capsules) casts a shadow on all public software.

researchers at Israel's Hebrew University observed a growing lethargy in some graphics software. Only a flaw in the infecting virus led users to the ailment's source: the bug reinfected the same programs hundreds of times until the problem became obvious. The virus spread widely in two months and was meant to erase files on May 13 1988, the fourtieth anniversary of Palestine's occupation.

Thus, software terrorism was born. In this instance, it has actually been traced to a well-meaning reader letter from Italy, published in *Scientific American*. By explaining in detail how one virus had multiplied, it gave away the blueprint to virus design. Soon they'll teach Virology 101 at all the better computer science schools.

Already a number of companies make it their business to distribute "vaccines" and similar remedies[15,16]—including one in Pakistan that offered to send a virocide after receipt of $2000. But so simple and well known a measure as callback—whereby an accessed computer checks the calling system's phone number— could have repelled most virus attacks.[17] Yet, this cheap nostrúm remains unused. In any case, "No longer can you let your programmers run barefoot through the data fields," as one software guru aptly put it.

The bug stops here.   Why should you, as a software project manager, be concerned about viruses and Trojan Horses? That's what one MIS manager in a Minneapolis company thought until one of his own programmers built a sophisticated time bomb into a program—for job security. When he was fired he demanded $350 a week or he'd "shred" all company records by phone. Extortion is not the only motive, though. Another programmer felt insulted by his boss and changed the management access code. Neither carrot nor stick persuaded him to reveal it.

Of course, chances to get caught in a similar predicament don't run very high. Still, managing programmers does pose unique problems. Sociologists have found programmers to be a special breed even in sober Cobol shops. Of all employee groups, programmers exhibited the biggest need for professional challenges and the smallest needs by far, for social rewards. No wonder so many burn the midnight oil, even in an age where "getting CPU time" no longer serves as a viable excuse.

Compulsive hacking does pose health risks not explainable by weird hours and odd feeding habits. Nordvang Hospital in

Copenhagen actually specializes in "computer syndrome" cases (95% are boys 14 to 16 years old). So, if you hear somebody mumbling "20 goto bathroom; 30 if no paper check next booth . . ." a trip to Denmark would be in order. (This is *not* a sick joke. Some computer freaks actually believe they are computers!) The average software project manager may never see a case of computer syndrome, but programmers' solitary disposition definitely hampers communications and, hence, supervision.

Alright, so hacker-style programmers may be a bit strange, but you certainly should get your money's worth when you hire a Ph.D. from a reputable computer science school, right? Reports are mixed. Among the PC era's 20 most prominent and creative programmers, few thought computer science contributes much to a software designer's competence, and some even termed it detrimental.[18]

The problem is that mathematicians have claimed computer science as their own, and many experienced software professionals take violent exception to the whole idea.* Even more outspoken criticism comes from Ian Somerville[10] who declared that computer science is "hung up on the study of trivial programs" and "obsessed with keeping [software] a science [although] it's not based on hypothesis and test." Until courses in bona fide software engineering become mandatory elements of the curriculum, hiring a computer science graduate doesn't guarantee peace of mind for the boss.

Security need not cost too much. How does the software manager ensure both project control and system security while employing bugbusters? As to security, we are not talking about the cryptographic kind that a bank needs to prevent fraud.[19] (In 1986, such shenanigans cost Volkswagen alone a chilling $259 million!). Primarily, we are concerned about general system security, for which you as a project manager might be responsible. Access to the payroll file is probably much less of a risk than defining who can get at whose code. As the horror stories of rampant virus epidemics prove, security in

---

*Paul Bassett, vice president of research at Netron, once branded Edsger Dijkstra's admonition to write only "provably correct" software as "mathematical chauvinism in computer science that I consider quite detrimental . . . . Proving programs correct is usually irrelevant and will never be more than an academic pastime." More about this controversy in Chapter 14.

most software shops is so abysmal that it can be boosted with little effort. However, it's a known fact that even the best "gate-keepers"—human or otherwise—will be circumvented unless they help rather than hinder the user.[20]

CASE packages and so-called version control systems (to which we'll return) usually include enough access control to satisfy most needs. In fact, the vast majority of security breaches can even be stopped with a little prudence in picking passwords. You may keep intruders at bay by posting a sign at every terminal (right below the daily bug report):

> THIS SHOP DOES NOT USE "LOVE," "SEX,"
>
> OR SPOUSES' FIRST NAMES AS PASSWORDS

These are the favorites in American computer rooms, while the English prefer FRED, GOD, PASS, HACKER, and GENIUS. Quite interesting, wouldn't you say? (If you know who Fred is, call collect. Perhaps Sir Freddy Laker of Skytrain fame?)

⌐ Riding Herd on Software Flocks

Programmers' lust for independence (including choice of working hours) may largely account for the fact that software projects are notorious for lack of control (see Figure 4.4). CASE tools for project tracking outnumber all others (one-third of surveyed companies own them), but they often fail (85% of surveyed programmers expect them to). Such tools go well beyond the common GANTT chart, so familiar to most managers. In a software shop it will likely bomb because its milestones furnish only the crudest yardsticks. Besides, it is prone to the Waikiki effect. (Glad you asked. As deadlines pass, the top bars keep growing to the right, while the bottom one with its delivery date remains fixed. When the top overhangs the bottom, bring your surfboard.)

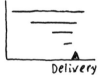

Delivery

PERT charts, thanks to their critical path, provide more help. Under computer control they can actually be used to calculate the probability of project completion, both as a function of time and of funds. Even when the effort for each individual task can be projected within a few days, in the aggregate the uncertainties add up quickly. On a two-year project, the spread between 10% and 90% probability of completion can easily grow to many months—valuable information if you possess it even before the project starts.

Figure 4.4 This parchment distills the legendary lack of control in software projects into poignant "laws." They would be funnier if less widely obeyed.

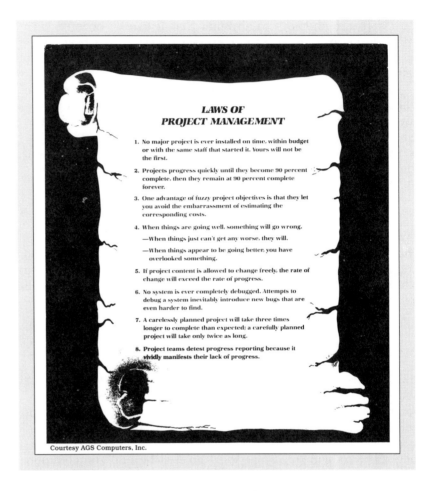

LAWS OF PROJECT MANAGEMENT

1. No major project is ever installed on time, within budget or with the same staff that started it. Yours will not be the first.

2. Projects progress quickly until they become 90 percent complete, then they remain at 90 percent complete forever.

3. One advantage of fuzzy project objectives is that they let you avoid the embarrassment of estimating the corresponding costs.

4. When things are going well, something will go wrong.
   —When things just can't get any worse, they will.
   —When things appear to be going better, you have overlooked something.

5. If project content is allowed to change freely, the rate of change will exceed the rate of progress.

6. No system is ever completely debugged. Attempts to debug a system inevitably introduce new bugs that are even harder to find.

7. A carelessly planned project will take three times longer to complete than expected; a carefully planned project will take only twice as long.

8. Project teams detest progress reporting because it vividly manifests their lack of progress.

Courtesy AGS Computers, Inc.

Practical impact, though, is a different matter. Just imagine, the boss asks for your project's cost estimate, and you say: "Would that be for a 20%, 50%, or 90% confidence level, sir?" The response will likely be: "Never mind the facts, just give me the bottom line." At one large electronics company all attempts to introduce such a forecasting tool succumbed to management resistance at high levels. Could that be one reason why this once prominent outfit no longer exists?

In contrast, some successful companies whose life depends on software have worked out effective methods for project management. For example, each phase of a project can be viewed in several dimensions: time flow (as in GANTT charts), task networks (as in PERT), information flow (resembling a bubble chart), and expenditure of effort (actual versus planned spending). Naturally, at least the senior team members must be involved in the creation of such a complex model from the start, and upper management must be committed to it as well.[21]

With the help of detailed task definitions you'll see immediately when a project goes off the track; at that point, you can either revise the plan or modify staffing. Even the best-laid plans and monitoring methods, however, can't substitute for personal contacts, which are especially important when dealing with loners. Often the most successful managers operate without formal plans. They may just tour their fiefdoms every morning and, like good gardeners, observe who needs a little water, some pruning, or a bit of fertilizer.*

A software view of management. One management control tool deserves a few more words because in its original incarnation it served as a software analysis tool. In that function the Structured Analysis and Design Technique with its SADT diagram will pop up again in Chapter 6. An SADT task box distinguishes between three kinds of inputs: data (usually entering from the left), control (entering from the top), and methods or mechanisms (captured at the bottom). Outputs originally emerged from the right face of the box but are now often leaving at the bottom as well.

A simplistic project control diagram might resemble the one from **Meta Software**'s CASE tools shown in Figure 4.5. For the design phase, inputs consist of specifications and the budget, the customer's plan acceptance constitutes a control, and the product plan figures as the applied method. To keep the "piping" between boxes in bounds, you need not indicate feedback with a separate connection, but can just add an arrow pointing backwards. While SADT is a proprietary tool designed at **Softech Inc.**, a public domain version known as IDEF0 is gaining popularity in Europe. It seems to be winning the hearts of (primarily French) data processing managers to describe information and control flow in business organizations. Oh, well—*c'est la vie*.

---

*We are not talking about the type of fertilizer so vital to the Mushroom Theory of Management: keep your employees in the dark, feed them plenty of horse manure, and when they are nice and mature, can them.

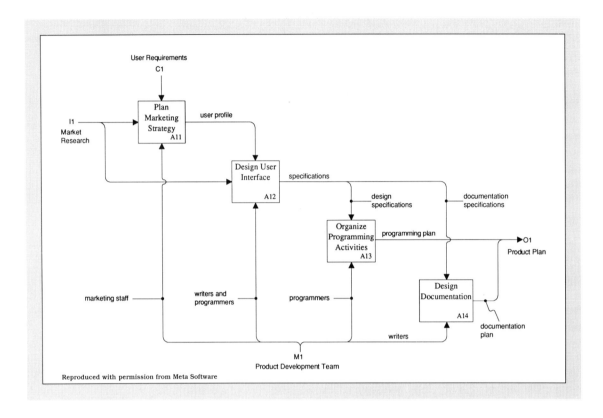

Figure 4.5 The venerable SADT diagram now finds more use in project management than in its original purpose of programming.

Because software is so intangible, professional consultants advocate frequent formal code reviews. Take their advice, but add a pinch of salt. Formal "peer review" can be merely a euphemism for propagating the status quo—a practice well known from medical and other scientific journals. You may be better off getting individual programmers into your office, perhaps together with the technical project director (who also goes by such names as chief programmer, head analyst, or system engineer). The more formal meetings should be reserved for major design reviews.

This brings us to another maxim: tracking a project's progress and cost without proper documentation means little.[22,23] When the term "documentation" comes up, most software managers will instantly think of reports and manuals. These are certainly part of it, but a much more important document is the source code itself. Code is to software what blueprints are to hardware, and it demands the same attention.

A car maker, for example, meticulously documents each change in each part's drawing and any impact the change may have on other drawings and components. Only very formal (and often cumbersome) change controls can ensure that, let's say, the stockroom's pistons will fit the recently changed cylinder bores. Furthermore, hardware engineering uses hierarchies of blueprints—layers of assembly drawings with different views. This provides a great deal of redundancy, which rarely exists in software.

CASE + care = quality software.   The CASE paradigm will rectify this deficiency with such views as functional decomposition diagrams, data entity and relationship graphs, and, perhaps most importantly, information flow views, mostly in the form of data flow diagrams. Naturally, all views must be rooted in a common project database, as discussed further in Chapter 18. However, one difference from traditional controls remains: drawings still are passed around in some hardcopy form, while source code is not. Worse yet, even a software project laid out and partitioned with utmost circumspection can still yield poor fits between pieces more easily than any mechanical endeavor.

The reason should be obvious. If two physical parts don't fit, a distant interface is seldom affected. In a complex software package—especially when it's designed improperly—almost any line of code can affect almost any other line downstream. Furthermore, programmers on major projects must work in teams, and they usually have instant access to their colleagues' work. Unless they are exceptionally vocal (and social), they may laboriously build a perfect match to somebody else's interface, only to discover at review time that the mating part was changed.

How to keep entropy in check.   As a software manager, you should read *Thriving on Chaos*[24] to help keep your projects under control. Other help is on the way as well. We briefly mentioned version control software earlier, as exemplified by CCC (change and configuration control) from **Softool Corp.** CCC incorporates such vital utilities as audit trails, consistency checkers, and source code analyzers. By identifying much-used code segments, the latter permit the programmer to speed up execution by, for example, recoding "hot" sections in assembly language. A related package also checks compliance with DOD-STD-2167A (which you won't escape for long in your job, or in this book).

Not only has version control software gained luster, it is rapidly becoming the backbone of emerging CASE systems. In fact, an *SPS* survey identifies change management as the activity that benefits most from CASE (with a rating of 2.0), ahead of maintenance (1.4), requirement specification (1.12), and system design (1.07). Some version control systems, such as PVCS from *Polytron*, emphasize management controls and reports.[25] Others, such as CM from *Expertware*, form part of more comprehensive project management systems. Still others, like *Context*, concentrate on documentation.

In Europe, Istar, from London-based *Imperial Software Technology*, has been catching on; it offers a Unix-based development framework, optimized for large projects. At the center of the system resides a contract database surrounded by communications and tools interfaces. It can thus serve as a "software bus" for a wide range of software tools, similar to Backplane from *Atherton Technology*. The underlying concepts of such tools will be discussed in more detail in Chapter 18 on standards.

More ways to skin the CAT.   The computer-aided tools (CATs) described so far, by and large assume that your project will follow the venerable waterfall model. However, most can be applied just as well to other software design approaches. For example, you can take the "3-D" tack: define (with the customer by your side), design (replace the quick and dirty code with the real thing), and deliver. If you can accomplish the whole project in just three phases (or dimensions), your project planning takes less effort, and you'll sleep better (and definitely longer) after you submit the estimate. But even if such a prototyping approach is feasible for your project, you still must make the same kinds of decisions as in the waterfall world. Life will become more predictable once a CASE system that has earned your trust automatically keeps track of progress.

CASE vendors like to brag that their products will turn every software project into a prototyping effort. After all, with CASE you can run through a top-down decomposition quickly while the customer watches, right? Not necessarily, even if only a simple data processing package is under negotiation, because top-down refinement can result in a clash between the program's and the database's structures. In fact, for most complicated software, the best bet seems to be a kind of creeping prototype approach that combines top-down with bottom-up solutions. It will be examined in later chapters.

CASE is still a young industry, very much in flux. Vendors still must learn what helps users the most. Users still must learn the most efficient ways to apply specific CASE tools. Most anything in print is (almost by definition) obsolescent, although a few books may help you make a reasonable choice,[26,27] CASE reviews appear in many periodicals, although few at sufficient depth to keep you abreast of the latest wrinkles. Newsletters such as CASE Outlook[28] from *CASE Consulting Group* fill that void, and there is no shortage of conferences and exhibits. In fact, brace yourself against a veritable deluge. Decide which companies to visit before showtime, or you'll never hit paydirt. One more thing: keep your cognitive scalpel honed as you watch demos, and be ready for on-the-spot radical hype-ectomies.

⸗ References

1. David Kull, "Anatomy of a 4GL disaster," *Computer Decisions*, February 11, 1986, p. 58.

2. Frederick Brooks, *The Mythical Man-Month*, Addison-Wesley, Reading, MA, 1975.

3. Barry Boehm, *Software Engineering Economics*, Prentice-Hall, New York, 1981.

4. Jon Roland, "Software metrics," *Computer Language*, June 1986, p. 27.

5. Lowell Jay Arthur, *Measuring Programmer Productivity and Software Quality*, Wiley Interscience, New York, 1985.

6. Capers Jones, *Programming Productivity*, McGraw-Hill New York, 1986.

7. Edward J. Joyce, "Reusable software: Passage to productivity?" *Datamation*, September 15, 1988, p. 97.

8. General Electric (staff), *Software Engineering Handbook*, McGraw-Hill, New York, 1986.

9. Richard Fairley, *Software Engineering Concepts*, McGraw-Hill, New York, 1985, p. 67.

10. Ian Somerville and Ron Morrison, *Software Development with Ada*, Addison-Wesley, Reading, MA, 1987.

11. Anne Smith and Thomas Harris, "Software productivity measurements," *Digital Technical Journal*, February 1988, p. 20.

12. Roger Baldwin, "Reportage on Spring 1982 IEEE Computer Conference," *ACM Sigsoft, Software Engineering Notes*, April 1982, p. 13.

13. Bill Landreth, et al., *Out of the Inner Circle: A Hacker's Guide to Computer Security*, Microsoft Press, Bellevue, WA, 1985.

14. Ross M. Greenberg, "Know thy viral enemy," *Byte*, June 1989, p. 275.

15. Tom Manuel, "The assault on data security is getting a lot of attention," *Electronics*, November 1988, p. 136.

16. Tom Manuel, "Computer security," *Electronics*, March 8, 1984, p. 121.

17. Jim Smith, "Callback schemes ward off unwanted access by telephone," *Electronics*, March 8, 1984, p. 131.

18. Susan Lammers, *Programmers at Work*, Microsoft Press, Redmond WA, 1986.

19. Harry T. Larson, "Can you keep a secret?" *Hardcopy*, July 1985, p. 21.

20. Thomas Tilbrook, et al., "A new look at some old problems," *Unix Review*, March 1988, p. 49.

21. Jafar S. Nabkel, "Crystallizing plans makes for quality software," *Electronic Design*, May 14, 1987, p. 125.

22. Tom DeMarco, *Controlling Software Projects*, Yourdon Press, New York, 1982.

23. Woody Liswood, "Project management—for professionals only," *PC World*, November 1988, p. 144.

24. Tom Peters, *Thriving on Chaos: Handbook for a Management Revolution*, Knopf, New York, 1986.

25. Jim Vallino, "Tracking code modules," *PC Tech Journal*, September, 1987, p. 50.

26. Alan S. Fisher, *CASE: Using Software Development Tools*, Wiley, New York, 1988.

27. Roger Pressman, *Making Software Engineering Happen*, Prentice-Hall, Englewood Cliffs, NJ, 1988.

28. Gene Forte, "The CASE state-of-the-industry report," CASE Outlook, May/June 1989, p. 5.

5

LIFE
BEGINS WITH
REQUIREMENTS

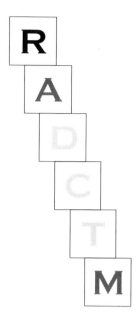

The spec is your contract
What you see is what you get
Enter software psychology

The time has come to follow His Majesty's advice to Alice and begin our journey down the software waterfall. The top basin is labeled "requirements," and finding out what the customer really wants is indeed a good way to begin. In fact, you can theoretically reduce the whole waterfall to a single box by starting out with a perfect and complete requirement specification. All you need to do is feed it into a perfect and complete CASE system, hit "Start," and pick up the code a day or two later.

Unfortunately, even if the perfect CASE tool were available, this scheme won't work in practice.[1] All you would get is what the *computer* thought you meant when you keyed in what *you* thought the customer *really* meant when he told you what *he* thought he wanted. How to compose requirements specifications has therefore grown into a discipline of its own that blends equal parts of computer savvy, psychology, and *je ne sais quoi*.

Let's take a very simple case. As a bonded computer consultant you get the following letter:

Dear Mr. Hacker:

I want to automate my bakery and I need a program. I think it will be small enough not to jeopardize my mortgage payments. You see, I only produce pound cakes. So, for every pound of flour in my dough I use a pound each of sugar and butter. Baking powder is already mixed in with my flour, as is the egg powder (please don't tell anyone!). Because of varying demand I do have to change the size of the charge for my kneading machine. The minimum is 2 pounds of each ingredient, and the maximum is 10 pounds. My oven is self-adjusting, so you don't have to worry about that. All I want to accomplish is to get the ingredients weighed on my PC-compatible scale; right now I have to punch in the same number three times and then hit the "K" key to get my kneader started. For this I have to drive 10 miles on the freeway, instead of playing a few sets while courts (and doubles partners) are still available.

Sincerely yours,

Cookie Baker

Being a tennis player yourself, you can sympathize with Ms. Baker. You're anxious to get the simple program done in a hurry, but you do have to submit a bid first, together with an airtight spec. In fact, the problem is so trivial that you can practically copy a formal specification from your predicate calculus text and feed that into your Lisp computer. (Naturally, the machine supports all those strange symbols about which the typesetter made such a big fuss when you wanted to publish your master's thesis.) You can also use the Lisp machine to get a real professional-looking letter out in a hurry:

Dear Ms. Baker:

Thank you for your RFQ, which indeed poses no problems. If I understand you right, your requirements are as follows:

$$(\forall x)(x \in X \to (\exists r)(\exists s)(\exists t)(r \in R \land s \in S \land t \in T \land x = C_1 r + C_2 s + C_3 t))$$

In your present setup all the constants are equal,
but you may want to change your mix someday. I can
produce the required program for your PC–DOS
compatible system within one week after you return a
signed copy of this letter. I am pleased to quote
you the special price of $99.95, plus five of your
delicious cakes. (How do you do it without real
eggs? You could have knocked me over with a floppy!)
I'll throw in one year of maintenance, and even
waive my standard disclaimer, because I really enjoy
cake and coke for lunch.

With best regards,

C. Hacker

(Glad you learned, Mr. H. Signing your letters $C++$ *Hacker* was
a bit pretentious.)

To be perfectly honest, you (still standing in for Mr. H.)
already have the code, automatically cranked out by your AI
machine. You therefore know that the formal spec you sent to
Ms. Baker is a correct well-formed formula (wff). But since you
still want to eat your cake, you must play the RFQ game. The
question is, will you really be surprised when Ms. Baker never
responds to this incredibly generous offer? Some computer science teachers (and even one or two AI company chairmen) would
be aghast at such mindlessness.

Mr. Hacker hopefully learns his lesson. The requirements revolution is not yet at hand. For the time being, we must communicate with software buyers in some "human-readable" language—
say, English++. The "++" stands for pictures, because far more
people would sign a contract based on a CASE system's bubble
chart than on a wff.

Let's face it, even in this enlightened age intraspecies communications remains a soft science at best. Worse yet, our gray
matter is subject to rote behavior—habits acquired over millennia die hard. (Remember Karl Marx? He promised a paradise on
earth if only people would rationally abandon such abominable
habits as greed and sloth.) In this chapter we are concerned not
so much with human psychology (and all its trap doors and con-

notations) as we are with "cognition"—that is, the way our brains register, store, and manipulate their inputs.

Battle of the hemispheres.   Brain research remains rather a gray area, but now that right brain–left brain talk has even scored in TV commercials, a few words about current theories are in order, especially since the subject impacts not only the man-man but also the man-machine interface (which we'll take up later in this chapter).

Supposedly, the two halves of the brain perform different functions. The right half is set up as a parallel processor, in which many sensory inputs can interact with (often subconscious) memories simultaneously. The processed objects may embody several dimensions, because the processing is pattern-oriented. Results are often very intuitive, if not unpredictable. How this half of the brain ties different and often unrelated experiences together and sometimes arrives at brilliant conclusions remains a puzzle. We call it inductive reasoning, inventiveness, or sometimes even genius. Painters and composers thrive on such messy thought processes.

The left hemisphere, on the other hand, is said to work more like today's conventional (serial) computers. It analyzes things in a linear sequence, which is just perfect for reading, talking, writing—and programming. No wonder computer scientists tend to be analytical, symbol-oriented, and given to abstraction. Their reasoning, like that of most scholars in most fields, tends to be deductive and cumulative. They take things apart in their mind and sort them into logical bins. Mathematicians epitomize this abstract, symbolic, and neat working of the brain's left hemisphere. Although left-brainers often enjoy the orderly fabric of classical music, they rarely compose anything more musical than études.

None of this implies that one hemisphere is superior to the other. Some well-educated professionals can't read a map. They prefer code: "Go straight through four lights (shucks, should I count the one where I asked?) and turn left into Main Street." Others instantly form an internal map after one glance at the picture you draw them, and they rarely get lost. Throughout history (probably since the discovery of fire), right-brained artisans have hit upon new ways of doing things by intuition, sometimes in their sleep. Then they have struggled on to perfect their discoveries by trial and error.

Philosophers—a more recent breed—have looked at man's and nature's creations and extracted underlying principles. Only during the last century or so did they require tools other than a pen or even a stick on a sandy beach. Still, they did have to "visualize" their abstractions to pass them on to their disciples. (Philosophers have always needed disciples. Telling others about their discoveries has been their greatest—and often only—reward.)

And what, you may ask, has all of this got to do with software specifications? Actually the rift between software practitioners and computer scientists extends through the whole software "life cycle," but it's most meddlesome in the definition phase. By understanding how we learn and how we pass our knowledge on to others, we can communicate more effectively. This, in turn, might lead to better specs, which should provide better software, which can save a lot of money, and perhaps even a few lives.

The chicken and the egg(head).   The student-teacher relationship has sparked great advances, but more often it remains antagonistic. Take the field of engineering. Physics professors tend to regard engineers as mere implementors of the scientific principles that they had taught them. Mature engineers, in contrast, know that school learning forms just the crust of the "knowledge pie," which they sell their employers slice by monthly slice. All the "filling" stems from experience; eventually it gets incorporated into the scientific knowledge base—or is lost.

Unfortunateley, it often takes decades (sometimes centuries) before scholars analyze this mix and derive the recipe, to be passed on to future generations of engineers. A recent example illustrates the process: high-temperature superconductors sprang to life when practitioners followed their intuition more than established theory. Now the academics are hard at work reconstructing solid-state theory to suit the newly discovered facts and to formulate laws that will level the way to further progress. Let's see how long that will take.

The software field is no different. Perhaps computer scientists will someday find laws of nature that put software design into a larger perspective; perhaps they won't. Meanwhile, software engineers must keep trying and erring (as engineers have always done), because we can't put progress on hold until science catches up. This does not mean we should ignore formal logic and automata theory—only that there's more to software than what you find in textbooks.

In Appendix A, which reviews computer evolution, you'll encounter the same chicken and egg cycle. Perhaps you'll wonder how our world would look if the cycle's span had been shortened. Indeed, it could be compressed to a few years, but only if we manage to persuade innovators to "commute" between industry and academe. As long as the schism between computer science and practice persists, the cycle is bound to remain agonizingly slow. Half a century has passed since Turing explained to mathematicians how a serial computer "thinks." The insights gained since then reflect a poor return on the expended brainpower.

You would probably not be reading this book unless you believe in the power of graphics for software design. We know that a video channel occupies a thousand times the bandwidth of a speech channel—an insight not lost on AI scholars. In fact, one major CASE vendor (IDE) calls its product "Software through Pictures." But like cartoons, software cannot live by pictures alone. It's the combination of text and graphics that opens up the information flow for software.

Athena is one company that applies this combination to requirement specifications (we'll encounter an example in Chapter 7). By and large, however, requirements are defined by text; perhaps this is the reason why between 40% and 80% of all software errors have been blamed on faulty requirements. Unfortunately, as Figure 5.1 proves, most mistakes are discovered much later and fixed at extremely high costs—often thousands of dollars a throw.

Perhaps once we rely more on graphics for requirements, the dismal record will improve. Obviously, we can't expect unsophisticated customers (like Ms. Baker) to write an airtight requirement. But even customers who should have the necessary know-how produce specs that need 50% more revisions than equivalent specs written by software vendors. To make matters worse, larger systems involve not just a customer and a designer, but whole chains of command.

Requirements tax bureaucracies.   Assume the H. R. Blank Company needs a new tax package. Mr. Blank tells his vice-president of 1040-related services that he'd like to see a single package used throughout the country. Can that be accomplished by tax time? The VP calls the chief technology officer and tells

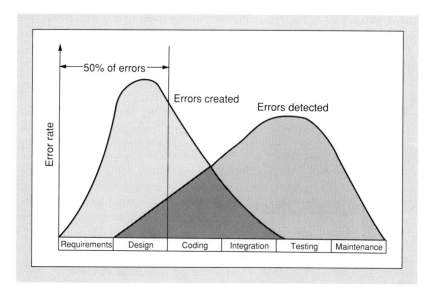

Figure 5.1 To no one's surprise, error discovery lags behind error creation. Few, however, realize by how much. Worse yet, bugs may cost 100 to 1000 times as much to exorcise during maintenance than during coding.

him that he needs the 1042A and 1044C programs combined by December 15, so that all the operatives can become familiar with the new system over the holidays. The CTO browses through the two programs, counts printout pages, and calls the director of Cobol projects. After consulting with his chief analyst, the director reports back that he lacks the manpower.

That's why Ada Lovelet, president of Coder & Hack, finds an RFQ in her mail and passes it on to her chief programmer. He knows little about Cobol but draws up a program plan for Ada to review. She cuts the proposal's cost by 15% and sends it on to Mr. Blank, who cuts two weeks from the delivery date before turning it over to his chief analyst. Already we are talking about six levels of management, each with different management skills and domain knowledge. In the case of a defense project, at least three such chains (the contractor's, the subcontractor's, and the Pentagon's) are involved.

Obviously, neither a formal spec, nor a structure chart, nor a data flow diagram can communicate all the required information to all of the parties involved. At least half a dozen specs with a dozen graphs and tables will be drawn and redrawn before the contract gets signed. In such a situation, not even rapid prototyping will help much, except perhaps when the two companies' analysts get to talking in the corner bar. But they will probably never even see each other, and you better keep that in mind when you read a specification. Chances are it has been "filtered" several times. Although American corporate culture frowns on employees who bypass levels of command, it may pay off to frequent some hacker hangouts.

Not that hardware projects fare much better, drawings or not. When you bid on a system, the drawings most likely just specify an interface and a maximum form factor (contractese for outline). So, even though a picture may be worth a thousand bytes, it can't guarantee competent interpretations along the management ladders.*

⌐ More Than Meets the Eye

We must realize that to the trained eye a drawing tells a lot more than just shapes and dimensions. Think of a journeyman who travels to Reims in 1289 to marvel at the new cathedral. He's impressed by the beauty of the flying buttresses and sketches the structure for his father. The old master would not exclaim "How beautiful!", but "What an ingenious way to keep the ceiling arches from collapsing!" Such domain knowledge can't be passed in a requirement spec that is written as much for corporate lawyers as for the implementors.

So, how should software requirements be specified? Borrow a page from the hardware designer's book. After all, the hardware implementation of an algorithm is functionally equivalent to a software implementation. And when a computer designer adds a multiplier chip to his machine, it usually will indeed multiply. The physical drawing of the integrated circuit with pin dimensions and labels naturally helps little, but the architectural schematic will show adders, counters, registers, and so on. That gets the prospective user into the ballpark, but not quite into the game, because something's missing—the details.

---

*I once directed a team that spent a year trying to meet a difficult requirement. One of the team members solved the problem and with much hoopla received a special company award. However, a competitor with an inherently inferior design got the contract. As it turned out, the specification supported two interpretations, and we had picked the wrong one. A few words with the customer could have prevented the fiasco. Moral: Though the project manager banned direct contacts. I should have ignored him and risked the blemish on my record (with indelible Dayglo ink). Ironically, the same man soon thereafter engineered the dismemberment of our organization anyway.

You follow the same process whether you shop for an IC, or for a window air conditioner in a Sears catalog. You can see at a glance whether a unit is meant for a car, a house, or a room. Next to the window models you'll find a table that gives you the specifics: room size, BTU, power consumption, measurements, and weight. Similarly, you'll find a table with all the working details for the multiplier chip—voltages, speeds, and driver load—in the IC catalog.

Someday, requirements for software packages will look similar, except that tables will concentrate on inputs and outputs—not unlike those already common in user manuals. In fact, such manuals would frequently serve very well as parts of a requirements spec, spelling out commands and meaningful error messages. Too bad the manual usually gets done last.

For machine-oriented software such as utilities, the formal kind of spec we saw earlier (for Ms. Baker, you'll recall) could also prove useful. It may not play well on Main Street, but it's readily understood at 1011 Ivory Towers. The symbols used in software calculus remind us of Egyptian hieroglyphs or Mandarin ideograms—earlier forms of written languages that could only be understood by scholars and scribes.

Later, phonetic languages broadened the customer base, and similarly logicians have added a language called SETL to their bag of tricks.[2] It translates symbolic logic into English (sort of), which at least helps the typesetter. C. Hacker's proposed spec would (roughly) translate into SETL as follows:

```
procedure Baker
   if (forall Charge in {'6','9','12'...'27','30'}
         (exists Flour in {'2','3',...'10'} and
         (exists Sugar in {'2','3',...'10'} and
         (exists Butter in {'2','3',...'10'}
     suchthat Flour = Sugar = Butter)
     then PC_input := 'K';
   end if;
end procedure Baker;
```

Yet another job for Ada. For pictophobes, another alternative to formal logic is being promoted by the Pentagon. As the world's biggest software customer, DoD certainly has a stake in clear requirements specs. As the world's biggest promoter of the

Ada language, it would like you to write software specs in Ada. This may sound strange at first, but all computer languages are really specifications.[3] A line of Ada code spells out for an Ada compiler what to do during execution. Furthermore, to an experienced Ada programmer, anything resembling the language is certainly a lot more readable than any wwf, and it is less ambiguous than English. (Especially if Ada indeed becomes the dominant language of the international aerospace industry.)

The Pentagon's efforts have resulted in another alternative called "PDLs" (program description, definition, or design languages). They can accomplish for a program what an outline does for a book. In fact, some gurus even advocate the use of "outliners," as you get them with some word processors, for high-level program description.[4] They may serve a purpose in small, largely tree-structured programs, but systems software and embedded programs resemble jigsaw puzzles more than textbooks and will benefit little from outliners.

Perhaps best known among PDLs is Byron from **Intermetrics**. While definitely a blood relative of Ada, a parent this Byron is not. As you may remember from Chapter 3, Ada uses "− −" (two minus signs) to mark the start of a comment. Hence an Ada compiler ignores everything from − − to the end of a line, and you can write a whole sonnet in "Ada syntax" as long as each line starts with − −. To distinguish Byron text from normal Ada comments, the symbol "|" follows the two minus signs.

Let's try to write Cookie Baker's requirements in Byron:

```
--| REQUIREMENT for Baker's automation program
--| Charge is the total weight to the kneader
--| Flour, Sugar, Butter indicates ingredient weights
--| K_Go is the starting signal for the kneader

PACKAGE Baking IS
--| Preamble with declarations
PROCEDURE Weighing IS
--| From the input value Charge
--|   determine the values Flour, Sugar, Butter
END Weighing
PROCEDURE Start IS
--| Send K_Go to PC
END Start
END Baking
```

This spec contains six Ada lines—the procedure and package declarations and the corresponding terminations. Even an Ada novice can derive from this spec that the program will have the form of a "package" that includes two procedures. Such information might help a knowledgeable customer to judge the vendor's approach. It will probably not influence Cookie Baker one way or the other, except that it won't frighten her off for good.

Not all PDLs—even in the Ada circuit—are created equal. Some allow you to use pseudocode (or even conversational English) in the requirements version of a program, and substitute Ada in the code version. In ADADL (Ada design language), from *Software Systems Design*, you might start out with the following:

```
IF the three ingredients have been weighed
   THEN turn on the kneader
   ELSE continue weighing
END IF;
```

and finally wind up with this code:

```
IF Number_weighed = 3
   THEN Signal := K_Go
   ELSE Weighing
END IF;
```

Here we created Ada code from the PDL pseudocode by hand. Source code can also be generated automatically, provided all necessary information is available to the CASE system. You just have to provide the actual transformations, which are usually described by assignment statements. The built-in syntax templates of most CASE systems also simplify the generation of conditionals or DO loops. However, you'll be well advised to thoroughly verify any assurance of automatic code generation. As you'll see in the implementation chapters, few CASE packages go beyond creating templates.

If a specification can be written entirely in real Ada, rather than mixed with pseudocode, it is obviously executable. Similarly, if a customer knows how to write an executable spec in formal logic, he needs no software house. Provided he owns the right CASE system, he can push the "Transform" button and vacation in St. Croix with the saved time and money. Well, not quite. We must remember that in both cases the code probably represents only a "quick and dirty" implementation of some algorithms. To obtain "production" code, which will work efficiently in the final program, a great deal of work remains to be done (and probably not in St. Croix).

⸖ What You See is What You Get

If a PDL accomplishes no more than rapid prototyping, it still can pay off handsomely. Customers don't always know exactly what they want and by showing them a first cut at the requirements, you can quickly converge on their real needs. However, the biggest advantage of the "WYSIWYG" (what-you-see-is-what-you-get) approach may not be so much technical as administrative. Prototyping forces vendor and customer to sit down together and come to a meeting of the minds. Furthermore, both parties gain the opportunity to work with actual data from the start, and that's a tremendous advantage.

Naturally, prototyping works best if a substantial part of the needed code already exists, perhaps from a previous project. When no code exists at all, there is nothing to demonstrate. A computer needs executable code just to put simulation results on a screen. A special prototyping lab with a substantial (and continuously growing) software collection can indeed evolve into a very practical tool. TRW Defense Systems in Redondo Beach, California calls the method "User Engineering," [5] and has practiced it since 1982, with productive gains of 40%.

That's great for TRW, you may think, but what about me? You can construct your own prototyper fairly easily via object-oriented languages such as Smalltalk or **Stepstone**'s Objective C. As we saw on p. 86, the company's Software ICs can leverage your coding time tenfold. If you're partial to Ada, you may stock up on basic packages (queues, lists, trees, etc.) by signing up with **EVB**. When your package store gets big enough, you'll appreciate EVB's search tree (see Figure 5.2), which can lead you to the wanted component very quickly. Categorizing components and building matching interfaces will become indispensable once code reuse catches on.

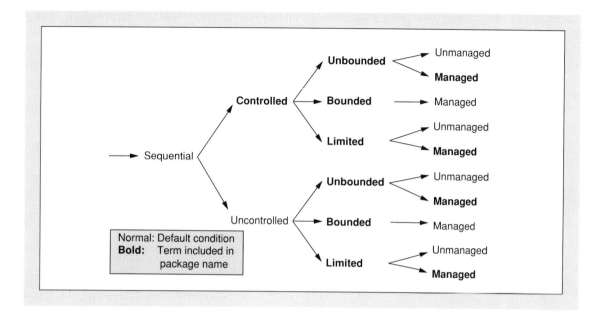

A tested shortcut.   Quite a different answer to the require-ments puzzle has been proposed by Robert Poston of *PEI*. The company offers packages for software testing, and we'll hear more about them in Chapter 15. Poston maintains that the simplest way to check out requirements specs is to test them right away—short-circuiting the whole waterfall, as it were. To do so, the spec must be executable, of course. PEI has developed an English-like requirements language called T that the company's software can read.

   Assume the requirement reads "4. The system shall deter-mine the later of two dates, Date 1 and Date 2, and output it on an indicator." In T, that spec would read

Figure 5.2 Efficient prototyping depends on access to a library of software components. However, to find the right module you need a sound taxonomy, such as this one devised by EVB for its Ada modules.

```
R04     is_to        indicate
                      later_date
        using         date_1,
                      date_2
        producing     indicator
```

If this requirement clashes with another one or proves to be incomplete, the T system will let the user know in very specific terms.

The syntax of T was partly inspired by PSL/PSA (problem statement language/problem statement analyzer—a first-prize candidate for brevity!) from **MetaSystems**. A problem statement under this method begins with a list of elements, followed by lists of entities, groups, inputs, interfaces, outputs, and processes (see Figure 5.3). Relationships between objects are defined with such verbs as "consists of," "uses," "derives," and so forth.[6] The PSA part of the system then analyzes the inputs and produces reports. Perhaps most important among them is the "contents report," which amounts to a data dictionary and includes an interaction matrix, where rows stand for data names and columns represent process names:

```
    1 2 3 4   5 6
   +---------+------+
 1 | D     R | D    |
 2 | D D   R |   R  |
```

Here, D means that row I is derived from column J (for example, data item 1 is derived from processes 1 and 5), and R indicates that row I is used by column J (e.g., item 1 by process 4). Most other CASE systems lack such analytical powers and are content with creating lists of labels (for objects, procedures, etc.) from the specs. The names are later checked against labels used in the graphic models to flag any inconsistencies. We'll encounter a few examples in the implementation chapters.

Word-processor math. So far we have implicitly treated functions as if they provided more or less mathematical transformation. But the days are long gone when computers served primarily as number crunchers. In fact, more PCs are used for text manipulation than for any other purpose.

What does *It* mean? Amuse yourself with the definitions in Appendix C.

On the surface, **office automation** chores may appear much easier than, say, calculating Bessel functions. However, in spite of numerous requests, no computer scientist has so far volunteered to produce a formal specification for a word processor—never mind a style checker such as *Grammatik*. Unfortunately, it isn't much easier to define such systems graphically either. However, a word-processing addict (say, an author) could definitely benefit by knowing the rationale behind the assignment of keys to functions—information that could best be expressed graphically.

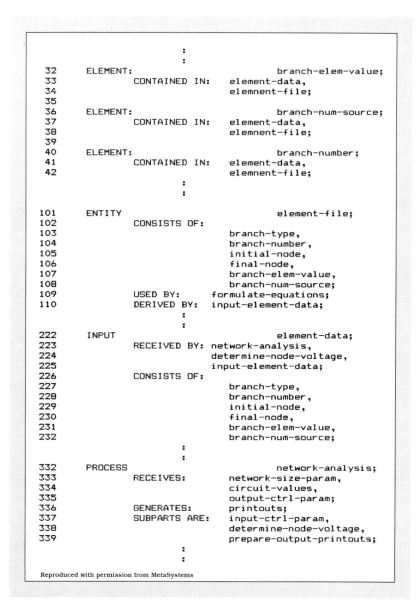

```
                                 :
                                 :
32      ELEMENT:                         branch-elem-value;
33            CONTAINED IN:    element-data,
34                            elemnent-file;
35
36      ELEMENT:                         branch-num-source;
37            CONTAINED IN:    element-data,
38                            elemnent-file;
39
40      ELEMENT:                         branch-number;
41            CONTAINED IN:    ·element-data,
42                            elemnent-file;
                                 :
                                 :

101     ENTITY                         element-file;
102           CONSISTS OF:
103                           branch-type,
104                           branch-number,
105                           initial-node,
106                           final-node,
107                           branch-elem-value,
108                           branch-num-source;
109           USED BY:       formulate-equations;
110           DERIVED BY:    input-element-data;
                                 :
                                 :
222     INPUT                          element-data;
223           RECEIVED BY:   network-analysis,
224                          determine-node-voltage,
225                          input-element-data;
226           CONSISTS OF:
227                           branch-type,
228                           branch-number,
229                           initial-node,
230                           final-node,
231                           branch-elem-value,
232                           branch-num-source;
                                 :
                                 :
332     PROCESS                        network-analysis;
333           RECEIVES:      network-size-param,
334                          circuit-values,
335                          output-ctrl-param;
336           GENERATES:     printouts;
337           SUBPARTS ARE:  input-ctrl-param,
338                          determine-node-voltage,
339                          prepare-output-printouts;
                                 :
                                 :
```

Figure 5.3 PSL/PSA defines such software units as processes, entities, or input data by means of their components, inputs, and other attributes.

Of course, the lack of such a rationale would be one valid reason for keeping mum about it. Like much consumer software, word processors have grown with the hardware, getting started, for example, on keyboards without function keys. Once the extra keys arrived on the scene, they were assigned to new tasks rather than to speed up often-used steps. The latter alternative would have destroyed "upward compatibility"—a sacred cow for the marketing manager. Any change means unlearning all the old rules. This is difficult, because after cranking out a few Mbytes on a given system, the fingers know exactly what to do, and the brain has a rough time stopping them.

In other words, specs for consumer software can get rather baroque and devoid of logic. How do you formalize a requirement that in essence says: "Build a system that exactly emulates our previous model, but also includes features X, Y, and Z"? In fact, in this context we can define "consumer software" as broadly as we wish—including even updates of a complex operating system such as Unix.

Word processors and desktop publishing packages also furnish excellent examples for software systems in which the man-machine interface dominates functionality. The only CPU–intensive processing takes place during searches and sorting. Moving blocks of ASCII characters about poses little challenge for even the simplest computer. Yet, as we saw in the first chapter, the human interface has been appallingly neglected. Early software designers set the trend, and to this day human engineering (sometimes called "software ergonomics") remains a Cinderella. Only in AI systems has the user interface moved from the ash heap to the royal palace.

⌁ Software Psychology—A Soft Science

A whole new science, software psychology, has sprung up to deal with such problems.[7] Behind the fancy name stands a growing stockpile of insights and the facts and figures to back them up. Aspiring programmers owe it to themselves and their customers to get acquainted with the work of at least one "software cognition" guru.[8,9] The human ability to interpret visual inputs should really stand at the beginning of every design for interactive software, not at the end as is presently the rule. Practically every PC user knows the frustration of such disregard. (Just recently one trade press editor reviewed a few new programs and then proposed that all software sellers uttering the term "user friendly" should be shot on the spot.)

Even the two most basic rules of software psychology remain all too often unheeded: (1) the user should be able to undo every keystroke, and (2) the computer should react to every input. The first rule is so obvious that its continuing violation ranks among the supreme riddles of the PC culture. Only the AI community has tackled the problem wholeheartedly, often assigning a single key to undo preceding commands, one by one. Even today's smallest machines can usually afford to retain some recent memory images. The mythological "DWIM" (do what I mean) button, however, remains beyond the horizon.

The second rule is best illustrated by an example. In 1987 a broker wanted to sell $25 million worth of stocks from his *terminal*. He hit the Enter key (why is it still called Return?), and nothing happened. After a minute, he hit Enter once more. Again, no response. Still nothing after the third try. But the fourth try worked—sort of. Before he fainted, the broker read this confirmation:

```
Trades executed. Debiting your account
$100,000,000.00
```

Choice of the proper method for man-machine interaction in any given application may well determine your software's success or failure. If a package is meant only for "power users" (sporting power ties), mnemonic commands are preferable to menus. If a product serves primarily intermittent (or novice) users, menus generally win out.[10] But menu hierarchies must be carefully thought out. A large majority of users get lost in even a two-layer structure.

To make matters even tougher, most consumer software is meant for both novices and experts; therefore, it should offer a path for graceful migration from menus to commands. The latter naturally are much more prone to mistakes. Users tend to hit wrong keys and forget the syntax, especially when commands are inconsistent. PC utilities, for example, occasionally ask you to respond Y(es) or N(o). Sometimes the choice must be followed by Enter, sometimes not. Here lurks a mean bug because a superfluous Enter remains in the keyboard buffer and may get the user into uncharted territory later on (like our stockbroker).

Tests have shown that both beginners and experts make lots of errors, so providing an escape chute remains mandatory. In one test, novices were using a subset of 15 commands for a text editor (which is really just an embryonic word processor). No less than 19% of the commands were in error. Experienced users (who were not restricted to the subset) still struck out 10% of the time. In another test, where inefficient command selections were also counted as errors, the rate exceeded 30%. If only 1% of these errors led the user into a dead end, every working day could have required several reboots. The days are over when users tolerate such a waste of their time.

Heimlich maneuver needed. Without a doubt, twentieth-century civilizations will eventually perish by choking on forms. Since forms have taken over so much of our lives, programmers often use them to capture user inputs. While forms require little learning, their drawbacks are severe: (1) flexibility approaches zero, and (2) everybody hates doing it. In short, don't specify this method unless the hardcopy version of the same form is essential (e.g., passenger tickets in an airline reservation system or IRS forms in a tax package).

A new and far superior approach to user interfaces is gaining popularity—that is, direct manipulation. Today this solution is limited to software that can trace its ancestry to AI (which includes the icon-and-mouse school). To give an example, the screen might show a staggered stack of files, a garbage can, and an empty file drawer. You select one of the files with cursor or mouse, "drag" it to one of the two containers, and release it. This approach requires no syntax knowledge at all, and thus practically disposes of rote learning altogether.

Before you decide to use *icons*, though, make sure to consult your lawyers (plural intended). As the raging trashcan war between Apple and Hewlett-Packard manifested, software companies are trademarking their way through the *Picture Duden*. This (originally German) picture dictionary permits the user to take in at one glance, say, all types of fruit or shapes of containers. Once available on CD ROM, this book should greatly help your lawyer to trademark whole categories of iconable everyday objects, both in look and feel. In fact, Apple's HyperCard can be viewed as a first step toward a "CD-Duden." It bodes well for America's favorite indoor sport: litigation.

Seriously, keep the legal beagles in mind when it comes to the vendor-customer interface. Unless your company cherishes the look and feel of a takeover candidate (or works undercover for *HALT*), it can't afford even a nuisance suit. Documenting customer requirements thoroughly will not come cheap. One of the oldest CASE vendors, **Nastec Corporation**, estimates that software designers spend 40% of their time preparing specification compliance documents. The company offers a special tool called RTrace (aimed at the VAX environment) to keep track of them. One particularly useful feature is the "orphan allocation report," which flags components that lack requirements. In other words, you'll find out which modules you needn't ship.

If you recall the Motor Vehicle disaster in New Jersey from Chapter 4, one vital aspect of the man-machine interface deserves special concern—response time. Loads of data have been amassed on the subject for decades. They all confirm the gut conclusion that faster is better, but just how much may surprise you. In one study, two groups of students were given menu selection tasks, one on terminals with 1200-baud transmission rate—about 120 characters per second—the other on 300-baud screens. The average number of correct searches jumped 50% with the higher speed.[9] Similar results were obtained for transaction processing as well as for engineering applications. It would appear that our attention span is a lot shorter than we think.

↳ References

1. Bernard H. Boar, *Application Prototyping—A Requirements Definition Strategy for the 80s*, Wiley, New York, 1984.

2. Charles Rich and Richard C. Waters, "Automatic programming: Myths and prospects," *IEEE Computer*, August 1988, p. 40.

3. Wladyslaw Turski and Thomas Maibaum, *The Specification of Computer Programs*, Addison-Wesley, Reading, MA, 1987.

4. Willis E. Howard, "The outline processor: A tool for program design," *Computer Language*, January 1987, p. 75.

5. Larry L. McLaughlin, "User engineering: A new look at system engineering," Conference on Space Operations Automation and Robotics, Houston, 1987.

6. Michael S. Deutsch, *Software Verification and Validation*, Prentice-Hall, Englewood Cliffs, NJ, 1982.

7. Ben Shneiderman, *Software Psychology: Human Factors in Computer and Information Systems*, Little, Brown & Co., Boston, 1980.

8. Barry H. Kantowitz and Robert D. Sorkin, *Human Factors: Understanding People-Systems Relationships*, Wiley, New York, 1983.

9. Ben Shneiderman, *Designing the User Interface*, Addison-Wesley, Reading, MA, 1987.

10. Judith R. Brown and Steve Cunningham, *Programming the User Interface*, Wiley, New York, 1989.

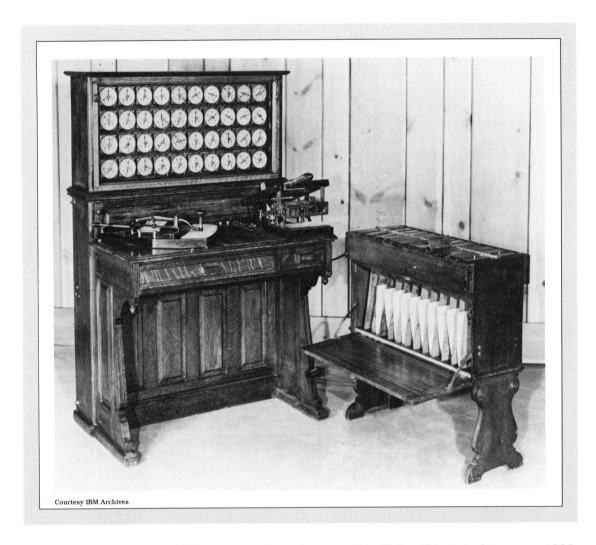

Courtesy IBM Archives

Office automation began with Hollerith's tabulator ca. 1890, combining punch cards with electricity. User interfaces have improved since then—somewhat.

6

GRAPHS BOLSTER ARCHITECTURAL DESIGN

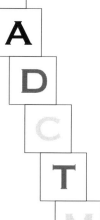

Pick the best of many views
Software's integrated circuits
Hooking up software modules
Put reality back or else

You recall from Chapter 1 that software and hardware have much in common, because both implement logic structures. In fact, one form can be converted into the other without much trouble. In Chapter 2 we discussed how computers evolved along two paths, one dedicated to computation and hence dominated by data flow, the other to control applications, where data play a secondary role. In the preceding chapter we finally dipped a toe in the software waterfall, and now we are ready for a good swim.

The software game begins in earnest with the translation of the customer's requirements into some kind of more formal specification—preferably one that makes sense to both a computer and a human being. You can view the alternatives as forming a triangle: natural language at the apex, executable specifications at one bottom corner, and mathematical specifications at the other. Requirements have traditionally been written in what passes for a natural language, which poses a problem for

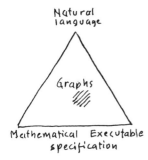

Natural language

Graphs

Mathematical specification   Executable

computers (or will at least until the year 2001, when HAL-9000 will not only understand English, but also read our lips).[1]

In the meantime, we must find a compromise if we want the computer to help us design software. Graphic representations have long helped humans with the systematic, top-down design of software, but only the recent technology of bit-mapped graphics have turned pictures into inputs that computers can "read." We can visualize graphics as placed near the center of the specification triangle, but closer to executable formulations than to algebraic ones.

With CASE systems that turn computers into prolific draftsmen, modifying software "blueprints" as they evolve no longer exacts sweat and tears. A wide range of well-tried graphic tools, augmented with a thriving crop of more recent additions, stand ready to speed software design. Which specific tools you choose depends on what kind of software you are trying to construct—the computational kind that primarily transforms input data into output data (called "procedural") or the controller type that is embedded in some kind of machinery (known as "reactive").

Most software bears traits of both types, and some fits neither category well (e.g., a graphics interface). However, the bulk of all programs used in business, as well as engineering or science, fits under the procedural umbrella. Traditionally written in Fortran, Cobol, Basic, or Pascal, this is the type of software we must deal with first. If you lust for object-oriented or declarative programming, later chapters will oblige. Nevertheless, you should stay aboard for the following introduction to the graphs used in most CASE tools.

Piecemeal conquest.   "Divide and conquer" has been good advice for generals and rulers from time immemorial, and it has served just as well in conquering (often unruly) software tasks. In fact, until you are able to break a problem down into smaller pieces, chances are you don't quite understand it. The breakdown process usually goes by the unappetizing name of "decomposition." At the coarsest (or architectural) level of design, tree structures have been the most popular representation. They are known to the structured school as decomposition, dependency, or HIPO (hierarchical input-process-output) diagrams. These trees (which in the unreal software world always grow downward) resemble organization charts, adorned with "reporting" (or calling) relationships (see Figure 6.1.)

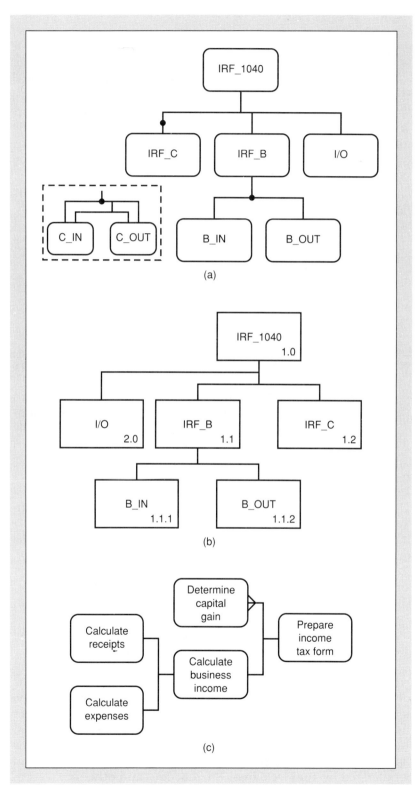

Figure 6.1 Relationships between software modules have been expressed in many ways, including decomposition (*a*), HIPO (*b*), and dependency (*c*) diagrams.

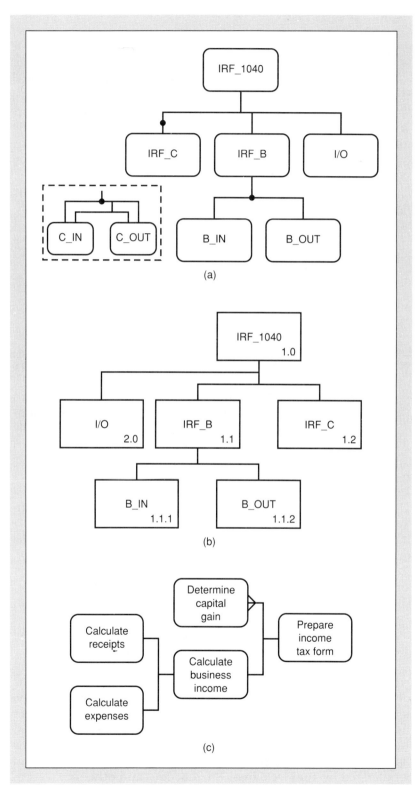

129

Unlike an organization chart, however, the software equivalent cannot be viewed as a snapshot of a system, because not all of its parts exist simultaneously. The higher levels of the hierarchy often represent only the names of subsystems or of module groups, and only the "leaves" (at the bottom, naturally) represent actual code or data. A simple example will most easily explain the terminology.

Let's assume you need a program to calculate your income tax as a consultant. At the highest level, you might call the package IRF_1040 (you know, "Infernal Revenue Form"). It will get its inputs from IRF_C (on which you'll have to confess your broker's capital mistakes) and IRF_B (which reports on your business acumen). The latter breaks down further into B_IN (the pleasant part) and B_OUT (where you get back at the tax man). To keep this book within one volume, we'll assume unrealistically that you won't need any of the multitude of remaining forms. Figure 6.1 shows the makeup of IRF_1040 as a decomposition diagram, a HIPO chart, and a dependency diagram. Later, in Figure 6.2, we'll add a structure chart and a data flow diagram, which offers a somewhat different view.[2]

The decomposition diagram (see Figure 6.1*a*) sports two black dots; one indicates that the capital gains section is optional, the other that business income and expenses are mutually exclusive. While the in/out decision is obvious for any given entry, in the totals you could come up with either income only (bad planning) or expenses only (tough luck). The inset shows the correct representation for all eventualities.

The HIPO chart of Figure 6.1*b* closely resembles the decomposition diagram, but its numbering scheme adds more information. For example, it identifies the program's I/O section as a process that's basically independent of the IRF_1040 package. The dependency diagram (Figure 6.1*c*) looks like a HIPO chart turned on its ear, but it provides further hints about the package. The crow's foot at the "determine capital gain" box, for example, lets the programmer know that this calculation may be required more than once—say, for short-term and long-term gains. All three diagrams are used primarily in the DP community.

In the structure chart (Figure 6.2*a*), arrows leave no doubt which way data are flowing. In fact, it even makes provisions for control flow (black-headed arrows). One such arrow in the figure shows that the business income is done first, and the other indicates end of file (EOF) for the business income section. Thus, the structure chart turns out to be a close relative of the data flow diagram of Figure 6.2*b*—the graph favored by CASE vendors and popularized by Tom DeMarco, Ed Yourdon, and others.[3,4]

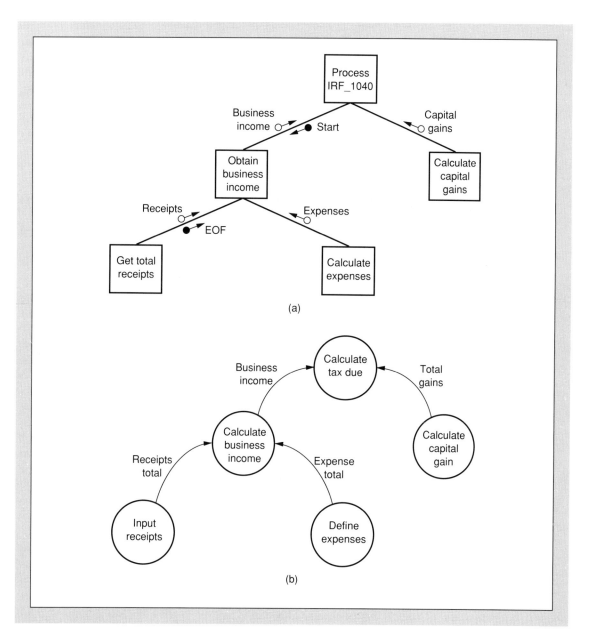

Figure 6.2 Structure charts (*a*) are most popular in front-end CASE, while the data flow diagram (*b*) reigns supreme throughout the sprawling CASE kingdom.

Before Washington started fine-tuning its take each year, it would have been reasonable to implement our tax program in hardware as well—say, as a desk calculator. The "leaf" boxes in the decomposition graphs would turn into schematics or chip layouts. But how would they relate to the other two boxes in the decomposing tree?

A nested representation evades such questions and can be applied to software as well as hardware (see Figure 6.3a). The system could be realized, for example, with two custom integrated circuits (ICs), IC_IN and IC_OUT, sitting on a small circuit board (B_BOARD). We could implement IRF_C on another board, perhaps made up of standard components. Finally, the figure's outermost frame would represent the calculator "box," combined with the I/O subsystem. After all, we need a keyboard to enter all those numbers and a display to read out the tax due. (Unfortunately, there can be no refund—we made no provisions for estimated tax payments.)

A picture is worth 1024 bytes.   With the help of such a diagram, you can put the right half of your brain to even better use and depict IRF_1040 as a three-dimensional structure (see Figure 6.3b). There, each level of detail occupies a plane of its own. For more complex systems, a layered view permits each subsystem to be shown in as much detail as desired, without running off a small PC screen. Those predisposed toward left-brained reasoning can also benefit from the "3-D" representation. Each plane clearly identifies a level of abstraction, with the highest on top. The letters in the figure merely identify information streams, shown as arrows.

The visual "language" of Figure 6.3b is not new. It had a promising start in the form of SADT (structured analysis design technique) diagrams but went into a decade of hibernation.[5] Recently, integration of such diagrams into CASE systems has begun, albeit at a snail's pace. A comparison between Figure 6.3a and 6.3b shows that the SADT format ties in nicely with software as well as hardware. Because in SADT an operand can be any object and an operator can be any event, the diagrams can be applied to things other than software, as we discussed in Chapter 4. In fact, the IDEF0 version of the SADT concept is now more at home in MIS circles—illustrating intracorporate information flows—than in software systems.

Another modeling technique, the state transition diagram, is shown in Figure 6.4. This diagram resembles the data flow diagram, except that arrows now identify processes, while the

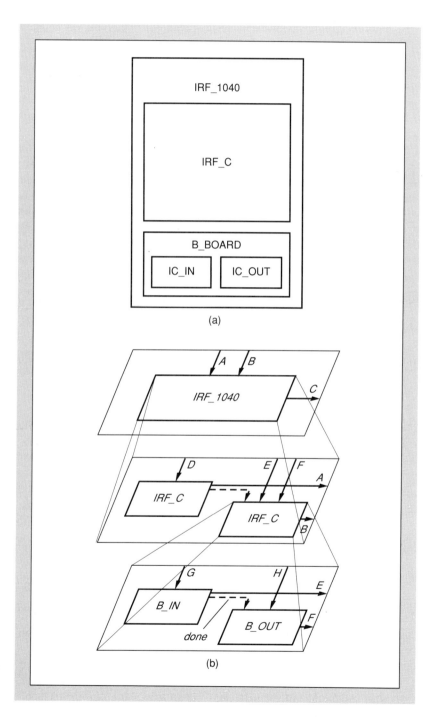

Figure 6.3 A tax package serves to illustrate decomposition into smaller units. The system can be shown as a nested graph (*a*), or an exploded SADT diagram (*b*).

Figure 6.4 State transition diagrams serve well to supplement SADT information at all system levels.

bubbles represent states (in which execution stands still). All these graphs lend themselves to hierarchical layering, so that individual parts can be decomposed further without affecting other modules. Such modularity is less prominent in yet another methodology, developed by Englishman Michael Jackson.[6] The data structure graph in Figure 6.5 addresses data-intensive systems typical of DP or transaction processing, but is rarely found in real-time CASE tools. Although preceding the CASE boom, the method is noteworthy because it comes close to producing provably correct data structures.

Of all these graphs, SADT is the most comprehensive and best attuned to general-purpose programming. Data generally are shown as entering a procedure box from the left and exiting at right, while controls enter at the top. Where specific tools or methods must be identified, they are indicated by arrows entering from the bottom. In contrast, normal data flow representation, as we encountered it in Figure 6.2*b* displays procedures as bubbles and permits both data and control flow to enter and exit wherever it's convenient.

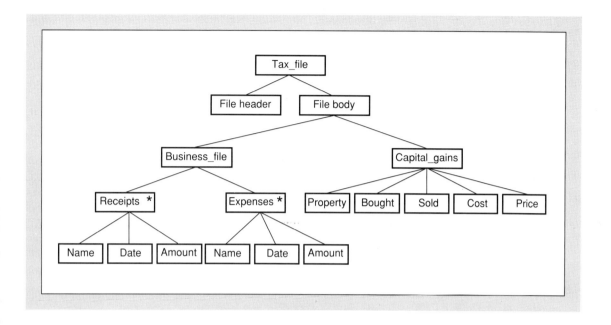

⁘ Announcing the All-New IP

Because the SADT format conveys more information visually, it will be adopted—and adapted—for this book. Modifications serve to make the graphs easier to read and to stay closer to the hardware (IC) analogy. In fact, we shall call our software modules IPs (for integral packages, processes, procedures, programs, or anything else that strikes your fancy). Data will enter an IP at the top and exit from the bottom, while control can enter or exit on either of the sides (see the margin figure). This convention quickly identifies the system type. If most lines emerge from IPs horizontally, you are clearly dealing with a control-rich reactive system that can also be represented as a *state machine.*

Don't regard the IP as YAM (yet another methodology), but rather as a common denominator. To set IPs apart from other symbols, they are marked with a dark corner at the top. (Practically all better-looking shapes have already been incorporated in the many extant diagramming systems.) That black corner, however, provides a fringe benefit—you can regard it as a "nil" input, which is equivalent to the ground connection on a hardware component. Naturally, each IP can be subdivided into

Figure 6.5 The data structure representation pioneered by Michael Jackson (the English one) helps to organize data-intensive applications in a reliable fashion.

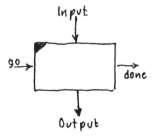

more detailed ones, just like the procedures in an SADT or data flow diagram. You might ask, if so many graphic representations already exist, why add another one? Primarily, to establish continuity as we move from one CASE vendor's graphs to another's. Figures 6.1 to 6.4 probably convinced you that learning them all would be quite a chore and would confuse the issues to boot.

The concept of IPs may seem far-fetched to some, but it is really identical to that of the previously discussed "reusable software," which is our best hope to solve the software crisis. Prepackaged modules, for example, form one of the attractions of the Ada language, invented expressly to save some of our tax dollars (see the discussion in Chapter 1). New, off-the-shelf components (usually in the form of Ada "packages") appear with each trade show. It would have been nice to call the IPs "Software ICs," but **Stepstone** has trademarked the term to convey the "plug-in" nature of its software libraries written in Objective C. (We'll return to this language in Chapter 12.) With software reusability very much on people's minds, it's no wonder that vendors are locking up such descriptive terms as "Software IC" or "Software Chip" (a form of firmware components).

Unlike these plug-in modules, our IPs will primarily serve as software design tools. Because they can be decomposed through many levels of detail (or abstraction), a naming convention will prove helpful. To keep things simple (and close to standard practice), we shall employ numerals separated by periods. For example, IP.3.5 designates the fifth IP in the breakdown of IP.3, which in turn makes up the third IP of the system. Practical experience with system decomposition mandates that no level should contain more than nine components, so we can limit each IP level to a single digit. (In a pinch, you can always switch to **hex** notation.)

The top level always consists of a single IP. Because it looks the same in any system, we shall call it IP.0 (as in Figure 6.6a). At the IP.0 level, input data flows into the system from some file and results are stored in another file. Scholars like to call the former "afferent" and the latter "efferent" data.[7] (Pity the students whose teacher is not blessed with a crystal-clear enunciation). At this level, there is only one control input that starts execution and one output that either signals completion or sounds an alarm. (We'll return to this second output later in this chapter.)

We have chosen the term "IP" because it conjures up the analogy with an IC, whose designers have learned to master up to a million transistor "switches" (e.g., in the Intel 80486). As we saw in Chapter 1, software and hardware "circuits" are essentially mirror images of each other. Many software gurus (especially aca-

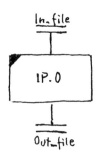
In.file

IP.0

Out_file

demics) have argued that software is the twin of calculus and, at best, a remote cousin of hardware. Some of them now admit to the equivalence of hardware and software, but they insist that it holds only at the level of elementary statements. Real-life software, they claim, is infinitely more complex than hardware.

Let's examine the facts. The popular 68020 microprocessor from Motorola contains about 200,000 transistors. The chip incorporates relatively little memory, whose regularity would indeed defy a software equivalence. If we assume that a logic gate—the atom of digital circuitry—demands four transistors, we arrive at a count of roughly 50,000 gates. Assuming the equivalent of three gates per average statement in a software implementation, we arrive at over 16,000 lines of code. That's no match for DOS (which has grown to take up nearly a whole floppy in object code), but it still produces about 300 pages of printout.

Some will dismiss this equivalence calculation as idle speculation, but we can easily prove them wrong. To expedite the design of ICs, engineers use many software tools. One of them models a processor like the 68020 in the form of a program that accepts the same inputs (including assembly instructions) as the chip and produces the same outputs. Such a "functional model" for the 68020 happens to comprise about 15,000 lines of C code. In spite of the supposed regularity of a 32-bit processor, this model comes pretty close to our guesstimate.

Put 10 components of similar complexity on a circuit board, and you have a respectable 150,000-line software equivalent. That corresponds to an effort of nearly 20 staff-years, except that the hardware version will contain far fewer bugs than the 300 to 1000 expected for a program of that size. (On Intel's 80386, somewhat larger than the 68020, an unusually high number of 21 bugs were found, mostly in a novel part of the architecture. Even so, that's only the equivalent of 1.5 errors per 1000 lines of code—orders of magnitude below par.)

The analogy with silicon chips should teach us something about designing their software counterparts as well. To remain consistent, we'll apply as much of the IC terminology as possible. For example, like the IC, an IP has connections (or "pins"). In general, one signal (usually in the form of a variable) is "wired" to one pin—even if it is a complex data structure, like an n-dimensional array. The pins will be labeled with lower-case letters for inputs and upper-case letters for outputs. To distinguish more easily between control lines and data (or "signal") lines, pins for the former (always located at the left or right face of an IP) will be identified with letters near the end of the alphabet.

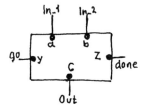

ꝏ Hooking Up an Audio System

Before the IP can start to execute, all its input signals must obviously be present (which represents a logical AND relation). Sometimes, however, only one of several inputs may be needed, and we shall connect those to the same pin, as ORed inputs. Although such inputs can substitute for each other, they may differ in details. Therefore, ORed "pins" can be split, as an example will show. Assume, you want to set up an audio amplifier. To function, it must receive two inputs: power and an audio signal. This particular amplifier produces audio output for only one of two pairs of speakers, labeled A and B (Figure 6.6b).

Now we'll convert this piece of hardware into a software equivalent.* We can model the amplifier system like the switches in Chapter 1:

```
IF Radio OR Phono OR Tape is ON
    AND Power is ON
THEN Stereo_A OR Stereo_B is ON
```

In the form of an IP (Figure 6.6c), this statement closely resembles the hardware wiring diagram of Figure 6.6b, but it retains all the information of the code. Logically, only one of the three inputs need (or, in fact, may) be present. However, because one input level (e.g., phono) may be lower than the others, the IP permits us to describe them separately.

The amplifier is, naturally, only part of a complete audio system; we'll call it IP.1. Some other component—say, the receiver—controls when the amplifier will actually start to work. (Audio systems delay the amplifier turn-on to avoid weird sound effects during power-up.) So, a control signal, go, also enters IP.1. In our state-of-the-art audio system, the user can expect to be notified if something goes awry; hence we provide a control output labeled xcpt for "exception" in Figure 6.6c. (Control variables can be recognized by their lower-case initials.) If, let's say, neither pair of

---

*The days are fast approaching when audio signals will indeed have the form of binary data streams, all the way to the loudspeaker. Even power can be regarded as just a special type of a binary signal, in spite of its huge amplitude and drooping shoulders.

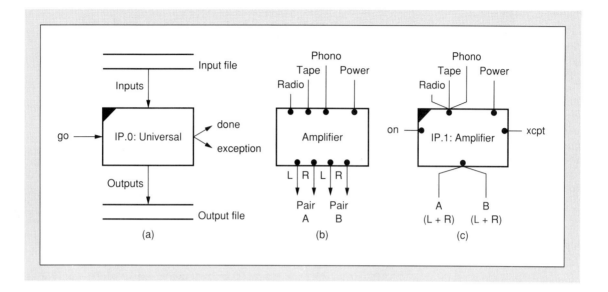

loudspeakers is switched on, the exception signal can activate a flashing display on the receiver's readout panel.

In a real computer system, the go and done flags (usually single-bit variables) should by rights be carried throughout the system's complete decomposition. A separate IP called "Flags" might be assigned to their evaluation (see Figure 6.7). But since any multitasking operating system takes care of getting a task started that is ready and waiting, such scheduling controls will be omitted from now on. For the sake of simplicity, we can just assume to be dealing with a dataflow architecture, in which any node automatically starts processing as soon as all its "raw materials" (namely, the data) are available. In fact, multiprocessor systems of the future will function that way, assigning specific processor ICs to individual IPs according to availability and priority.

The functions of the exception flag are not as easily described as those of the flags labeled go and done. Failure to include exception handlers has been responsible for many a software disaster, although their usefulness has been understood for many years. (Exception handling was, for example, available in PL/I, and DoD included it in the requirements for the Ada language.) "Exception" is not just a euphemism for error. Rather, the term signifies a condition that cannot be resolved by the hardware or the software. Overflow is a common example for the former; a negative array index might exemplify the latter.

Figure 6.6 Derived from SADT diagrams and resembling schematics, IPs at the highest (system) level show data input and output as vertical flows, while controls flow horizontally (*a*). The hookup of an audio amplifier (*b*), when represented as an IP (*c*), includes control signals and ORed connections.

Figure 6.7 In most cases, a computer's operating system controls the startup of software modules when their precursors are done (broken lines). To show all these internal controls would needlessly obscure essential control flow (solid lines).

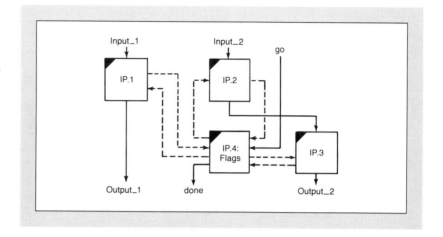

Exceptions don't have a true hardware equivalent; perhaps crosstalk between telephone lines would come closest. In pharmacology, exceptions might correspond to side effects or to interactions between several medications. Exceptions are often as hard to foretell as such side effects, and they can be quite as deadly. Consequently, a software designer should at the very least make provisions for some orderly system shutdown. Too many hackers just make provisions for the ensuing funeral—for example by displaying the message "General system failure" after the unexpected has happened.*

In the amplifier example, we decided to connect the exception signal to a blinker input in the display. That link will not fix any bugs in IP.1. However, when the system suddenly goes silent, the flashing display tells the puzzled user that the selected station is not really off the air; he may just have inadvertently hit the "Speakers A" button. (When all is black on black, who can tell?)

Setting unused inputs of the Display package to null represents another precautionary measure that is all too often ignored

---

*Being poets at heart, some hackers resort to more imaginative displays. At General Motors, a Multics crash recovery program once displayed the following message: "*Hodie natus est radici frater.*" A former altar boy supplied the translation: "Today onto the root is born a brother." After much discussion, a Multics sage solved the riddle: there can only be a single root in the file system, and an "impossible" event must have taken place. Good old Murphy at work again—even under Multic's crib at venerable MIT!

by software designers. They learn the hard way that software is not immune to "crosstalk" when the system suddenly crashes. One cause might be that storage assignments for two variables get mixed up. By setting unused variables explicitly to zero, any mixup can be spotted easily, if not avoided altogether.

Enter the talking car. For an example as simple as the amplifier, breakdown into two components may well complete the architectural design phase. A more practical application will provide us with better insight into the design process. Take the approaching flood of automotive electronics. You may refuse to buy a car that talks back to you, but you won't be able to evade, say, an electronic speedometer. The mechanical model consists of a flexible shaft, usually connected via a worm gear to a front wheel. At the shaft's other end, behind the instrument panel, sits a kind of combination generator-motor. The generator part induces a current proportional to the wheel's rotations per minute (rpm). The motor part produces a torque proportional to that current, which deflects the speedometer's spring-loaded pointer (see Figure 6.8a).

In the electronic version, we could replace the troublesome flexible shaft by putting a "generator" next to the worm gear and

Figure 6.8 A mechanical speedometer derives readings from wheel (and sometimes crankshaft) rotation (*a*). Implemented in software, one IP can handle the data conversions and another the display (*b*). A data flow diagram for the same system reveals much less detail (*c*).

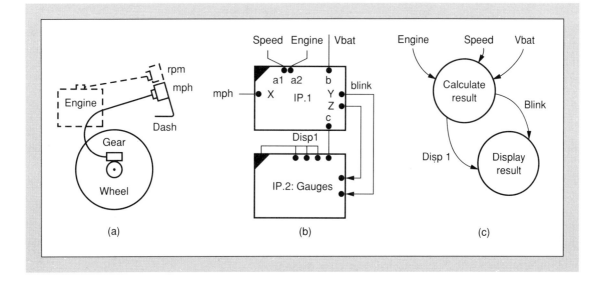

(a)   (b)   (c)

running a wire to the dashboard. But if we go digital all the way, we save money to boot. A digital rpm sensor is cheap (consisting of a small rotating magnet and a field probe), and all we need is a chip that counts the number of pulses in a given period of time—say a tenth of a second—and outputs the count, which we'll call Speed. We can now translate the count to miles per hour (or mph, if you prefer) and display it via IP.2.

On second thought, let's link another generator right to the crankshaft, so we can also register the engine's rpm. Why is this reading so dear to the heart of all true sportsmen? An rpm display permits the zealous driver to keep the engine running at its point of highest power, and for such macho information he is willing to pay good money. We'll call this second sensor's output Engine. There should also be a way to check the battery, so we hook up a digital voltmeter and run another signal, Vbat, to the dashboard. This IP representation (see Figure 6.8*b*) rather resembles the audio amplifier's IP, except that we have added an explicit display module.

Now IP.1 can choose between the input signals for rpm and mph. On the control side, the IP has a flag that tells it whether to display speed or rpm. IP.1's output goes to IP.2, whose unused input "pins" are connected to "ground." Again, the display will blink if IP.1 reports an exception, triggered by a low battery or a malfunction. Chances are, your CASE system provides no IP graphics, so let's see what a standard data flow diagram for our design looks like (see Figure 6.8*c*). You'll probably agree that it offers less insight than the IP does.

Remember to look up *jargon* in Appendix C.

Before proceeding to more detailed design, you should apply rapid **prototyping** to find out whether the design satisfies the customer. This way you can establish, early on, a baseline for the dangerous journey through the algorithmic design phase. (Faulty algorithms, according to reports, account for no less than one-third to one-half of all software malfunctions.) A good CASE environment should permit you to exercise your architectural structures with a **simulator**; we'll see one at work in Chapter 7. Without CASE, execution usually must wait until all the code is written.

To simulate the architectural design, it is of course necessary that at least a "quick-and-dirty" (q&d) implementation of the chosen algorithms is available. Only CASE systems that generate code automatically can bypass this hurdle, but rarely at the architectural level. All we need for a q&d model of our system are a few lines of pseudocode:

```
IF Vbat > 12
        IF mph_flag = true THEN
                Disp1 := Speed * F
        ELSE Disp1 := Engine * 600
ELSE xcpt := true
```

Here, `Disp1`—the signal going to the digital display—is set either to the rpm generator count times 600 (to convert from the count in 0.1 second to the count in one minute) or to the speed sensor's count, times a factor F. This factor depends on the size of the car's wheels and may have to be modified for calibration. For this reason, a symbolic name, F, is preferable to a numerical constant. Finally, the exception flag will be turned on if the battery voltage is too low.

It might not be a bad idea to add another line to the code—one that turns on a second blinker permanently. This precaution would effectively prevent the prototype from being turned (inadvertently, of course) into the delivered product. **Softworkers** brought up under the doctrine of **information hiding** could otherwise wind up in trouble. Why? Unless we take special precautions in defining IPs, their users can easily make false assumptions about the software modules' content. Indeed, as our example will soon demonstrate, information hiding (like its political counterpart) can trick us into spreading disinformation.

Now let's invite the customer to a demo. He hooks up his sensors and revs up the engine. We are immediately rewarded with a display, but all the numbers are flickering badly. Thanks to rapid prototyping, we find out early in the game that our model disregards a minor fact: the generators produce a reading 10 times each second, and the display changes too rapidly for our eyes to read it. Spooked by the flickering readout, the customer finds he really doesn't like the digital displays, even when they hold steady. The traditional analog gauges are much easier to read. Furthermore, our client determines that he wants both mph and rpm displayed simultaneously. Well, back to the drawing board.

Still, we have learned some valuable lessons. A q&d model, though quick, can be too "dirty" to be useful. The mechanical gadget we want to replace apparently has properties we weren't aware of. We overlooked the fact that the speedometer's mass evened out minor variations. Furthermore, a little vibration of a gauge needle bothers nobody, while flickering digits are worse than useless. Try to read them, and you could wind up in an accident, which would certainly defeat the purpose of mandatory speedometers. We also noticed during the demo a top-speed reading of 1500 mph—about Mach 2. Since we didn't plan to design a jet fighter instrument we must have goofed somewhere.

Rapid prototyping has prevented us from getting caught in a corner. Recall that we contrived the architectural model's simplistic code to show the customer quickly how the human interface works. That includes operation of the gauges, but not the details of the speed calculation. Without prototyping, we would have built a numerical readout, found out that it was useless, and told the customer "Well, your specification doesn't work. We need more green to start all over." Thanks to prototyping (which verifies the "what" of the spec against the "how" of the design) we can quickly decide to use a commercial IP that provides gauges galore, and keep a happy client.

⌁ How to Put Reality into Software

Prototyping or not, we must always be sure that our system does not produce impossible values. This goal is extremely important, because only by carefully imposing constraints on our software can we accomplish what the laws of nature do for us in the real world. For example, if somebody races the engine in neutral, the rpm indicator may go off the scale (which probably turns red at 6500 and ends at 8000). But we can be fairly sure that the actual count will never exceed 10,000, and that the engine will sound awful before it flies apart.

The software model, however, knows no restraint. Unless we explicitly tell it that 10,000 is the upper limit, it will happily go on to calculate a million rpm (or, for that matter, a negative million). And it will neither whine nor smell hot on the way up to Mach 2. But if something does go haywire, we should certainly be told about it. In other words, an exception handler should take over.

We must therefore establish limits for all the variables we use in the model. The variable Speed can range from 0 to +5.0, which corresponds to 180 mph, assuming an F of 36.0. A typo had set F to 360 in the demo, which means the vehicle would have to move 10 yards with each turn of the wheels. (The car's wheels would turn five times in 0.1 second.) We may not want to actually display more than 100 mph, but because other parts of the futuristic car's electronics (e.g., a radar system) could be tied to speed, we must have its value available for the whole possible range. As for Engine, we will permit 10,000 rpm, or 16.67 crankshaft rotations in 0.1 second. For the battery voltage, we could set limits of −30 to +30 volts, which should take care of hooking up wrong batteries, even backwards. However, we want to get an exception for any unusual voltage, so we'll put the limits at 11.5 to 13 volts.

Setting limits for each variable in a program does more than restore constraints that are lost when we map a real-world device into the never-never land of software. It also greatly narrows the solution space, which, in turn, translates into simpler test procedures and higher confidence levels in a program's correctness.

For these reasons, constraints on variables' values were built into the Pentagon's Ada language, primarily designed for mission-critical applications (e.g., a rocket guidance system). Any violation of an established limit within even the largest program triggers an exception handler that propagates the error flag all the way up to the human interface. Since the designer can control the path of propagation, he (rather than luck) decides exactly what a rocket should do, no matter what goes wrong.

While in Ada the variables' constraints are part of the language, in our IP system they must be part of the module under design, because coding will come much later. When splicing IPs (or actual, purchased software components) together, we must make sure that the outputs of an IP (the producer) don't exceed the limits that are acceptable to another IP (the consumer). In the present example, sloppy definitions can cause no harm, because we are only building a prototype model that will be thrown away after code refinement. But remember that today the fate of industrialized nations is enmeshed in perhaps close to a trillion lines of code, and only a tiny fraction incorporates even nominal safeguards. That's a rather scary thought.

According to the "wiring diagram" of Figure 6.8b, the "pins" on IP.1 will have to be defined as follows (remember that ORed pins like "a" can be split):

```
a1:  0 ..   5.0
a2:  0 ..  16.67
b:  11.5 .. 13.0
C:   0 .. 10000
x:   true = mph
Y:   true = exception
Z:   true = q&d_model
```

Now we must make sure that IP.2's pins actually accept the values we intend to feed into them. For a digital readout, this may well turn out to be a problem because it must go only as high as 180 for speed but up to 10,000 for the rpm reading. We should probably modify our model to display rpm ÷100, which is also standard practice on mechanical gauges. In that case, the fourth line would read

```
C:   0 .. 180.0
```

because now the mph reading of 180 is greater than the rpm reading of 100.

To establish the compatibility of just a dozen IPs by cross-checking their specs would be quite a chore. Most programmers refuse to define even the type of their variables, never mind the range. (Because Ada requires painstaking interface definitions, few software designers use it—unless they must, in order to get paid.) Yet, in the hardware world engineers not only can design circuits with 200,000 logic gates, but can also *place and route* the corresponding million transistors for the generation of IC masks. And usually they can get it right the first time.

In the software world, on the other hand, we run into trouble with a dozen modules, each containing a page of code. The discrepancy has an obvious explanation. In the hardware case, a computer automatically checks the electrical and mechanical design rules by means of the CAE (computer-aided engineering) tools used—a process known as "electronic design automation" (EDA). But CASE-less software must rely on some (usually well-hidden) checks contained in a compiler or in the language we happen to use.

End the anarchy.   Obviously, if we want to build large software systems safely, we must apply the lessons learned in hardware design to software. A graphic representation permits you to hook up software components simply by feeding data outputs into the proper input "pins," exactly as engineers "capture" an IC schematic. That by itself does not prevent errors, but it permits you to apply a design rule checker akin to those built into every CAE system. That checker can quickly ascertain that only inputs and outputs of the same type are interconnected, that no connections are left dangling, and that the declared limits of an output "signal" do not exceed those of the target input.

Fully specified modules like the IPs have an important fringe benefit. In older languages, defining the scope of variable names (i.e., where in a program they are valid) has been considered an often intractable problem. Even in Ada, scoping rules can be quite complex (as discussed in Chapter 3). The problem largely disappears under the IP paradigm, because *all* symbolic names are local. The "net list" (which in hardware schematics catalogs all interconnection networks) determines which values are passed to which variables.

For example, in the speedometer, the variable on pin IP.1.C is internally called "Disp1"; when the data arrive at IP.2, they are referenced by whatever name the vendor of Gauges has seen fit. Unfortunately, until somebody implements an IP-based system, programmers must abide by the rules of their specific CASE tools, and not all of them require scope declarations.

An Ada compiler must check for such declarations in the package interfaces to link external names to internal ones. Of course, it also checks for a variable's type and permissible values (via the "range" declaration) and for resolution (by means of the "digits" clause). What such a compiler cannot do, but a rule checker could, is to assure that variables are expressed in the proper units and that units don't clash between modules.

You may recall an SDI laser experiment that the space shuttle Discovery was to perform on June 19, 1985. The test had to be repeated because the shuttle flew upside down over Maui, where the laser was located. It flew that way because its mirrors were programmed to point to a coordinate at 10,023 feet altitude. Unfortunately, the computer expected dimensions in nautical miles, and 10,023 miles up is where the mirrors in fact pointed, Ada or not.

A rule checker could also ensure that variables hold the proper dimensions (in the physics sense). For example, the multiplication of two variables with the dimensions "volt" and "ampere" must result in the dimension "watt." An Ada compiler can make sure that variables of different types aren't added together, but unless the programmer declares types volt, amp, and watt, the compiler will obligingly add volts to amps and divide the sum by watts. Even so, the compiler won't know what type the product of volts and amps should be, except base type real. Nor can the compiler assure accuracy. If, say, the voltage is known to six significant digits, but the current only to three, a rule checker could alert the designer that the resulting power is accurate to only three digits. No language offers such a capability.

Waste not, want not.   In our speedometer example, however, the problem will not be accuracy; it will be economy. The first architectural prototype was rejected primarily because of troubles with the display. The wish to have both mph and rpm displayed poses no problem. IP.2, a ready-made package, has built-in gauges, so we can easily hook up two of them. But what can we do about the flickering? We must simulate the mechanical instruments' inertia by taking an average over, say, half a second and display that.

In our first try, we assumed that the speed sensors would deliver numbers in binary form rather than just pulses. That would require two digital counters, when one can easily handle both instruments by alternating between the pulse strings. In the revised prototype, we'll therefore have two single-bit inputs, a clock input (which is available from the microprocessor that handles the whole dashboard), and a battery line. We might as well hook the latter up to IP.2 as well and make it blink if the voltage strays outside the set limits.

In theory, we should not have to worry about algorithmic details during architectural design, but (as Goethe's Faust put it) "Dear friend, all theory is gray." In the real world, we must have some idea how we'll turn pulse trains into binary numbers for the gauges, or simulation would be impossible. So, let's assume there will be two infinite DO loops to count the pulses from the two generators. Every half second we'll switch from one to the other and set the unused loop back to zero. That will make for a somewhat jumpy display, but we'll iron that out during detail design. (We could, for example, use moving averages instead of straight counts.)

Expressed in IPs, the design now shapes up as shown in Figure 6.9a. IP.1 has been broken down into two subsystems; IP.1.1 contains the counting loops, while IP.1.2 provides their switching flag `loop`, derived from the variable `Time`. We'll also use IP.1.2 to produce blinker flags by monitoring the ranges of all the measured values: mph, rpm, and battery voltage. Because mph and rpm are closely related, we'll just let the rpm meter blink.

Now that the battery voltage is also hooked up to a gauge, it doesn't really need a separate blinker—let's just OR the `volt` flag with the general exception signal. As you can see in Figure 6.9a,

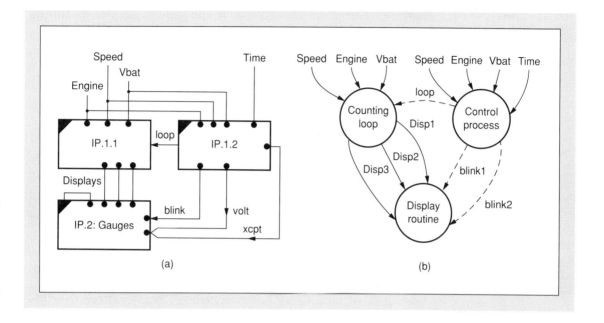

(a)

(b)

two of the blinker controls emanate from the bottom of IP.1.2, rather than from the side. When a Boolean variable is derived from a numerical operation (as in checking the battery voltage), it's up to you whether to make it a data or a control output. You may recall from Chapter 3 that we'd favor control status for Boolean variables, while the control variable for a DO or CASE construct could be of almost any type and hence must be treated as data.

To express the speedometer design in the form of a data flow graph turns out to be much tougher than for the first example. We now deal with a real-time system, for which the original bubble graphs weren't designed. We must add control flow (e.g., via the Ward-Mellor[8] extensions), as in Figure 6.9b. Even so, it is clear that the IP representation contains more information than the data/control flow diagram (D/CFD). Depending on the specific CASE system you are using, you may have to find other means of adding such information as logically ORed signals.

Figure 6.9 Taking the design from Figure 6.8b one step further, we can break IP.1 down into one module containing the counting loops and a second one providing real-time control (a). Such real-time aspects are harder to define by data flow alone (b).

Off the rack. The software package we use for the dashboard gauges gives us less trouble. We assume it was bought ready-made (indeed, a package called Gauges is available in Smalltalk), and all we need to worry about is the valid ranges of its inputs and into which "pins" to feed them. That's the beauty of reusable software, which will make an even bigger dent in software productivity than CASE as such. But reusable software has had a rough time getting off the ground, though advocated for more than a decade.

Why so? After all, previously used software modules are not just cheaper; unlike used cars, they also inspire greater confidence than brand-new merchandise. Still, the actual amounts of code being reused are often overestimated. At a 1987 workshop on software reuse in embedded systems,[9] attendees were asked to identify what part of their most recent designs would be reusable. Estimates ranged from 60% to 75%; however, those who measured actual reused code came up with a paltry 15% to 25%.

While the NIH syndrome may contribute to the poor showing, confidence is probably the main reason. After all, even in scientific subroutine libraries that have been popular for decades, bugs still surface. Does any programmer really believe that his new package will be less bug-ridden? Probably nothing short of credible certification can bring about the enormous savings that reused software promises.

The questionable accuracy of ready-made packages may also contribute to skepticism. While rightly brushed aside in a prototype, accuracy is all too often overlooked in finished software as well. Ever since computers were applied to scientific and engineering calculations, users have been loosing track of accuracy—often with fatal results. Even in double precision, it only takes a handful of trigonometric operations before results turn flaky. An example should convince you.

Years ago, aerospace engineers moved a Fortran program they had used for more than a decade from an IBM machine to a VAX. They were at a loss when the the message "argument for sin too high" appeared; it had never been seen before. The software, as it turned out, used the modulus (or remainder) of a number as the argument for a sine. When that number reaches 10^{20}, obviously all the precision available in a 20-digit calculation is gone. Because the IBM machine never complained, the engineers had designed airplanes with essentially random numbers for at least a dozen years.

So far, the computer industry has only faced up to the problem of accuracy in some hardware standards (e.g., IEEE 754 for floating-point arithmetic). In software, the only accuracy rule remains *caveat emptor*.

↳ **REFERENCES**

1. Arthur C. Clarke and Stanley Kubrick, *2001: A Space Odyssey*, Ballantine Books, New York, 1968.

2. James Martin and Carma McClure, *Diagramming Techniques for Analysts and Programmers*, Prentice-Hall, Englewood Cliffs, NJ, 1985.

3. Tom DeMarco, *Structured Analysis and System Specification*, Yourdon Press, New York, 1978.

4. Meilir Page-Jones, *The Practical Guide to Structured System Design*, Yourdon Press, New York, 1980.

5. D. T. Ross, "Applications and extensions of SADT," *Computer*, April 1985, p. 25.

6. Michael Jackson, *System Development*, Prentice-Hall, Englewood Cliffs, NJ, 1983.

7. Roger Pressman, *Software Engineering: A Practitioner's Approach*, McGraw-Hill, New York, 1982.

8. Paul Ward and Stephen Mellor, *Structured Development for Real-Time Systems*, Prentice-Hall, Englewood Cliffs, NJ, 1985.

9. Tenth Minnowbrook Workshop, July 1987, Blue Mountain Lake, NY.

Courtesy IBM Archives

Babbage's Difference Engine was never completed but is widely given credit as the first true computer. Its "mill" (the arithmetic unit)— shown here—imposed excessive demands on the gear-cutting art of its day.

7

TAKE
THE TRAIN,
FOR EXAMPLE

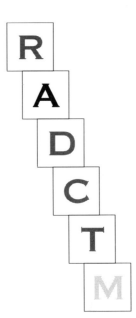

Railroad of the future
Be the station master
Can today's CASE hack it?
Athena's ardent answer

In Princeton University's undergraduate catalog you'll find a course "Microprocessors for measurement and control." If you try to enroll in it though, you'll probably be told to come back in a year. This course has been oversubscribed ever since the opening of its "lab"—a large toy train layout that the students can use to implement their choice of a measurement and control system. You may say "boys will be boys," but trains do hold a strange fascination for many of us.

What does this have to do with CASE? As you know, we are going to examine a range of CASE tools in this book, and the example to which all of them will be applied is a train. (If it works in Princeton, why shouldn't it work here?) Our example, though, is not an ordinary train. In 1965, an article by H. K. Edwards[1] proposed a novel kind of train, that runs in a tube that tunnels deep into the earth. Pulled by gravity, the train can reach speeds in the hundreds of miles per hour. To reduce friction, the tube will be evacuated. As the train passes the air lock, the atmosphere helps accelerate the vehicle some more, much like the pneumatic capsules used in drive-in banks. In fact, a pneumatic-tube train ran under New York's Broadway over a century ago (see Figure 7.1). But *our* train will fly on magnetic cushions.

Let's assume the year is 2001, and room-temperature super-conductors provide affordable levitation. The Pentagon is very much interested in this technology and ready to fund a test track for such a "Gravity Train." The track will be 200 kilometers (km) long and will run between Washington and Philadelphia, where the digging is easy. Naturally, the scheme has been labeled a boondoggle by narrow-minded journalists; indeed, the *Georgetown Inquirer* has called the project "Gravy Train." The name seems to stick, but we'll stay neutral and call the project "G-Train" for short.

Figure 7.1 Running a passenger train in an evacuated tube may be a brilliant idea, but it's certainly not new, as this engraving from the March 1870 issue of *Scientific American* neatly illustrates.

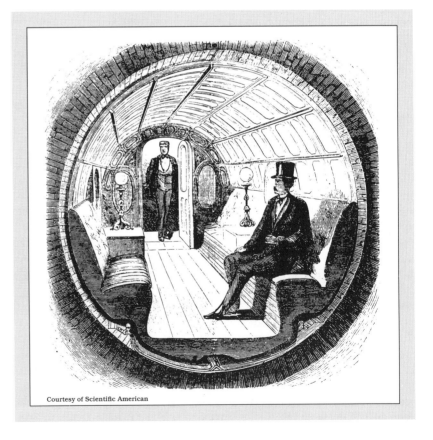

Courtesy of Scientific American

Like everything else in 2001 the single-car test train will be entirely controlled by computers, both on board and at the station. However, to keep the example manageable, we only include the stationary parts of the system in the demo. The Pentagon's request for proposal (RFP, to those in the know) is accompanied by a superfloppy with 66 Mbytes of requirements, from which we have extracted the relevant section below. Abiding by the waterfall rules, we sent this spec to all the potential "subcontractors" (i.e., CASE vendors):

Requirements for G-Train Project X-1865/2001/PDQ

G-TRAIN is a control system for a test track to evaluate a novel (levitated) train with a maximum speed of 500 km/h. The system consists of three subsystems, WEIGHT, SPEED, and DISPLAY. All use the same computer (e.g., a PC variant).

WEIGHT resembles the gates of airport metal detectors. A green light indicates that the gate is clear; a red light shows that weighing is in progress. The passenger steps on a sensor that provides the weight in pounds as a three-digit number to the computer. Ten seconds after the weight has been obtained, the green light goes on. Weighing continues until either 100 passengers have boarded, or the Depart button has been pressed. Weighing then stops, and the red light stays on.

SPEED sends signals to the computer from sensors along the 200-km track, mounted at 5-km intervals (38 sensors). All are connected to the same serial controller input. At maximum speed, a Signal arrives every 36 seconds. Each Signal consists of two pulses; the Delay between them indicates the train's speed:

$$T_s = 2500/Delay$$

So, at 500 km/h, the pulses are 5 milliseconds (ms) apart, at 100 km/h 25 ms, and so on. (Propagation delays along the sensor wiring are neglected.)

DISPLAY presents on the monitor screen the following data: number of passengers, total passenger weight in kg (1 kg = 2.205 lb), and train speed (Ts) in km/h. In addition, the screen will contain the following graphics:

Mandatory: Show the train position on the track, which is represented by a curved line. This line is a circle segment whose

Figure 7.2 The monitor for a gravity-propelled train will serve as an application example in future chapters. Its requirements specify the shown system components.

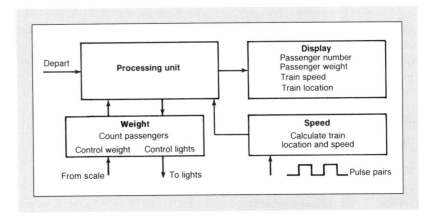

end points are 100 units apart and whose midpoint lies 25 units below the end points. At rest, the train is shown as a bright spot at the left end point. For every Signal (i.e., double pulse) received, the spot moves along the line one horizontal increment to the right.

Optional: The speed may also be displayed graphically on the screen by means of a round gauge resembling an automobile speedometer.

DRAWING: The enclosed drawing (see Figure 7.2) sketches one possible system architecture. Its sole purpose is to clarify the preceding text.

⤷ The Architecture of the G-Train Monitor

Before we examine any of the contributions from CASE vendors, we'll apply our IP system to the G-Train example. As the spec suggests, we'll break it down into three subsystems, Speed, Weight, and Display, all tied into a small computer. Instead of drawing up a formal specification, we'll work with the requirements and scrutinize them a bit.

The subsystem Speed monitors the train's speed and location by measuring the time intervals within pulse pairs arriving every 30 to 360 seconds, if the train travels at speeds between 600 and 50 km/h. We'll assume that the pulses are induced by two magnets (located on the train), as they pass stationary coils mounted along the track, spaced 5 km apart. All of these coils are connected in series, thus requiring only a single serial input to the computer. (*Exercise:* How far are the train's magnets apart to produce a 5-ms pulse interval at 500 km/h?)✝

The second subsystem, Weight, consists of a gate similar to those abominable contraptions in airports that force us to empty our pockets and bare our knee braces. But the G-Train's gate merely serves to determine the train's gross weight, an important variable for the on-board computer. All the data collected by our monitoring computer are transferred to the on-board system when the Depart function takes over. (How? Never mind, just "beam them up, Scottie.")*

A green light on the gate signals the waiting passenger to enter the gate, luggage in hand; a red light then goes on until the weighing is complete, and it stays on for another 10 seconds before it switches back to green to beckon the next passenger. (Let's not worry about crowd control—this is a DoD operation. All personnel shall be directed to enter on green and remain on the scale for a count of five.) The weighing procedure ends when either 100 passengers have passed the gate or the station commander depresses a Depart button. The red light then stays on indefinitely.

Run, spot, run.   The last subsystem, Display, drives a monitor (e.g., the screen of the system's terminal) that shows the number of boarded passengers, total transported weight, train speed, and location along the track. A bright spot, moving along a curved line that approximates the parabolic shape of the track, marks the train's position on the screen. The speed is displayed as a three-digit number, supplemented (optionally) with a speedometer gauge.

The G_Train system has been set up this way so it comprises three major software types: real-time (for the speed calculation), number crunching (figuring total weight), and graphics (the display). Figure 7.3 shows the first cut at an IP implementation. Three packages represent the subsystems: IP.1 for Weight, IP.2 for Speed, and IP.3 for Display. IP.1 needs two input "signals," Scale and Time, as well as two control inputs, open_gate and departing. The former launches the boarding process, and the

---

✝See p. 172 for the solution.
*Obscure reference to a popular twentieth century television show, which often resorted to bitwise and instantaneous transport of facts and figures.

Figure 7.3 Using the IP paradigm we can break down the G-Train system easily into the components identified by the requirements specification.

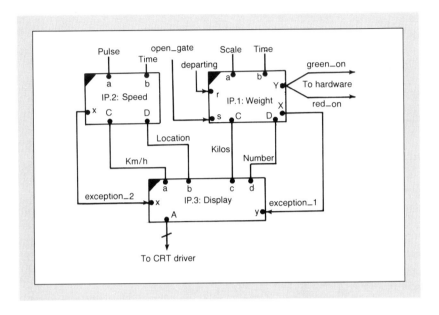

latter sets the train in motion. The outputs include Kilos (total weight) and Number (total passengers), as well as green_on and red_on. The last two are, of course, mutually exclusive (ORed) states of the light display. (Note that only data-carrying variables have upper-case initials.)

The "pins" of IP.1 can be defined as follows, with the convention that inputs use lower-case letters and outputs upper-case:

```
a: type weight, 0..399 lb
b: type time, 0..20.000 s
C: type weight, 0..0.20000E5
D: type count, 0..100
r: type bit, true = departing
s: type bit, true = open_gate
Y: type bit, true = green_on
```

True to our faith in realistic models, the data types in this list go beyond the traditional definitions as integer or real. Such base types are implied by the range values: weight and count are integers while time and weight are real numbers. Time has a resolution of 0.001 seconds (1 ms), while weight is defined as a five-digit floating-point number. The three control variables require only single bits, whose values are defined as shown— one starts the boarding process, the other terminates it. "Pin" Y will eventually have to be split, but there's no need for that now because outputs share the same type and value.

IP.2 also needs two inputs, namely `Pulse` and `Time`. From their values it calculates two outputs, `Km_per_h` and `Location`. We can define them as follows:

```
a: type bit, true if pulse = 1.0..10.0 V
b: type time, 0..0.36000 E8 ms
C: type speed, 0..500.00 km/h
D: type count, 0..38
```

The valid ranges are determined by the system's character- istics and by the conditions for which we want to trigger an exception. Pulse voltages under 1 volt, for example, could be noise, while pulses over 10 volts could only be produced if the train's magnets crash into the induction coils. (For the detail design phase, we'll remember that the latter condition must set off an especially trenchant alarm.)

The time variable in IP.2 has a resolution of 0.01 microsec- onds to provide adequate accuracy for the speed calculation. The variable's range limit of 10 hours may seem high, but it accom- modates an emergency pusher "loc" with a speed of 50 km/h in case of an accident. We must later set a blinker inside IP.3 to alert the operator to speeds lower than 100 km/h in track segments 2 to 36. (It will be easy—the IP catalog from which we picked the Gauges component indicates limit "switches" for each dial.)

All specs are flawed.   A good "design-rule checker" would notice that the two time variables (on IP.1 and IP.2) are incom- patible, because one counts seconds and the other milliseconds. If both IPs have their own clock, this poses no problem, but any attempt to "wire" the two together (e.g., at the computer) should sound a warning. Since such flaws are the rule rather than the exception in specifications, a CASE system should be able to spot them. But keep in mind that present systems can at best dis- tinguish between types, so use typing liberally if your preferred language permits it.

Finally, IP.3, which creates the display, is the same Gauges package we used in Chapter 6. We know from the catalog (available by January 2001) that the displays for weight, speed, and passenger count present no problem. However, the train location may pose a challenge. The spec given previously explicitly states that during boarding the train is identified as a bright spot at the left end of the scale. Whenever a sensor coil is passed, the spot moves to the right, until it reaches the last sensor. But because there are only 38 sensors, the last 5-km stretch remains unaccounted for—another flaw in the specification.

Furthermore, the spec is silent about the remote train terminal. One can reasonably assume that its setup duplicates the near terminal, so that speed and location could be calculated from the same sensor pulses. The Speed IP at the far terminal could be initialized to 40 and count backward. If the train never gets to the far terminal, however, the whole location scheme breaks down, and the passengers would definitely be in trouble. Rapid prototyping or *dynamic* simulation should bring such problems to the designer's attention, and we can shelve our concerns for the moment.

To avoid that the *last* track sector turns into a *lost* track sector, we could place multiple induction coils at each sensor location; they could generate a unique identifying vector for each train position. But right now—having years to go before the G-Train contract will be awarded—we need not worry about this problem yet either. We'll assume that only a monotonically growing distance has to be measured.

Because we are still in the architectural phase of the waterfall diagram, none of the discussed flaws is holding up progress. But let us examine Figure 7.3 closely to see how the system functions. IP.1 will start working when actual data for both Time and Scale become available. We can assume that the former is supplied by the computer hardware, but no weight values will materialize unless a passenger steps on the scale. This in turn can only happen after the control signal open_gate (supplied by the operator) turns the gate light to green. Once we break IP.2 down further, we must make sure not to forget this initialization step, but at the architectural level we can ignore this detail too.

Although the spec neglected to define system initialization, we just made some reasonable assumptions to get going. But you can't expect a commercial CASE system to outguess the spec. Remember that today's computers can at best match the intelligence of a reptile. The steps we just took may be obvious to programmers or even to high-school graduates, but what can you expect from an iguana brain? (Only in remote galaxies do such critters master computers.)

Most of the CASE vendors that contributed to the book also had to make assumptions to placate their grumbling machines, and these guesses may well be wrong. You should not hold that against the company's CASE product though—after all, how many CASE designers have constructed railroads before?

Blank screens are like blank checks.   A closer look at IP.3 raises another question. We have four signals coming in, and according to the rules of the IP game laid down in the preceding chapter, all of the inputs must be available to produce any output. So what happens while the G-Train is boarding passengers? No speed pulses have come in yet, hence there will be no value for km/h, and the whole screen will be blank (except for the >C prompt, perhaps).

Actually, the four displays in Gauges work independently of each other, and only the speedometer may be hibernating. Still, that's not what we want, is it? If you recall our comment about "grounding" variables, the answer becomes obvious: speed must be set to zero (e.g., during initialization) until other values are ready for consumption. Leaving any value undefined is an invitation for garbage (or even worse, a virus) to settle in the allocated storage space.

Eventually, we'll have to tie the software system of Figure 7.3 to some hardware or, more precisely, to the computer's operating system (OS). We need not be concerned with the OS details quite yet, but some architectural decisions must be made. For example, do we need a multitasking system? Must we have more than one processor? Will we need special utilities? After all, PCs are normally not hooked up to traffic lights or induction coils. If it turns out that a simple, asynchronous system (on which we'll base our cost estimate to the Pentagon) does not suffice, it's back to square one.

Because of such backtracking, some software pundits take exception to the whole waterfall model, which stipulates that detail design be followed by coding, not by rewriting the spec. Of course, the same argument applies to any kind of design; if your first idea does not work, you start over. Is that any reason to abolish PERT or GANTT charts? Apparently management tools are not subject to the same rigorous scrutiny as software tools.

Luckily, the weighing function and the speed calculation never occur simultaneously. A main program can first wake up the weighing routine, and when the Depart button is pressed, pass control to speed measurement. The display, of course, must operate during both phases. Still, no problem. The weighing routine takes a 10-second break between passengers, and the Speed IP also remains idle most of the time. Even at top speed the pulse pairs are 36 seconds apart, leaving the computer idle 99.9% of the time. In fact, we should make provisions for some background work to keep it busy (e.g., letting the operator work on his 1040 forms or write the sequel to *Gone with the Wind*).

Only the 5-ms spacing between the two pulses of each pair at top speed is time critical. To get an accuracy of 2%, the pulse spacing must be known to within 100 microseconds. Hence we must poll the buffer that accepts the pulses at least 10,000 times a second. Time is available according to our specification of IP.1 in 0.1-microsecond increments, which implies that we'll have a 10-MHz clock in the box. But even a processor running at a sluggish clock rate of 1 MHz would still have 100 ticks available just to stash away the first pulse and get ready to look for the second one. So, the simple computer system we postulated should suffice quite nicely.

⅂ How CASE Systems Capture the Design

Because G-Train is such a simple example, the breakdown into the three subsystems concludes the architectural design. Now let's see how commercial CASE tools handle the initial (or upper) steps of the waterfall diagram. One of the oldest and most widely used "upper CASE" tools is Excelerator from *Index Technology.* The tool's RTS version can handle real-time applications and could represent G-Train as shown in Figure 7.4.

Here, peripherals appear as external entities, and the time input is obtained from the file Calendar. Four procedure "bubbles" complete the system "Fig. Mov." (figure movement, for speed and location), "Fig. Load" (for weighing and passenger count), "Disp. Value" (the display driver), and "Chg. Sig." (for controling the red/green switch via the dashed control line). By setting up the last function, the Excelerator model differs somewhat from the IP breakdown of Figure 7.3.

When you enter the system description as a requirement (via text or graphs), the CASE system constructs a database that

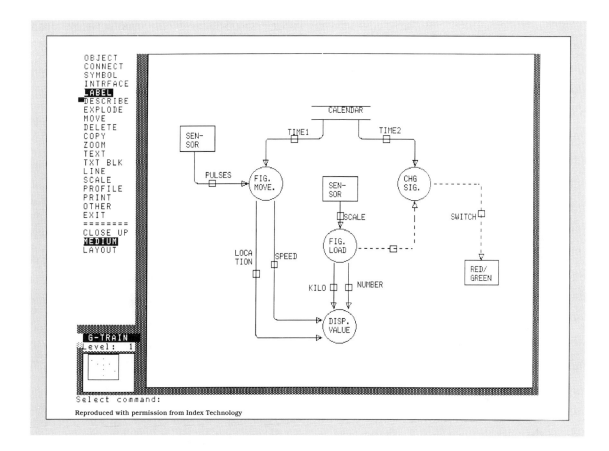

captures your design. We demonstrated textual input via the PSL/PSA tool in Chapter 5, and you've just seen two graphic examples in this chapter. (As we proceed to implement G-Train, many more will follow.) Either way, the system will ask you for more information than you would normally consider so early in a project. This naturally means you'll spend more time in the requirement and architecture phases than you have in the past. Even so, you'll find that CASE tools can save time and money in the long run. For example, code generation and testing will proceed much faster and, best of all, CASE will eventually dispatch maintenance as we know it to the proverbial dust bins of history. Such predictions are more than idle hype. *Teledyne Brown*, a prominent CASE vendor in the engineering field, has accumulated some hard evidence for the efficacy of its TAGS system. For two recent projects, originally projected to run into millions of

Figure 7.4 At the system level, Index Technology's Excelerator tool decomposes the G-Train monitor in a somewhat different way than the preceding figure.

dollars, cost savings came in at 50% and 75%, respectively. Both projects were completed about three months ahead of schedule—a remarkable feat in itself.

Naturally, not all CASE tools are created equal. You should evaluate candidates for clarity of graphics, editing ease, diagnostics, adaptability, team support, documentation, and dynamic modeling, among other things. We'll return to these issues in Chapter 17, after getting acquainted with nearly a dozen CASE systems. In the G-Train example, the participating CASE vendors chose a variety of approaches, and you'll be able to decide which ones suit your applications best.

If you deal with real-time systems, for example, the tool of your choice must incorporate time as a variable and allow you to represent hardware. Systems derived from data flow diagrams (DFDs) tend to be weak in this regard, because specifying such things as bit-by-bit storage allocation runs counter to DFD philosophy. Remember that DFDs were introduced to help software designers in the DP community. Their applications were meant to run on as many computers as possible—in other words, hardware independence figured as an important goal. DP systems also require means for relating sets of data elements via schemas. Technically oriented CASE systems rarely flaunt their (often skimpy) schemas.

If you're at home in both worlds, you may have a problem. At present, most CASE tools offer the flexibility of a strait jacket. But as CASE database structures improve, their ability to propagate revisions from one design view to another will overcome present limitations. In some cases, the relationships between views are hierarchical, as discussed in Chapter 6; in others, they are *orthogonal*—technobabble for independent.

For example, assume IP.1 is broken down into IP.1.1 and IP.1.2. You are looking at two levels of the same information. (IP.1 collapses the details of the two subsystems IP.1.1 and IP.1.2.) A change in the higher level definitely affects at least one of the lower-level components, thus barring true orthogonality.

The myth of orthogonality. As an example for orthogonal views, think of a hierarchy chart (see Figure 6.1*a*) and a data flow diagram (see Figure 6.2*b*). You might compare the DFD to the floor plan and the hierarchy chart to the elevation view of a building. However, these views are not quite as independent of each other as the term "orthogonal" suggests—neither for software nor for a building. A change in the roof style, for example, will be clearly visible in the elevation, but barely noticeable in the floor plan. That's pretty orthogonal. Now take the floor plan and interchange the kitchen with the (equal-sized) dining room. You may not expect to see much in the elevation view, but take a closer look. In spite of the apparent orthogonality of the two views the underlying infrastructure for the whole house— say, electricity and plumbing—may change dramatically. What you really have to do when you move the kitchen is to revise a three-dimensional model of the house and then produce new floor and elevation views.

Applied to CASE tools, they must be capable of compiling and storing the complete "three-dimensional" software structure, and from that model you extract the desired views. Even more demanding, they must permit the user to change any given view and incorporate the changes *properly and automatically* into the total structure. CAE (or EDA) systems—the hardware designer's equivalent to CASE tools—can do precisely that with the help of elaborate software. As always, the cobblers are only now beginning to make shoes for their own families.

An encouraging development along those lines is the evolution of software "backplanes," which will facilitate communications between CASE tools from different vendors. This will ease transitions not only between different views of the same software package, but also between control-oriented real-time and data-oriented DP systems. Formidable hurdles must still be overcome, but at least CASE vendors are traveling on the right road. For the time being, however, don't presume that you'll attain reliable designs of large software systems just because you are plugged into a fashionable CASE tool.

Although G-Train cannot be called large by any definition, some of the contacted CASE vendors dropped out of the "contest," pleading lack of manpower. Judging by comments from those who persevered, analysis to the level of pseudocode in one of the subsystems should constitute about one or two days' work. In some cases, the solutions included simulation, which requires executable code and thus takes longer. In fact, about half the participating vendors have built the G-Train example into their training courses, solving the problem in full detail.

Even though the majority of vendors concentrated on just one or two G-Train subsystems, some of the entries include dozens of graphs and many more pages of automatically generated documentation. Obviously, only a small fraction of this material can be included in the book, but vendors might be willing to provide the full workup upon request. We must not generalize, but CASE systems that can't provide simulation or that require more than a few staff-days to implement it for G-Train may well not be up to snuff.

⤷ Echo the Requirements—with Foresight

When someone mentions specifications, this passage might well flash through your mind: "Make thee an ark of gopher wood; . . . the length shall be three hundred cubits; the breadth of it fifty cubits; and the height of it thirty cubits." The description goes on for several verses, but to this day scholars can't agree what Noah's ark should have looked like. Thanks to CASE graphics and simulation we can do better with another mythical vehicle— our G-Train.

For addresses of highlighted *companies* see Appendix D

Let's examine one CASE tool that specializes in the early design phases, Foresight from **Athena Systems.** Its primary mission lies in capturing the requirements in executable form to allow rapid prototyping. Foresight uses both graphics—as in the top-level diagram of Figure 7.5—and text. The latter applies a new requirements language (ESML), developed by a number of aerospace firms. This "Extended Systems Modeling Language" was designed specifically for real-time systems and is about to develop into an industry standard.

First, we'll take a look at some graphs. Figure 7.5, described as a logical context diagram, displays the system's data flow. Double-headed arrows indicate continuous data (e.g., those retrieved from a buffer or physical switch). Peripherals, such as sensors and switches, have been combined in one box labeled `Gravity Train`; the rest of the system follows the breakdown used in the spec. The system's DFD, shown as an inset, depicts a range of data sources from the Foresight library.

In Figure 7.6 the weighing subsystems appear in the form of an annotated state transition diagram. Each of the used variables can be regarded as a simple flag with the states True or False, except for `passengerStatus`. This label defines a record with two fields: the number of passengers and the total boarded weight. Because this subsystem is fully described by the figure, no ESML description need be added.

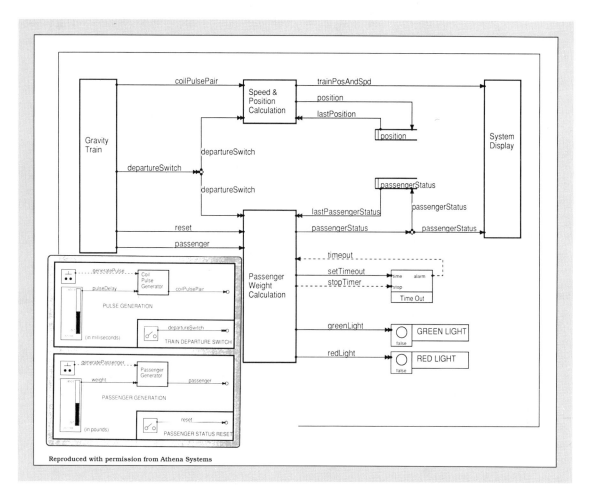

Reproduced with permission from Athena Systems

Speed and position calculation, however, require a "mini spec." It consists of a nested IF construct that defines the end positions, followed by the equations for calculating train speed and position along the way:

```
BEGIN
   IF (departureSwitch = FALSE)
      THEN trainPosAndSpd.trainSpeed := 0.0
           trainPosAndSpd.trainPosition := 1;
   ELSIF (lastPosition = 38)
      THEN trainPosAndSpd.trainSpeed := 0.0
           trainPosAndSpd.trainPosition := 40;
           position := 39;
```

Figure 7.5 With a tool such as Athena's Foresight, G-Train's requirements are readily turned into an executable graph. The inset represents the data flow diagrams for speed (*top*) and weighing (*bottom*). "Thermometer" bars represent simulated inputs for delay time and weight.

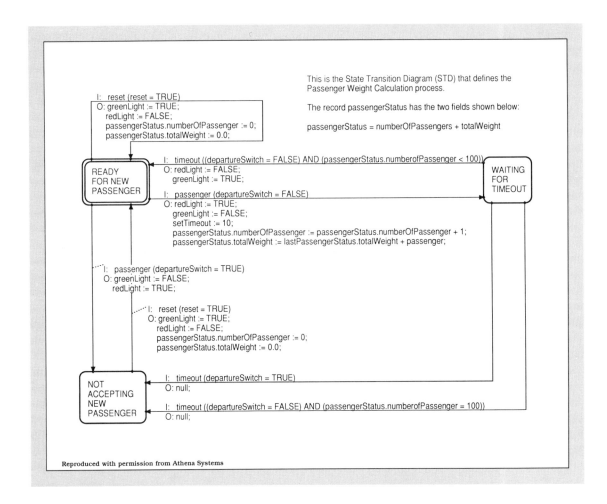

This is the State Transition Diagram (STD) that defines the Passenger Weight Calculation process.

The record passengerStatus has the two fields shown below:

passengerStatus = numberOfPassengers + totalWeight

I: reset (reset = TRUE)
O: greenLight := TRUE;
   redLight := FALSE;
   passengerStatus.numberOfPassenger := 0;
   passengerStatus.totalWeight := 0.0;

I: timeout ((departureSwitch = FALSE) AND (passengerStatus.numberofPassenger < 100))
O: redLight := FALSE;
   greenLight := TRUE;

I: passenger (departureSwitch = FALSE)
O: redLight := TRUE;
   greenLight := FALSE;
   setTimeout := 10;
   passengerStatus.numberOfPassenger := passengerStatus.numberOfPassenger + 1;
   passengerStatus.totalWeight := lastPassengerStatus.totalWeight + passenger;

READY FOR NEW PASSENGER

WAITING FOR TIMEOUT

I: passenger (departureSwitch = TRUE)
O: greenLight := FALSE;
   redLight := TRUE;

I: reset (reset = TRUE)
O: greenLight := TRUE;
   redLight := FALSE;
   passengerStatus.numberOfPassenger := 0;
   passengerStatus.totalWeight := 0.0;

NOT ACCEPTING NEW PASSENGER

I: timeout (departureSwitch = TRUE)
O: null;

I: timeout ((departureSwitch = FALSE) AND (passengerStatus.numberofPassenger = 100))
O: null;

Figure 7.6 The Weigh subsystem is here defined by a state transition diagram. The detailed annotations obviate the need for separate minispecs.

```
ELSE -- the train is in route
     trainPosAndSpd.trainSpeed := 2500.0/pulsePair
     trainPosAndSpd.trainPosition := lastPos + 1;
     position := trainPosAndSpeed.trainPosition
  END IF
END;
```

A data dictionary that compiles all used labels and identifies some as user-defined types rounds out Foresight's G-Train description.

The value of simulation was born out in the preparation of this example. One glance at the draft version of the display (see Figure 7.7) revealed a misunderstanding about the track

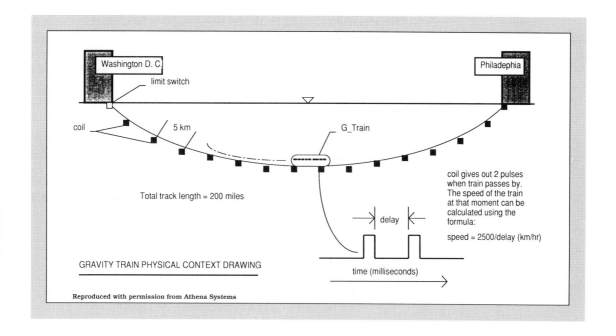

GRAVITY TRAIN PHYSICAL CONTEXT DRAWING

Reproduced with permission from Athena Systems

representation that could have led to a great deal of wasted effort. An error in the RFQ-specified number of sensors also stood out readily, and in fact causes a discrepancy between two position variables in the preceding minispec. A 10-minute study of Athena's "proposal" furthermore revealed more subtle glitches. As we pointed out before, most specs contain errors and ambiguities, and Foresight identified several readily.

Responses to RFQs are always due tomorrow, and such was the case for Athena. The immediate feedback offered by an executable spec can thus be invaluable in real-life situations. For example, rapid prototyping could have saved the F 16 project some embarrassment. A demo simulation revealed the plane's inability to right itself when flying exactly upside down (caused by a deadlock in the software). But then, every student of "Universal Design Theory" (so elegantly formulated by Professor *Murphy*) knows that the tenacity of mistakes is inversely proportional to the havoc they can wreak.

Figure 7.7 When all the G-Train subsystems are specified, Foresight executes the requirements. A graph of the "roadbed" permits the user to view the operation.

What's in the CARDS for you?   Since G-Train includes real-time features, we should contemplate another CASE tool specifically created for such applications—that is, CARDtools from **Ready Systems**. It is aimed at the aerospace market, which demands comprehensive requirements analysis. The reviewed part of Ready's G-Train workup runs nearly 50 (though often sparsely populated) pages, including the following sections: data and control flow diagram (D/CFD) of the requirements model; display screen mockups; control maps, including hierarchy charts and pseudocode; data type dictionary and invocation tree (a brief hierarchy description); cross-references for functions, data, and procedures; a DOD-STDD-2167 requirements document (18 pages); and a listing of data flow errors.

The last item can point out potential flaws in the specification before any effort has been invested—for example, with this output:

```
BOX    : g_train_C
ITEM   : Passenger Weight
WARNING: Internal feedback. Danger of
         use of uninitialized variable.
```

The feedback warning was simply triggered by the fact that the weight is taken repeatedly, and the designer must make sure that one set of data has been digested by the hardware before the next one arrives at the scene. The second "gotcha" chides the requirement for not specifying that the weight must be set to zero before the count starts. Although obvious in the present case, missing initialization can indeed be dangerous to your health. It has led to crashes not only of computers, but of more lethal hardware, such as cruise missiles.

CARDtools' top-level task map provides context in the form of the D/CFD in Figure 7.8, which also summarizes the system's icons. The notation differs from that of other control flow diagrams because CARDtools' control flow (lightning-type arrows) discloses such details as event flags, queues, and mailboxes. For example, the subsystem Tachometer passes data labeled Speed_Signal directly to the device service routine Speed. The control arrow labeled Speed_Sensors, however, must pass through the *interrupt* service routine Speed_Sens_Int, which activates Speed via an event flag, Speed_Event.

The system now performs a timing analysis for the Speed subsystem and prints out the results as in Figure 7.9. The analysis proves that, even with queue and flag delays, the system can easily meet the worst-case spacing between speed pulses of 5 ms.

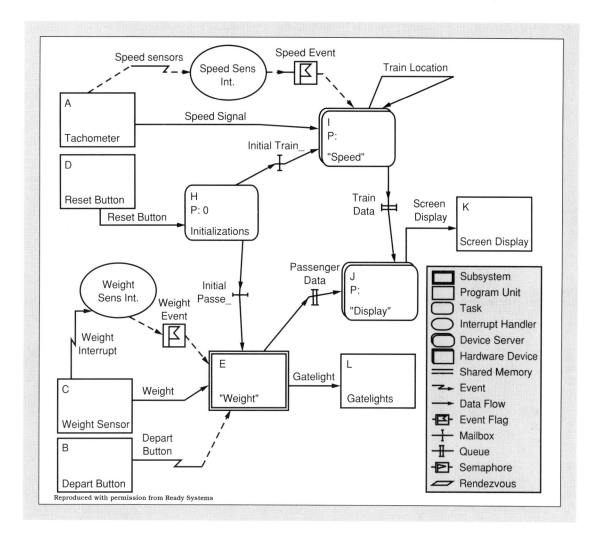

Reproduced with permission from Ready Systems

In the subsequent design stages, control map and pseudocode can be refined and the pseudocode expanded. A new invocation tree and decomposition hierarchies can then be constructed, and new cross-reference charts compiled.

CARDtools next cranks out the DOD-STDD-2167 top-level design document to be filed in the Pentagon with all the other documents required for the G-Train project. As the design advances, detail design documents, test and validation documents, and so on (and on), will follow in due course. (Judging by some past projects, a real G-Train might weigh less than the paperwork it will create.)

Figure 7.8 Ready Systems' CARDtools emphasize G-Train's real-time aspects (even in this top-level representation) by including mailboxes, queues, and flags. The loop atop the Speed module triggers a feedback warning.

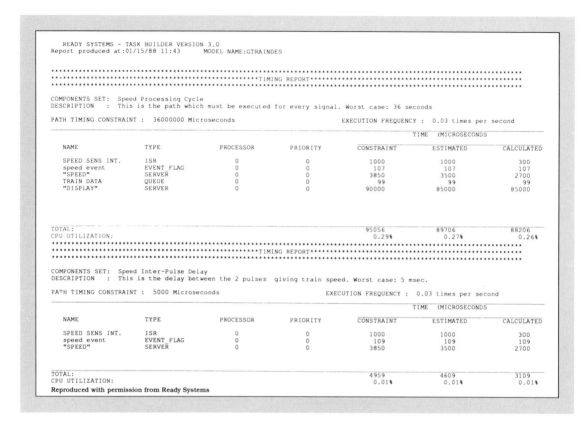

```
READY SYSTEMS - TASK BUILDER VERSION 3.0
Report produced at:01/15/88 11:43     MODEL NAME:GTRAINDES


*****************************************************************************************************
**.*********************************************TIMING REPORT****************************************
*****************************************************************************************************
COMPONENTS SET: Speed Processing Cycle
DESCRIPTION   : This is the path which must be executed for every signal. Worst case: 36 seconds

PATH TIMING CONSTRAINT : 36000000 Microseconds                      EXECUTION FREQUENCY : 0.03 times per second

                                                                        TIME  (MICROSECONDS
    NAME             TYPE           PROCESSOR      PRIORITY       CONSTRAINT       ESTIMATED        CALCULATED

    SPEED SENS INT.  ISR               0             0              1000            1000              300
    speed event      EVENT_FLAG        0             0               107             107              107
    "SPEED"          SERVER            0             0              3850            3500             2700
    TRAIN DATA       QUEUE             0             0                99              99               99
    "DISPLAY"        SERVER            0             0             90000           85000            85000


TOTAL:                                                             95056           89706            88206
CPU UTILIZATION:                                                    0.29%           0.27%            0.26%
*****************************************************************************************************
*****************************************************TIMING REPORT***********************************
*****************************************************************************************************
COMPONENTS SET: Speed Inter-Pulse Delay
DESCRIPTION   : This is the delay between the 2 pulses giving train speed. Worst case: 5 msec.

PATH TIMING CONSTRAINT : 5000 Microseconds                         EXECUTION FREQUENCY : 0.03 times per second

                                                                        TIME  (MICROSECONDS
    NAME             TYPE           PROCESSOR      PRIORITY       CONSTRAINT       ESTIMATED        CALCULATED

    SPEED SENS INT.  ISR               0             0              1000            1000              300
    speed event      EVENT_FLAG        0             0               109             109              109
    "SPEED"          SERVER            0             0              3850            3500             2700

TOTAL:                                                              4959            4609             3109
CPU UTILIZATION:                                                    0.01%           0.01%            0.01%
```
Reproduced with permission from Ready Systems

Figure 7.9 Timing reports examine G-Train's Speed module. In the top chart, spacing between pulse pairs is analyzed and easily passes muster. The bottom chart applies the same scrutiny to interpulse timing. Together the two processes use up at most 0.3% of CPU time—an important measure for a real-time system.

Oh yes, eventually, a few pages of code will also be included in the report, which (unlike all the other documents) is actually bound to be read—namely, by the computer that monitors the test track. You can imagine how much documentation will be piled up on, say, a communications satellite. No wonder the Pentagon prefers documents in computer-readable form and nurtures expert-system development. Exactly in which century AI will marshal enough intelligence to evaluate a pile of 2167 reports, however, remains top secret.

⅃ Reference

1. H. K. Edwards, "High speed tube transportation," *Scientific American*, August 1965, p. 30.

---

†Distance = speed × time. We convert all units to meters and seconds at a speed of 500 km/h: 500,000/3600 × 5/1000 = 0.694 meters, or 2 feet 3 inches.

8

AT THE HEART,
ALGORITHMS

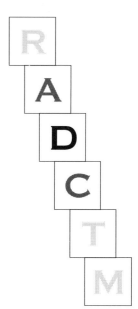

Mathematical recipes
Boarding the G-Train
In the picture with IDE

So far we have sampled the two top tubs of the waterfall diagram—requirements specification and architectural design. In the previous chapter, we actually applied some CASE tools to the architectural phase of the G-Train example. The next dive gets us into **algorithm** (or detail) design. One might think that CASE tools are most indispensable in this phase of software design; after all, among major error categories, faulty algorithms take the prize with 30%. (Improper data handling follows with 24%.)

Unfortunately, such is not the CASE. You can guard against architectural decomposition errors by adhering to a strict methodology. You can guard against coding errors by employing a code generator or by writing your program twice, in different languages. Neither precaution will prevent algorithmic errors. That's why algorithms represent the most difficult and most rewarding part of software design. Algorithm design has indeed become a discipline in its own right.

One can argue that algorithmics was started by a school boy named Karl Friedrich Gauss about 1785. To gain some time for correcting papers, Karl's teacher had asked the class to add up all the numbers from 1 to 1000. He refused to believe the answer little Karl presented within minutes: 500,500. The boy had mentally "folded" the string of numbers, so that 1000 came to rest under 1; 999 under 2; and so on. Clearly, each pair added up to 1001, and there were 500 pairs.

The anecdote catches the essence of algorithm design—finding a "recipe" to accomplish some task efficiently. Of course, solutions are not always as compelling as Karl's formulation. Take a simple matrix multiplication:

$$\begin{bmatrix} a & b \\ c & d \end{bmatrix} \times \begin{bmatrix} e & f \\ g & h \end{bmatrix} = \begin{bmatrix} ae + bg & af + bh \\ ce + dg & cf + dh \end{bmatrix}$$

Such matrix products dominate the solution of systems of linear equations—for example, in resource allocation or electronic circuits. In the latter case, matrices can grow to tens of thousands of elements. Because calculation time increases with the third power of the number of elements, the product of two 100×100 matrices will take 16 times longer to work out than the product of four 50×50 matrices.

Should it be possible to replace each large matrix with four smaller ones, we could cut CPU time by almost 94%. No wonder efforts continue to exploit every imaginable breakdown into submatrices. Unfortunately, this is only possible in special cases—primarily when specific elements of the matrix are absent. One rather devious algorithm needs no such restrictions, yet it reduces the calculation from order 3 to order 2.81.[1] That may not seem like much, but for matrices with 10,000 elements, the savings could theoretically amount to 82.6%. But alas, there's no free brunch. The "high school" procedure given earlier requires 8 multiplications and 4 additions. The new algorithm makes do with 7 multiplications but needs 18 additions and subtractions. Depending on the executing computer, the onset of savings varies, but matrices with under 10,000 elements need not apply. One could say that this algorithm attacks at the tactical (detail design) level, while Gauss's struck at the strategic (architectural) level.

Another example may affect far more users than matrices do. You have probably seen learned discussions about the relative merits of sundry searching and sorting algorithms.[2-4] Just by picking the most suitable one, you can cut the search for specific data on a reel of tape from days to minutes. Solving problems like these efficiently is the sort of challenge mathematicians revel in (Gauss, of course, grew up to be one).

Eternal quest for elegance.   Few computer users can hope to improve on the mathematicians' solutions to generic problems. Trouble is, how do you find them when mathematicians hide them under cute code names? For example, when would you look up papers on the "Towers of Hanoi" (a constrained sort) or on the "Dining Philosophers" (a queueing task)? Furthermore, the uninitiated may wonder why they should care about "elegance"— a term dear to the heart of scholars and rampant in learned papers. But what does the word really mean?

The dictionary is of little help, offering descriptions like "tasteful," "graceful," "superior," or just plain "excellent." When it comes to the elegance of mathematical algorithms, we could call them efficient, clear, astute, clever, or even beautiful. (Elegance, like beauty, lies in the eye of the beholder. To some the Brooklyn Bridge is elegant, to others just quaint. To some a Mercedes engine may represent the epitome of elegance, for the rest of mankind it's just a power plant.)

Elegant or not, an algorithm can speed up the solution you need by orders of magnitude, so it's well worth looking for. Someday you will be able to access a taxonomy of algorithms from your keyboard, but for the time being, visit the library.[5-12] After all, finding the best algorithm dominates detail design, because it must precede both further decomposition and code generation. It's no use turning on the oven if you don't have the recipe yet.

But algorithms need not be solutions to *mathematical* problems—the fastest way to get to City Hall is also an algorithm. So is a voter registration program that prevents double registration. One was set up in Brazil, but its simplistic algorithm (comparing last names, addresses, and birthdays) disenfranchised half of all twins. Neither mathematical expertise nor reliance on CASE systems could preclude such a blunder. Better research could have prevented some red faces in Quebec, however, where an election forecasting system for two television networks credited votes to the wrong candidate because of an erroneous sorting scheme.

More insidious goofs run rampant, even in IQ-laden places. On March 16, 1986 the Stanford Research Institute's E-mail computer thought it was December 7, 1984, which wreaked havoc with the mail. The reason? In the interest of accuracy, the computer's calendar was routinely reset with a time reading averaged from several sources. When one of them hallucinated (thinking it was 1972!), the Stanford system followed it doggedly. Of course, a good averaging algorithm throws out obviously bad data, right? Well, the worldwide ozone monitoring system was set up to do exactly that. So, for nine years it threw out the "obviously errant" data that reported a growing hole over Antarctica—another case where data hiding didn't pan out.

A matter of life and death. Unfortunately, more calamitous errors have been reported as well. One man was killed and two seriously burned during "treatment" with the Therac 25 irradiation machine. It can provide either an electron beam or X-rays, which are produced by positioning a heavy metal target in the beam's path. In the X-ray mode, the beam must be much stronger, posing a potential danger to the patient. That was no problem as long as the mechanical "algorithm" used an interlock to firmly couple beam strength to target insertion. Modeling that safeguard in software turned out to be elusive. To make matters worse, a program editor provided a shortcut that spared the operator the exertion of punching in each treatment from scratch. (For this part of the problem a hardware fix was easiest to implement: remove the edit key.)

A similar shortcut may have contributed to the fate of flight KAL 007, which cost 269 passengers their lives. A postmortem panel of aviation experts suspects that the crew used an autoload feature to bypass triple-redundant entries of flight coordinates (about 100 digits). We might shrug off this flaw by labeling it a man-machine interface problem. However, finding a recipe that ensures safe loading of programs and data is indeed part of algorithmic design.

In the design of algorithms, experience (aka domain knowledge) still reigns supreme. Naturally, in the absence of common sense, neither expertise nor simulation can save the day. When the designer of the Three Mile Island reactor console decided that the printout should read "?????" when the temperature exceeded 700°, neither his boss nor a government inspector set him straight. Simulation or rapid prototyping might have induced some onlooker to ask "What's with the question marks?" Now we know better.

The testing phase can cull out blunders as a last resort—provided at least *one* reviewer is alert—or a **validation** contractor might smell a rat. In the case of the questionable question marks, no one did, and the erosion of public faith in reactor design resulted. It has already cost this country billions of dollars, and all mankind will eventually suffer from a side effect—the burning of more fossil fuels. Yes, algorithm design is inherently tricky and should not be taken lightly, especially when human life hangs in the balance.

Academic research into automatic algorithm generation attempts to harness artificial intelligence for this software design phase. However, success so far has been limited to very narrow domains.[13] In fact, no current computer (AI or otherwise) could even come up with Gauss's simple addition algorithm on its own. It's just as well—once computers can innovate without human help, what will they do with us? (You do recall what HAL did in *2001*, right?)

Simulation of proposed algorithms has saved the day for many an aerospace system. It caught, for example, an algorithmic blunder that flipped (imaginary) F16s over on their backs whenever they crossed the equator. Because that plane flies under computer control (and becomes statically unstable without it), it could not even be tested without extensive simulation. Still, all possible scenarios will never be covered in make-believe flights, and we hear about the resulting disasters in the evening news, as discussed in Chapter 3. (As one skeptic put it: "If simulation is so great, how come insurance premiums for test pilots are still going up?")

Although the CASE paradigm imparts no magic, graphic representation of an algorithm does offer hope for cleaner and more reliable design. Whether you use flowcharts, data flow diagrams, or IPs, the graphs are meant to clarify an algorithm's inner workings. Just how far the process of visual decomposition should be pursued, however, is a matter of taste. Eventually, graphs still must be converted to code, even if automatically.

Purists insist on graphic problem breakdown to the level of primitives (mostly statements), and some CASE environments actually implement this philosophy. Ardent coders, however, may prefer to skip even flowcharts since code produced by continued graphical refinement is rarely elegant. But then, the code need only satisfy the customer's computer, which might just emulate Rhett Butler's sentiments in *Gone with the Wind*: "Frankly, my dear, I don't give a damn."

More importantly, semiautomatically generated code may not only be ugly, it may also be very inefficient. And that's a very different story, especially if speed is of the essence. Many CASE packages include "analyzers" that point out execution bottlenecks ("hot spots"). Here again, human interference remains the only viable solution.

A time to decompose, a time to code.   In general, decomposition serves no further purpose when an IP or its equivalent contains only serial code or can be imported as a single module. This point has definitely been reached when no control constructs remain within the leaf-level procedures. So, whatever graphic method you choose, it's essential to minimize ambiguities in the control structures lest they misrepresent the current level of abstraction.

In our IP system, for example, an IF/THEN/ELSE construct can always be activated with a control input. DO loops pose a much greater challenge. First of all, serial thinking has predisposed many designers to see DO loops where none really exist. Take the addition of two vectors, each consisting of, say, *N* integers. The low-level implementation in a specific language on a single CPU may indeed require a loop that performs *N* integer additions. But an IP (let's call it VectorAdd) would simply show two input signals of type Vector, each with a "bus" symbol to indicate the dimension (see Figure 8.1*a*).

In contrast, a factorial calculation cannot be implemented in parallel. It calls for either a DO loop (see Figure 8.1*b*) or for recursion (Figure 8.1*c*). In the former case, the argument is also a

Figure 8.1 How far to decompose graphically remains a matter of taste. IPs permit a vector operation (*a*) to be defined as a loop (*b*) or recursive operation (*c*).

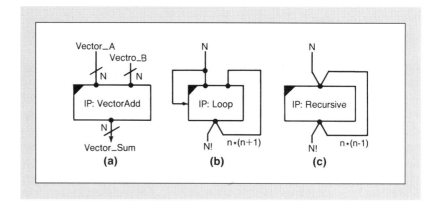

control value; in the latter, it is purely a data "signal." Obviously, the distinction between the two gets blurred at this point, but breakdown to the level of machine code clarifies the difference. The loop version must test a control variable and set a jump switch when *N* has been reached. A recursively called IP would just have to check the (successively decremented) argument for the value 1, and exit at the proper branch of an ORed output.

At times, refinement will lead to IPs that show far more control "wires" than data lines. An operating system or even a word processor may break down in this manner, signaling a control rather than a process subsystem. A growing number of CASE environments permit the user to switch from data and control flow diagrams (D/CFDs) to a different visual format—say, state transition diagrams or even truth tables.

What a character.   Since so far we've concentrated on data-driven design examples, let's now look at one that illustrates your choices when control flow dominates data flow. Assume you want to determine how many records in a file begin with a given search character. The algorithm is perhaps best illustrated with the flowchart of Figure 8.2*a*. A DO loop compares each record's initial letter with the search character, char, and ratchets up a counter N whenever a match is found. When the search reaches EOF (end of file), the value of N is printed out.

A state transition (or just state) diagram, in essence, reverses the roles of the flowchart's lines and boxes (see Figure 8.2*b*). Circles indicate states—a condition when nothing happens within the program and, consequently, within the executing computer. However, because every clock tick usually produces some state change in the hardware, state transition diagrams reflect a higher level of abstraction. The state diagram in Figure 8.2*b* nicely illustrates the choices in our fairly trivial example. But large state diagrams can become quite unmanageable.

An IP diagram, like the one in Figure 8.2*c*, displays the same information in a more hierarchical form. Again, the IP version adds one more function to the program: if an exception arises, the system prints out the value of the loop variable to simplify the search for the error's cause. EOF could also be handled as an exception, but that would be a questionable practice. After all, we know that each run ends with the reading of EOF, and exception handling should only be reserved for the unforeseen.

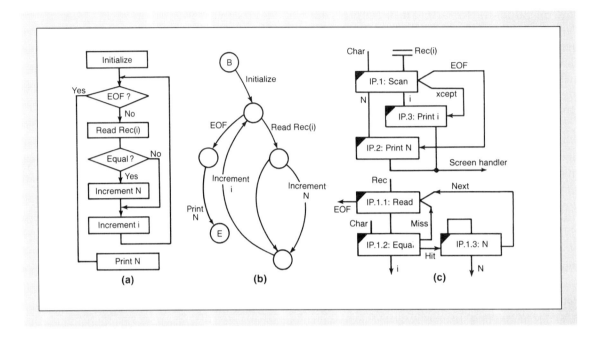

(a) **(b)** **(c)**

Figure 8.2 If control flow dominates an algorithm, flowcharts (*a*) usually eclipse state diagrams (*b*). An IP implementation of the same search algorithm combines the features of both (*c*).

In the illustration, IP.1 has been broken down further to show more detail. Without a doubt, the IP description reveals more information than the flowchart, which in turn provides more than the state diagram.

In most CASE systems' detail design phase, the coding step follows (sometimes automatically) the graphic representations. Experienced programmers and computer science graduates, however, itch to get into code as quickly as possible. Therefore, they may be tempted to bypass visual design tools. If you belong to that school, consider this: even if you have all the code already "in your head," generating a graphic representation can provide valuable documentation.

Furthermore, detail design also includes a program's internal organization—we might call it the meta-algorithm. For example, a technique called "funneling" (which separates interfaces from algorithms) can go a long way to simplify later changes. For instance, by separating access routines from the main program, you can get at a data structure regardless of where it's stored—main memory, disk, or file server. To sketch out such organizational details, full-fledged CASE systems may not be the most efficient tools. Mouse addicts may opt for an inexpensive graphics tool; it beats pencil, paper, and (economy-sized) eraser in such chores. A better alternative are object-oriented CASE systems, which we'll examine in Chapter 13.

If you still want to use text-oriented CASE throughout detail design, literally truckloads of language-specific debuggers, loaded with sundry bells and whistles, stand ready to serve you. Thumb through the pages of journals such as *Byte* and *Computer Language*, and get on the mailing list of specialty distributors like **The Programmer's Shop** for specifics. If you play in the big leagues, examine such toolboxes as **Digital Equipment**'s VAXset or (for Ada addicts with the needed moolah) **Rational**'s R1000 Development System.

↳ All Aboard the G-Train

Let's put our algorithmic wisdom to the test by composting (sorry, decomposing) the G-Train system some more. Some of the nitty-gritty decisions that were postponed in the last chapter can be taken up again at this time. In the weighing section, we decided that on power-up the light should be red and the weight zero. As long as the scale platform remains vacant, the analog-digital converter of the scale should show the value "000" (we only need the approximate weight, so fractions will be truncated). But these scales do need calibration, so we'll use the initial reading as a correction. We must not forget to set the total weight to zero as well.

Next the console operator hits a specific key (e.g., F1), and the green light turns on until a passenger steps on the scale. At that point the light turns red, and we must wait until the weight reading stabilizes. Cleverly, we have ordered the Thinking Scale from Brain & Brawn Inc., whose display tells the user to stand still until the reading is stable. (You think that's cheating? OK, as an exercise work out a solution for a dumb scale.) The scale, which was originally designed for a fat farm, now displays the weight and sends it to a PC as input. As soon as this input arrives, we can start up the specified counter and let it tick off 10 seconds. Then the gate light turns green again.

As algorithms go, this one is simple enough and can easily do without any help from a mathematician. It seems reason-

able to break down IP.1 from Figure 8.2 down into two IPs—
IP.1.1, which interfaces with the peripherals (scale and lights),
and IP.1.2, which performs the remaining functions. That way
we can revamp the hardware later, without affecting IP.1.2. In
fact, we can even implement IP.1.1 as hardware if we so desire
or integrate it with the Thinking Scale altogether. It would even
make sense to put the lights into the scale's display.

Now our Weight subsystem shapes up as follows (see Figure
8.3a): IP.1.1 receives the raw scale readings with limits of −2.0
to 401.0. (For the calibration we allow a range of ±2 lbs.) The
scale we picked outputs four-digit real numbers. Values outside
the defined range trigger the exception flag xcept (which differs
in function from the one in Figure 8.2). True_Weight will be an
integer with the previous limits of 0 to 399 pounds. In addition,
IP.1.1 controls the lights, but the two outputs are no longer ORed
together. We are now free to overlap the red and green cycles, as
is still common in some states (and foreign countries) for traffic
lights. Making such tradeoffs early in the game is exactly the
purpose of top-down refinement.

Figure 8.3 Further
IP breakdown of
Figure 7.3 permits
us to calibrate the
weighing scale (*a*)
and even produce
error messages (*b*).

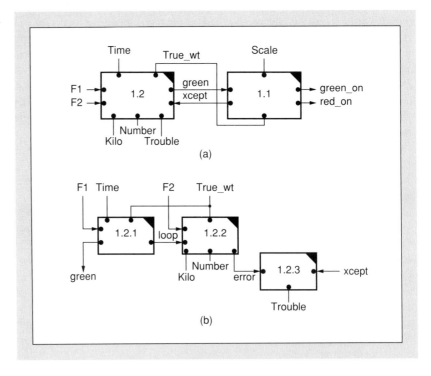

Built-in trouble shooter.   The control inputs for IP.1.2 now carry the labels F1 for "open gate," F2 for "departing," and green as the Boolean output that controls the lights. Time, Kilos, and Number remain unchanged. A new output variable, Trouble, serves to feed exception data into the display, replacing the original plan of turning on an (ambiguous) blinker. The carrier of such information can be defined by

Trouble: error ASCII, @..@@@@@@@@@@

The @ symbol stands for "any", and we specify that the number of symbols will range from 1 to 10. The messages might include "ok", "weight", "time", and "?????". (In this case, question marks are just fine.)

We still need an algorithm to change the lights and calculate the number of boarding passengers. The only input available to IP.1.2 is True_Weight, which during boarding will jump from 0 to an integer lower than 400 and back again. For example, we can look at this variable every second, and, if a reading over 20 follows one under 20, turn the light red and raise the count by one. Simultaneously, the timer starts ticking away and, when it reaches N, turns the light back to green. By using the symbolic value N for the lapse time, we lock in the benefits of hindsight— for a skier on crutches the specified 10-second interval may prove inadequate.

Only one chore remains—figuring out the total boarded weight. That's easy enough. Whenever we increase the passenger count, we convert the current weight reading to kilograms and add the result to the total. In fact, let's compare the total to a constant, Max_Weight, just in case G-Train can't handle 18,141 kg— the total if every passenger weighs in at 400 lb (luggage included, naturally). In that unlikely event, we can trigger the message "overweight". (Hence the ten @ symbols).

Just for practice, we'll decompose IP.1.2 further, according to the implementation decisions we just made. IP.1.2.1 can sense the weight transitions, IP.1.2.2 can perform all loop operations, and IP.1.2.3 can produce the error messages (Figure 8.3*b*). Because we want to check the weight once a second, IP.1.2.1 needs a Time input. So, we might as well obtain the red-green delay in this IP too. We gain greater flexibility this way because we don't necessarily have to count full-second ticks, as in the weight monitor. Once IP.1.2.1 senses a weight drop, it passes the control signal loop to IP.1.2. The IP also initializes the system when it receives F1 to start boarding.

IP.1.2.2 converts the weight to kilograms, calculates the total, and also passes the increment index as the passenger count. Because it can experience different error types, we show the exception handler not as a control flag but as a signal named Error. However, it enters IP.1.2.3 as a control signal because it will probably manipulate a case statement that generates the values for Trouble. The xcept control from IP.1 also enters here because it will trigger yet another error message.

We have now reached the point where further graphic decomposition of the Weight subsystem serves little purpose, except if we rely on the Nassi-Shneiderman diagram as the next step. For the Weight module, it might have the form shown in Figure 8.4, but you'll rarely encounter it. Most commercial CASE tools resort to pseudocode at this point to describe the function of each module. (Presently, few CASE tools generate executable source code without intervention, but most plan to implement autocoding eventually.)

Pseudocode descriptions are sometimes called minispecs and can serve as the requirement spec for a component or a whole system. In the latter case, we should use a program design language, better known as PDL. (In the Ada world, Ada-like PDLs are

Figure 8.4 Nassi-Shneiderman diagrams typify alternatives to purely graphical decomposition. From this representation of the weighing module, some CASE tools could generate source code automatically.

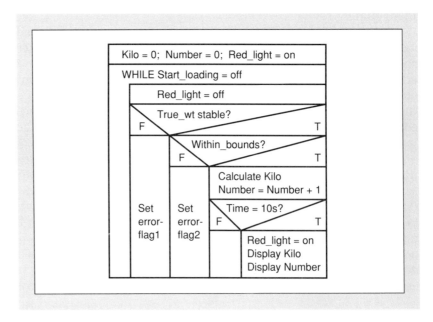

not only preferred, they are often prescribed.) For IP.1.2.3, the pseudocode might look as follows:

```
IF xcept = true THEN error := 99;
CASE error =
        0: Trouble := "ok"
        1: Trouble := "time"
        2: Trouble := "overweight"
       99: Trouble := "scale"
     ELSE: Trouble := "?????"
END CASE
```

Remember that all IP variables are local, so the difference between a data variable Error leaving IP.1.2.2 and a control variable error entering IP.1.2.3 is immaterial. What counts are the pin definitions, which read for IP.1.2.3 as follows:

```
A: type char, @..@@@@@@@@@@
x: type bit, true = exception
y: type integer, 0..99
```

Because IP.1.2.3 is an exception handler, we have to convert the Boolean exception flag from IP.1.1 to an error message. But why the value 99? The problem here is that part of the exception handler has been built into IP.1.2.2, where we distinguish between time-related errors and overweight. We have a choice: play strictly by the rules and output a general exception flag in addition to the variable Error or convert the flag inside the IP:

```
IF xcept = false THEN Error := 0
                 ELSE Error := 90
```

The value 90 was chosen arbitrarily. Should we later decide to expand the exception handler to a dozen messages or more, we won't have to change anything else.

The distinction between control and data variables may seem ludicrous to the average hacker and unimportant to the average software engineer; however, many computer scientists find it vital. Software algebra would have us place a "guard" in front of executable statements that evaluate to true or false, which, in effect, would turn every assignment into an IF statement and thus simplify correctness proofs. However, we'd have to give up constructs that require a control integer—like DO loops and

CASE statements. Although control and data should indeed be kept apart, as pragmatists, we choose convenience over purity.

⌐ Get in the Picture with IDE

One of the most mature of today's general-purpose CASE systems, Software through Pictures (StP, for short), can show us how it would help the lucky (sic) winner of the G-Train contract. Developed by *Interactive Development Environments* (IDE), the system follows the Yourdon-DeMarco methodology with real-time extensions. StP sports more flexibility than most because the system supports the Xwindows and Sun NSE interfaces, and its files are compatible with PostScript. Better yet, the user can access all of StP's tool interfaces for customization. Although not yet capable of full code generation, it does provide code skeletons (templates) in Ada, C, and Pascal syntax. StP can also access the cross-development tool InterACT from *ACT Corp.* and DEW from *SES* as discussed in Chapter 11. The package also caters to object-oriented programming (see Chapter 13) and supports DOD-STD-2167.

We start out with the system view in the top left window of Figure 8.5, where the zero-level process control g_train interfaces with the sensors and the display. The other three windows deal with the subsystems: one determines the train's speed (bottom left), one computes the weight (top right), and the last gets the data ready for display (bottom right). For each leaf process, a Pspec (or minispec) is generated, for example:

```
Process 2.2: compute_wt_no
    This process has 4 data flows
        weight_of_passenger, number_of_passengers
        total_passenger_weight, green_pulse
    input data flows
        weight_of_passenger
    output data flows
        total_passenger_weight,
        number_of_passengers, green_pulse
    This process has 0 control flows
end pspec
```

A description is also included which reads: "This process computes the total passenger weight by increasing the current passenger weight every time a passenger steps on the scale. It also finds the number of passengers on the g_train." Except for

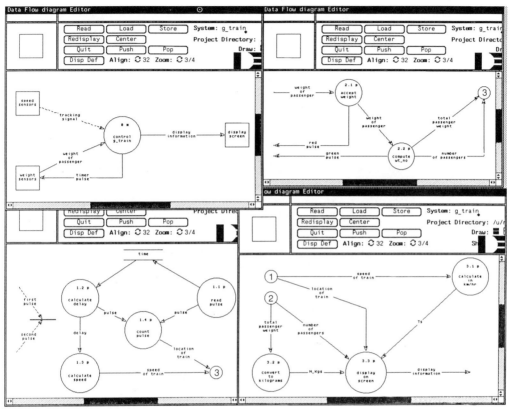

Reproduced with permission from IDE Inc.

the description, the minispec is generated automatically. Process 2.2 receives its input from process 2.1, and we might as well take a look at its Pspec too. For the sake of variety, however, we'll request it in the Ada format:

```
# "accept_weight"
----------------------------------------------------
-- accept_weight was generated from diagram:
-- /u/project/g_train/2.sce
----------------------------------------------------
-- This process accepts as input the weight of a
-- person who steps on the scales when the light is
-- green. As soon as the passenger steps on the
-- scales the red light goes on to indicate that
-- the scales are in use.
with ${} ;
package body accept_weight is
end accept_weight;
```

Figure 8.5 At the highest level of its G-Train implementation, IDE chooses to introduce a control module (top left). Weight (top right), speed (bottom left), and display (bottom right) follow the requirements specification.

You'll recall that only the last three lines represent executable Ada code (once a valid name replaces ${ }), while all the rest will be disregarded by a compiler as comments.

Explore a second dimension.   We could now continue to decompose the Weight subsystem further as we did for the IP implementation, but that might get rather boring. Instead, let's put another StP view to the test. A second view not only helps us to disentangle the executing processor's "food chain," it also adds some redundancy—a rare commodity when working with computers. Yet it is redundancy in human communications that permits us to understand, for example, a sentence that . . .

Ideally, a software system should be broken down into a tree structure to minimize module interdependence. Some CASE tools examine a system's deviation from a pure tree and from that calculate a complexity rating. Judging by the looks of Figure 8.6 (top), the StP solution passes muster. Now we just have to see whether the two views we have fed into StP's database mesh with each other and with the G-Train requirements. By pushing the proper mouse buttons, we can goad the system to yield a module traceability report that looks like this:

```
1. Modules satisfying a process requirement
            Module                    Process
         cal_weight            compute_wt_no
         find_loc              count_pulse
         start_train           control_g_train
         to_screen             send_to_screen

2. Modules NOT satisfying a process requirement
            accept_pulse_1
            accept_pulse_2
            cal_speed
            calculate_delay
            count
            reset_scale
```

With our ecstasy somewhat clipped, we return to the drawing board. Our two views of G-Train require, as accountants so neatly put it, reconciliation. We'll pull up another data structure tree (at left in the bottom screen of Figure 8.6) and add D/CFDs, which might stifle some of the criticism that the module traceability report showered upon us. To start with, we'll decide whether

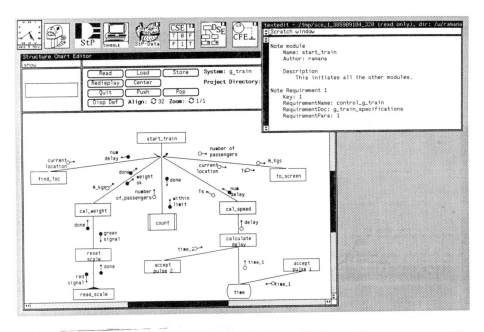

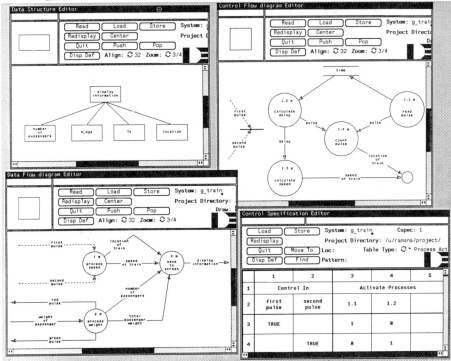

Figure 8.6 The G-Train structure chart of the top screen clearly shows that the IDE solution comes close to the goal of a tree-like system structure. (The small window serves to edit the root module description.) In the lower screen, a data structure editor (top left) and a control specification editor (bottom right) facilitate corrections.

the speed pulses should be called first and second pulse or pulse 1 and 2. Then we'll grapple with the related terms for delay and speed calculation.

Together with the bubble charts we've also put a decision table on the screen that complements the Speed module. It is almost trivial since it merely tells the system that process 1.1 is activated by the first pulse and process 1.2 by the second. We'll go into more detail on the speed algorithm in the next chapter, which deals with the G-Train's real-time aspects.

⁀ References

1. John L. Bentley, "An introduction to algorithm design," *IEEE Computer*, February 1979, p. 66.

2. Sanford Hersh, "String searching in C," *Computer Language*, December 1988, p. 63.

3. K. O'Toole, "Sorting in place," *Computer Language*, December 1988, p. 41.

4. Dan Khoushy, "Practical algorithmic development and tradeoffs," *TC Interface*, January 1987, p. 21.

5. Milton Abramowitz and Irene Stegun (Eds.), *Handbook of Mathematical Functions*, Dover Publications, New York, 1965.

6. John L. Bentley, *Writing Efficient Programs*, Prentice-Hall, Englewood Cliffs, NJ, 1982.

7. R. B. Coats, *Software Engineering for Small Computers*, Reston Publishing, Reston, VA, 1982.

8. David Harel, *Algorithmics*, Addison-Wesley, Reading, MA, 1987.

9. John F. Hart, et al., *Computer Approximations*, R. E. Krieger Publishing, Malabar, FL, 1978.

10. D. E. Knuth, *The Art of Computer Programming*, vol. 1 & 2, Addison-Wesley, Reading, MA, 1969.

11. Robert Sedgewick, *Algorithms*, Addison-Wesley, Reading, MA, 1983.

12. Pat H. Sterbenz, *Floating-Point Computation*, Prentice-Hall, Englewood Cliffs, NJ, 1974.

13. Elaine Kant and Allen Newell, "Problem solving techniques for the design of algorithms," *Information Processing and Management* (UK), vol. 20, 1984, p. 97.

9

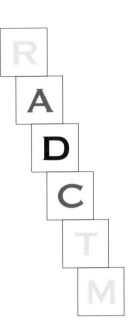

WHEN SOFTWARE TOUCHES THE REAL WORLD

Cruising into real time
Take the G-Train's pulse
A view from Mentor Graphics

In the previous chapter we examined the G-Train's weighing system, which connects a scale to the computer that runs the show. The subsystem does in fact reach out to touch the real world, but at a leisurely pace. From the computer's point of view, light-years pass between passengers. Things get a lot livelier in the subsystem that measures the G-Train's speed. When the two speed pulses arrive, the hardware better be ready to greet them, or they enter a black hole. As you know, nothing ever returns from there, unless our universe was made from 26-dimensional strings.[1]

To accentuate such dismal prospects, systems this strongly rooted in reality are branded "real-time" machines. But one system's real time is another's eon. When a vendor of transaction processing equipment talks about "real-time response," he means that the screen reacts to an input before the operator can doze off—say, within a few seconds. An F 16's control computer, on the other hand, must respond 1000 times in that period to keep the unstable flying machine in the air. Still, even this computer dawdles compared with one that must intercept data on a megabaud channel, because it has less than 8 microseconds to swallow each arriving byte. As Einstein realized long before the computer era, time is indeed relative.

Software by itself is rarely aware of time's passing. The same `store` instruction can put a bit away in a millionth of a second or once a year. When we deal with fleeting events, we just have to confirm that the system—hardware plus software—responds fast enough. To develop such software on a CASE system, we must first make sure that it can handle time dependencies at all. The original Yourdon-DeMarco data flow diagram was designed for data processing. It needed no provisions for dynamic system behavior or even for hardware interaction. By now the diagram has been extended, and its bubbles can be made to obey the beat of more than one drummer.[2]

Needless to say, the bubble charts were enhanced more than once. CASE vendors generally follow either the Ward-Mellor approach,[3] the Hatley-Pirbhai method,[4] or both. Although their underlying dogmas differ, in practice you primarily notice some differences in their graphical notations. Hatley and Pirbhai follow the Yourdon-DeMarco method more closely and focus primarily on processes and procedures, followed by data storage needs. Thus, the approach could be classified as procedural.

Ward-Mellor view the system as a black box that responds to external events. In this view, processes result from stimuli, which forces the designer more quickly into design specifics. You could regard this methodology as more event-driven than Hatley and Pirbhai's approach. The next logical step should be a truly object-oriented paradigm, and one has indeed evolved at **Project Technology**.[5] (We'll discuss it further in Chapter 13.) First a comparison between the Ward-Mellor and Hatley-Pirbhai methods. We can relate the two easily because the basic text from both schools implements (among other examples) a cruise control system. Let's get acquainted with it first.

Just cruising along.   Unless you own a car with a cruise control (CC for short), you may not know how it really functions. The purpose of the gizmo is to give your gas foot a rest when driving long monotonous stretches of interstates. (Oldtimers may remember "hand gas"—a lever on the steering wheel that accomplished the same end in a low-tech way.) Before you can engage CC, you have to get your car into the leftmost lane, where chances are lowest that you'll have to brake for a dump truck at the next entrance ramp. Then you bring the speed to 55 mph (or more if you travel in an enlightened state) and push the CC button.

The automatic system engages to keep your speed constant, over hill and dale, no matter what your right foot does. (For safety's sake, most CC owners like to keep it lightly on the brake pedal, just enough to blind any pursuer with blazing tail lights.) How do you resume control? In Massachusetts and parts of California you'll find out the moment some wise guy passes you on the right and cuts you off. You step on the brakes, and the CC disengages.

Now we already know that the CC system consists of at least the following subsystems: the driver, the brake, a speed sensor, and a throttle mechanism that maintains the speed. All of these subsystems are peripherals of the CC monitor, as shown in Figure 9.1a. (To simplify matters, we assume that the car is already in motion.) Hatley and Pirbhai show data and control flow in separate graphs to avoid confusion. Ward and Mellor prefer to combine both flows, as in Figure 9.1b, which deals with speed management. The double-headed arrows represent continuous data, such as those measuring the rotation rate of the drive wheels. (Ward and Mellor call it "time-continuous flow.") Single-headed arrows identify discrete data ("time-discrete flow"), like the stored value of the target speed.

In the IP representation in Figure 9.1c we deal only with the software. At the IP.1 level we break the system down into two subsystems; IP.1.1 manages the whole CC, and IP.1.2 controls the throttle. (We dispense with a separate brake control; mountain drivers don't like cruise controls anyway.) IP.1.1 needs only one input—the drive shaft's rotation rate. When the car has reached the desired speed, we activate the "set" control; to disengage the system we just tap the brake pedal.

IP.1.1 outputs two values: (1) the current speed reading for the speedometer and (2) the difference between current and desired speed, which governs IP.1.2. If the value is negative, the controller opens the throttle more; if it's positive it reduces the intake flow. There is one more input, namely current throttle position. This reading, combined with the speed differential, tells the governor how fast the throttle position should be changed for best gas mileage.

As a fringe benefit, IP.1.2 can set a flag when the throttle is completely open and pass that flag to IP.1.1. The throttle flag, combined with the current rotation reading, can activate a yellow overload light and turn the CC off. This also douses a green light, which indicates that the CC system is engaged. We have therefore ORed the two lights, but it might be a good idea to keep the overload light functional even when the CC is disengaged.

Although all three parts of the figure depict fairly high-level notions, they obviously represent different views of the CC system. In Figure 9.1*a* the driver is part of the system and exchanges information with the computer. If you want to pick nits, you could insist on arrows between driver and brake pedal—after all, the pressure sensors in the foot do provide important information. Figure 9.1*b* concentrates on the data transformations caused by stimuli—very much resembling a Yourdon-DeMarco bubble chart. (If you like bubbles, the three volumes of Ward and Mellor's book dispense enough to make your cup run over.) But let us go on; we'll see more bubbles of both persuasions soon enough.

The IP view of Figure 9.1*c* concentrates on the signals flowing through the CC system. Six of the I/O lines carry data, and six carry control flags—a nice balance for a microprocessor system. If all lines carried control signals, the CC could just as well be implemented with relays, albeit at much higher cost. (Few could have imagined such a perversion 20 years ago: relays dearer than computers!)

⌐ Cruising from State to State

In the absence of any data signals, the CC system could be implemented by a pure state machine, which will be discussed at length in the next chapter. Suffice it to say here that CASE tools generally describe state changes by means of squarish diagrams, similar to the one Hatley and Pirbhai give for the CC (see the slightly simplified version in Figure 9.2*a*). You always enter the CC in the cruising state (i.e., at the current speed) and always leave it by stepping on the brake. The only other state changes take place between cruising and accelerating—the CC's normal activities until somebody cuts you off.

State graphs are sometimes supplemented with state transition tables (as in Figure 9.2*b*), or with action tables (the one in Figure 9.2*c* goes with the chart of Figure 9.2*a*). Action tables add a bit more information to the diagram than transition tables,

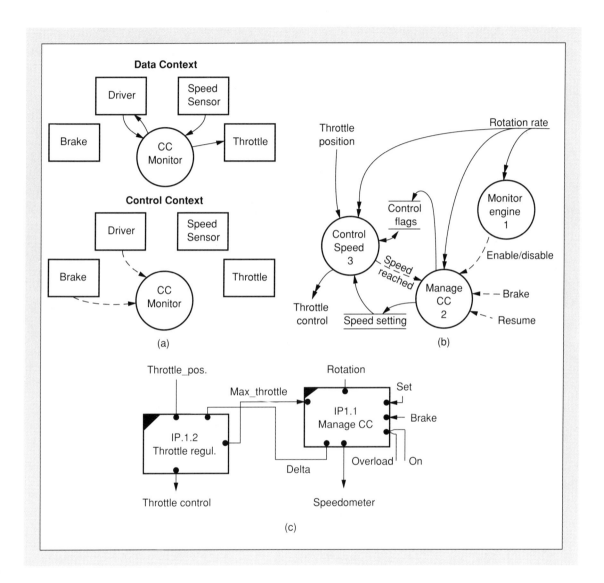

Figure 9.1 The cruise control (CC) remains dear to the heart of real-time system designers. A subset (which assumes that the car is in motion) in the Hatley-Pirbhai version shows data and control flow separately (*a*), while the Ward-Mellor method prefers to combine them (*b*). An IP version (*c*) will resolve any confusion, of course.

Figure 9.2 A state diagram of the simplified CC states its case clearly enough (*a*). However, some prefer state tables (*b*) or brain teasers called "action tables" (*c*).

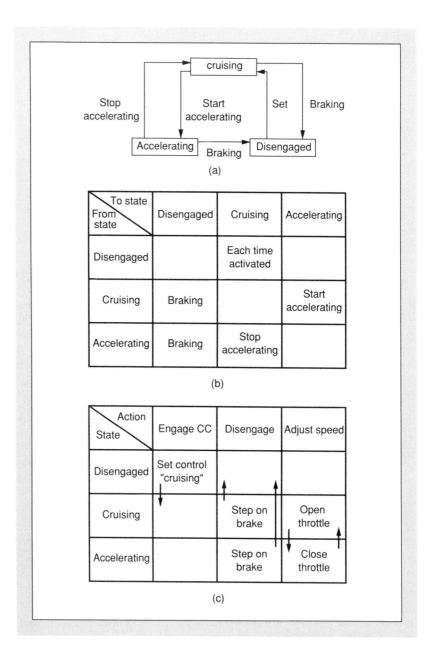

(a)

From state \ To state	Disengaged	Cruising	Accelerating
Disengaged		Each time activated	
Cruising	Braking		Start accelerating
Accelerating	Braking	Stop accelerating	

(b)

State \ Action	Engage CC	Disengage	Adjust speed
Disengaged	Set control "cruising"		
Cruising		Step on brake	Open throttle
Accelerating		Step on brake	Close throttle

(c)

but they are harder to follow. The arrows shown in Figure 9.2c are normally not included; instead, the names of the transition arrows are listed, and you have to find them in the main diagram. For the simplified CC system of this figure, the tables are mostly ornamental. In a more realistic setting, they can get messy.

Some CASE systems also implement Ward and Mellor's token flow, which serves well to animate the execution of a data flow diagram. Figure 9.3 reflects the process bubble labeled "2" in the CC graph of Figure 9.1b, which sets the cruising speed. Events are shown for three time slices: At first the process receives continuous input data (double arrow) from the rotation sensor (see Figure 9.3a), but produces no output until the token on the Enable line actually turns the process on. After the next clock tick, the bubble comes to life (Figure 9.3b) and soon output starts flowing (see Figure 9.3c).

Not the only game in town. We have studied the Ward-Mellor and Hatley-Pirbhai methodologies at some length because they dominate CASE implementations. But other approaches are maturing. At Hughes Aircraft, for example, a multiview paradigm adds a stimulus/response chart to the Ward-Mellor method. It sustains different scenarios for a given system and includes unambiguous verification diagrams.[6] This brings us back to the stimulating concept of *Project Technology*, known as OOA (object-oriented analysis).

OOA tries to effect the reliability of real-time models by describing various objects' attributes—as we have done before

Figure 9.3 Ward's token flow helps the CASE user to follow program execution. This sequence (a, b, c) visualizes the events that set the CC's speed.

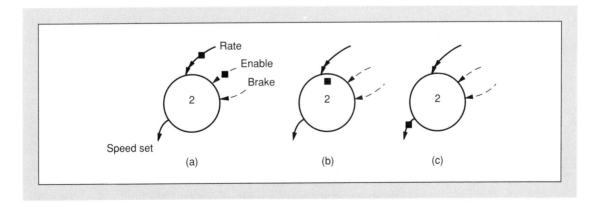

with IP models. However, OOA reduces its models to instances (or "incarnations") of objects, expressed by the tables of a relational database in *third normal form*. Events signal that something happened, and what it happened to (e.g., a car going from the engine-on to the engine-off state). There is one "action" (usually embracing several "action processes") for each state, and that action takes place as soon as a state is reached. Action processes can make queries, generate events, or set timers. When a timer expires, it can generate new events.

In each state model, a separate data flow diagram is constructed for each state. Only attributes from the information model are permitted to appear on the data flows. Since all data have been defined previously, a data dictionary becomes superfluous. Although process models add no new information, they can help to identify redundancies or similarities, suggesting the possibility of simplification. Furthermore, data flow diagrams pinpoint any missing data, which after all was their original purpose. So far the OOA method has proven itself in well over 100 applications, and several CASE vendors are planning to include it in their tool kits.

Still other approaches to real-time system modeling will be explored in later chapters. Nonprocedural languages have also been proposed, but since predictability must reign supreme in real-time systems, some scholars question their viability for such applications.[7]

There is no free champagne.   In the hardware world, few people question the maxim that there is no free lunch. If you want more functions, you pay more. Contrary to hacker dogma, the same is true for software: there is no free martini. (In the CASE world, where bubbles tickle the mind, a champagne breakfast seems more appropriate.) When it comes to partitioning a system, CASE tools will readily produce all the bubbles you want, but how you link them and subdivide them can't be automated.

Ward and Mellor offer about the best rule to govern the procedure: "You should partition [in such a way that] the decomposition results in the minimum number of connections between the subsystems . . . " Only practice perfects this skill. (That's why there are so many "top-down" books on the market, with so many examples.) But without question, the chore of decomposition is toughest for real-time applications.

One trick often employed in Ward and Mellor's examples is to define pure control structures wherever possible—bubbles that are only associated with broken arrows. (These control bubbles are marked as a broken circle.) The nice thing about pure control procedures is that they form state machines that can be defined with decision tables. They do, however, clutter up the diagram, and we decided to remove them in Chapter 1 by decree: "Whenever all inputs are present, an IP (or process) will execute."

In real-time systems that's not always possible, at least not for the most detailed levels of those modules that brush against the hardware. In fact, at that level every system turns real-time, as a simple example will show. Assume you want to refine the IP in Figure 9.4a, which performs a vector addition. Your model must actually take into account the processing time of each addition—information that you would not need in an ordinary data processing or scientific calculation. Let's assume for the solution given in Figure 9.4b that the members of the two vectors, A_1 to A_n and B_1 to B_n will be taken from cache memory, so we need not worry about their rate of arrival. However, we do need to know whether a new value has entered the cache.

If the program is written in C, we may just have to watch the pointer to the storage location B_n, and then set the addition in motion when the "Change?" module—IP.1.1—sends out a True. IP.1.2, the "Scheduler," is tied into a clock and at intervals (determined by the hardware) loads the values A_i and B_i into the "Adder"—IP.1.3. The scheduler also keeps track of the count (1 to n) and outputs total lapse time when it receives the last "done" flag from the adder. For good measure, Figure 9.4c reveals the system's meager state diagram. Normally, these transitions are effected by a computer's operating system; however, if we want to build a special-purpose machine (e.g., for the G-Train monitor), these are the things to worry about. In fact, the exercise could help us decide later which IPs could become ICs by implementing them in hardware.

⅃ Timing the World's Fastest Train

In the preceding chapter we broke down part of the G-Train's IP "blueprints"—subsystem Weight—to illustrate algorithm design. We have saved the Speed subsystem of IP.2 until now because of its real-time implications. To refresh your memory, the G-Train's speed must be determined from a sequence of double pulses that arrive at the computer on a single wire loop. It would be nice if we could just plug that wire into a serial port and write a program that scans some memory segment, looking for the single bits and

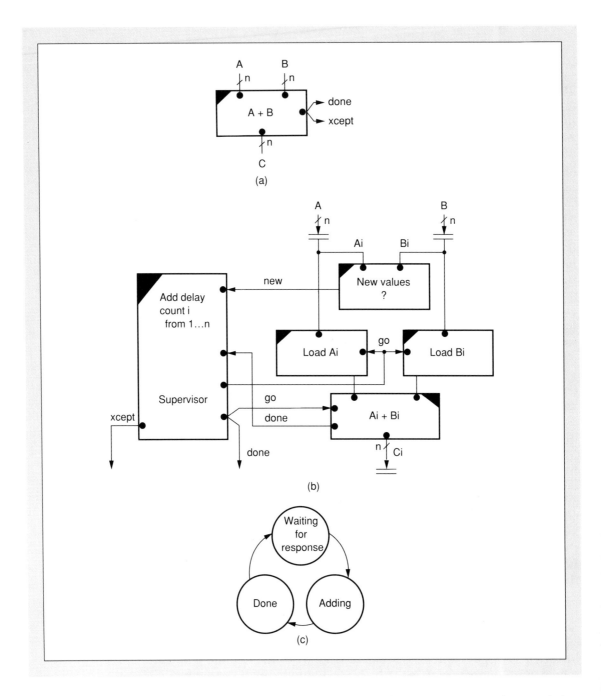

Figure 9.4 At the hardware level, every program has real-time implications. Implementing a simple vector addition (*a*) serially can lead to complex IPs to account for timing (*b*), even though the state diagram may seem trivial (*c*).

figuring the speed from the memory location. However, such an approach is flawed: it ties up a lot of memory, and the pulses are neither shaped properly, nor do they conform to any communications protocol.

The easiest way to solve the problem would be to build a little plug-in board called IP.2.1 that contains an analog-digital converter with "trip points" for minimum and maximum voltage. We'll call the corresponding flags f_min and f_max. The first must be True to trigger the speed calculation, and the last must be False to validate the reading. The fractional seconds of the system clock will be copied simultaneously into two registers. Copying will be stopped in one register by even-numbered and in the other by odd-numbered incidents of f_min, brought about by a flip-flop. Let's call the two resulting readings Time_1 and Time_2. If the pulses fall outide the trigger range, IP.2.1 also produces an exception flag that sets off an appropriately severe warning in the Display module, IP.3.

The time readings are absorbed by IP.2.2 in Figure 9.5a, which derives the train's speed and location from these values. That's a very simple job. The speed is obtained easily enough by calculating

```
Speed := 2500/(Time_2 - Time_1).
```

To get the train's position, we need a counting loop whose initial value is set to zero and which ratchets up one notch with each execution of the Speed assignment.

To conform to the specs of IP.3—the Gauges package—we still must convert the count integer to a percentage of full travel, using the statement

```
Location := Loop_counter * 2.5.
```

When the count reaches 40, we thus feed IP.3 the required value of 100. (How do we know the Gauges spec? Why, by looking it up in the Fall 2002 IP catalog from Integrated Package Inc., naturally.)

This module is hardly hardy. One small problem remains. If any of the pulses gets wiped out by noise or bad luck, the whole scheme falls apart. We have committed the ultimate sin of

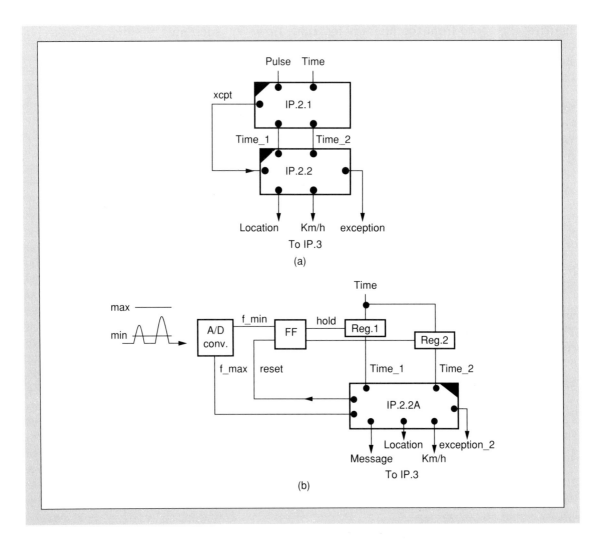

Figure 9.5 To determine G-Train's speed we must time the two sensor pulses (*a*). One approach might be to implement IP.2.1 in hardware via latching clock registers (*b*).

programming and produced a brittle algorithm. We did provide an exception handler for bad pulses, and we could use that to make the location display flash or turn red with embarrassment. But that's little consolation if something goes awry on the test track and we don't know where the expensive vehicle lies stranded.

A better alternative for the location algorithm is to save the time differential from the previous segment and extrapolate the time when the vehicle should approach the next checkpoint. At that moment, we move the indicator to the next location, but let it blink. When the expected speed reading pulses come through, we turn off the flasher—unless xcpt from IP.2.1 turns True.

However, can we rely on the even-odd switch in IP.2.1? What if one pulse in a pair drops out? We would attempt to calculate the speed using one pulse each from two successive pairs, and the result would be only a calculated speed of 69.4 to 694 *meters* per hour (2500/36,000 at top speed). We did set limits for the speed at 50 and 600 km/h, and the resulting exception would trigger an alarm. Still, one dropped pulse would invalidate all future speed readings, so we better replace the even-odd scheme with a more reliable one.

It's not that tough. Even at the train's slowest expected speed of 50 km/h the pulses in a *single pair* are still a mere 50 ms apart, even at 500 km/h the spacing *between pairs* remains 36 seconds. So, let's modify IP.2.1 by resetting the flip-flop, say, 1 second after each attempted speed calculation. Now the next pulse will go to the register that was meant to capture Time_1. We might also connect the "pulse" exception to IP.2.2 and display the message "BAD PULSE AT LOC n". That way we not only can distinguish among several pulse failures, but we also can store all generated error messages for later evaluation.

We could increase confidence further by setting the pulse converter not for two but for three levels: one barely above normal noise level, one at 2 volts for the time readings, and the third above all reasonable values (e.g., 10 volts). If worst came to worst, we could then fall back on the 2-volt readings to determine where the train is. All these revisions would barely affect the looks of the second-level IPs in Figure 9.5a, but certainly would make a difference if we proceeded to a pseudocode description (e.g., a minispec). Since we want to implement IP.2.1 in hardware, we note that Figure 9.5b, which shows the new reset flag and the output Message, contains the information to be displayed on the screen.

ꙍ The G-Train According to Mentor Graphics

Useful as an IP representation is, you'll probably prefer a ready-made CASE tool that understands real-time needs. One that diverges from the main flock somewhat is Analyst/RT, the CASE system developed originally at Tektronix and now maturing under *Mentor Graphics'* wings. It handles both the Ward-Mellor and the Hatley-Pirbhai methods, providing us with another

Figure 9.6 Mentor Graphics' Analyst begins with the creation of a context diagram (top left) and a data flow diagram (top right) in the Hatley-Pirbhai style. Both bottom windows deal with dictionary creation.

chance to view the two alternatives side by side. Furthermore, Analyst/RT can be classified as an upper-CASE tool, meant to prepare the ground for Designer, which nurtures the detail-design and coding steps. A third tool, the Auditor, complements the others with traceability and documentation support.

Analyst/RT's automatic link to **Digital Equipment**'s Code Management System (CMS) provides the project leader with the means to control shared file access and track changes (as well as progress). System specification, Analyst's main goal, begins with the creation of a context diagram, as displayed in the top left window of Figure 9.6. The zero-level data flow diagram (0/DFD)

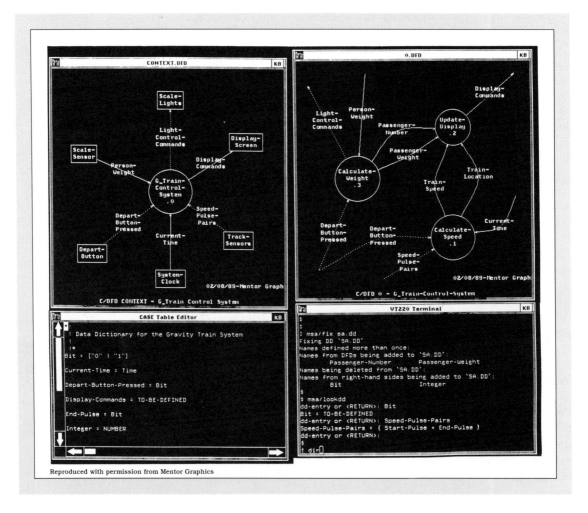

Reproduced with permission from Mentor Graphics

next to it adheres to the Hatley-Pirbhai methodology, which combines data and control flow. Further decomposition will provide additional detail for specific subtrees. Analyst/RT can merge such subtrees automatically into a parent diagram, or it can dissociate the children again.

At the bottom left of Figure 9.6, you can observe the creation of the data dictionary. One entry is marked "to be defined" by the system to make sure that all levels in the data flow diagrams' hierarchy are accounted for in the dictionary. The final (bottom right) window provides work space for fixing up the data dictionary, where Speed.Pulse-Pairs has just been defined.

Next level: speed calculation. Descending one level, we find the child diagram for deriving the G-Train's speed from the arriving pulses at the top right of Figure 9.7a. In its top left corner three control flow arrows end in a vertical line, known as a CSpec bar. You could regard it as the side view of the state transition table displayed (partially) in the top left window. Below it, you find a minispec for the speed calculation. The bottom right window reflects the VMS command editor in the process of selecting the next file.

As promised, the next illustration switches to a Ward-Mellor diagram of the same Speed module. At the left of Figure 9.7b, you see a simple state diagram that takes the place of the table in the preceding figure. From the initialization state at the top, the system switches to waiting for the first pulse, then to waiting for the second pulse, and back to the first pulse. At the right, you'll find the same data flow diagram as in Figure 9.7a, except for the expanded control flow representation.

Now that we have specified and simulated the Speed subsystem, we shift from Analyst to Designer. The system transforms the Analyst's data flow hierarchy into a flattened bubble chart, as depicted in Figure 9.8. Then you pick one of the bubbles as the "boss" to produce a structure chart (see Figure 9.9). It appears a bit more entangled than the one in the preceding chapter, but a glance at its progenitor discloses why; data-related processes had clustered around the top and left side of the screen, while control and display functions gravitated toward the bottom right.

The Designer's complexity evaluator, which grades your design according to its deviations from a pure tree structure, produces a mildly critical report:

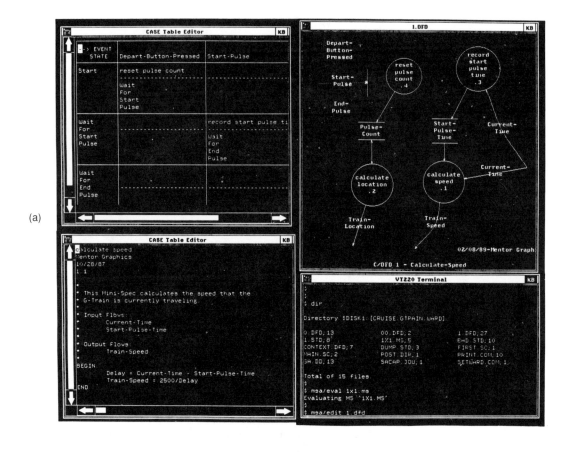

(a)

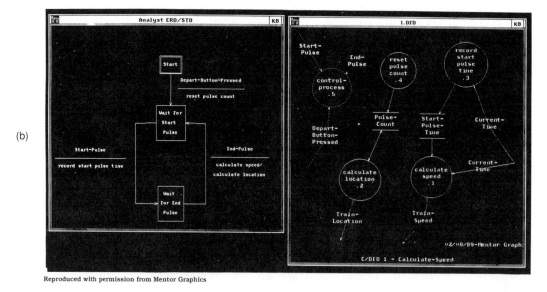

(b)

Figure 9.7 At the child level of Figure 9.6 a diagram for the Speed module results (*a*), enhanced with a minispec (bottom left). The Ward-Mellor data flow diagram (*b*) is supplemented with a state diagram.

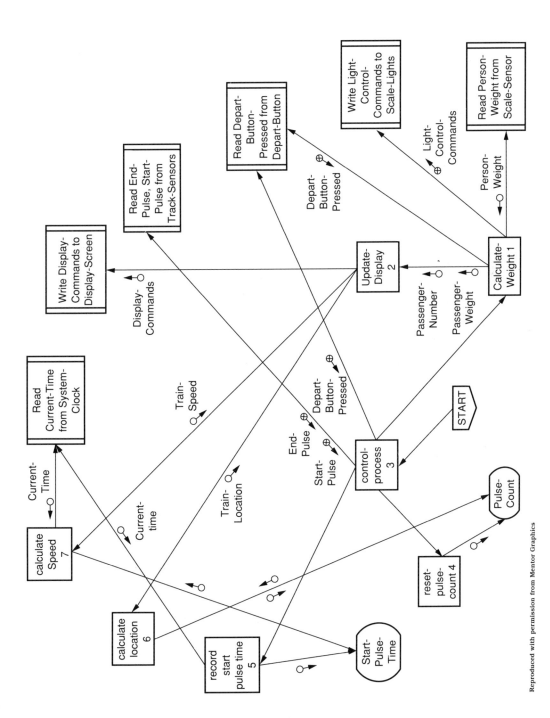

Reproduced with permission from Mentor Graphics

Figure 9.8 The Designer tool flattens the Analyst/RT's data flow diagrams into a network adorned with arrows that preserve the data and control flow relationships. (The latter's circles are marked ⊕.)

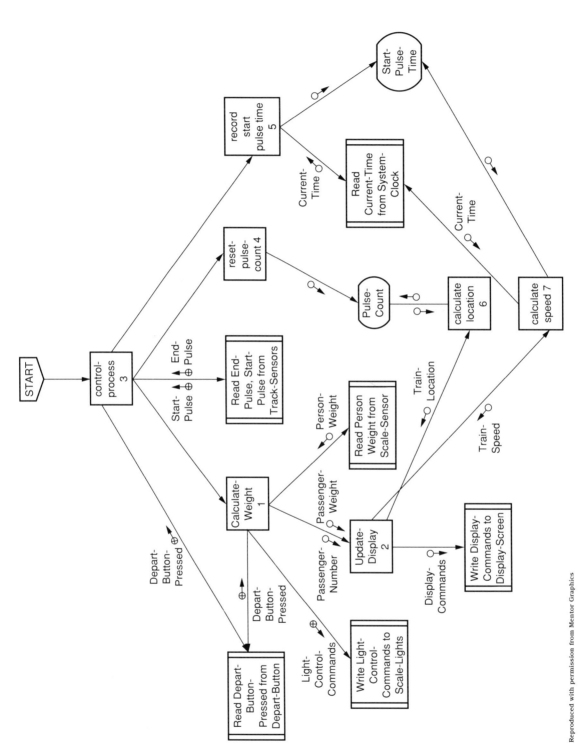

Figure 9.9 This structure chart results when one of the boxes in Figure 9.8 is selected as the root (or "boss") node. A complexity test confirms that the structure is less than an ideal tree and requires more work.

Level	Items	Calls	Complexity	Tree Impurity
0	1	0	0	0.00
1	3	3	0	0.00
2	3	3	0	0.00
3	2	4	2	0.20

Not to worry, though. You can either designate another "boss" module or rearrange the details of level 3, where the complexity problem crops up. This procedure makes a good case for CASE; without such tools, the relocation of a system's parts would surely introduce new errors, not to mention the wasted effort.

If we continued the design into coding, we would start the transformation of the procedure bubbles by adding code stubs in the minispec. In fact, we could even demonstrate *reverse engineering*, because you can put the Designer in reverse and have it convert source code into structure charts. We'll return to the joys of reverse engineering in Chapter 16.

⁀ References

1. Stephen W. Hawking, *A Brief History of Time*, Bantam Books, Toronto, 1988.

2. Gene Forte, "CASE tools for real-time analysis and design," *CASE Outlook*, January 1988, p. 1 (see Case Consulting Group).

3. Paul T. Ward and Stephen J. Mellor, *Structured Development for Real-Time Systems*, vols. 1,2,3, Prentice-Hall, Englewood Cliffs, NJ, 1985–86.

4. Derek J. Hatley and Imtiaz A. Pirbhai, *Strategies for Real-Time System Specification*, Dorset House, New York, 1987.

5. Sally Shlaer and Stephen Mellor, *Object-Oriented System Analysis*, Yourdon Press, Englewood Cliffs, NJ, 1988.

6. Michael S. Deutsch, "Focusing real-time systems analysis on user operations," *IEEE Software*, September 1988, p. 39.

7. John A. Stankovic, "Misconceptions about real-time computing," *IEEE Computer*, October 1988, p. 10.

Courtesy IBM Archives

Charles Babbage, credited with the concept of modern computers' basic architecture, never saw his inventions fully implemented.

10

VISIT TO THE STATE DEPARTMENT

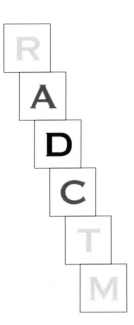

State machines offer control
G-Train according to i-Logix
Cadre simulates the supertrain
Petri nets from Germany

In the preceding chapter, we repeatedly found ourselves snared in state machines, though not the kind deployed by legendary Chicago Mayor Daley. They were related to real-time systems, but they need not be. In fact, we had already classified a word processor as an example in Chapter 8, because each time you depress a key you may alter the machine's state. How then can we recognize a state machine? The best approach would be to look at a leaf-level control/data flow diagram (C/DFD) or an IP representation of the system. When data flow plays second fiddle to control flow, state machines are bound to pop up in some leaf-level procedures. If all the data flow has dried up and only control flow remains, you are looking at a pure state machine, because control signals can only produce state changes.

Since real-time systems usually incorporate on/off devices such as switches and clutches, CASE systems bent on toiling in real time always incorporate state machine diagrams of some

Baffled by *jargon*? See Appendix C.

kind. Traditionally, the states in a state transition diagram (a *directed graph*) have been represented as circles, but we've already noted in the preceding chapter that CASE vendors have by and large chosen rectangular state outlines. The arcs (also called *edges*) that connect states are usually labeled with the activity that brings about the state transition.

State machines fit well into the computer programmer's binary spirit; they too deem answers other than "yes" and "no" as inspired by Satan. We can, for example, assign the cruise control system from the preceding chapter only two states: engaged and disengaged. When engaged, we can again define two states: accelerating and cruising. The result would be a nested diagram as shown in Figure 10.1*a*—bubbles blowing more bubbles. Since the human eye can easily distinguish up to seven objects at a glance we can "flatten" the diagram without unleashing anxieties (see Figure 10.1*b*).

But at this lower level we can get into trouble because a state machine can only describe on/off switches. While a cruise control can be implemented by oscillating between full throttle and idle, a smooth transition is much more desirable, to say the least. We might weasel out of the predicament by defining a state transition "accelerate," which opens the throttle by one notch until we get back to cruise speed, but then we would need another one, "decelerate," for downgrades. In one of Ward and Mellor's examples in Chapter 9 the "cruising" state is replaced by two

Figure 10.1 Nested state transition diagrams, such as the one for cruise control (*a*), can be "flattened" (*b*). However, a multiplicative explosion often results.

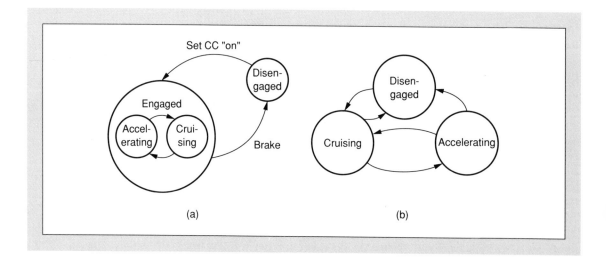

(a)   (b)

states: "maintaining speed" and "resuming speed" which is defined as "return to previous speed." But how? The basic problem remains: we are still trying to force a round peg (the analog throttle) into a square hole (the finite-state model).

We can now understand why in textbooks the most common example for state machines is a different reactive system—the elevator. While state transition diagrams (or state diagrams, for short) function well in such an application, they are still beset by ailments. Think of a very modest elevator controller in a four-floor building. Two floors sport two buttons each (Up and Down), providing four combinations of pressed and unused buttons. Add the first and fourth floors' single buttons, and there you have 34 states already.

Inside the elevator cabin, the four destination buttons provide 10 states, and the cabin itself has three (ascending, descending, and standing still). Multiply the combinations out, and you get over 1000 states, before even considering doors, alarms, or malfunctions. No screen can flaunt that many bubbles. When you trade the textbook for the real world, things get even worse. Consider that just two successive keystrokes on a PC may create nearly 10,000 state transitions and you quickly realize why state diagrams have not taken over the CASE world. Of course, there's a solution, and we have just looked at it—in a small way—in Figure 10.1.

↳ The G-Train According to i-Logix

Like other diagrams popular in CASE systems, those defining state machines can be partitioned and presented as a hierarchy. One vendor, *i-Logix*, managed to base a complete CASE system on this concept. The firm's Statemate tool simplifies matters further by culling out tasks that are independent of each other. Examples are the weighing and speed functions of G_Train, because they never even occur at the same time. To describe a system's data flow, data storage, and other functions, i-Logix complements Statemate's Statecharts with Activity and Module Charts. Each chart type represents a complete, executable graphical language, so that Statemate models can undergo dynamic simulation.

Module Charts let the user organize a system into separate structural units and allocate activities to specific hardware or software modules—much like generalized structure charts.

Activity Charts represent a system's functional view. They resemble data flow diagrams, displaying data and control flow for the G-Train, as in Figure 10.2 on the color page. Activity charts differ from our old friends the bubble charts in two ways: (1) circles are replaced with rectangles and (2) several levels of a hierarchy can appear simultaneously.

For example, the subsystems Weight, Speed, and Position are shown side by side, each displaying its internal structure. Yet they interact with G_Train_Control, which is part of the plane labeled G_Train, and communicate with such peripherals as lights, sensors, and the passenger. In a hardware design system, such a graph would be called a mixed-mode representation; G_Train could be a mother board; each of the subsystems could be a circuit board; and procedures like G_Train_Control or Spd_Handler could be IC components.

The decision to decompose directly into subsystems was taken because Weight and Speed are independent of each other. Position was separated from Speed, forming three subsystems. The Display module was split up between the three because each has a separate display. Like some other contributors to this exercise, i-Logix found that the spec for the Weight subsystem did not provide for error conditions; consequently they added a "cancel" switch linked to a reset button.

Well-behaved states. The vital Statechart—Statemate's very heart—describes a system's behavioral view. As mentioned before, this diagram encapsulates state hierarchies (to any depth), which requires a mechanism for interconnecting its layers. In the G-Train example of Figure 10.3 on the color page, the state space is broken down into two clusters, one covering the conditions before and the other after departure (labeled In_Transit).

Statemate simplifies matters further by culling out orthogonal (i.e., independent or separate) components in the same state cluster with dotted green lines. For example, the lights have been separated from the weighing function because i-Logix considers the 10-second wait for the light change a design detail that should not be introduced at the specification level. (The timeout function could otherwise be used to tie the lights into the Handle_Wgt state.)

At rest, the Green_Light and Handle_Wgt states prevail. The dot at the end of a transition arc identifies the default (or

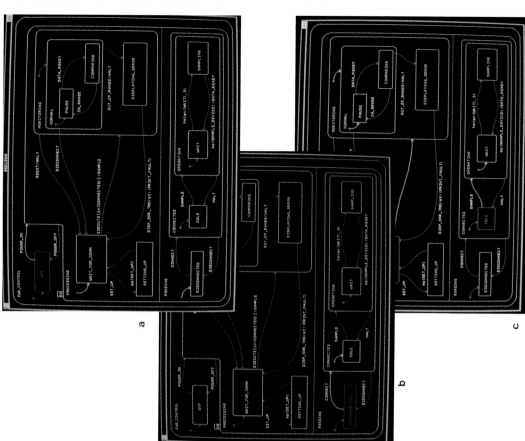

Figure 10.2 The i-Logix system describes G-Train's data and control flow with an Activity Chart. A control sub-system centralizes control functions.

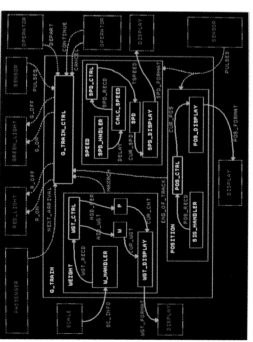

Figure 10.3 The Statechart, a complete graphical language, describes G-Train as a state machine consisting of four nearly independent sections.

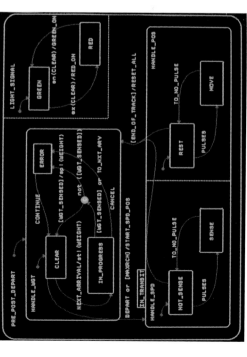

Figure 10.4 Colorful simulation helps the i-Logix user analyze his design. Here the blue lines spread as a communications system is put through its paces from power-up (*a*) to the connected (*b*) to the execution state (*c*).

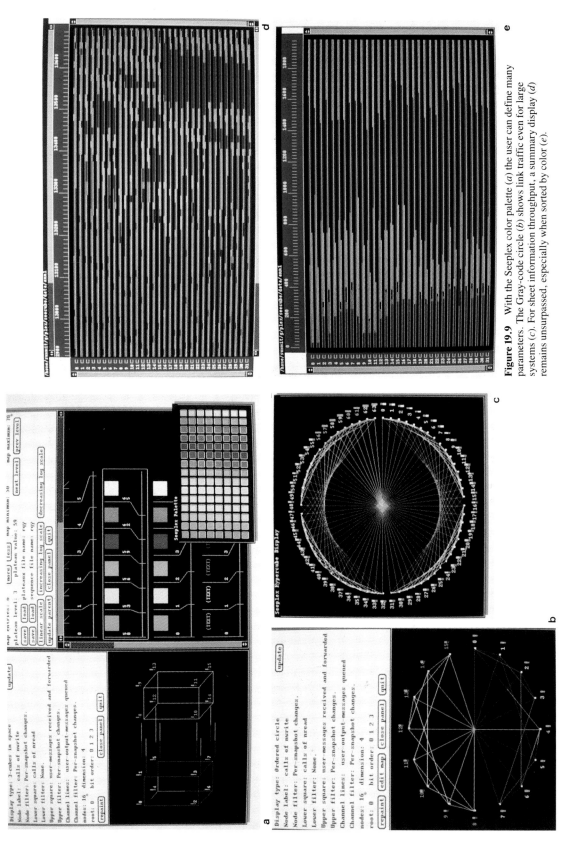

Figure 19.9 With the Seeplex color palette (*a*) the user can define many parameters. The Gray-code circle (*b*) shows link traffic even for large systems (*c*). For sheet information throughput, a summary display (*d*) remains unsurpassed, especially when sorted by color (*e*).

base) level, thus sidestepping the need of arcs to cross boundaries of hierarchy levels. The discussed arc's arrow points to Clear. When a passenger arrives, a transition to In_Progress takes place; when he leaves the gate, the system returns to Clear. Should the passenger start aerobic exercises on the scale, the weight sensor's erratic readings would push the system into the Error state, from which it can return to Clear only via a special Continue signal.

The arc to Error divides at a blue connector symbol identified as a conditional split by the letter "C." The conditions are noted along the split arc: if the weight was not sensed properly, the Error state is chosen. Another arc, labeled Cancel, seems to duplicate this branch of the split arc. It serves, however, quite a different purpose—namely, to let the Weight state terminate itself. For example, a malfunction in the weighing process or the requirement for a 10-second pause could trigger the cancellation (with the help of a watchdog timer in the latter case).

Once the system moves from the Handle_Wgt to the In_Transit state, two concurrent subsystems wake up: Handle_Spd and Handle_Pos. When pulses arrive, the state Not_Sense gives way to Sense in Handle_Spd, and Rest yields to Move in Handle_Pos. When the train reaches the far end of the track it triggers the Reset condition, and the system returns to the Handle_Wgt state.

Thus, the lack of any end-of-line conditions in the G_Train spec has been resolved. That's the beauty of state representations; dangling ends are not permitted. Statemate was originally developed for aerospace and weapons systems, where loose ends can really spell trouble. (In one extant missile system, Statemate discovered a firing mode of which the designers had been unaware. Yikes!)

Show and tell. Once a system's Statemate descriptions have passed muster for completeness and consistency, the real fun begins. You can put your design through its paces before you invest resources in implementation detail. During a simulation run, both the state boxes and the connecting arcs change color as they are exercised. But why talk about it when pictures can tell the story much more persuasively?

As you'll recall, the G-Train spec made no provisions for the test track's remote terminal. Luckily, i-Logix has already designed a communications package for a remote display terminal that we just need to plug in. The first snapshot in Figure 10.4*a* on the color page reflects the system status right after power-up. The blue Power_On arc has activated the high-level Processing and Reading states, whose base arcs have changed color and in turn fired up the states Wait_for_Comm and Disconnected.

In Figure 10.4*b* the Processing state's section remains unchanged but in Reading the arc Connect has activated the state Connected. Its base arc consequently changed color and turned on the Idle state. Finally, Figure 10.4*c* reflects that the operator has initiated Execute (e.g., by pressing the Return key), which sets off a series of events. Activation of the Monitoring state has propagated to the Normal state and, in it, the Pause condition. According to the label at the Execute arc, execution also fires up the Sample arc in the Connected state. As a result, we see Operating enabled and napping in the Wait state. As soon as data arrive, they can now be displayed.

Naturally the same simulation ability will come in handy as you proceed through detail design and on into the coding phase. In fact, if it's Ada code you're after, Statemate will generate it automatically. Furthermore, the simulation scenarios used during the early validation stages also establish test criteria for system integration. This means the total system, not just the software system, since Statemate simulates hardware states as easily as software states.

Get your tokens from Cadre. Remember that i-Logix does not hold an exclusive on simulation. As we saw in Figure 9.3, any C/DFD can be loaded with tokens, and we can expect all surviving CASE systems to offer such capabilities eventually. One tool, Teamwork/ES from *Cadre* had demonstrated an animated cruise control some time ago[1] and now does the honors for our G-Train as well.

Assume you have already worked your way through the upper layers of the system's hierarchy and are ready to tackle the speed calculation. In the two top windows of Figure 10.5, you see some of your previous work: the context diagram and the top-level C/DFD. A detailed data flow diagram of the speed subsystem takes up most of the screen, augmented with a simple state diagram (bottom left) and some status information (top right). A small clock face registers the ticks of the system clock, and an execution histogram registers how active each of the three main bubbles have been.

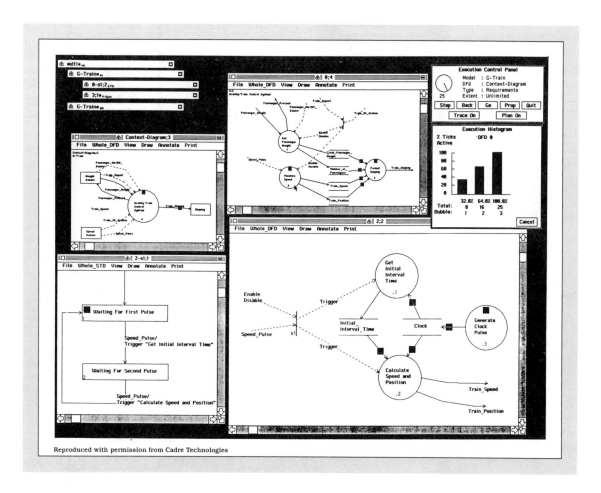

Reproduced with permission from Cadre Technologies

In the top-level C/DFD, the weighing process has been completed (bubble 1 has no token, but its bar at the right indicates past activity) and the speed measurement is under way (a token has activated the Measure Speed bubble and the corresponding bar proves that this happened some time ago). Additional tokens also indicate that all the required data are being displayed. In fact, the display function (bubble 3) is busy as can be. We are now waiting for another pulse from the speeding train; the state chart tells us we are expecting the first pulse.

The rest of the simulation has been combined in Figure 10.6. First, a token had appeared on the control flow arrow Speed_Pulse, but it has already been consumed, triggering the process in bubble ".1" (labeled "Get Initial Interval Time"). The

Figure 10.5 In these Teamwork/ES views, G-Train's top-level C/DFD appears in the top center window. Context and state graphs are at the left, while the main window shows the Speed subsystem, primed for execution. A clock and execution histograms (top right) add more information.

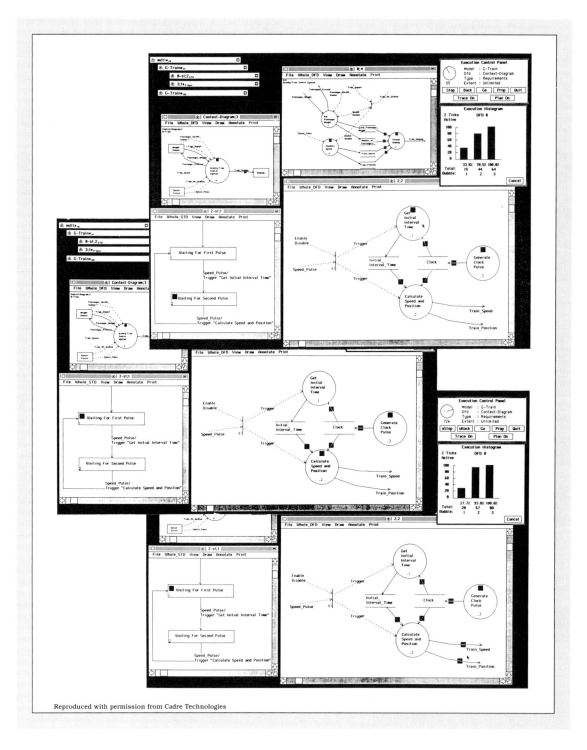

Reproduced with permission from Cadre Technologies

Figure 10.6 Simulation of the Speed subsystem, which began in Figure 10.5, continues here. The token flow in the main window traces one execution cycle's sequence of events.

state diagram indicates we're waiting for the second shoe (sorry, pulse) to drop.

After its arrival bubble ".2" (tagged "Calculate Speed and Position") boasts a token, while the one in the top bubble is gone. Again, we are waiting for the first pulse, which, as we know, will be a while coming. In the last screen, the calculation is complete and two tokens make it clear that the results (`Train_Speed` and `Train_Position` at bottom right) are on their way to the display.

Now that the first excitement has worn off, we would like to know how this simulation has come about. Internally, the whole G-Train system is represented as a flattened state machine with certain enhancements, known as a ***Petri net***. (Chemists take heart—no kin to Petri dishes.) To find out where this imaginary web comes from, let's look back for a moment.

⸌ **Rendezvous in Germany**

In Chapter 8 we had encountered the Nassi-Shneiderman diagram, a more orderly form of the venerable flowchart. This diagram and its still neater cousin, the ***Structogram***, are rarely seen in the United States, but they frequently show up in a German *Pflichtenheft* as required documentation. While flowcharts and Structograms can represesent procedures in a lucid way, they fail when it comes to state machines.

Fortunately, a German computer scientist combined the two software views in a single, orderly diagram and named it the Petri net, after himself. Is it any wonder that a German CASE company called GPP (you don't want to know the full name) has included both Petri nets and Nassi-Shneiderman diagrams in its tool kit? We shall return to the vendor's American connection shortly. Fuji Xerox (Japan) also got caught in the net, and their version is now available in the United States from a Xerox spinoff, the Smalltalk house ***ParcPlace Systems***.

Petri nets use circles to identify states and rectangles (or vertical bars) to denote events. Like state diagrams, Petri nets provide excellent vehicles for dynamic system simulation. As in state notation, you need tokens to set the mechanism in motion. A state bubble is considered "marked" when it harbors a token, but a transition can only be activated when all states linked to the target event are loaded with tokens. Sometimes token flows must be combined between states in the absence of an event. In such cases, Petri's theory requires a dummy event, shown as a bar across the state transition arcs.

Figure 10.7 In a Petri net, state circles are supplemented with event bars and procedure boxes. Here the first speed pulse has arrived, as the token dot shows.

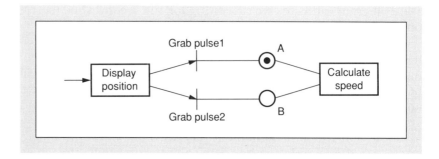

Let's examine a small fragment from the G-Train's speed calculation (see Figure 10.7). Since state transitions in a Petri net can be interrupted by procedures (or "events"), they can be made time dependent—a very useful feature for real-time simulations. (In fact, the mailboxes and queues of CARDtools in Chapter 7 could be represented in this manner.) In Figure 10.7 state A will become active before state B because the latter suffers a longer delay. Clearly, the speed calculation can only proceed when both A and B are loaded. Just as in our IPs, a function can only "fire" when all inputs are present.

Let Epos tell the story. The CASE company **SPS**, distributor of German GPP, puts Petri nets to good use in its Epos tool—a womb-to-tomb CASE system. Petri nets could be set up at all levels of detail design, depicting the main relationships within G-Train, but they naturally become most valuable where different tasks must interact with each other.

Before we proceed with the G-Train example, a few words about Epos. You can begin system design (including hardware) at the requirements phase, dubbed level 0, or even at level −1, called the environmental level. Epos-R serves as the formal language at this phase. Architectural (or in SPS terms, system) design begins at level 1 and may at times require one or two more levels of modules. When detail design begins, Epos adds another representation largely made up of "actions." An action strongly resembles our IP, except that data flow from left to right and control flows from top to bottom. Epos-S serves as the description language in these two design phases.

Continued refinement may then lead to Nassi-Shneiderman diagrams or Petri nets, and we'll see how the latter work in the G-Train system. Take the task Control in Figure 10.8. It

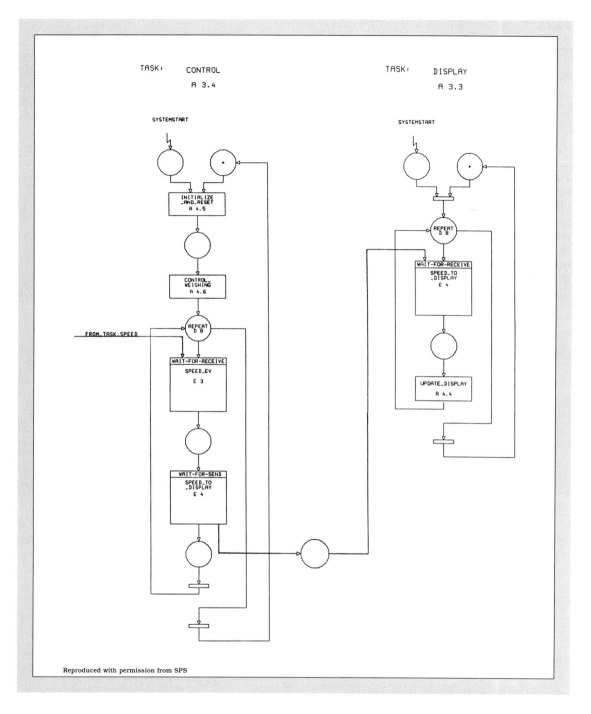

Figure 10.8 In its Petri net guise, the G-Train Control task manages information flow from Speed to Display. As the two dots at the top indicate, both subsystem loops are waiting for start signals before processing another cycle.

contains a reset routine, the subsystem Control_Weighing,
and two communications blocks, one for receiving inputs from
the Speed task and one for sending outputs to the Display
task. At the moment, execution lies within the weighing loop,
as the token dot in Control's top right state circle indicates.
The Display task is also waiting for a signal to recycle through
the Update_Display loop, which can only be executed after
the Control task signals a new speed. In the Petri net representation, Wait procedures (shown as narrow rectangles) syn-
chronize the events.

Only one of the two tasks can take control of the processor,
so we are embarking on the classic Ada Rendezvous mission.
SPS has introduced a special graph to depict the situation (see
Figure 10.9). The two competing entries, New_Display and

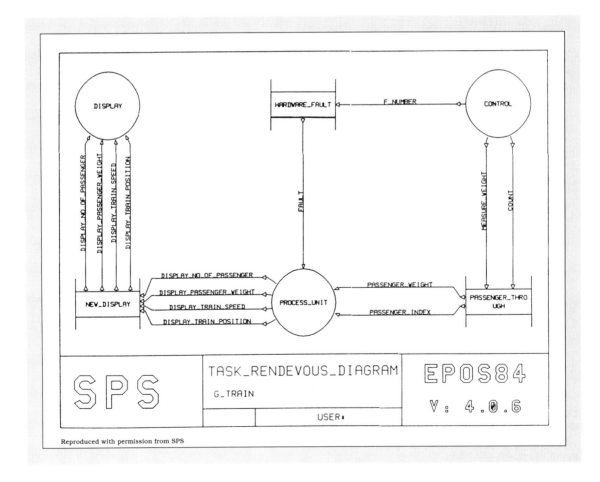

Passenger_Through, occupy the bottom corners. Arrows connect them with their parent tasks (top left and top right circles) on one hand, and Process_Unit on the other. These arrows are labeled with the data to be transmitted. A third entry (top center) comes to life only in case of a hardware failure.

Whatever form they may take, graphs based on the state machine concept clearly serve a vital function in real-time systems. To date, state machines may have been synonymous with embedded systems, from digital watches to spaceships. But soon another computer species will drag synchronization problems into other walks of life. Once multiprocessor systems are as commonplace as PCs are today (which may be sooner than many think), every programmer will have to worry about states. We'll return to this problem in Chapter 19.

⅃ **Reference**

1. Max Schindler, "CASE kit supports open system, adds simulation features," *Electronic Design*, June 23, 1988, p. 63.

To simplify error-prone calculations with complex numbers, Bell Laboratories' George Stibitz built his first relay computer in 1939. The inset displays the machine's terminal used by trained operators.

11

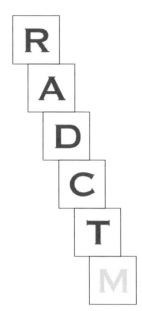

How to Beat the System

Not by software alone
G-Train on the DEW line
A game of TAGS for engineers

When we started out on our journey down the waterfall diagram, the purpose was a quest for nothing less than 24-karat software. But ever since the G-Train joined the endeavor, we've been discussing hardware as well. In the world of embedded systems, it turns out, hardware and software form an indivisible union called a system. But why should you have to worry about the quirks of real-time computing when you may only want to write a program for updating your résumés?

True, most application programmers need not be concerned with hardware interfaces, but in the evaluation of CASE systems its real-time features play a dominant role. In fact, a growing number of vendors interpret CASE as Computer-Aided *System* Engineering. We have also found that time plays a vital role in multitasking programs; when we discuss the programming of computers with several processors, the importance of timing will become even more apparent. However, even if you never plan to venture beyond DP or MIS programming, you'll find that timing simulation can help you optimize any kind of software.

Transaction express on track.   The system we explore next adds the concept of transaction flow to those of data and control flow. Developed by *Scientific and Engineering Software* (SES), formerly Information Research Associates, the CASE tool DEW (Design and Evaluation Workbench) indeed caters not just to combined hardware and software, but to distributed systems as well. Since they are certain to dominate the computing scene within a decade, SES should have its hands full. Another feather in DEW's cap is the integration with *IDE*'s CASE tools, discussed in Chapter 8.

DEW, a greatly improved revision of the company's PAWS tool, uses directed graphs that supplement a system description with the procedural information needed for simulation. Thus, DEW combines object-oriented with procedural system definition and top-down views with bottom-up views. Furthermore, DEW graphs (like our IPs) let you postpone the decision of which part of a system is to be built in hardware and which in software.

In its performance simulation, DEW combines five methodologies: (1) work-load analysis, (2) network queuing, (3) load simulation, (4) load measurement, and (5) simulation modeling.[1] Such factors as peak loads in transaction systems, network congestion, bus overloads, and buffer delays can be modeled accurately in DEW, using the graphic language GPSM (graphical programming of simulation models). The system not only issues detailed reports for node and system response times, but it also informs users of node population and utilization. Mean values are supplemented with variance and standard deviations. Therefore, a system can be put through its paces and optimized even before the hardware is available.

To furnish such detailed simulation, DEW comprises an unusually rich menu of icons to describe hardware and software functions (see Figure 11.1). In GPSM, the processed unit of information is called a "transaction"—a unit of work which closely resembles our IP "signals." GPSM icons describe the transactions' activities as they travel through the system from entry (or creation) to exit (or destruction). Each transaction is associated with a "category" (a class similar to user types) and "phases" (tags indicating a transaction's state). Phases can change as a transaction proceeds along its path.

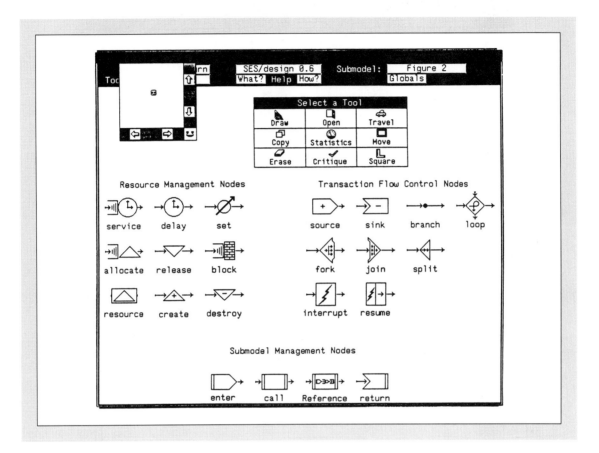

Figure 11.1 A rich icon menu permits the DEW user to express complex hardware/software systems graphically.

To get a bit more concrete, let's see how DEW models the G-Train system. At the highest level, it breaks G-Train down into four subsystems that handle departure, weighing, speed measurement and display, the last being accessible both from the Weigh and Speed nodes. Represented by icons, nodes are connected to form "information processing graphs" or (IPG)s. We'll concentrate on the weigh module, as represented by the IPG in Figure 11.2a. A Source node generates transactions in a sequence that simulates the random arrival of passengers. The transactions pass through an icon that stands in for the module weigh_sw and then go on through either closegate or relgate (which simulates passenger queuing). Transactions then encounter a Split node and proceed via a subsystem call (that updates the display), or they bypass the call if boarding has ended.

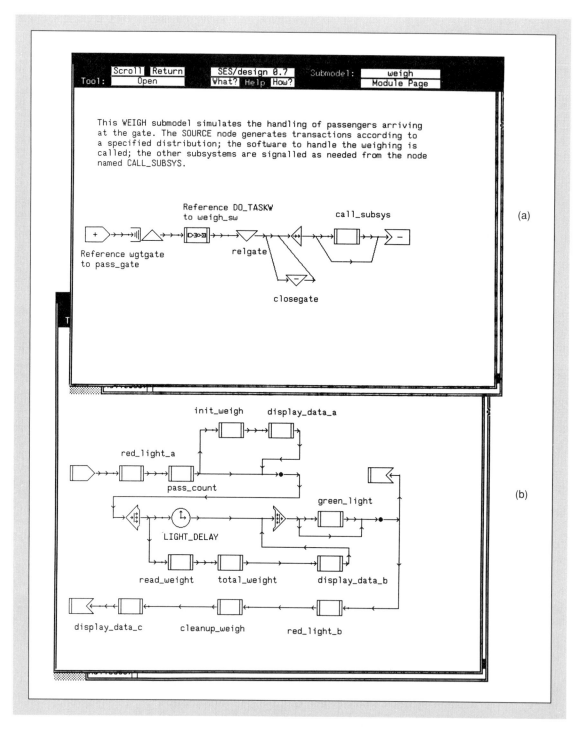

Figure 11.2 G-Train here zips along an Information Processing Graph (*a*). Descending one level we can follow the processing of passengers in greater detail (*b*).

They shall be weighed and counted.   Descending one level into the weighing model's innards, let's observe the processing of passengers (see Figure 11.2*b*). Each thread through the graph represents a possible calling sequence, depending on the state of the simulation (identified by a transaction's phase). Each of the Call nodes (empty rectangles) invokes the specified tasks (usually subroutines), whose names are self-explanatory. A Fork node spawns a sibling for the transaction, facilitating concurrent processing. Thus, the timer can tick away while weight readings are processed and displayed. When both transaction siblings are done, they reunite at the Join node and proceed toward the Return node. (In two places black dots indicate that branches have joined again.)

Each GPSM icon can be opened to add C code to the model. In Figure 11.3 a large window into the open Enter node displays code for the computation of the total passenger weight and number. A distribution function has been included that provides realistic passenger weights for the simulation. Furthermore, the code determines the `weigh` subsystem's state by checking whether the passenger count has reached 100, at which time boarding must be terminated.

Finally, the bottom window in Figure 11.3 describes the G-Train system's resource manager—essentially a minimal operating system. The only resources to be managed are the four ports: one input each for scale and track sensors, and one output each to switch the scale's "traffic light" and to feed the display. If we ever want to use the same computer for more than one G-Train, or employ parallel processors, this graph could best reflect such changes. Eventually the day will come when a system like G-Train can be linked with canned models of real-time operating systems and executed on models of specific computers (or processors). Whether you're a train or a missile buff, such stores of software and hardware models will greatly simplify the simulation of embedded systems. Indeed, there is no reason why DEW shouldn't support the object-oriented paradigm as well, by combining related hardware and software functions.

⅄ For Engineers, A Game of TAGS

Alphabet soup may not be to everybody's taste, but sometimes acronyms are indispensable. For example, TAGS for a tool called "Technology for the Automated Generation of Systems." That's

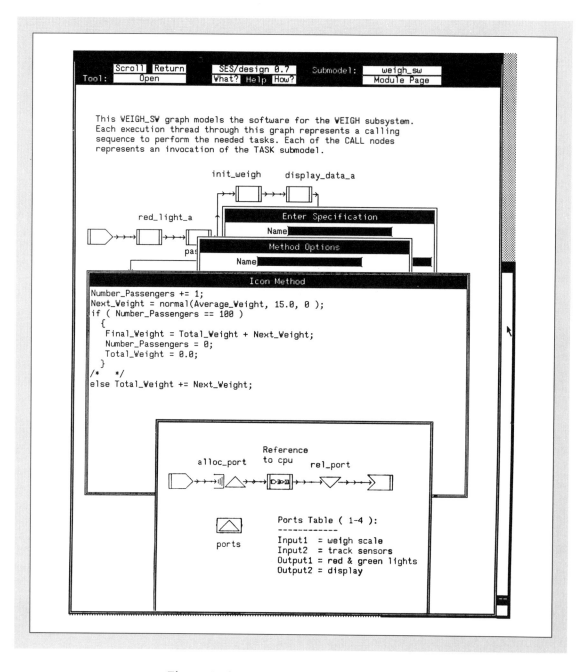

Figure 11.3 DEW icons—like the Enter node at the top left—can be opened to define activity details via C code. The bottom window (which would normally occupy a separate screen) reflects G-Train's resource manager, in essence a minimal operating system.

a mouthful but at least the name spells out with abundant clarity what its developer, *Teledyne Brown Engineering* has in mind. The defense and aerospace firm defines TAGS as a "Computer-Aided Software and Systems Engineering Environment," or CASE[2] for short.

Unlike some me-too CASE entries, TAGS has proven in "battle tests" to be comprehensive, down to the level of code generation. TAGS has modeled complex embedded computer systems from the space shuttle to SDI. The tool rises from a foundation called IORL (Input/Output Requirements Language), which encompasses a graphical system description vocabulary. IORL and its methodology enforce the careful definition of specifications throughout all phases of system design.

Like few others, Teledyne Brown understands that software design must follow the same track as integrated circuit design. In fact, TAGS can take its users from the requirements specs all the way to executable code—Ada for software components and Ada-derived *VHDL* for the hardware. The IORL language supports not only the hierarchical decomposition of the system itself, but its description in related "documents" as well. They comprise, in addition to graphics and tabular pages, code and comments. Such a mix is hard to beat: the pictures convey a great deal of high-level information at a glance, while the other documents fill in the details.

Each IORL page is identified by system name, document ID, and page number. To understand the relations between the graphs for the G-Train system first look at the bottom line where "SEC" declares the graph's identity: SBD for Schematic Block Diagram (showing data flow), IORTD for Input/Output Relationship and Timing Diagram (showing control flow), PPDs (Predefined Process Diagrams) help with stepwise refinement, and IOPTs and IPTs identify tables. IORL's graphics symbols are displayed in a screen window, as in the G-Train diagram of Figure 11.4*a*. You'll find the meaning of the icons defined right underneath in Figure 11.4*b*. But a few words are needed to define the definitions.

Like our IPs, IORL descriptions must be able to handle both ANDed and ORed inputs as well as outputs. Unlike the IPs, IORL uses different symbols for all the combinations. All are based on circles, but it's what's inside them that counts. The logical OR is sometimes designated by the symbol + (to confuse the layman, who will interpret that symbol as AND). The AND, in turn, can be recognized by a dot, which here stands in for the × used by some

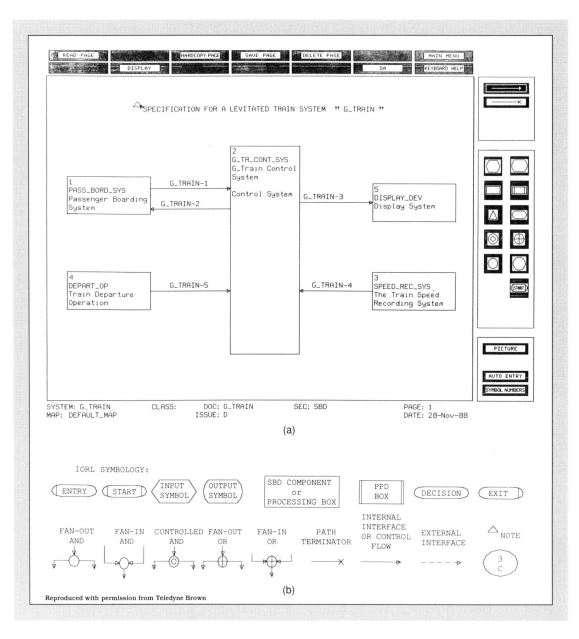

Figure 11.4 The Schematic Block Diagram in the TAGS view of G-Train identifies the subsystems (*a*). An icon menu at the screen's right edge is explained further, below the screen shot (*b*).

logicians. When signals are combined, TAGS speaks of "fan-in" and of "fan-out" when they are split. (These terms are popular among hardware engineers.) To identify which is which, just look at the arrows. When more are coming in than are going out, it's a fan-in; otherwise, it's a fan-out.

One fan-out has its special symbol—namely, a smaller circle inside the usual fan-I/O circle. This "controlled AND" has one entry and several exit paths, but it isn't really a fan-out. As an AND symbol, it requires that every path must be taken; however, only one can be active at a time, as determined by timing constraints. We did not need such a symbol for our IPs because in real-time IP mockups a Time input determines the sequence of events internally. Still, the special symbol alerts the user to time-sensitive events in the system under study.

Because IORL diagrams are limited to the size of a standard page, another symbol is needed—a "connector." Its purpose is to link signal lines between pages, and it consists of a somewhat larger circle than the "fan" symbol, labeled with an identifier. Of course, the same ID can be found on the page where the diagram continues.

Playing TAGS in the G-Train.   After these preliminaries, we can return to Figure 11.4*a*, G-Train's schematic (formally designated "SBD"). We see that the system has been broken down into five modules. The one labeled "Control System" does just what its name implies; consequently, it serves as the clearinghouse for all data. Three of the modules *produce* data signal for the controller, and one (Display) only *consumes* them. We'll return to these signals after a look at the decomposition of module 1, which handles passenger boarding.

In Figure 11.5 we have combined the two pages of the IORTD-2 diagram. The first processing box after the Start symbol contains just initialization assignments for some variables. The second box has more to say. At the top, we find a line of predicate calculus defining the index variable *I*. Translated into English, its first clause reads "For all values of *I*, where *I* is a member of the set [1,2, . . . 38]." Mere mortals would just write FOR 0<I<39 DO or, in the clearer KISS syntax, ! I = 1,2..38. (Why clearer? It doesn't force you to modify the starting and ending values 1 and 38—a step likely to breed errors.)

After activating a process labeled "50", the control "signal" splits when it encounters a controlled AND. Process 100 executes

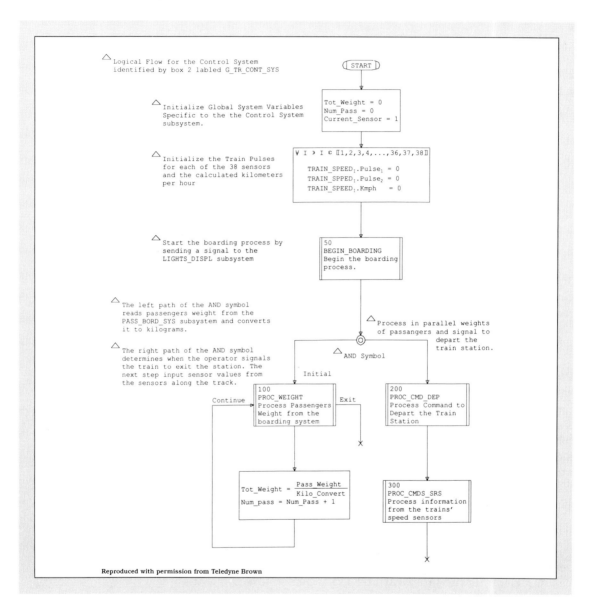

Figure 11.5 Combining two pages of the IORTD-2 graph, yields an overview of the system's execution. Note the formal spec (box near top) and Process 300, depicting the Speed system.

first; it has the form of a DO loop, which calculates the total weight and passenger count. When this job is complete, the process exits to a termination, symbolized by an "X". Now the other branch gets its chance; first it waves the train goodbye (process 200), and then it calculates the speed (process 300).

When we open up the processes 50 and 100 in Figure 11.6, we learn all about the fate of the two data signals from Figure 11.4a—G_Train-1 and G_Train-2. (In Figure 11.6, the two pages PPD-50 and PPD-100 have been combined to save space.) From the Entry symbol, control proceeds to the command $Light_Switch = "Green" and then on to two output symbols. The first has been dubbed "Call," and the second is called "Send." Going back to the "schematic" of Figure 11.4a we find out that Call is calling the passenger boarding system. The parenthetical expression after Call contains a time range for the call, in this case "right now, or else!" (minimum and maximum are both zero). A similar expression after Send just defines that the transmission will occur at a rate of exactly 0.6 kBaud.

At the other end of the line, an input process, Listen, stands ready. Its arguments state that the listening begins at the same time as the calling and will continue precisely till the end of

Figure 11.6 These two processes provide details for the data links of the top left subsystem in Figure 11.4a. Errors in Process 100 will be resolved later.

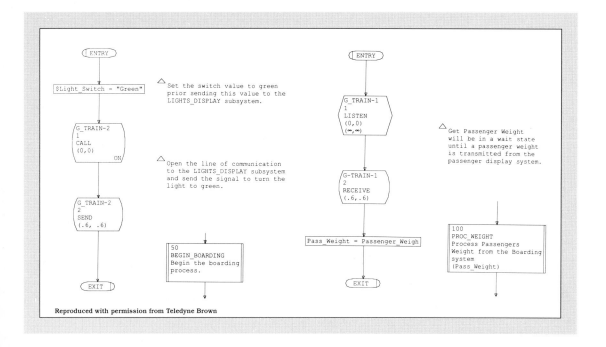

Reproduced with permission from Teledyne Brown

time. Of course, once the message (namely, a passenger's weight) has been received (at 0.6 kBaud as stated), hell has definitely frozen over and Listen returns to time zero. Since the premise of infinity was not stated in strict mathematical terms, we can accept such a disparity in good grace and proceed to Figure 11.7, the SBD of the document Pass_Board_Sys. It provides more detail about the passenger boarding system.

This second-level SBD has been broken down into three subsystems, one of which proves particularly instructive. The object in box 3 is labeled "Passenger" and has both input and output. In fact, unless the passenger sees the green light and actually steps on the scale, the whole boarding process grinds to a halt. (At this point, only fuzzy logic might produce a life-like simulation.) Of course, once the supply of the passenger object has been exhaust-

Figure 11.7 Details of the passenger boarding subsystem reveal a "hidden" system element: the passenger. Unless he steps on the scale when the signal turns green, boarding stops.

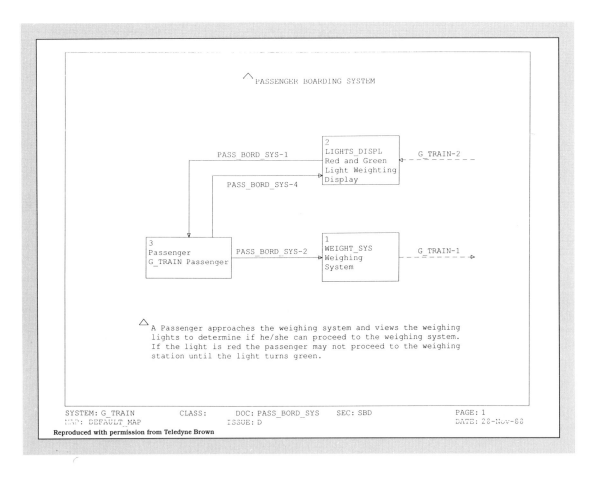

ed, we must proceed to the right-hand branch in Figure 11.5 and depress the Depart button.

Before we take off, let's examine a parameter description table (see Figure 11.8). The first three entries simply note some variables' limits (the I-like symbol means "any integer"). Train_Speed defines a data structure of 38 records—an array we'll deal with shortly. The next section, between B−−B (for begin) and E−−E (for end), defines the speed, which is to be calculated from the variable Pulse. The latter again turns out to be an array, though only with two records apiece. Group 4 defines something quite different—the commands we briefly reviewed earlier. In the right column, the notation [22,22] tells the compiler that each command must be exactly 22 characters long. Thus, the table fills in the information not available from the IORTD.

Figure 11.8 Tables such as this serve to define parameter details that are not easily captured graphically.

GRP	PARAMETER DESCRIPTION (DIM)	NAME	VALUE RANGE	UNITS/VALUE MEANING
	Number of Passengers Boarded	Num_Pass	{0,1,...,99,100}	
	Total Weight of all passengers	Tot_Weight	I	Kilograms
	Sensor Number	Current_Sensor	{01,...,37,38}	
	Train Speed Information Records (38)	TRAIN_SPEED		
		B---------B		
	Kilometer Per Hour	Kph	I	
	Pulse information sent by each sensor (2)	Pulse	I	
		E---------E		
	Passengers Weight	Pass_Weight	I	[OUTPUT]
	Kilo Conversion Constant	Kilo_Convert	2.205	
	This group contains the information which is transmitted from the G_TRAIN Control System on interface G_TRAIN-2			
	Message Text	$Command	{"Start Boarding Process", "100 Passengers Boarded", "Depart Button Pressed", "Shutdown Boarding Sys"}	[22,22]

SYSTEM: G_TRAIN   CLASS: DOC: G_TRAIN   SEC: IPT-2   PAGE: 1
MAP: DEFAULT_MAP   ISSUE: D   DATE: 10-Feb-89

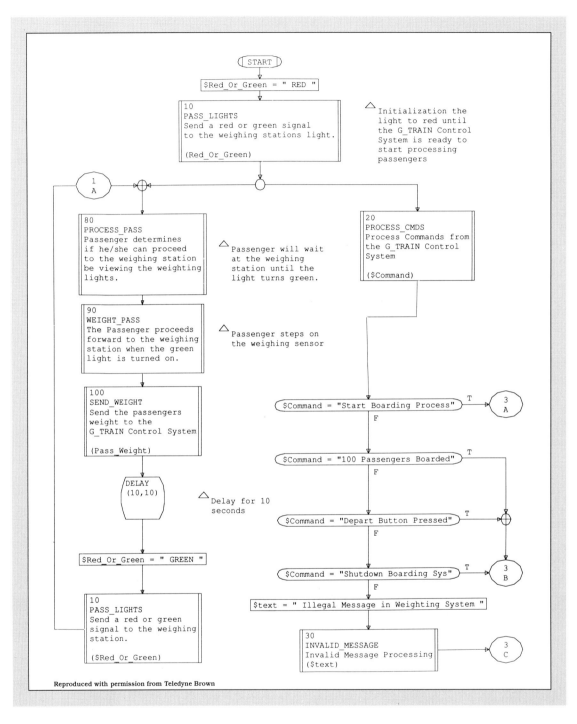

Figure 11.9 Details of the boarding subsystem are revealed in this composite graph. The right branch identifies commands the system must scan during boarding. Numbered polygons are connectors.

All aboard!   To see exactly how the boarding system functions we take a look at IORTD-1 of Pass_Board_Sys, as shown in Figure 11.9 (which combines two pages of the document). The left branch holds no surprises; passengers examine the light and step on the scale, after which a 10-second delay takes effect. Once the light has changed, control proceeds to connector 1A—which brings us back to the top of the left branch.

Simultaneously, the system must pursue the right thread, which examines a number of commands. The last one, "Shutdown Boarding Sys," tells us that it's up to the station master to keep an eye on the boarding queue and either turn the boarding light red or press the Depart button. This approach relieves the system designer of the need to provide a camera that looks out for stragglers and perhaps an expert system to evaluate the picture. Another million tax dollars saved.

The missing parts of the IORTD don't easily fit into Figure 11.9 because the connectors 3A, 3B, and 3C are scattered about. But it's easy enough to describe where they lead. The first "wire" sets the signal to green, the second sets it to red, and the third goes straight to a fan-in OR where all three are combined for return to 1A, the beginning of the loop.

We now turn our attention to the speed calculation; it is defined by PPD-300 in Figure 11.10. With process Get_TR_Sensor, we first obtain the two time readings at which the pulses arrive. Then we calculate the train speed from a rather complex data structure—the array of records defined in Figure 11.8. Train_Speed carries the suffix Sensor_Num, which is the array counter. Each of the records contains values for Kph, Pulse1, and Pulse2. The second and third equations merely assign values from the array to Pulse1 and Pulse2, thereby keeping the length of the first equation manageable. The final equation calculates the train position from the array index.

After process 550 updates the display, we still must check the array index and close the loop until its value reaches 39. This step concludes process 300, which is shown once more in Figure 11.11, Part A—after its transfiguration into Ada package G_TRAIN_PPT_PPD_300. The package body includes a line "use OVER_OPS", which refers to a library package where overloaded operators are defined. They are needed below the label <<PAGE_1_SYMBOL_3>> for the array components, as described previously, on p. 237. Similarly, the definitions of Figure 11.8 (Table IPT-2) are converted to the package G_TRAIN_IPT_2 in Figure 11.11, Part B.

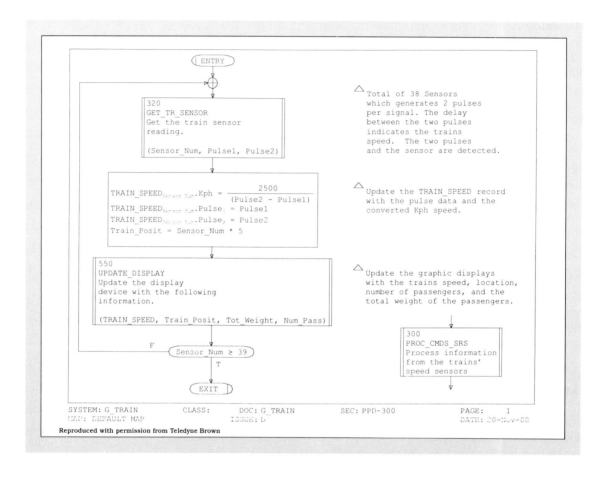

The diagram contains:

- ENTRY
- 320 GET_TR_SENSOR — Get the train sensor reading. (Sensor_Num, Pulse1, Pulse2)
  - △ Total of 38 Sensors which generates 2 pulses per signal. The delay between the two pulses indicates the trains speed. The two pulses and the sensor are detected.

$$\text{TRAIN\_SPEED}_{\text{Sensor\_Num}}.\text{Kph} = \frac{2500}{(\text{Pulse2} - \text{Pulse1})}$$

$$\text{TRAIN\_SPEED}_{\text{Sensor\_Num}}.\text{Pulse}_1 = \text{Pulse1}$$

$$\text{TRAIN\_SPEED}_{\text{Sensor\_Num}}.\text{Pulse}_2 = \text{Pulse2}$$

$$\text{Train\_Posit} = \text{Sensor\_Num} * 5$$

  - △ Update the TRAIN_SPEED record with the pulse data and the converted Kph speed.

- 550 UPDATE_DISPLAY — Update the display device with the following information. (TRAIN_SPEED, Train_Posit, Tot_Weight, Num_Pass)
  - △ Update the graphic displays with the trains speed, location, number of passengers, and the total weight of the passengers.

- F — Sensor_Num ≥ 39 — T
- 300 PROC_CMDS_SRS — Process information from the trains' speed sensors
- EXIT

SYSTEM: G_TRAIN   CLASS: DOC: G_TRAIN   SEC: PPD-300   PAGE: 1
MAP: DEFAULT MAP   ISSUE: D   DATE: 28-Nov-88

Figure 11.10 The definitions from Figure 11.9 make another appearance in this diagram of the Speed subsystem. Speed and location data reside in an array of records.

Finally, Figure 11.11, Part C contains a code fragment from Figure 11.5 (IORTD-2) where a bevy of variables are defined and initialized. This code includes some Ada tasking (easily recognized by such giveaways as accept and entry) and a long comment explaining that the logic symbol "for all" is not supported by the code generator. Near the end, the code fragment also illustrates the darker side of automatic code generation—a variable name that runs across the whole page (just above end TASK_G_TRAIN_IORTD_2). But then, once it's compiled, not even the computer knows.

At this point let's run part of our design through the Ada compiler. It has some complaints (see Figure 11.12), all of them related to process 100 from Figure 11.6. The standard procedure

```
                ---- PART A ----

        package body G_TRAIN_PPT_PPD_300 is
            use TEXT_IO;
            use OVER_OPS;-- overloaded operators as in <<PAGE_1_SYMBOL_3>>
            use BUILTINS;

            procedure G_TRAIN_PPD_300 is
            begin
            <<PAGE_1_SYMBOL_3>>
                    G_TRAIN_PPD_320(sensor_num, pulse1, pulse2);
                    ASSIGN (train_speed(sensor_num).kph, 2500 / (pulse2 - pulse1));
                    ASSIGN (train_speed(sensor_num).pulse(1), pulse1);
                    ASSIGN (train_speed(sensor_num).pulse(2), pulse2);
                    ASSIGN (train_posit, sensor_num * 5);
                    G_TRAIN_PPD_550(train_speed, train_posit, tot_weight, num_pass);
                    if sensor_num >= 39 then
                        goto PAGE_1_SYMBOL_2;
                    else
                        goto PAGE_1_SYMBOL_3;
                    end if;
            <<PAGE_1_SYMBOL_2>>
                    return;
            end G_TRAIN_PPD_300;
        end G_TRAIN_PPT_PPD_300;

                ---- PART B ----

        with DATA_TYPES;
        with INT_PKG;

        package G_TRAIN_IPT_2 is
            use DATA_TYPES;
            use INT_PKG;

            Scommand: IORL_STRING(1..22);
            current_sensor_O: LONG_INTEGER;
            kilo_convert_O: constant FLOAT := 2.205000;
            num_pass_O: LONG_INTEGER;
            pass_weight_O: LONG_INTEGER;
            tot_weight_O: LONG_INTEGER;
            type train_speed_R_pulse_O_array is
                        array(LONG_INTEGER(1)..2) of LONG_INTEGER;

            type train_speed_R_rec is
               record
                    kph_O: LONG_INTEGER;
                    pulse_O: train_speed_R_pulse_O_array;
                end record;
            train_speed_R: array(LONG_INTEGER(1)..38) of train_speed_R_rec;

        end G_TRAIN_IPT_2;

                ---- PART C ----

        package body G_TRAIN_IPT_IORTD_2 is
            . . . .
            task body TASK_G_TRAIN_IORTD_2 is
            begin
                    accept task_entry;
                    tot_weight_O := 0;
                    num_pass_O := 0;
                    current_sensor_O := 1;
                -- Expression not Generated: FOR_ALL Operator not supported
                -- by code generation. PAGE: 1 BOX: 5;
                    ASSIGN (train_speed_R(i).pulse(1), 0);
                    ASSIGN (train_spped(i).pulse(2), 0);
                    ASSIGN (train_speed_R(i).kmph, 0);
                    G_TRAIN_PPD_50;
                    G_TRAIN_IORTD_2_TASK_CONTROL_PAGE_2_SYMBOL_2.task_entry;
            end TASK_G_TRAIN_IORTD_2;
            . . .
        end G_TRAIN_IPT_IORTD_2;
```

Figure 11.11 When all the details are in, TAGS generates Ada code.
Process 300 (which calculates the speed) converts to Part A. It uses
a package derived from Figure 11.8 (Part B). A slice of Figure 11.5
transforms into Part C—excluding the For-All clause.

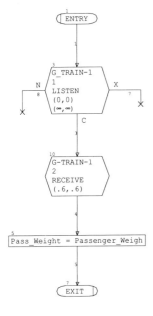

LISTEN demands three outputs, even though only one is used in our application. We get around that problem easily enough by terminating (or "grounding") the extra outputs. The message about illegal text stems from a typo. In the RECEIVE procedure we have entered G-TRAIN-1 instead of G_TRAIN-1. Finally, we have also picked the wrong icon for this procedure—it identifies an output type rather than an input type. After the needed corrections, process 100 looks as shown in the margin.

Simulation clinches the deal. Like any self-respecting CASE system nowadays, TAGS sports a simulator. The simulation compiler produces an executable system model from the IORL database. Modeling results can be collected and postprocessed to produce a trace listing of the execution. Dynamic error analysis can locate such problems as races or timing and control faults—essential for real-time systems. TAGS further enhances productivity by classifying errors as either fatal or severe; in addition, it issues warnings.

A good example of a fatal error would be the timing fault that caused a cruise missile to crash in August 1985 near Freeport, Florida. During program loading, an input routine outran storage allocation so that parts of the program were overwritten. (The cost? Check with your friendly neighborhood surplus store.) The "severe" category might be appropriate for another timing problem: A pseudo random-number generator once used a clock for seeding, but ran too fast for the clock-reading routine to keep pace. This problem exemplifies the value of dynamic simulation. With a normal debugger the error could not be found because this tool slowed down execution just enough to cover up the "clockenspiel" trouble. You might classify this error as a Heisenbug—when you look closely it disappears.

Back to the G-Train application, which also harbors an error. But although fatal, it won't even produce a warning. Improperly counted pulses from the trackside sensors could terminate the location routine too early, and we'd never know whether the train made it to the remote terminal. You may recall that the TAGS specification provides 38 arrays for speed data—one for each sensor. However, a 200-km track contains 40 segments of 5 km apiece. That's 39 segment boundaries, for which we need 39 sensors, not 38. G-Train is bound to become a Ghost Train after traveling 195 km. But it will take a system much smarter than today's CASE crop to flag such a requirements blunder.

```
ERROR#   LEVEL                    MESSAGE
─────────────────────────────────────────────────────────────────────────────
10002     S      Symbol has an illegal number of outgoing connectors.
                 DOCUMENT: G_TRAIN        SECTION: PPD-100    PAGE: 1  SYMBOL: 3

11509     S      Illegal or missing label(s) on connector(s) exiting a LISTEN symbol.
                 DOCUMENT: G_TRAIN        SECTION: PPD-100    PAGE: 1  SYMBOL: 3

 2004     S      Unrecognizable or illegal text.  In the vicinity of  train
                 DOCUMENT: G_TRAIN        SECTION: PPD-100    PAGE: 1  SYMBOL: 10  LINE: 1

10401     S      Missing or invalid interface designation.
                 DOCUMENT: G_TRAIN        SECTION: PPD-100    PAGE: 1  SYMBOL: 10  LINE: 1

10401     S      Missing or invalid interface designation.
                 DOCUMENT: G_TRAIN        SECTION: PPD-100    PAGE: 1  SYMBOL: 10

14321            Stage 1 of Compilation process completed: successfully


14322     S      Stage 2 of Compilation process completed: unsuccessfully


*** END OF FILE ***
```
Reproduced with permission from Teledyne Brown

You have now had a chance to observe several real-time CASE systems at work, but keep in mind that the CASE industry itself is still very much in motion. One trend stands out, though: a drift toward object-oriented solutions. While some would call TAGS object oriented, the output in a procedural language like Ada remains suspect. The next chapter takes a look at more orthodox object-oriented languages, and we will board the G-Train once more in Chapter 13.

Figure 11.12 Before compiling the Ada code for execution of a simulation run, the listed errors must be expunged.

⸬ References

1. Gordon E. Anderson, The coordinated use of five performance evaluation methodologies. *Communications ACM*, February 1984, p. 119.

Courtesy IBM Archives

The genre of calculating machines climaxed with the electrified Mark series built at Harvard University. IBM footed two-thirds of the bill for the Mark I, shown here only in part.

12

THE CASE FOR DESCRIPTIVE LANGUAGES

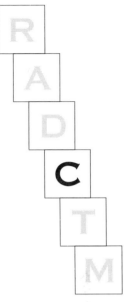

Object-oriented programming
Lisp started the revolution
From C to shining C++
Prolog—back to the future

Under the paradigm of top-down, stepwise problem decomposition, which we have explored so far, the desire to simulate a system right from the requirements spec encounters difficulties. Foremost among them ranks the lack of executable code in the early design stages—before you (or your faithful CASE tool) have written any. However, one school of software sages claims to have cut the Gordian knot. Their method is called object-oriented programming (OOP), and it is gaining support even among some straightlaced engineers.[1,2]

Like any style (say, impressionism), OOP is much easier to recognize than to describe—especially in view of the many sects that lay claim to the true faith. Most factions have one thing in common, though—languages that can model a system by describing it rather than by defining its activities. We should gain at least nodding acquaintance with the OOP school if we want to explore the brave new world of "Object Orientors" (honestly, that's the job title on some business cards). Actually, this "postindustrial" software paradigm should not be called object-oriented but subject-oriented—if grammar still counted for anything.

In Chapter 3 we discussed procedural languages, so named because they define the procedures applied to the given data. Inspired by the format of grandpa COBOL such languages are also called "imperative": ADD Numbers, SORT Files, and FIGURE taxes. Descriptive languages take a radically different tack.

The subject is taxes.   In the sentence "Cobol figures taxes," the verb defines an activity and the next word is the *object*—a data object to be precise. In the spirit of OOP, the sentence would have to read "Taxes wish to be figured"; the *subject* stands in the limelight, not the procedure. An OOP disciple will point out that the calculations needed for tax payments are fleeting at best, while taxes wax eternal (as Ben Franklin had discovered long ago). In contrast, a Cobol programmer's view would be that the calculations remain unchanged (until Congress tinkers with them again); only the numbers differ from one taxpayer—or accountant—to the next.

In other words, the Cobol programmer looks at tax data as the raw material that must be "crunched" until the bottom line appears. The object orientor sees a data structure called income tax—an empty vessel, if you will, that can be filled with different taxpayers' dollar figures but whose properties (income, expense, profit, loss, deduction, penalty) remain invariant. The question is not which view should be called right or wrong, but simply which one is more appropriate for a given task. To produce a table of Bessel functions, procedural Fortran works just fine. But if the task were to create the image of a (shirtless) taxpayer from a menu of shapes and colors, a language such as object-oriented Smalltalk would win hands down.

Fine, you say, but what makes the object-oriented view postindustrial? It is because procedural languages comply with the production line view of the world. You set up a process "Punch Holes," and whatever enters that mechanism gets punched, be it a copper strip or your wristwatch. In other words, the process remains constant while the data object changes. Under OOP's doctrine, you send the copper object a "message" (the OOP equivalent of a procedure call) that it needs holes, and the object then tells the tool to punch it. Send the same message to a wristwatch object, and it will laugh at such nonsense.

More formally, we can define an object as an instance of a class (so that "oak" *instantiates* the class "tree"). Objects possess storage in the form of "slots." (In hardware you could regard a multiplier chip as an object of class coprocessor; its slots would be the registers, and its method would be the multiplying algorithm.) Classes are associated through the "is-a" relation.* Thus, trees are a subclass of plants, because you can say "a tree is-a plant," and as such it can inherit certain characteristics from the parent class—say, the intake of carbon dioxide and the return of oxygen. From its grandparent, organism, tree could inherit reproduction and—to close on a cheerful note—death.

⌐ It All Began with Lisp

Even though some object-oriented pundits deny that Lisp qualifies as a proper language for their world, we must begin a review of nonprocedural languages with Lisp. After all, Lisp was barely edged out by Fortran as the oldest computer language. Thus, it helped set the tone for computalk etymology, even to this day. We already mentioned Lisp briefly in Chapter 3, because its spirit made itself felt back in the founding days of Algol (honorable ancestor not only of Pascal but of Ada).

As the name implies, Lisp is a list processor—even though it is not the first one. That honor goes to IPL, which ran on Remington-Rand's Johnniac computer in the mid-1950s. John McCarthy of MIT perceived the need for a declarative list processing language a few years later to facilitate symbolic (in contrast to numeric) computing.[3] Computers, unlike calculators, are really symbolic devices anyway. To add two numbers, we instruct the machine: "Take the contents of bin 12345 and add it to the content of bin 67890." McCarthy decided to operate with these pointers to values rather than with the values themselves for as long as possible. Thus, unlike Fortran, Lisp would not overwrite data once they had been used, but like the human brain it would manipulate the information in a nondestructive manner. That's the only viable approach to create what McCarthy was really after—*artificial intelligence*. From the start AI was meant to emulate human intelligence, including intuitive rather than rigorous math-like programming.

---

*The keyword "is" in Ada, however, merely stands for "is defined as follows." It has nothing to do with object orientation.

It took Lisp a while to make much headway, but by 1962 the language had been implemented. It provided a vehicle for symbolic calculation—in other words, computer algebra had been added to computer arithmetic. However, as Lisp caught on it soon threatened to drown in a tide of its own dialects. In time, Lisp's popularity spread even to the Pentagon, which had to prune the unruly growth. It picked Common Lisp as the DoD standard and it appears to be taking over rapidly.

As we'll soon see, Lisp's list approach to programming was not overly conducive to math, however. In fact, it led to a prefix notation that takes some getting used to. Generally, the first element of a Lisp list defines what to do with the remaining members of the list. Unless, that is, the prefix "quote"—as in '(a b c)—specifies that the first word is just another list member. Clearly, a prefix format simplifies list processing by telling the computer right away what to expect.

Let's take an instant course in symbolic calculation by writing the compund "list"

(PLUS x (TIMES 3 y) z).

This statement says that the product of 3 and y is to be added to list items x and z. Resembling the notation of some "reverse Polish" calculators, this format became known as "Cambridge Polish." Awkward as it seems for math, however, the prefix approach turns out to be essential for self-modifying programs— a vital aspect of AI research.

List members are linked by pointers; one half of a Lisp word may contain data, while the other half contains a pointer to the next list item that can be manipulated by the program. As Figure 12.1 illustrates, Lisp can easily vary the volume of information tied to a specific object—simply by expanding the lists. This feature has endeared the language to the AI community but, as the figure demonstrates, at the cost of high memory demands. An array that may take 10 memory locations for storage in Fortran can take 21 in Lisp—an overhead of 133%. Furthermore, getting to the nth element may mean unraveling n levels of pointers.

Today, when memory is counted not in words but in megabytes, such inefficiency may be a small price to pay for flexibility, but it was not always so. Some Lisp idiosyncrasies date back to the days of tight resources. In fact, the very core of the language challenges one of AI's most sacred canons: "Never mind the underlying hardware." Lisp's elementary functions reflect

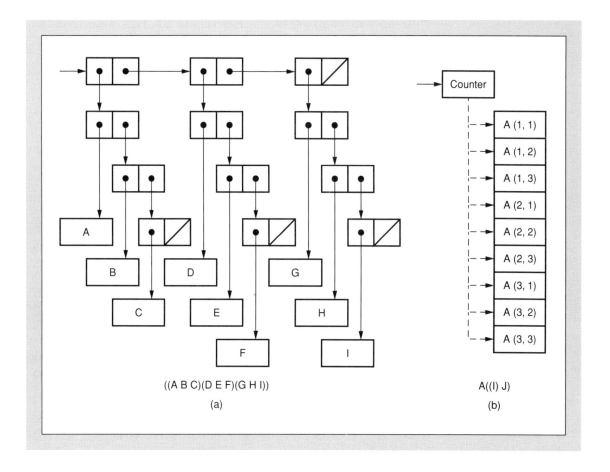

((A B C)(D E F)(G H I))

(a)

A((I) J)

(b)

the old spawning ground of the IBM 704: CAR (head of a list) and CDR (the remainder and pronounced "kuh-der") stand for "content of address register" and "content of decrement register," respectively. (By today's standards, this machine's assembler treated address and decrement backwards.) CONS can put (Humpty Dumpty) back together.

The function EVAL evaluates an expression and was originally invented to avoid the hardship of designing an interpreter. Today it encourages Lisp users to erect specialized languages on top of a Lisp skeleton—a very attractive feature not only for artificial intelligencers, but for object-oriented programming as well. Here is another interesting quirk: the IBM 704 had a 15-bit address, 15-bit decrement, 3-bit prefix, and 3-bit tag. Prefix and tag were soon omitted, which left a single type,

Figure 12.1 Lisp's biggest drawback stems from the list linkage mechanism. An array of 9 values can use up 21 storage locations (*a*), when it only needs 10 in Fortran (*b*).

with a 15-bit address. Much, much later the tags were rediscovered and put to good use in specialized Lisp machines as hardware-based type checkers. Lisp machines also set aside memory space for working storage—aptly called a "heap," through which a garbage collector roams periodically to clear out data no longer linked to a pointer.

(You (can't (win (them all)))). Some other early choices in Lisp's design proved less fortunate, leading, for example to cascades of nested parentheses that have to be unraveled during execution. Originally, the parentheses around data assisted in hand-coding I/O; they also proved necessary to demonstrate program correctness mathematically. Nowadays parent matching (a dating service for p*arents*) is fairly automatic and can even help to ferret out errors.

It should not surprise us that pointer-based arithmetic turned out to be rather tedious—10 to 100 times slower than with procedural languages. To speed up Lisp-based software (e.g., expert systems), it has become popular to translate it into a more conventional language. Not surprisingly, the language most amenable to emulating typeless Lisp turns out to be weakly typed C. Not only that, but C's pointer mechanism lets the language mimic Lisp rather nicely. Is it any wonder that two object-oriented C versions are already available?

IF word = *jargon*
GOTO Appendix C

Enough procrastination. Let's discuss list processing—Lisp's *raison d'être*. Whatever happens to be in the parameter list of a Lisp function (invariably named **FOO**) will be processed—letters, numbers, or graphics. In symbolic processing (used for equation solving), numbers need not replace variables (i.e. "symbols") at the very beginning of execution as in procedural languages ("early **binding**"). Rather, the symbols can be manipulated under normal rules of calculus, before values are assigned ("late binding"). The function SETQ permits explicit binding, thus mimicking the assignment statement of conventional languages. For example, the statement (SETQ List1 '(A B C)) makes (A B C) an instance of List1. The quote prefix suppresses evaluation.

Because the EVAL function undoes the quote, Lisp lets you manipulate an expression as a list and then execute it. Take, for example, (EVAL (CONS 'TIMES (CDR List1))). The absence of a quote before the last term leads to its evaluation, replacing (CDR List1) with (B C). Now the whole expression evaluates to a product of the list variables; if they are bound to the values 3 and 4, the result is 12. Thus, Lisp lets you manipulate lists of words and then turn those lists into programs.

In most cases, a Lisp programmer can enact these feats interactively and associate a given symbol first, say, with a number, next with a string, and then with a nested list. Naturally, only an untyped language can handle such antics, so the price Lisp exacts for its flexibility includes a disposition toward unsafe code. (Run-time type-checking is possible, but only by examining each symbol's property list.)

Lisp's dynamic binding of a symbol to first one and then another object depends on the sequence of events and the scope of the involved objects, so side effects often haunt Lisp programmers. Nevertheless, dynamic binding greatly eases object-oriented programming; in AI the ability of programs to modify themselves plays a similarly important role. (But when it comes to running, say, a nuclear power plant, a procedural Ada program ranks as a much safer bet.)

Via Oslo to Palo Alto.   We had mentioned before that Lisp affected the thinking of Algol's founding fathers. But it also had an impact on the designers of Simula at the Norwegian Computer Center, who wanted to expand Algol for time-sensitive simulation. Simula can be considered the first descriptive or declarative language, defining *what is* rather than *how to act*, as procedural languages do. The Simula work predated object-oriented programming with such conceptual objects as stations, systems, producers, and customers—all of which were "classes." (Because simulation demands the quasi-parallel execution of processes, a `select` clause similar to the one in Ada was also concocted, but that's a different story.)

Simula-67 notions played a major role in the evolution of Smalltalk at Xerox PARC (Palo Alto Research Center), the object orientors' Camelot.[4,5] Smalltalk flourished and sprouted a whole new software methodology known as visual programming—a close relative to many CASE systems. By combining Lisp with Smalltalk and Prolog features, Xerox researchers eventually created an extremely versatile AI language they called Loops (but that's getting ahead of the story).

As to Smalltalk, it was long regarded by computer-language mainstreamers as idle chatter. By now Smalltalk has managed to establish its own subculture—jargon and all. Objects (or, in some cases, "actors") are organized in a class structure; classes can be broken down into subclasses and grouped into super-classes, thereby forming big semantic trees. Actually, we should talk about semantic shrubberies because at the root of all super-classes lie the base classes. (If this sounds like mixed metaphors, keep in mind that software trees grow from the ceiling down. This inversion occasionally gives rise to vaporware.)

All these classes struggle to inherit properties (plural manda-tory) from their superiors (i.e. their parents). It's up to object-oriented programmers to decide who inherits what, which gives them the power to reduce code duplication and thereby boost productivity. (Laziness—the urge to find an easier way—has pow-ered Western civilization for millenia. The Incas probably did themselves in by declaring laziness a capital crime.)

What class objects actually inherit are **methods**—newspeak (make that Newtalk) for procedures. You could have a class "vec-tor," with subclasses for integer, real, and complex numbers, and even characters. All could share methods for copying or dele-tion, but only the numerical ones could inherit addition and multiplication, although the methods would differ between, say, integers and complex numbers. An alphabetical (or character) vector would obviously require very different methods, which it might share with another class—say, "word" in the superclass "language."

Smalltalk supports such multiple inheritance, so the pro-grammer would not have to write new methods for concatenation or sorting. But the neat (perhaps even elegant) semantic tree now turns into an untidy semantic network, like the ones you'll find in expert systems and other knowledge bases. The more such a network tries to emulate the behavior of real objects in the real world, the messier it gets. Just as messy as the real world, which can't readily be organized the way Linné classified plants and animals.

As we inferred before, the classless society of conventional languages may inherently suit many applications better than classy Smalltalk. Still, the latter could win a programming bout because, after a decade and a half of incubation in research labs, Smalltalk has emerged as not just a language, but as a complete programming environment. The variant available from Xerox spinoff **ParcPlace Systems**, Smalltalk-80, comes with over 200 "prefab" classes and thousands of methods. The next chap-ter should convince you that these riches turn Smalltalk into a very viable prototyping language,[6] especially since it can draw on

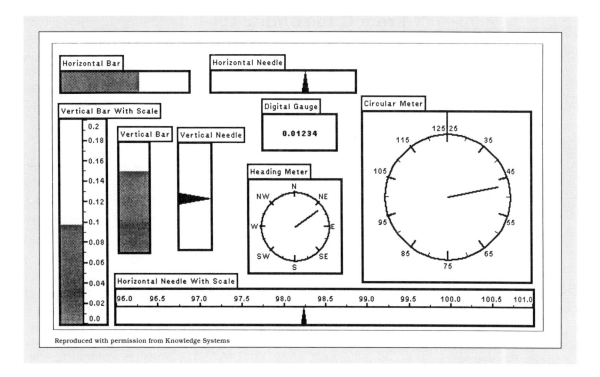

Reproduced with permission from Knowledge Systems

a package called "Pluggable Gauges" from *Knowledge Systems* (see Figure 12.2).

Needless to say, workstation-oriented Smalltalk-80 has company. The Mac and PC worlds draw their objective chatter from Smalltalk/V, a product of *Digitalk*. The company works closely with Canada's haven of OOPdom, Carleton University in Ottawa. This link ensures a steady flow of such goodies as Goodies #1, #2, and #3.[7]

Working on relatively small systems, Smalltalk/V retains the spirit of '72, when Smalltalk was implemented with 1,000 lines of Basic. The language pays much attention to resource conservation—how to call the garbage collector or get rid of instances and the like. For example, when you create windows, "ghost" images (object code) from earlier (unsuccessful) attempts to open the windows may clutter up the RAMscape. Hunting them down can be rather tedious, because it's not an automated process. Worse yet, if you don't watch your step you might kill off some base classes in the process.

Figure 12.2 Object-oriented languages like Smalltalk lend themselves to pre-configured software modules such as "Pluggable Gauges" used for this display.

⅃ From C to shining C++

Learning a new language is hard enough for most of us; getting used to a strange civilization like OOP naturally meets with a lot of resistance. Luckily, there's a way to ease into object orientation, namely C++ (a play on C's increment operator). Because C++ is a superset of C (meaning most C programs run on most C++ compilers), the fairly new language is usually described by means of C code. That's little help for those unaccustomed to C-fare. Right after assembly code, C must be the favored language of Humpty Dumpty, whose motto was "a word means just what I choose it to mean." So we'll keep C code to a minimum and stick with English −− (a concise subclass of English).

We have already mentioned an affinity between C and Lisp; both are given to computing with pointers more than with data. In fact, object-oriented programming can be practiced in "plain-vanilla" C.[8] But while in theory OOP may accord equal opportunity to all tongues, C is much more equal than the rest of the procedural clan. No wonder it was converted to the object-oriented faith with relative ease.[9] In the process, some of C's original sins were exorcised as well, and C shops are plus-plusing their idiom in growing number.[10] The word is spreading that C++ saves time two ways: (1) inheritance facilitates code reuse, and (2) enforced type checking reduces errors.

Mismatches between the type of a function argument and the type expected by the called function have long haunted C programmers. Now you can define, say, double precision for both input and output quite simply:

```
double sqrt (double arg)
```

Uninitialized variables—another well-known error source—should decline as well, because in C++ declarations can be placed wherever a normal statement can go. New is the concept of a "reference" as an alternative name for an object so that function arguments can be called by name rather than just by value.

Naturally, these improvements rank well behind the real innovation: user-defined types called classes. If you want to write a chess program, you might declare class Chess_piece and use it as the base class for your program.[11] Such attributes as name, color, or position would be private for this class; other attributes aren't. Let's scrutinize an example:

```
class Chess_piece {
        public:
            int color
            void display_me
            void list_moves
              ...
```

You would then add classes Bishop, Knight, and—perhaps last, but certainly not least—Pawn. After all, one of them might wed the king:

```
class Pawn : public Chess_piece
            int queened;
              ...
```

If you don't speak C, you might think void is related to black holes or cancelled checks. Syntactically, the C++ type void—unlike the C version—no longer masquerades as an integer. As the "basest" of types, it may be used only as part of a derived type; there are no objects of type void. Thus, it can be used for pointers to objects of an unknown type. Why would a type be unknown? Like other object-oriented languages, C++ boasts virtual functions—similar to Ada's generic packages. Only at runtime will the computer know whether, say, the data in the object Vector will be integers or characters.

All of this spells "dynamic binding"—an essential prerequisite for OOP. But while this feature can be very costly in some languages, in C++ a virtual function call requires only a few operations more than a normal call.[12] In Smalltalk, by contrast, a list of all methods must be stored in such a way that they can be found at runtime. Compared with Smalltalk, C++ generally needs half the storage space—and often runs ten times faster.

No arguing with success.   Virtual functions also connote operator overloading; move_me certainly means different things for queens, knights, or pawns. All told, virtual functions probably deserve the prize as the biggest time saver in C++, especially since they don't chew their way through half the memory. Each type maintains its own storage management in the form of a "destructor" that mops up superfluous classes. No garbage collector is needed to assist the destructors.

However, C++ is not perfect. It lacks an exception handler (although one can be faked with pointers to "exception objects"), and it lacks Smalltalk's "prefabs." Perhaps more importantly, the inheritance mechanism in C++ is more limited although multiple inheritance has been added in Version 2. Still, some maintain that C++ classes are no match for otherwise comparable Objective C.[13] When one—perhaps slightly bigoted—user of that language called C++ inheritance "next to useless," another quickly improvised a fix (which turned out *comme C, comme ça*). Some dislike the fact that in C++ the *recipient* of a **message** determines object type, while in Objective C it's the sender. (Defects involving data hiding were corrected back in release 1.1.)

Such gripes must please **Stepstone Inc.** (formerly known as PPI), developer and vendor of Objective C. Using an external description of its class hierarchy (maintained in so-called phylum files), Objective C code is translated to normal C before compilation. The resulting object code is linked with two sets of runtime libraries, those of C and of Objective C, before execution. Objective C commands an extremely flexible message-passing scheme, but a programmer remains responsible for getting messages to the proper destination. Objective C also applies true late binding, (rather than dynamic binding) but can't create new classes at runtime. The class struggle of the Cs will likely continue.

But C++ enjoys two major advantages over its rival: (1) it's in the public domain, and (2) it provides graceful migration to "objectivity" from today's most popular language. Objective C, on the other hand, just received one major shot in the arm. Together with Common Lisp[14] it resides in every NeXT machine.* (What nExt, STeVe?) No matter how the object-oriented cruisade will develop, NeXT does point to the future, if the past is any guide. For example, the proper mix of object orientation and Lisp has given rise to expert systems.

Object-oriented C extensions will nevertheless remain a compromise when compared with, say, Smalltalk. So must Ada when pressed into the class struggle. Therefore, we should at least look briefly at a language that was specifically designed for Ada-style real-time programming in the object-oriented manner. Eiffel, developed by **Interactive Software Engineering**, could almost

---

*If you get tired of waiting for the 90-ms optical disk to catch up, you can always read *Much Ado About Nothing* on the side. All of Shakespeare comes with NeXT.

be called Ada++. The language features multiple inheritance, generic classes, and dynamic binding. Eiffel also combines Ada's strong typing and exception handling with Smalltalk's separate class compilation. To be truly evenhanded, Eiffel generates C files and thus gains access to the vast majority of computers.

To convey Eiffel's "look and feel," let's take a peek at an implementation of states—an essential ingredient of real-time systems (see Figure 12.3). We are dealing here with part of a flight reservation network that answers schedule inquiries.[15] Because the states are not yet known, the declarations are labeled "deferred"—corresponding to "virtual" in Simula-67. The class description for STATE defines the pattern common to all states, but each state has to provide implementations of the deferred objects.

You might ask—and rightly so—whether we really need yet another language. If the result is better and perhaps less expensive code, by all means. You could even regard Eiffel not as a language, but as an environment. After all, the resulting source code is standard C, and the input will soon accommodate CASE-style graphics. In fact, the Eiffel solution eclipses the Ada solution because it permits the addition of safety features and rule

```
deferred class STATE export
   read, check, message, one_state, choice
feature
   choice: Integer;
   read: Answer is deferred;
   check (a: Answer): Boolean is deferred;

   one_state is
      local
         a: Answer; correct: Boolean
      do from correct := false
         until correct loop
            a := read;
            correct := chack(a);
            if not correct then
               message(a)
            end
      end; -- loop
      choice := a.next_choice
   end; -- one_state
end -- class STATE
```

Courtesy Interactive Software Engineering

Figure 12.3 An object-oriented language specifically for embedded systems? Yes, Eiffel masters all of Ada's tricks but adds class inheritance too, as this fragment from a schedule inquiry system shows.

checking without affecting the language standard. Ada can only be improved by a procedure as cumbersome as a constitutional amendment, even when sudden hardware evolution demands change. (More about evolving ADA 9x in Chapter 19.)

Speaking C with a Lisp. Back to the affinity between Lisp and C, which rests on the fact that both stay rather close to the underlying hardware. We mentioned that Lisp lends itself as support for specialized home-brew languages like those needed in expert systems. One of the first languages to be built atop Lisp for this purpose was OPS.[16,17] But with the advent of workstations, proprietary expert systems began to migrate from Lisp to C— which was healthy for the AI industry but no help to those who want to roll their own artificial expert.

Many expert system languages (often in the form of complete "shell" systems) pack the market today. As an example, we'll peruse OPS/83 because it's a direct heir to founding father OPS4/OPS5. The language (available from **Production Systems Technologies**) runs not atop Lisp, but atop C. Furthermore, OPS/83 demonstrates the confluence of object-oriented and procedural programming. And OPS's rules embody yet another nonprocedural branch on the language tree of Chapter 3—formal logic.

To accommodate standard PC keyboards, OPS/83 uses "synthetic" logic operators: $/\backslash$ for AND, $\backslash/$ for OR, and $\sim$ for NOT. You can recognize variables by the prefix **&** and characters by their single quotes, as in `'\0'`,`'\n'` (the former designates null, and the latter a new line). Symbols are character strings that stand for some value; matching such symbols plays an important role in an expert system. The following OPS/83 function conveys the flavor of the language:

```
function fold(&C:char):char
    {
      local &I:integer;
      &I=ord(&C);
      if (&I < ord('a') \/ &I > ord('z')
          return(&C);
      else
          return(char(&I + ord('A') - ord('a')));
    };
```

This function converts lower-case characters to upper case and leaves everything else unchanged. Within the code, ord(&C) accepts a character as the parameter and returns the corresponding integer value in the host machine's character set, while char performs the inverse operation. The IF checks for letters, and the last line performs the actual conversion.

Expert systems' stock in trade are rules and pattern matching. Let's look at two rules that check whether the value of variable &C is 10 or less:

```
rule count
{
    &C (cnt  val <= 10);
    -->
        write() &C.val <= 10);
        modify &C (val = @.val+1);
} ;

rule stop
{
    &C (cnt  val > 10);
    -->
        remove &C;
} ;
```

In these rules, the text before the arrow matches the value of the variable with the given condition; the rest defines what action is to be taken. If we execute the rules starting with val = 1, the first rule will fire 10 times and print out the counter, yielding the sequence 1 2 3 4 5 6 7 8 9 10. Then the second rule fires and removes the variable from memory. In an expert system, such rules—together with facts and relationships—form the knowledge base on which the system's *inference engine* operates.[18]

⌐ The Future is Prolog—Perhaps

In Act 1 of *The Tempest*, Caliban gripes: "The red plague rid you for learning me your language." What language might that be? The riddle is solved in Antonio's reply: "perform an act whereof the past is prologue." Certainly Colmerauer was aware of that passage when he called his language Prolog in 1973. So what is Prolog? It's not just another declarative language, but, in many ways, Prolog is an implementation of Boole's logic. Proponents call it a **VHLL** (very-high-level language), but then Zuse's *Plankalkül* should also be classified as such.

More precisely, Prolog is an implementation of predicate calculus.[19] It easily expresses such relationships as

```
dominates (math, software)
```

which is a predicate that mathematicians love. Actually, a growing number of engineers are adopting Prolog as well. Prolog proponent **Quintus** points out that the language can very nicely describe such logic structures as computer components. After all, as we saw in Chapter 1, logic gates are just realizations of logic expressions.

Generally, in logic programming you create a database of axioms, and you execute it by entering a theorem and asking the system to find a proof. A Prolog program encompasses collections of facts and rules (called "predicates")—much as in an OPS program. In addition, a built-in **backtracking** algorithm can answer logical questions.[20,21] Take the statement

```
works_for (John, Mary)
```

If you want to know who's the boss, you type

```
? works_for (John, x)
```

and the system will dutifully reply x=Mary.

Next let's try out a rule:

```
manages (x,y) :- works_for (y,x)
```

This rule defines that "manages" is the inverse of "works for," and if you query

```
? manages (x, John)
```

you now get the answer x=Mary. You still may not know who works for whom—for that we need a Prolog syntax primer. Just put the predicate between the parameters and you know: Mary is the boss. (You must have guessed by now that : - just means IF, but a true mathematician will never accept an operator as obvious to the layman as IF.)

Like any other public computer language, Prolog has its dialects, currently dominated by *Borland*'s Turbo-Prolog. We have chosen a version in which constants are capitalized, while lower case identifies variables. Unfortunately, in the major Prolog implementations, it's the other way around. That, however, is Prolog's smallest problem. Unlike a typical expert system language, Prolog has a one-track mind: it can only backtrack, and only in the order the facts are arranged.

An awful trip—and a fix.   You could use a Prolog program to determine how best to get from Washington to Paris. First, let's define some travel methods:

```
travel(A,B) = walk(A,B,) |ride(A,B) |fly(A,B)
```

where | stands for OR. To complete the hierarchy, we break down the mode "ride":

```
ride(A,B) = car(A,B) |train(A,B) |bus(A,B)
```

(Luckily, Prolog can't tell a noun from a verb.) We'll have to inform the program which transportation modes need roads, which need tracks, and which need airports. We'll also have to provide a list of cities and how they can be accessed.

Prolog will try all the possible combinations of cities and travel methods until one of them clicks. Even if we only enter data for Washington and Paris in the database, we could have eight false tries. If the number of covered cities went to 10, we could wind up with over 32 million attempts—not a very practical travel planning service. No wonder proposals to add heuristics to Prolog never cease.[22]

In the context of this chapter, we aren't out to find practical means to solve specific problems, but only to get acquainted with methodologies for CASE applications. Prolog serves well to demonstrate predicate calculus, even though other languages may overwhelm it in the long run. In fact, Japan's Fifth Generation Computer project found conventional Prolog inadequate and has developed several specialized *logic languages*. Counting all expert system approaches to logic programming, it's fair to say that new solutions run into the dozens each year.

One that deserves a closer look is Trilogy from **Complete Logic Systems**. The language derives its name from the goal to unify three paradigms in one language: procedural, database, and logic programming. For procedural programming, Trilogy summons Pascal's data types and the modularity of Modula-2, enhanced by the ability to include C and assembly subroutines. To tackle database problems (in the style of languages like dBase III), Trilogy contains a relational database. Not only is such a database much more versatile than the lists of Prolog, but, combined with predicate logic, it can provide answers to complex queries. For its logic, Trilogy relies on constraint programming. Elimination of Prolog's blind backtracking results in large speed gains (10,000-fold or even more, according to the developer). To get the feel of Trilogy, let's explore an example, again taken from the province of travel.[23]

This time, we'll plan a trip through Alabama (it's the first map in the road atlas). As Figure 12.4 shows, we start with type declarations and a database containing the necessary facts (L defines a long integer; constants are capitalized). Next, we add a predicate that defines a trip's "legs" and tells the program that all of the listed routes in the relation object AL can be used in either direction. (| again stands for OR). The second predicate combines legs into a trip by defining that we can go from `start` to `end` through the cities in the set `path`, driving the specified number of `miles` (barring false turns). The final parameter, `tries`, sets up a second list that we'll discuss shortly.

Two alternatives in the predicate are separated by a logical OR. The first alternative defines that any `leg` can be a `trip`, while the second specifies multilegged trips. The line `through in tries` should be read as "the city in `through` does not belong to the city list `tries`" and prevents trips passing the same `leg` more than once. Finally, we calculate the mileage total from the length of the component legs.

We can now ask the program which trips of 200- to 400-mile length go through Birmingham:

```
all path :: list City &
Birmingham in path &
miles > 200 & miles < 400 &
Trip (start, end, path, Nil)
```

```
City = Birmingham | Chattanooga | Huntsville |
       Mobile | Montgomery
Dist = L
Route = City, City, Distance
AL : ( list Route = (
      (Birmingham, Chattanooga, 145),
      (Birmingham, Huntsville, 95),
      (Birmingham, Montgomery, 91),
      (Chattanooga, Huntsville, 105)
      (Mobile, Montgomery, 172),
      Nil )

pred Leg (start :: City, end :: City, miles = Dist) iff
         (start, end, miles) in AL
       | (end, start, miles) in AL

pred Trip (start :: City, end :: City, miles :: Dist,
           road :: list City, tries :: list City) iff
      Leg (start, end, dist) &
      road = (start, end, Nil)
    | Leg (start, through, leg_miles) &
      (through in tries) &
      Trip (through, end, trip_miles, end, (start, tries)) &
      road = (start, end) &
      dist = leg_miles + trip_miles
```

If all goes well, the system responds with the following sightseeing tours:

```
path = Chattanooga, Birmingham, Montgomery, Nil
path = Huntsville, Birmingham, Montgomery, Mobile,
       Nil
```

(Hopefully, Tennessee will forgive the slight incursion in the first excursion.)

The Huntsville tour concludes our trip through the realm of nonprocedural languages. Surely some will cry foul because their favorite language (or religion) has been omitted, but the references provide many pointers into additional fiefdoms. And what about Ada? Is it an object-oriented language or not? Good question. Although Ada can do most of the things C++ can, it lacks one feature: inheritance. And that, according to the true believers, marks Ada as an upstart heathen.

Figure 12.4 A logic language such as Trilogy readily produces programs that operate like expert systems, thanks to a combination of logic and procedural programming.

⤷ References

1. Bruce Shriver and Peter Wegner (Eds.), *Research Directions in Object-Oriented Programming*, MIT Press, Cambridge, MA, 1987.

2. Bertrand Meyer, *Object-Oriented Software Construction*, Prentice-Hall, Englewood Cliffs, NJ, 1988.

3. Patrick H. Winston and Berthold K. Horn, *LISP* 2nd ed., Addison-Wesley, Reading, MA, 1984.

4. Adele Goldberg, *Smalltalk-80: The Interactive Programming Environment*, Addison-Wesley, Reading, MA, 1984.

5. Adele Goldberg and David Robson, *Smalltalk-80: The Language and its Implementation*, Addison-Wesley, Reading, MA, 1983.

6. Timothy Budd, *A Little Smalltalk*, Addison-Wesley, Reading, MA, 1987.

7. Barbara Noparstak (Ed.), "Partnership formed with Carleton University," *Scoop Newsletter*, Spring 1988, Digitalk Inc.

8. Stephen C. Bailey, "Designing with objects," *Computer Language*, January 1989, p.34.

9. Bjarne Stroustrup, *The C++ Programming Language*, Addison-Wesley, Reading, MA, 1986.

10. Steve Witten, "Introduction to C++" *TC Interface*, March 1988, p. 11.

11. Nancy M. Wilkinson, "Virtual functions in C++: best fit," *Unix Review*, August 1988, p. 57.

12. Bjarne Stroustrup, "What is object-oriented programming?" *IEEE Software*, May 1988, p. 10.

13. Brad J. Cox, *Object Oriented Programming—An Evolutionary Approach*, Addison-Wesley, Reading, MA, 1986.

14. Guy Steele, *Common Lisp Reference Manual*, Digital Press, Maynard, MA, 1984.

15. Bertrand Meyer, "Reusability: The case for object-oriented design," *IEEE Software*, March 1987, p. 50.

16. Charles L. Forgy, *OPS/83 User's Manual and Report*, Production Systems Technologies, Pittsburgh, PA, 1986.

17. C. L. Forgy and J. McDermott, "OPS, a domain-independent production system," in *Proceedings IJCAI* (International Joint Conference on Artificial Intelligence), 1977.

18. Max Schindler, "Artificial intelligence begins to pay off with expert systems," *Electronic Design*, August 9, 1984, p. 104 (30 pages including glossary).

19. R. A. Kowalski, *Logic for Problem Solving*, North Holland, New York, 1979.

20. K. L. Clark, *micro-PROLOG: Programming in Logic*, Prentice-Hall, Englewood Cliffs, NJ, 1984.

21. W. F. Clocksin and C. S. Mellish, *Programming in Prolog*, 2nd ed., Springer-Verlag, New York, 1984.

22. Paul V. Haley, "A search strategy for commonsense logic programming," *Byte*, October 1987 p. 173.

23. Peter Grogono, "More versatility with Pascal-like Trilogy" *Computer Language*, April 1988, p.83.

Courtesy IBM Archives

IBM seriously entered the computer business with the SSEC, which combined tubes and relays. For years it remained the only publicly available number cruncher.

13

HOLISTIC PROGRAMMING LIFESTYLES

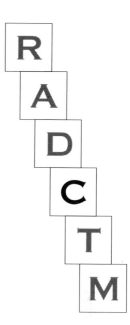

It takes all kinds of OOPs
View from the Ada train
Train ride with Smalltalk
Quick-draw 001 spins Axes

In the preceding chapter, you got an earful on object-oriented programming (OOP), which has been hailed by some gurus as the wave of the future in software design.[1] Others brand it as the "structured-everything" fad of the 1980s, which also meant something different to every advocate. This chapter will provide you with opportunities to judge for yourself where prophecy ends and hype begins. It will not be an easy call because one pundit's object orientation is another's snake oil. We must also keep in mind that the following deals with object-oriented design (OOD), which is not quite the same as OOP.

A number of OOD schools lay claim to the true faith: GOOD (general object-oriented design), which addresses the early phases of Ada-based programming; HOOD (hierarchical object-oriented design), whose objective is a direct mapping into Ada code; MOOD (multiple-view object-oriented design), which targets concurrent processing and is liberal enough to accept tasks as well as objects; OOA (object-oriented analysis), which object-orients the Mellor method[2]; and OOSD (object-oriented structured design), which tries to combine the best of the OOD and SD (structured design) worlds. And then there's *HOOPLA!*, which might mean "all of the above," but is the magazine of OOPSTAD (Object-Oriented Programming for Smalltalk Application Developers).[3] Object orientors do have a sense of humor.

Since Ada figures in several of these schools, we'll have to deal with that language even though many OOPSTAD zealots deny it the certificate of baptism. The Ada school itself lacks unity, but it seems only right to begin with its founder and main evangelist, Grady Booch. He sums up the difference between functional and object-oriented programming roughly like this: "Read the specification of the software you want to build. Underline the verbs if you are after procedural code, the nouns if you aim for an object-oriented program."[4] In the G-Train example (which you'll soon encounter again), the "verb" alternative led to subsystems that calculate speed, determine net weight, and display result. The "noun" choice might lead you to a train object, a passenger object, and a station object.

A proponent of the Simula-Smalltalk school and developer of the Eiffel language (discussed in the preceding chapter), Bertrand Meyer, cautions that looking for nouns would produce too many objects. Rather, the choice of objects (or classes) should not so much depend on what an object does or has, but what it is. (We discussed the "is-a" relationship in the previous chapter.) Classes and metaclasses (classes of classes) indeed don't readily map into Ada types and subtypes, which lack inheritance features. It seems we must deal with two distinct views of the object-oriented world, and we'll tackle the Ada hemisphere first.

STOOP with Ada. For lack of an established acronym, we'll call the Ada version of object orientation STOOP (structured object-oriented programming). Commercial implementations are mostly based on graphics developed by Buhr[5] and are an extension of the Booch methodology. Buhr diagrams—which can help you even during conceptual design—have been implemented, for example, in *Cadre*'s Teamwork/Ada. A top-level cut at G-Train illustrates a Buhr diagram in Figure 13.1. Packages take the shape of parallelograms into which tasks can be "plugged." Heavy arrows connote access (if conditional they turn into a fishhook). The small buoy-like arrows portray data flow, as usual. The STOOP spirit becomes evident when you study the illustration. The three main objects are labeled Train, Passenger, and Sensor. Train contains four routines, one

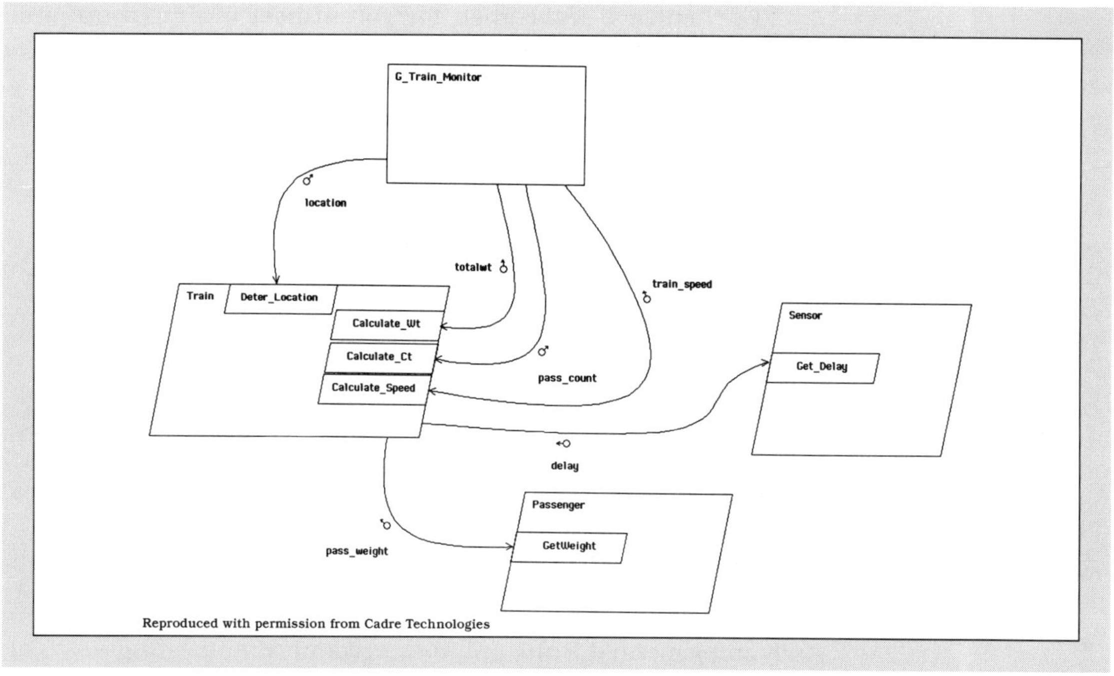

Reproduced with permission from Cadre Technologies

for finding the train's location, and the others to calculate total weight, passenger count, and speed. Passenger and Sensor only contain one function each, yielding a rather unbalanced system. But then Train really is the only important object in the example.

Even at this high (architectural) level, Teamwork/Ada produces an Ada template corresponding to the figure:

Figure 13.1 To implement G-Train under the Buhr model of Ada, Teamwork/Ada provides the necessary tools, including a code generator.

```
with Train; use Train;
package body G_Train_Monitor is
        function return is
                begin
                Deter_Location;
                Calculate_Speed;
                Calculate_Ct
                Calculate_Wt;
        end;
begin
        null;
end G_Train_Monitor
```

The "entries" (Ada lingo for coroutines) in Train are still empty at this high level:

```
task body Train is
begin
        accept Calculate_Speed do
                null;
        end Calculate_Speed;
                ...
end Train;
```

Except for the names, the other three functions look identical. Keep in mind that the graphical Buhr notation is not yet cast in concrete. In fact, work in progress at **IDE** will expand the graphics in such a way that they can be used with languages other than Ada as well.

If you're into Ada to the exclusion of other idioms, you might want to examine Adagen, a PC CASE tool from **Mark V Business Systems**. Unlike the more conventional CASE tools, fully implemented Buhr graphics accommodate nesting—say, of entries within tasks within packages. Adagen complements the top-down approach with bottom-up facilities, including support for libraries of reusable code fragments. Built-in "reverse engineering" can convert such code back into graphics for easier integration. Code generation resembles that of Teamwork/Ada discussed previously.

Beware the IDE en marche.   A broad methodology is not only the goal of the revised Buhr graphics. Another effort still underway goes even further: OOSD from **IDE**. You'll certainly remember the company's Software through Pictures (StP) from Chapter 8; now it's on the march with a novel object-oriented methodology. OOSD, as we mentioned briefly, tries to mate the Ward-Mellor methodology with the Booch and Buhr objectives.[6] The (hopefully happy) twosome will, however, keep an open mind about languages as well as methodologies. Ideally, OOSD should become a design tool for all software seasons, but a firm wedding date must still be set.

The system's basic building blocks, dubbed (with little hoopla) information clusters, can represent C++ or Eiffel classes, Ada packages, or Modula-2 modules. Design normally begins with an enhanced structure chart that discloses the relationships between the main objects. Once you descend into the nitty-gritty, however, deviations from both the standard structure and Buhr diagrams become more apparent.

Take the case of a stack, which frequently serves as a popular example in Ada texts. In the Buhr representation you'd find a parallelogram with two "sockets" to accommodate the push and pop operations. In the OOSD graph of Figure 13.2, a number of novel features show up: two diamond inserts, over and under, for exception handling; the corresponding data arrows; an indicator for the empty stack; and an arrow at the left with a dashed data symbol.

It's the last addition that connotes OOSD's kinship to class structures. You regard the object of Figure 13.2 as a generic stack generator, to be stored in a library and called up like our IPs. (That's why the rectangle appears with broken lines.) To create an instance of the stack, you provide values for size (say, 100) and stktype (say, character). The result is a module called smallstack with solid outlines but all the functionality of the generic ancestor.

But G-Train has no stacks, so we'll convert the speedometer IP module (oops, make that speedometer object) of Figure 9.5 to

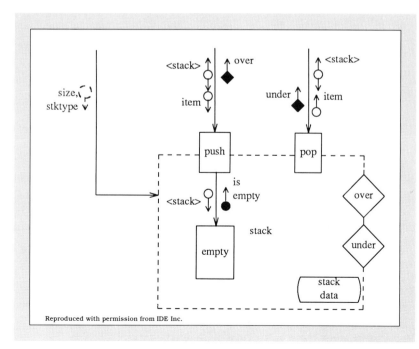

Reproduced with permission from IDE Inc.

Figure 13.2 Generic components like this stack generator go a long way toward reusable code. IDE has now incorporated object-oriented OOSD graphs like this one in its StP tool-kit.

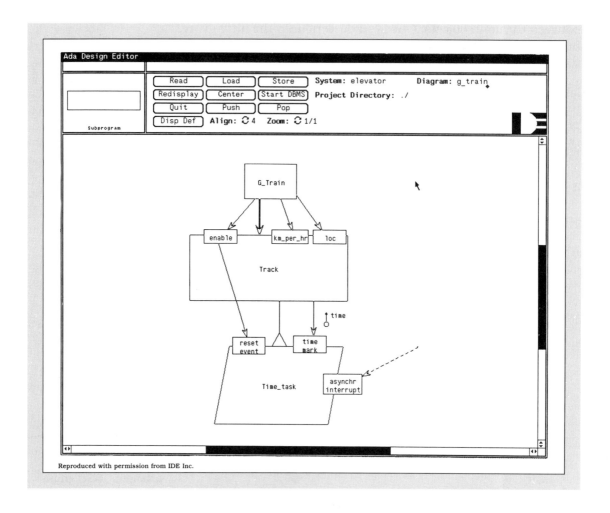

Figure 13.3 Using OOSD on the G-Train example, we get this representation of the speed/location module. The broken line depicts an arriving pulse "event."

OOSD format. In Figure 13.3 the small rectangle "time mark" inside Time_task corresponds to the signal Time in Figure 9.5, and the rectangle "asynchr interrupt" reflects the signal Pulse. The broken line identifies an event and the parallelogram a task, as in Figure 9.1. The G-Train model was created easily after a brief study of Wasserman et al.[6]

Objects enter the mainstream. We mentioned another object-oriented methodology, object-oriented analysis (OOA), from *Project Technology* in Chapter 9. Let's take a closer look at the kind of objects that OOA has dealt with so far. They are not as abstract as some object-oriented literature would have us believe, and include valves, electrical circuits, samples, programs, even work crews, shift supervisors, quality specifications, and, yes, trains (as well as their schedules).

In other words, just about anything in the physical and the management world has been modeled as an object, with attributes such as states (on, off), physical properties (voltage, pressure), and labels (part number, version). Operations (or methods) on such objects run a similarly broad range, from monitoring and controlling hardware to measuring and recording the results of product evaluation, and to archiving and validating specifications.

Relationships between objects cover the full range of database models: one-to-one, one-to-many, many-to-many, conditional (with unmapped instances on only one side), and biconditional (unmapped on both sides). Not only do we have to consider the wide spectrum of relationships, but also the fact that they tend to change with time. These are certainly vital concerns when the objects are software modules, and it's clear that conventional database approaches tend to break down under such stress.

No wonder then that the much more flexible object-oriented database techniques are beginning to move into the CASE mainstream. In fact, some CASE pundits believe that the whole CASE structure will soon come crashing down unless tool vendors adopt object-oriented databases. As you'll see in Chapter 18, the reasons are compelling—different users need different tool combinations. No vendor can support everything, *ergo* a common interface will be needed. And, because of the complexity of software and its graphic views, object-oriented databases have the best chance to accomplish the goal.

The hallmark of object orientation applies to databases as well: data objects and their manipulators (or methods) are packaged together in what one vendor likes to call "living data cells." Another view emphasizes that in a normal database management system (DBMS) the data structure is predefined by the normalized schema, while in an object-oriented DBMS both structure and behavior of the data are defined by the user. A third distinction stresses the system architecture, as shown in Figure 13.4. In the traditional system, the database interfaces with the operating system, while an object-oriented database interfaces with the user. (The manager can, however, still reside near the OS.)

To date only two object-oriented database systems have attained some commercial maturity: Gemstone from **Servio Logic** and Vbase from **Ontologic**. Gemstone's Opal database lan-

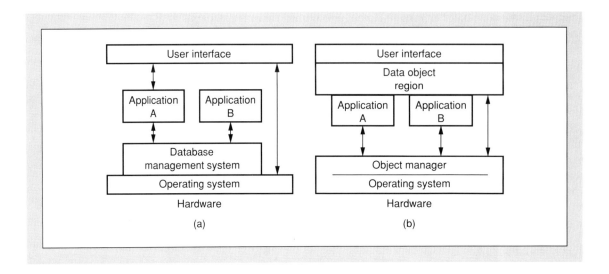

Figure 13.4 The main reason for the flexibility of object-oriented programming lies in data management. A traditional database is controlled through the operating system (*a*), while objects can be controlled directly by the user (*b*).

guage handles large amounts of data (up to a billion elements) and was developed in Smalltalk. It interfaces both with C and Smalltalk applications and was recently updated (Release 1.5) for faster operation on VAX and Sun machines. The younger Vbase runs on the same computers, plus Apollo workstations, and primarily caters to the C community. Not only is Vbase written in C, but it also offers C development tools. To no one's surprise, both databases have recently added interfaces for C++.

⅃ A Splendid View from the Smalltalk Train

After scanning the broad landscape of object-oriented design methods, would it not be interesting to see how a hard-core object orientor tackles the whole G-Train project? Luckily, we can oblige with an entry from *ParcPlace Systems* in Palo Alto. Going through this solution probably better illustrates the concepts of object-oriented programming than a textbook would. The problem was worked out with Smalltalk-80, which provides a comprehensive software environment. The user can draw on a large collection of existing classes, including Pluggable Gauges.

To tackle G-Train in Smalltalk, you start with a functional problem description (see Figure 13.5*a*), then you define the classes of objects to be used. Since classes inherit instance variables and behavior (in the form of methods) from their super-

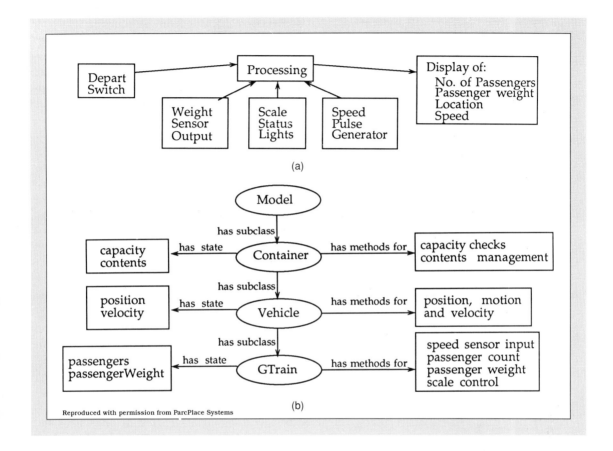

Reproduced with permission from ParcPlace Systems

classes, you must choose those as well. A train object could, for example, exhibit container and vehicle characteristics. An object in the Container class (which is defined as a subclass of Model) has states (attributes) called capacity and contents, with methods for capacity checks and contents management. A Container subclass could be Vehicle with states position and velocity and methods to manipulate them.

As Figure 13.5b illustrates, the subclass GTrain gets closer to the problem specifications. It embodies the states passengers and passengerWeight and the methods speed sensor input, passenger count, passenger weight, and scale control. Of course, GTrain also inherits the methods and instance variables from its superclass. The class has its "protocol," which defines the types of messages that can be sent to instances of the class. (As you'll recall, messages activate methods.)

Figure 13.5 To tackle G-Train in Smalltalk, we begin with a functional system description (a) followed by a definition of the class structure (b).

The train object will receive inputs from sensors (including the Depart button) and send messages to the display. The functions can be grouped into scale handling, light control, speed conversion, and decision making (e.g., train departure). The display can be handled with classes from the Smalltalk-80 library, including View, DisplayTextView, and CircleMeterView. Even the required track display can be handled with the built-in class Circle.

Smalltalk-80's "Model View Controller" helps you to implement class descriptions by providing a procedural interface that encapsulates states and method implementations. The dependency mechanism then stands ready to send update messages to all dependents whenever a method makes a relevant change. When the model sends itself the message changed, the dependent objects decide whether or not to take action (e.g., updating the display).

Point and click. You start to "program" by envoking one of the system's code browsers and clicking on add category (see Figure 13.6a). Asked for the name, you enter Simulation-GTrains (Figure 13.6b) and proceed to describe the class in the main window (Figure 13.6c). For example, you define subclass Container with a description of instance variables contents and capacity. To start adding messages to a class, you select "add protocol" (Figure 13.7a). Let's begin with the most basic one—the messages for accessing an object's variables. You select that choice in the third menu window ("accessing" in Figure 13.7b), and a method code template comes up that tells you how to define the method in the main window (see Figure 13.7c).

You repeat this process for all the GTrain methods; two of the more interesting ones appear in Figure 13.8. Once the coding is done, you can instantiate (create an instance of) GTrain and test it by sending some messages. Normally you would try to test one class at a time until you're satisfied that its methods work properly. A system view called an Environment serves as a kind of workspace to interact with objects. Say, you type in

```
OBS <- GTrain new initialize.
```

The expression creates a new instance of GTrain named OBS by sending the message new*; the message initialize provides

---

*In case you wonder: OBS stands for Otto Bach Special, in honor of O.K. Bach—still undiscovered brother of P.D.Q.

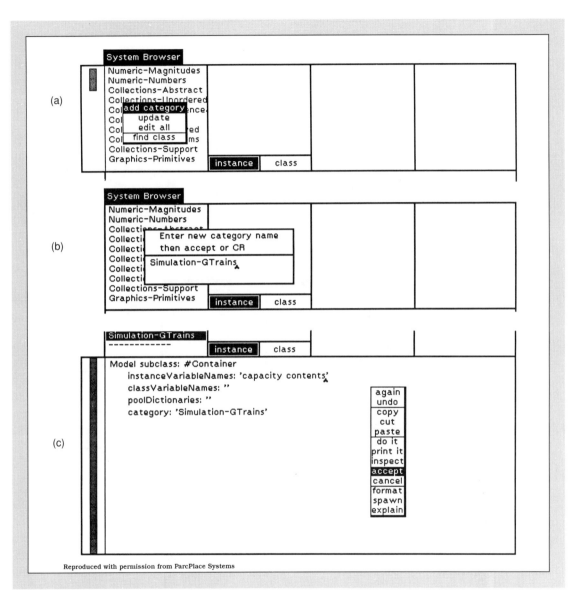

Reproduced with permission from ParcPlace Systems

it with default values. The compiler then prompts for a declaration for the new variable OBS, and you can choose, say, local from a menu.

Next, let's simulate a passenger's entry by typing

```
OBS passengerWeight: 150
```

and clicking on do it. An "inspector view" tells you about any

Figure 13.6 Thanks to a rich environment, "programming" gives way to mouse clicks and descriptions. We add a category (*a*), enter its name (*b*), and describe the new subclass (*c*).

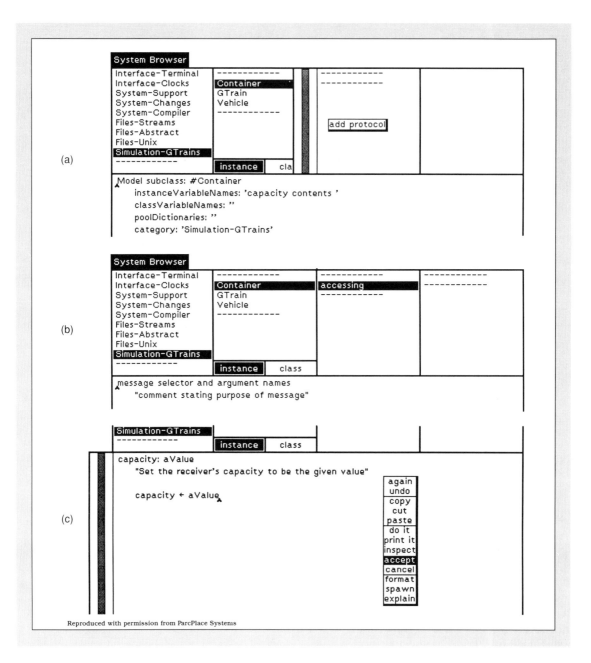

Figure 13.7 Next we select "add protocol" (*a*) for messages of type "accessing" (*b*). We can define it in the main window—for example, to return the value of the variable "Capacity" (*c*).

```
GTrain methodsFor: 'passenger meter'
passengerWeight: passWeight
        "Receive a value from the scale and update the passenger and weight counts.
        Turn the red light on for ten seconds."

        contents ← contents + passWeight.
        passengers ← passengers + 1.
        loading ← false.
        self changed: #loading.
        passengers >= 100 ifFalse: [
                (Delay forSeconds: 10) wait.
                loading ← true.
                self changed: #loading]
```

(a)

```
GTrain methodsFor: 'sensor input'
speedPulse
        "React to speed signal bits by counting them and taking a time-stamp.
        If this is the second of a pair, compute the new velocity and increment the position.
        Send the 'self changed:' message so the display will be updated."

        | now delay |
        now ← Time millisecondClockValue.
        pulseCount = 0 ifTrue: [                 "if this is the first pulse"
                pulseCount ← now ]               "remember the time"
            ifFalse: [                           "else"
                                                 "compute the velocity"

                velocity ← 2500 / (now - pulseCount).
                position ← position + 1.         "increment position counter"
                pulseCount ← 0.                  "clear the counter"
                self changed: #speed ].          "signal what's changed"
```

(b)

state changes resulting from your input (see Figure 13.9a). In this case, the inspector reports: a GTrain with 1 passengers (weight = 150), at position 0 moving with velocity 0.

It would appear that the targeted object has indeed gotten the message. Now let's try a message from speedPulse. The method counts pulses and toggles between first and second states; you therefore have to send the message twice and specify the delay

Figure 13.8 Two "methods" convey the flavor of Smalltalk procedures: one for the weighing module (a) and the other for the speed sensor (b).

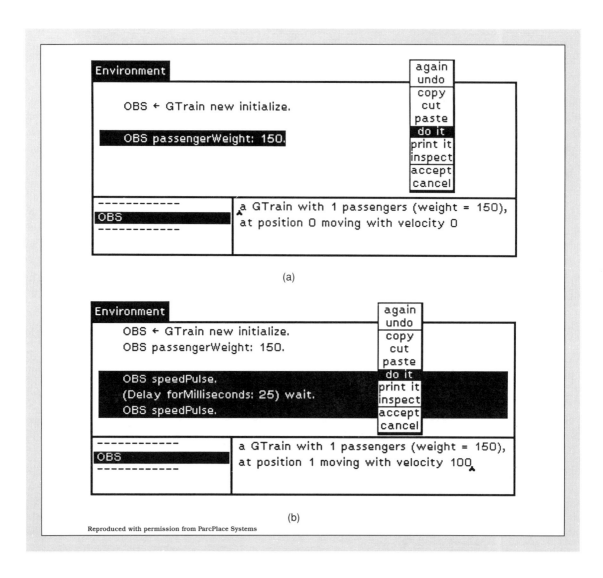

Figure 13.9 During simulation, an "inspector" reports on passenger status (*a*) and later on train velocity (*b*).

between pulses (see Figure 13.9*b*). Now the train is indeed moving, with its solitary passenger aboard. (It must be O. K. Bach.)

Display, change thyself. Of course, we don't really want to get the train data secondhand from an inspector; we just want to look at the display we had specified. So we must create GTrainPanelDisplay, which is not very time consuming, given Smalltalk-80's rich graphics capabilities. You can even create

```
GTrainPanelDisplay class methodsFor: 'instance creation'!
openOn: aTrain
        "Open a new GTrain simulation display panel with the given train.  Display the control
        panel in a view"

                        "create the top-level window to put the display into"
    topView ← StandardSystemView new.
    topView minimumSize: 667@200.
    topView borderWidth: 2.
    topView label: ' GTrain Display Panel '.

                        "create an instance of GTrainPanelDisplay"
    me ← self new.
    me model: aTrain.


                        "create the subview for the passenger counter display"
    thePassView ← DisplayTextView new.
    thePassView editParagraph: ('0' asParagraph).
    thePassView centered.
    me addSubView: thePassView
            in: (0.25@0.75 extent: 0.05@0.1)
            borderWidth: 1.

                        "create the subview for the passenger weight display"
    theWeightView ← DisplayTextView new editParagraph: '00' asParagraph
    theWeightView centered.
    me addSubView: theWeightView
            in: (0.4@0.75 extent: 0.08@0.1)
            borderWidth: 1.

                        "create the subview for the text speed display"
    theSpeedTView ← DisplayTextView new editParagraph: '00' asParagraph.
    theSpeedTView centered.
    me addSubView: theSpeedTView
            in: (0.58@0.75 extent: 0.08@0.1)
            borderWidth: 1.

                        "create the subview for the speed gauge display"
    speedHolder ← NumberHolder new value: 0.
    theSpeedGView ← CircleMeterView on: speedHolder
            aspect: #value change: #value:
            range: (0 to: 500 by: 50).
    me addSubView: theSpeedGView
            in: (0.67@0.08 extent: 0.3@0.8)
            borderWidth: 0.
                        "create the subview for the position display"
    thePosView ← ArcValueView new: 400@101.
    thePosView model: aTrain.
    me addSubView: thePosView in: (0.05@0.1 extent: 0.6@0.55) borderWidth: 1.

                        "plug the other subviews into the main GTrainDisplay view"
    me passView: thePassView.
    me weightView: theWeightView.
    me speedGView: theSpeedGView.
    me speedTView: theSpeedTView.

    topView addSubView: me in: (0@0 extent: 1@1) borderWidth: 0.

    topView controller open.
```

Figure 13.10 A method that creates the display panel in Figure 13.11*b* needs little more than a page of code.

your own logo for the "G_Train Co. of Palo Alto" with the help of the BitEditor (which you'll see in a moment). Once the display's components are defined, you can write the message that will lay out the display. This is done with a class message called openOn. Including comments, the compound message takes up some 50 lines of code (see Figure 13.10).

The Smalltalk declarations in the figure form a hierarchy; its top view is the system-level window, into which you plug the subviews. The variable me stands for the display at the top level and allows interaction with the system's multiwindow control and screen management objects . Objects within me are instances of the user-created class DisplayTextView. You provide text and a relative subview area—for example, the speed gauge comes from type CircleMeterView of the Pluggable Gauges package with a range of 0 to 500 and a location as defined by the line beginning with "in:".

To display a view, you must implement an update message that is invoked by the system's object dependency mechanism whenever the G-Train model sends itself the message changed (see Figure 13.11a). The attached Aspect symbol permits the view to react differently to changes in passenger count, speed, or location. At this point, the inspector tells us the train has moved to location 6, with five passengers aboard. When the display comes on, we get all the available G-Train information at one glance (see Figure 13.11b).

All seems well with our software, but the train itself has problems. It should have accelerated to about 400 km/h by now, while the speedometer shows a measly 125 km/h. Looks like the vacuum pumps have failed, and the five passengers (including a three-star general and the chairman of the G-Train Company) could be in trouble. The train does not have enough momentum to make it uphill to the other terminal. We'll have to send the little auxiliary Engine that Could after it, but that tops out at 50 km/h, so the passengers are in for a long night. (Fortunately, several copies of this book as well as many chapter references and HOOPLA! issues are aboard.)

While the G-Train project may be in hot water, object-oriented programming has passed the test with flying colors. The complete ParcPlace solution for G-Train's class and method descriptions (including numerous comments) take up less than 500 lines of text. The biggest single chunk goes for the logo—just about a kByte of dull numbers. You may question whether the Smalltalk solution really constitutes CASE. It's computer-aided

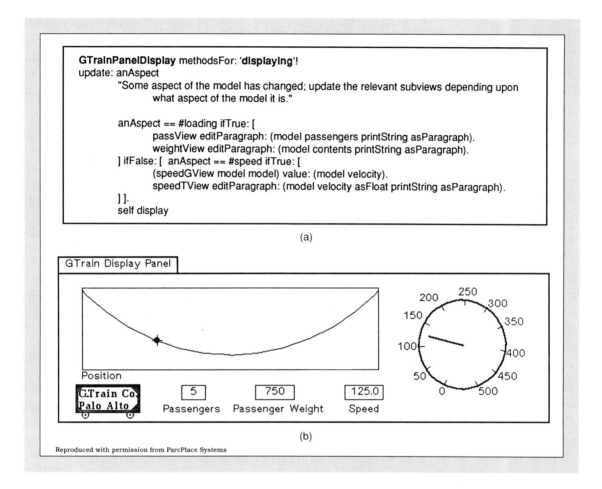

```
GTrainPanelDisplay methodsFor: 'displaying'!
update: anAspect
        "Some aspect of the model has changed; update the relevant subviews depending upon
            what aspect of the model it is."

    anAspect == #loading ifTrue: [
            passView editParagraph: (model passengers printString asParagraph).
            weightView editParagraph: (model contents printString asParagraph).
    ] ifFalse: [  anAspect == #speed ifTrue: [
            (speedGView model model) value: (model velocity).
            speedTView editParagraph: (model velocity asFloat printString asParagraph).
    ]].
    self display
```

(a)

(b)

Reproduced with permission from ParcPlace Systems

all right, but is it software engineering? No doubt object-oriented programming gives us a viable prototyping tool, but when it comes to "production code" for operating a real train system, many engineers will prefer a more conventional language.

Recently, ParcPlace has brought about a meeting of the two worlds with Objectworks for C++, which combines the Smalltalk environment with C++ coding. However, other languages and methodologies can be accommodated as well. Still, a died-in-the-wool train engineer may wish to obtain high-quality code without actual coding. For him, the next tool might just be the coming attraction of his choice.

Figure 13.11 Once we have set up the proper display message (*a*), we can observe the weight, movement, and speed of G-Train on this panel (*b*).

⌐ From Spaceship to G-Train, Courtesy 001

You have certainly heard of 007 (aka James Bond), but who is 001? Wrong question—*what* 001 is can't be explained easily in a few words, except that it's a CASE system from *Hamilton Technologies* (HTI). In fact, 001 might just rank as the oldest comprehensive CASE tool for real-time applications in existence.

To be more exact, we can trace 001's ancestry to the Apollo space program. Back in the 1960s, a project with several million lines of software represented a true challenge. (Today's Shuttle project involves about 40 million lines of code, and in the near future we can expect to see space projects comprising over 100 million lines.) HTI founder Margaret Hamilton started out on the roughly 20,000-line software for the Lunar Excursion Module (LEM)* and wound up managing all the spaceborne software.

Based on a postmortem analysis of her part of the Apollo program, Hamilton and some coworkers developed a system for creating "ultrareliable" software. It evolved into a product known as Use.It from (now defunct) Higher Order Software. It included a specification language called Axes, an Analyzer for it, and a code generator dubbed RAT (Resource Allocation Tool). These tools— although heavily revised—still form the backbone of 001, which can be viewed as a latter-day Use.It.

HTI describes 001 as a combination of object-oriented and functional programming environments that can improve productivity by one to two orders of magnitude, compress development time by between 3:1 and 8:1, and deliver error-free code. And not just because 001 produces the code automatically, but because Axes helps programmers to view systems in a new and very organized way. It makes sure that from the very beginning system definitions exclude ambiguities and that module interfaces can't clash. So let's take a brief look at this miraculous methodology, even though understanding it fully will take some additional study.[7,8]

Up and down the trees.   The 001 system relies on tree structures called maps for system definition and visualization, which poses problems for those used to bubble charts. Like struc-

---

*While Hamilton designed the LEM software, I worked on LEM hardware. But we didn't meet until years after the Eagle had landed.

ture charts, "Rmaps" represent a system's decomposition into smaller objects. "Fmaps" supplement them by defining the relationships of system functions. Take a system called build, which defines the construction of a public library with lots of built-in shelving. In dataflow graphics, build could be represented as the nested chart shown in Figure 13.12a. The ingoing data consist of building-mtl, shelf-mtl, and carpenter. (As we can see in the graph, two carpenters are competing to supply the shelving.) The two outputs are labeled house and shelving.

In 001 terms, the project can be represented as the tree in Figure 13.12b. At the top level, the function is defined by the statement

```
shelving, house = build(shelf-mtl, carpenter,
building-mtl)
```

and the tree junction is identified as "include," which says that the inputs of the parent are farmed out to the children, and the children's outputs are passed back to the parent. The right child turns out to be the leaf on the "house" branch of the tree, identified by the transformation

```
house = build house (building-mtl)
```

The left child (attached to the shelving branch) packs the statement

```
shelving = build shelving (shelf-mtl, carpenter)
```

and the junction is identified as a "join" operation. This operation deviates radically from data flow notation, because sequential events appear side by side. Inputs are passed from the parent to the rightmost child, whose outputs in turn pass to the sibling at the left, and so on until the leftmost child's outputs return to the parent as the parent's outputs.

In the example, the "build shelving" child has two offspring. The one on the right receives the shelf materials and constructs shelf units, which we'll call shelves. The child (actually, grandchild) on the left receives these units and assembles them into finished shelving. The right grandchild is identified by the statement

```
shelves = make shelves (shelf-mtl, carpenter)
```

Its purpose is not so much to make shelves as to demonstrate the third main 001 construct, the OR tree.

As you can see in the figure, both of the great-grandchildren do the same thing. There's only one difference: one branch embodies carpenter Jack, the other carpenter Jill. Of course, further breakdown might reveal that they really aren't that much alike. Jack might make his shelves individually, with hammer and nails, while Jill could run a high-tech shelving factory where robots cut, glue, and paint particle boards. In any case, only one of them will get a chance to contribute to the library.

So how does Figure 13.12*b* combine object-oriented and functional concepts? The functions are easily identified as the verbs behind the equal signs, complete with parameter lists in parantheses. The trees themselves provide the system's control structure. As to the objects, you have not yet seen their repository, the type control map (Tmap), but the expressions we used in the function control map (Fmap) in Figure 13.12*b* are all members of the data classes established in the Tmap. Should you violate the typing, the next run through the Analyzer (which can be used in all design stages) will inform you of your transgressions.

G-Train and all its branches. After this rudimentary introduction, you should be ready to grasp—at least superficially—the 001 view of our much-exercised Gravy Train. The HTI system took about two hours to set up the G-Train model's top tier, and the whole prototype, with its 3500 lines of C code, was completed in less than two weeks—thanks to 001's huge library of real-time modules.

While 001 permits rapid prototyping just like most CASE systems, its goal is to generate "ultrareliable" production code—say, in C. Therefore, design proceeds in a more rigorous manner than the object-oriented school normally observes. This means that actual inputs (e.g., the speed pulse wire) can be connected to the computer on which the model runs and produce the same display as the simulation. This in turn requires that all ambiguities in the spec must be resolved—a chore that can often be handled by "implied requirements," which are based on experience with a similar system.

HTI's designers broke G-Train down into five functional groupings: the three suggested by the spec (Weight, Speed, and

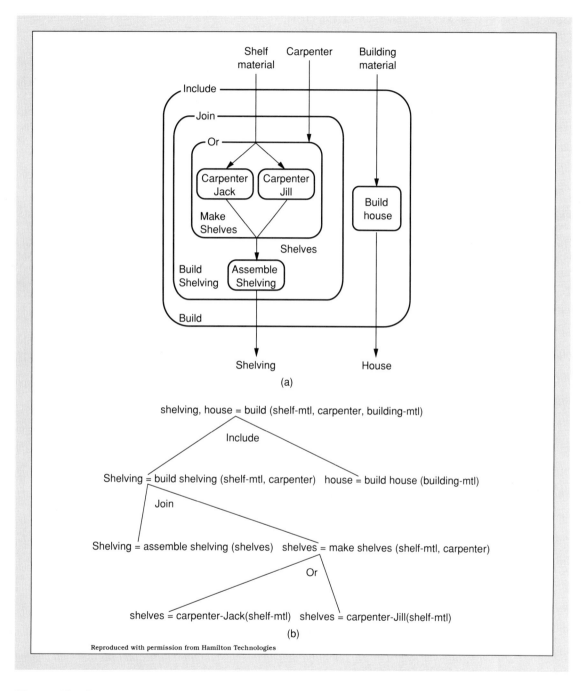

Figure 13.12 HTI converts the traditional data flow paradigm (*a*)— here applied to building a library —into a tree structure (*b*), which can be decomposed further.

Display) plus Asynch_Parent (responsible for asynchronous communications between the subsystems), and Environment, which imposes real-world requirements on the model. Thanks to Asynch_Parent the groups can be developed as independently testable units devoid of interdependencies. Even though the speed and weight calculations can't occur simultaneously, the two subsystems were designed to stand on their own. This approach permits reuse in a future, more complex system—say, one that runs several trains simultaneously.

Figure 13.13 An FMap tree for G-Train's Speed subsystem comprises three levels.

We'll concentrate on the Speed object, because it poses the greatest challenge. The subsystem's Fmap in Figure 13.13 exhibits a number of function types: primitive and nonprimitive leaf-node functions and structuring nodes. The top node,

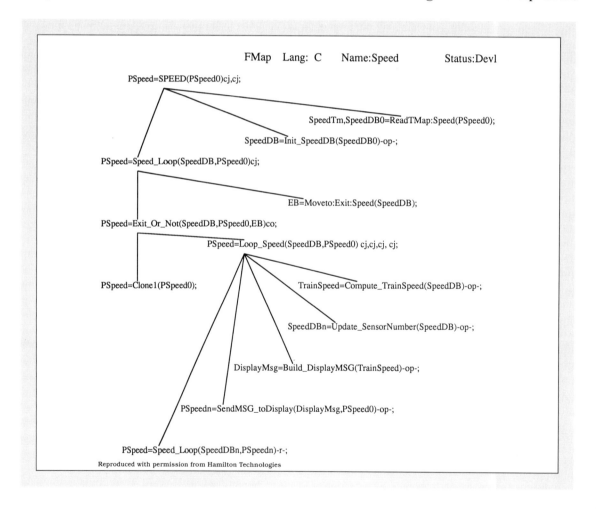

FMap   Lang: C   Name:Speed   Status:Devl

PSpeed=SPEED(PSpeed0)cj,cj;

SpeedTm,SpeedDB0=ReadTMap:Speed(PSpeed0);

SpeedDB=Init_SpeedDB(SpeedDB0)-op-;

PSpeed=Speed_Loop(SpeedDB,PSpeed0)cj;

EB=Moveto:Exit:Speed(SpeedDB);

PSpeed=Exit_Or_Not(SpeedDB,PSpeed0,EB)co;

PSpeed=Loop_Speed(SpeedDB,PSpeed0) cj,cj,cj, cj;

PSpeed=Clone1(PSpeed0);

TrainSpeed=Compute_TrainSpeed(SpeedDB)-op-;

SpeedDBn=Update_SensorNumber(SpeedDB)-op-;

DisplayMsg=Build_DisplayMSG(TrainSpeed)-op-;

PSpeedn=SendMSG_toDisplay(DisplayMsg,PSpeed0)-op-;

PSpeed=Speed_Loop(SpeedDBn,PSpeedn)-r-;

Reproduced with permission from Hamilton Technologies

SPEED(PSpeed0), is the first to become active. Its input is passed down into the top tree structure and returns to the parent when the children's work is done. This input is of type Process—part of the tool suite's library, facilitating communications among processes. Thus, when Asynch_Parent starts up SPEED, the parameter PSpeed0 serves as a communications pipeline.

After initialization in Init_SpeedDB, the Speed_Loop function becomes active. Its child, EB (exit Boolean), determines which branch of the node Exit_Or_Not becomes active next. If the flag is true, Clone1 gets the green light; it sets the output to equal the input (a multiplication with 1) and passes the output to the parent. In that case, great-grandfather SPEED terminates, because Clone1's parent and grandparent both have completed their assignments.

If EB is false, control passes to the node Loop_Speed and we can get some real work done. Four operations are called in sequence, from right to left, followed by Speed_Loop, whose label "-r-" defines it as recursive. It keeps its tree active until the EB object inside the Speed object becomes true. We are especially interested in Update_SensorNumber, because we intend to follow its actions more closely.

Agent 001: licensed to kill bugs.   The root node of the tree in Figure 13.14a is called from Speed only when a speed signal has been received successfully. Put simply, it springs into action when the G-Train has passed a sensor. The function gets SensorNumber from the SpeedDB0 object through its first (rightmost) child, updates the number, and puts it back. The second child checks whether the count has reached 38; if so, *its* children reset the number to 1.

Now let's get acquainted with Figure 13.14a's identical twin, Model/Update_SensorNumber—the subtree's textual form written in the Axes language:

```
SpeedDB=Update_SensorNumber(SpeedDB0)[cj/cj]
    SensorNumber,SpeedDB1=Get:SensorNumber_Speed(SpeedDB0)[p]
    nSensorNumber=Check_For_Reset(SensorNumber)[]
        Reset_orNot=EQ("38",SensorNumber)[p]
    nSensorNumber=Reset_orNot(SensorNumber,ResetOrNot)[p]
        SensorNumber=Add:Rat("1",SensorNumber)[p]
    nSensorNumber=K:Nat("1",SensorNumber)[p]
SpeedDB=Put:SensorNumber:Speed(nSensorNumber,SpeedDB1)[p]
```

Whichever form you have used to pass your design ideas to 001, chances are the description contains some errors. No problem, just envoke the Analyzer tool, and it will tell you within seconds where the bugs are (see Figure 13.14b).

According to that faithful servant, you have committed three syntax errors—not too bad. The first error message pops up when the tool checks the Axes code for tree consistency and completeness. It fails and lists two possibly faulty lines. The empty brackets [] immediately look suspect, and the second error message right below that line confirms your suspicion. It reads "Illegal function form," so you decide that line 3 should end with [j], the identifier for sequential operations starting at the rightmost child.

The last error message below line 6 chides you: "Same data is both input and output." Indeed, the left side of that statement contains a typo—the leading n in nSensorNumber is missing. In Axes, the same variable names can never appear on both sides of the equation. Confident that you're now in the clear, you run the fixed code through the Analyzer once more. Alas, it now informs you that the code still contains a syntax error plus one in a new category—"Data Flow."

Below line 3 the message "Offspring not communicating" divulges that your choice of functions did not pan out. You need a "cojoin" here, which permits variables to be passed down from the parent as well as transmitted from the right-hand sibling. Furthermore, you realize that [p] in line 5 defines a "primitive" structure, when in fact you wanted to specify an "or." That's easily taken care of by changing the marker to [o].

During the next analysis, another disappointment awaits. This run (which digs a level deeper and takes over two minutes) calmly proclaims "4 interface errors". Actually, a total of seven error message lines looks rather intimidating at first glance. But what the complaints all boil down to is a type clash between the "Nat" (natural number) and "Rat" (rational number) declarations. The system does not know which is wrong, so it tags all affected variables. You realize right away that the sensor number must be of type Nat—a thoughtless mistake that could prove calamitous in actual operation, were it not for 001's watchful eye.

Thanks to 001's nitpicking you can now convert the corrected package Update_SensorNumber in Figure 13.14c to source code, without having to worry about interface clashes. In fact, the next Analyzer run passes the code on to the Resource Allocation Tool, which generates C code. For this module, the

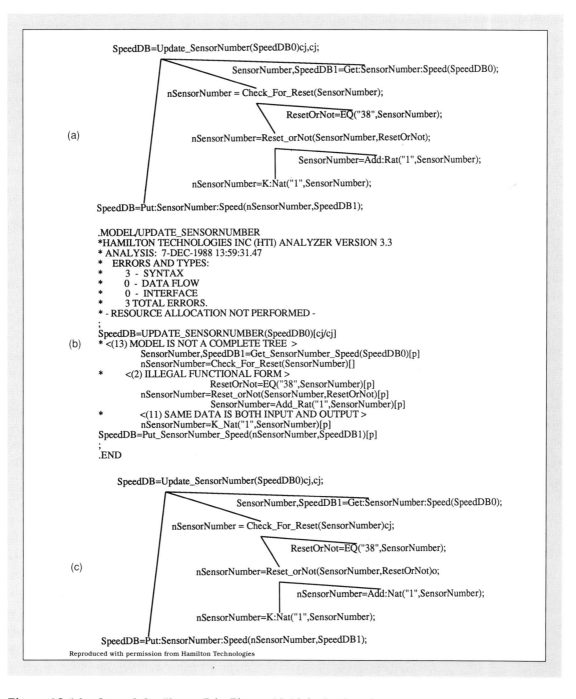

```
              SpeedDB=Update_SensorNumber(SpeedDB0)cj,cj;

                          SensorNumber,SpeedDB1=Get:SensorNumber:Speed(SpeedDB0);

                nSensorNumber = Check_For_Reset(SensorNumber);

                          ResetOrNot=EQ("38",SensorNumber);
(a)
                nSensorNumber=Reset_orNot(SensorNumber,ResetOrNot);

                              SensorNumber=Add:Rat("1",SensorNumber);

                nSensorNumber=K:Nat("1",SensorNumber);

       SpeedDB=Put:SensorNumber:Speed(nSensorNumber,SpeedDB1);


       .MODEL/UPDATE_SENSORNUMBER
       *HAMILTON TECHNOLOGIES INC (HTI) ANALYZER VERSION 3.3
       * ANALYSIS:  7-DEC-1988 13:59:31.47
       *   ERRORS AND TYPES:
       *      3 - SYNTAX
       *      0 - DATA FLOW
       *      0 - INTERFACE
       *      3 TOTAL ERRORS.
       * - RESOURCE ALLOCATION NOT PERFORMED -
       ;
       SpeedDB=UPDATE_SENSORNUMBER(SpeedDB0)[cj/cj]
(b)    * <(13) MODEL IS NOT A COMPLETE TREE >
               SensorNumber,SpeedDB1=Get_SensorNumber_Speed(SpeedDB0)[p]
               nSensorNumber=Check_For_Reset(SensorNumber)[]
       *    <(2) ILLEGAL FUNCTIONAL FORM >
                   ResetOrNot=EQ("38",SensorNumber)[p]
               nSensorNumber=Reset_orNot(SensorNumber,ResetOrNot)[p]
                   SensorNumber=Add_Rat("1",SensorNumber)[p]
       *    <(11) SAME DATA IS BOTH INPUT AND OUTPUT >
               nSensorNumber=K_Nat("1",SensorNumber)[p]
       SpeedDB=Put_SensorNumber_Speed(nSensorNumber,SpeedDB1)[p]
       ;
       .END


              SpeedDB=Update_SensorNumber(SpeedDB0)cj,cj;

                          SensorNumber,SpeedDB1=Get:SensorNumber:Speed(SpeedDB0);

                nSensorNumber = Check_For_Reset(SensorNumber)cj;

                          ResetOrNot=EQ("38",SensorNumber);
(c)
                nSensorNumber=Reset_orNot(SensorNumber,ResetOrNot)o;

                              nSensorNumber=Add:Nat("1",SensorNumber);

                nSensorNumber=K:Nat("1",SensorNumber);

       SpeedDB=Put:SensorNumber:Speed(nSensorNumber,SpeedDB1);
```

Figure 13.14 One of the "leaves" in Figure 13.13 is further decomposed (*a*), then analyzed (*b*), and finally corrected (*c*). Automatic code generation by the RAT tool can follow next.

code begins with a number of "include" statements (calling up a bevy of library functions), followed by declarations of variable and constant types. It concludes with a few lines of executable code—an IF construct with half a dozen function calls corresponding to those in the Fmap:

```
Get_SensorNumber_Speed(V_SpeedDB0.V_SensorNumber,
                                          V_SpeedDB1)
EQ_Nat(C6,V_SensorNumber,V_ResetOrNot)
    if (V_ResetOrNot<1)
        {   /*Begin FALSE and REJECT branch*/
            Add_Nat(C8,V_SensorNumber,V_nSensorNumber)
        }
    else
        {  /*Begin TRUE branch*/
        K_Nat(C9,V_nSensorNumber)
        } /*End IF */
Put_SensorNumber_Speed(V_SensorNumber,V_SpeedDB1,
                                          V_SpeedDB)
```

The work on Update_SensorNumber, which we just reviewed, took less than an hour at the terminal. But such a small program is not an adequate yardstick. Fortunately, HTI has implemented the whole G-Train example, an effort that provides not only the display of Figure 13.15, but also some hard numbers on potential cost savings with the 001 system. The project amounted to about 900 lines of Axes code, which—thanks to the system's library—converts into nearly 3500 lines of C code, or a 13-K chunk of object code.

What effort did it take? The bottom line comes to 120 hours, or roughly 30 lines of C code per staff hour. The best values in Figure 4.1 for C amounted to 10 lines per hour, but 3 to 5 lines per hour are more realistic. Judging by some of the aerospace and Ada projects surveyed, high-quality code still consumes at least an hour per line. If the HTI code indeed proves ultrareliable, 001 could boost productivity as much as 20- to 50-fold. Who says software will always be expensive? It's good to know that there's still hope.

This chapter also taught us something else: object-oriented programming is more a frame of mind than a methodology or even a paradigm. As to languages, we have encountered the whole spectrum from declarative Smalltalk to full-bodied Ada to lean

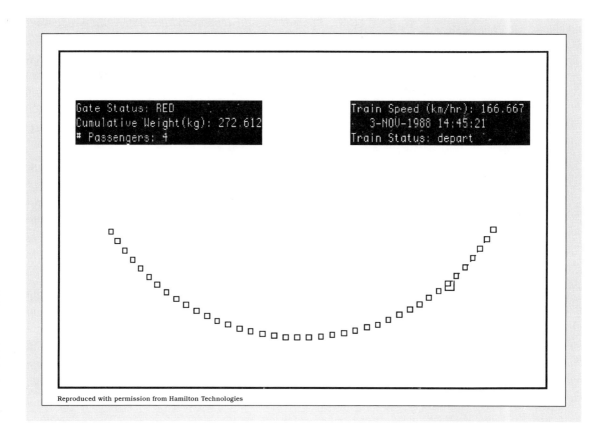

Reproduced with permission from Hamilton Technologies

(and, at times, mean) C. Of course, we can never rule out the possibility that object orientation lies not only in the eye of the beholder, but also in the pen of the public relations mastermind.

Figure 13.15 Simulation of the complete system uses the identical code as a real G-Train monitor.

⸬ References

1. Special Issue on Object-oriented Programming, *Byte*, August 1986.

2. Sally Shlaer and Stephen Mellor, *Object-oriented System Analysis*, Yourdon Press, Englewood Cliffs, NJ, 1988.

3. *HOOPLA!* (Hooray for Object Oriented Programming Languages) Quarterly, OOPSTAD, P.O. Box 1565, Everett, WA 98205.

4. Grady Booch, *Software Engineering with Ada*, Benjamin Cummings Publishing, Menlo Park, CA, 1983, p. 39.

5. R. J. A. Buhr, *System Design with Ada*, Prentice-Hall, Englewood Cliffs, NJ, 1984.

6. Anthony Wasserman, et al., "An object-oriented structured design method for code generation," *ACM Software Engineering Notes*, January 1989, p. 32.

7. M. Hamilton and S. Zeldin, "Higher order software—a methodology for defining software," *IEEE Transactions on Software Engineering*, March 1976, p. 25.

8. M. Hamilton, "Zero-defect software: the elusive goal," *IEEE Spectrum*, March 1986, p. 48.

14

SOFTWARE
MATH GAINS
A TOEHOLD

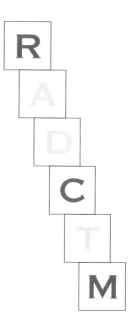

Software math vs Practice
Refresher on Logic 101
An abstract train Refined
Approximations pose problems

So far we have explored CASE tools that keep abstraction at a modest level, matched to the shortcomings of the human intellect. Although we've run into formal logic a few times, it has remained on the sidelines—even in the axiom-based HTI system, discussed in the preceding chapter. Now the time has come to give the left hemisphere of your brain its due by examining a foray of formal, mathematical programming into the commercial world. But first let's examine the roots of public skepticism for ivory tower solutions.

Throughout history, technology advances have tended to originate with practicioners, driven by specific needs. Often it has taken scholars decades (even centuries) to fit such advances into their prevailing models of the world. Even today, when news spreads instantly and universities work closely with industry, the lag persists. Just look at a recent example—the discovery of "high-temperature" superconductors. Once more, experiments have thrown science into disarray.

Scientific concepts have traditionally sprung from the *Gedankenexperiment*—a purely mental exercise, to wit Newton's abstract apple or Einstein's phantom trolley (which he imagined to zip along near the speed of light). Where does software fit into this scheme of things? Some vital contributions (Fortran, Unix, and spreadsheets, to name a few) stem from practitioners, while others (say, Pascal, expert systems, and X-Windows) were born on academic turf.

Many implicate software's uniqueness as the cause of this particular art's academic roots. Some insist that of all products made by man only software is expected to be perfect. Others consider software unique among human artifacts because it consumes no natural resources. But neither do novels or symphonies and, consequently, computer software finds itself legally lumped together with these earlier fruits of human creativity under copyright law. (Only recently has software gained a toehold on patent protection.)

The real reason why software evolved in parallel on both academic and industrial turf lies in the evolution of the hardware on which it is meant to play. The first modern computers were built at universities because in times of war industry tends to be preoccupied with more pressing demands. The purpose of these aboriginal computers (mostly funded by the military) was quite simply to compute things. So they naturally landed in the lap of mathematics departments. At the time few sponsors were concerned that the machines might be subverted there to solve, say, Fermat's Last Theorem or prove Goldbach's Conjecture.*

While fickle history can safely be blamed for some of software's schizophrenic evolution, we must also remember something else. Over nearly half a century, software progress has emerged both from purely intellectual pursuits and from the need to perform useful chores. (Let us quickly define "useful" as that for which outsiders are eager to trade more than a loaf of bread

---

*Pierre de Fermat asserted in 1631 that no integer solution exists for the equation $x^n + y^n = z^n$ when n is larger than 2. Up to powers of 150,000 at least, Fermat has been proven right. About a century (111 years, to be exact) later, the Russian bureaucrat Christian Goldbach proposed that all even numbers are the sum of two primes. Mathematicians have tested the conjecture up to 100 million, but so far have not been able to prove it right or wrong. Mankind awaits the resolution with baited breath.

and a jug of wine.) So far, we have dealt with software topics of immediate and practical concern—too mundane to whet researchers' appetites. But to understand where software is coming from and where it is really headed, we must peek into university laboratories as well.

Continuing tug of war.   Two academic forces vie for control of software's future: mathematics and artificial intelligence. The former (holding the advantages of incumbency) tends to claim software as its very own preserve with pronouncements like "software is so closely related to mathematics as to be indistinguishable."[1] Such claims have brought forth shouts of "academic arrogance" from practitioners and "one-track thinking" from other academics.

Whatever the merits of formal program derivation, they apparently remain unappreciated by most practitioners—in spite of the fact that by now the majority of them has been properly anointed with *predicate* calculus in school. Take the case of debugging parallel programs (to be aired further in Chapter 19), where normal bugs can be as elusive as viruses. At a recent conference, somebody suggested to use correctness proofs. The speaker—a reputable computer scientist—countered: "Our programs are longer than 10 lines."*

Artificial intelligence takes a sometimes diametrically opposite stance from *computer science*. It emphasizes intuition and the user interface, often at the expense of mathematical rigor. True to its psychological roots, AI remains focused on "cognition"—the process of understanding or learning. Preoccupied with the human side of the interface, AI often forgets the machine side. After all, we really just want the computer to *understand* us, not to imitate us.

Yet, in spite of its almost populist slant, AI finds the sortie from academe almost as arduous as does math. Even staunch supporters of AI in the defense establishment have started grumbling about "getting AI down to earth." Still, leaving untapped the huge reservoir of research data accumulated by both AI and math researchers would be foolhardy, to say the least.

---

*To be fair, automated theorem provers can tackle fairly complex relations, provided they can be expressed in binary (true/false) logic. A whole microprocessor called Viper was designed that way at the Royal Signals and Radar Establishment in England, and even a full Ada compiler has been taken on in Europe.

Figure 14.1 The marriage of math and AI has borne fruit at several levels. One offspring, Refine, can serve to implement our G-Train.

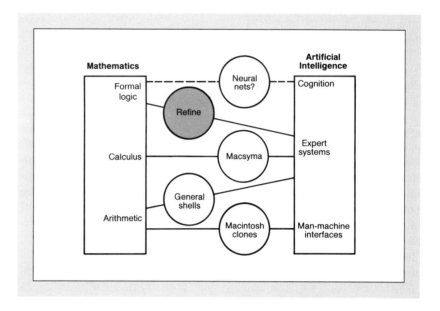

Industry, being more interested in practical results than issues of faith, can be persuaded to incorporate any useful technique in its software tool kits, even if it takes some time (see Figure 14.1). Take Macsyma, a well-established expert system developed at MIT that combines aspects of math and AI. It is capable of solving rather hairy equations symbolically. With Macsyma's help, scientists and engineers have been able to sever their ties to readily available "cookbook" solutions.

Another liaison between the two disciplines may soon bring similar advances to the software designer. Combine a software generator, based on formal logic and its provably correct transformations, with an expert system, and you get Refine from **Reasoning Systems**. You will soon see how it tackles our old friend, the G-Train simulator.

⌐ Refresher Course in Logic

Before we can take on Refine, we must examine the notion of provably correct software, as promised by software calculus. Basically, the idea is to expand the concepts of theorem proving to encompass all software—and even hardware. You define your requirements in strict mathematical form and, from there, move toward executable code in a series of refinement steps. Ideally, the requirements themselves should be executable, even though they lack algorithmic information. In other words, you should only have to specify *what* you want done, not *how* the computer should do it.

The primary tool in this pursuit is nothing new—Boolean logic has been around for a century (with little to show for it). Fortunately, a very readable book, *The Science of Programming*,[2] stands ready to guide you, albeit slowly, through this esoteric terrain (it takes 288 pages to get to the first piece of code). Because the concepts are important for a discussion of Refine, we have to find a faster approach. Rather than try to describe correctness proofs in abstract terms, let us examine a simple case. It was provided by C. A. R. (Tony) Hoare, perhaps the dominant figure in software math, toiling at England's Oxford University.[3]

Assume you need a program that finds the greatest common divisor, z, of two positive integers, x and y. You postulate:

1. z divides x
2. z divides y
3. z is the greatest number that satisfies 1 and 2.

Because you start from scratch, you must also define what "p divides q" means, namely:

4. There exists a positive integer w, such that $p \cdot w = z$

Furthermore, you have to define that

5. "z is the greatest integer" means the following: in the set S of divisors no other member is strictly greater.

These definitions would normally be written in a symbolic notation that generalizes normal arithmetic. The Boolean AND (or conjunction) would tie steps 1 and 2 together. Furthermore, you would generalize by saying "for all x . . .", which is written as $\forall x$ "there exists a z . . ." (the existential quantification, a generalized OR) written as $\exists z$. As you proceed with your conversion of the requirement into code, you develop correctness proofs at every step.

Haste makes waste.   Once you're sure that the requirement is correct you could in theory turn it over to a computer with the request to convert it into code. An algorithm that can randomly generate all provable mathematical theorems would take some time to do that—in Hoare's words "longer than it takes the whole universe to decay into photons." But don't despair. Just recast the requirements into a notation that is less "powerful" than universal mathematics. An idealized logic program provides such a vehicle, and all you need to express the problem are built-in predicates such as "isproduct" or "isgreater":

6. isdivisor (x, z) if there exists a w no greater than x such that isproduct (z, w, x).
7. iscommondiv (x, y, z) if isdivisor (x, z) AND isdivisor (y, z).
8. isGCD(x, y, z) if iscommondiv (x, y, z) AND NOT (iscommondiv (x, y, w) AND isgreater (w, z)); where GCD is the greatest common divisor.

We could perhaps attempt to execute the new definition with a Prolog-like system, but there is no guarantee that it will ever terminate. So, the new form must be restricted further, possibly by avoiding both disjunction (OR) and negation (NOT), which brings us to the style of algebra:

9. $x = $ GCD(x,x) for all x.
10. GCD$(x,y) = $ GCD$(x + y,y)$ for all x,y.
11. GCD$(x,y) = $ GCD(y,x) for all x,y.

These laws have been derived from steps 6 to 8 by algebraic reasoning, but Hoare points out that such a form may not preserve the clause structure of the original requirement. Therefore, both forms must be retained, and execution on a Super-Cray will be complete "when the whole universe reaches a uniform temperature of about 4 degrees K," according to Hoare. (Remember, he is formal logic's advocate, not its prosecutor.)

Conversion into a functional program (a concept devised by Fortran designer John Backus) comes to the rescue:

12. GCD$(x,y) = x$ if $x = y$.
13. GCD$(x,y) = $ GCD$(x - y,y)$ if $x > y$.
14. GCD$(x,y) = $ GCD(y,x) if $x < y$.

These equations permit the computer to work with specific values, for example by reducing GCD$(8,6)$ step by step to the form GCD$(2,2)$, which according to step 12 is 2. Now for the good news: with this transformation, execution has been speeded up dramatically—to a mere million years on a supercomputer with an integer range of 10^{20}.

Enter elegance.   At this point, brute computer force concedes to human ingenuity. Hoare proposes to rewrite the laws in such a way that the computer only has to deal with multiplication or division by 2, which amounts to a shift left or right and takes but a single clock tick. To become really efficient, the GCD program must also do away with conjunction—which lands us in a purely sequential, procedural program, written in Pascal or Fortran. Because such a program's structure differs radically from that of Hoare's original specification, each design step must be verified by a correctness proof.

It seems we are back where we started. Luckily the mathematicians offer a way out: you apply assertions about the program behavior before and after each transformation step, called precondition and postcondition. The precondition for GCD is that both x and y are greater than zero; the postcondition is

15. $Z = \text{GCD}(x,y)$

where Z is an intermediate value returned from a GCD subroutine. All that remains to be done is to find efficient intermediate steps and assertions that are provably correct. We can, for example, convert the search to a base-2 approach that suits digital computers especially well. Step 15 then becomes

16. $2^N Z = \text{GCD}(x, y)$

and we can write a DO loop that reduces N by 1 while doubling Z each time. This works for even numbers, but we still must find solutions for even-odd and odd-odd pairs of x, y. So we are back in the algorithm design business.

You will not be alone if you ask: "Was this (already greatly condensed) trip really necessary?" In fact, discussions on that point continue in the pages of *Computer* to this day.[4] Mark Weiser, a Xerox researcher in Palo Alto, comments: "We may never find what we seek of our programs if we look only at what can be formally specified." Professor David Parnas of Queens University in Kingston, Ontario (credited with the concept of information hiding) points to an even more acute problem—the use of discontinuous functions. (We'll return to that issue at the end of this chapter.)

Computer science majors who tend to shed their formal logic shortly after graduation day, however, have even better reasons for doing so. The software mathematicians lay claim to two benefits of their approach: (1) the code will be free of errors, and (2) the system is completely specified from the very beginning.[5] But our graduate soon finds out that the customer always starts out with a requirements specification that

(1) violates several laws of physics.
(2) asks for twice the achievable bang per buck.

Let's assume that after a week of exhausting negotiations the project leader succeeds in eliminating the obstacles of the first type and in whittling down the second kind to livable proportions. In the world according to software science, the negotiators should now rewrite the formal spec and sign it, never to argue about it again. In the real world, 't ain't necessarily so, and not just because of "requirements creep."

Why does this contrast between theory and practice persist? Simple economics. Newton, for example, had every reason to gloat over the fact that billions and billions of stars (and planets) would obey the same law as his apple. What if he had been wrong? The stars would not have changed their course, and the worst consequence would have been an abstract bump on the head.

A practitioner must be more cautious. Mindful of the admonition that "a haughty spirit goeth before the fall," we begin our exploits on *terra cognita*—with something that we know to work. Then we feel our way into the unknown, fully expecting some "law of nature" to fail us eventually. Otherwise, if we just went ahead with a Star Wars stage set and were proven wrong, the fauna of at least one minor planet could come to serious grief.

But even a more elementary force stands in the way of the mathematical approach to programming. It has also stood in the way of visionaries from Moses to Marx—human nature. People simply don't think the way software mathematicians think. To start with the most general abstraction of a problem and then constrain it until we get to the problem we really want to solve is inefficient. The human mind is much better suited to generalize from one specific case to the more general one than to "take it from the top." In fact, the ability to generalize has often been identified as the essence of human intelligence.

This test tells all.   A short example—common for IQ or aptitude testing—demonstrates the fact. Look at the series

$$1 \quad 4 \quad 9 \quad 16$$

and chances are you recognize the squares of the first four natural numbers. But the sequence could also be an addition of primes:

$$1 \quad +3 \quad +5 \quad +7$$

Generalization misfires here because of inadequate data. So let us add a second series:

$$1 \quad 4 \quad 9 \quad 16$$
$$9 \quad 16 \quad 25 \quad 36$$

Clearly, what we now have are two sets of squares of increasing integers:

$$\{N^2\} \text{ where } N = i \mathinner{.\,.} i + 3$$

first for $i = 1$ and then for $i = 3$.

So, if we accept the facts of life we reach this inescapable conclusion: to draw nonmathematicians into the correctness-proof business we must find a shortcut in the specification language— one that propels the solution a bit below the million-year level.[6]

⤷ How to Refine an Abstract Train

To prove that's possible we can turn to Refine and see how it combines math with reality. The tie that binds is AI, what else? While Refine implements stepwise refinement,[7] it does not start out with the quaint typography of the logician, as friend Hacker did in Chapter 5. Rather, the customer signs off on a specification that is cast in the language of the pertinent domain. For example, a communications system for G-Train might start this way:

```
the-comm-system G-TRAIN-COMM
    with-message-type              English-text
    with-system-bandwidth          4800 baud
    with-probability-of-error      0.00001
    with-channel-bandwidth         9600 baud
    with channel-characteristics   conditioned-line
    with-security-level            proprietary
```

When Refine parses this statement, it creates an object of class `communication-system` named `G-TRAIN-COMM` with the attributes listed in the spec. Refine is an expert system whose knowledge base already contains a great deal of engineering prowess about the domain of communications. For example, it knows that a transmitter protocol is only correct under the following conditions:

1. All its encoders and decoders are correct.
2. Their input and output data types match.
3. The ouput type matches that of the channel.
4. Noise immunization can't precede data encryption.

These conditions can be represented in the following Refine assertion:

```
Correct(protocol) <=>
    Empty(incorrect-coders(protocol))
    AND Empty(non-linking-coders(protocol))
    AND Coder-to-channel-match(protocol)
    AND Empty(noise-before-secrecy(protocol))
```

where, for example,

```
Coder-to-channel-match(protocol)
        = data-type-of(channel-of(protocol))
```

Assertions serve not only to impose design limits (or, if you prefer, constraints), but also to enforce consistency for version control. When all the specification detail is in place, refinement can begin. For this step, design details must be entered (e.g., that the system includes a receiver, a channel, and a transmitter). At the next refinement step, more detail is added (see Figure 14.2). To refine the task from one step to the next, Refine's expert system uses transformation rules from its knowledge base. Such rules are written in the form

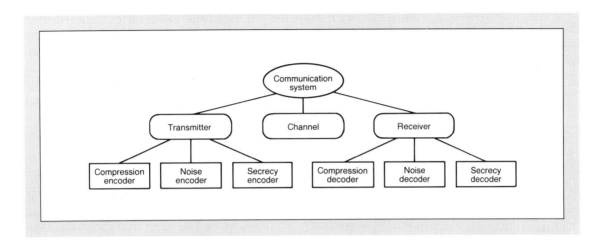

precondition -> postcondition

for example, "If the messages are English-text, then the protocol performs compression encoding." To put it more formally:

```
TRANS = 'the transmitter @_
        with-input-data-type @i-d-t'
        AND embedded-in(TRANS) = 'comm-system @_
->
compression-encoder(TRANS) =
    'compression-encoder @newsymbol("compressor")
     with-optimality 0.9
     with-compression-factor 1.3
     with-input-data-type @i-d-t
     with-output-data-type sequ(bit)'
```

Figure 14.2 An expert system like Refine needs domain-specific knowledge bases with engineering information at several levels—here for a communications systems.

In this rule, patterns are enclosed in single quotes; "@" marks a variable; and "_" identifies variables whose value is of no interest. (You'll recall from Chapter 12 that a pattern is a string that must be matched in the system's inference engine.) Repeated application of such transformation rules converts the original specification, step by step, into the working code of the communications system. Throughout the refinement, requirements of the original spec are transformed into constraints for the individual system components.

Transformation rules can also express **heuristics** that deal with problems beyond the reach of computation—say, system simulation with Petri nets or real-time behavior of a distributed system. In addition, the rule mechanism serves to automatically generate tests or even documentation. Whenever a new component joins the system, for example, transformation can create an entry in the project's documentation tree giving technical details, time of creation, and so forth. Once all subcomponents have been defined, the system cranks out Lisp code as the implementation language.

More training troubles.   Tackling the G-Train problem, however, poses additional difficulties. As a real-time system, it imposes on the theorem prover a new demand: to preserve the temporal sequence of events. The bad news is that for such tasks Refine does not yet encompass all the mechanisms we used in the communications example. The good news is that a prototype for real-time Refine exists, with whose help we can outline the Refine implementation of G-Train. For the time being, a parallel variant of Lisp must be used as the procedural code; Ada generators, however, will be phased in.

As in most other solutions, G-Train is broken down into the subsystems Speed, Weight, and Display. An operation Init sets appropriate parameters to zero; Weigh accepts a three-digit increment for total passenger weight (in kg), and Ts accepts a three-digit integer for train speed (in km/h); Depart halts the weighing; Green and Red control the corresponding lights; and Pulse receives the timing information. Pulse is a Boolean whose "moments of truth" are detected by a scheduler so it can start the speed computation.

Assumptions that must be satisfied will in the following be labelled **Assume**. Transformations that specify a module's behavior are identified by **Transform** and are supported by definitions. (The symbol --> marks the transform operator.) "Atomic" transitions from one state to the next ensure that their postconditions are true in the next state. The situation predicates Green and Red are determined by state properties rather than state transitions. We can now start to write the formal requirements:

```
Require      Always (Green or Red)
Variable     PCount:Integer=0 -- number boarded
Transform I  -->
             Display.Init and Green and PCount=0
```

Next we tackle the weighing task, which involves state changes and, consequently, temporal notions. Loosely defined, the variable Now, for example (used in Transforms 3 and 5), has a value that lies within the time limits of the current state. Numerical evaluation is indicated by [..], and for typographical reasons, we will use the Pascal-style assignment operator. A rule reading

```
A -->(B and c:=e)
```

is understood to correspond to

```
Forall(x)(A and x=e --> B and c=x)
```

where x is set to the value of e in the current state and c is set to x in the next state.

Transform 2   Weighing and Green and Weight.Weigh>0
         -->
         Display.Wt(Weight.Weigh) and
         [PCount := PCount+1] and Red

Transform 3   Weighing and (Red since(Now-10sec))-->Green

To complete the weighing function we need one more rule:

Assume 1 kg = 2.205 lb.

The next requirement defines G-Train's behavior during the interval from Depart to Initial. During this period, the sensor pulses must be evaluated with the help of a transformation that detects even-numbered pulses from Speed shortly after an odd-numbered pulse has arrived. By assuming a minimum train speed of 1 km/h we can minimize counting errors due to stray pulses, because then no two pulses, closer together than 2500 ms, can belong to the same pulse pair.

Transform 4   Depart --> Red
Transform 5   Forall(Delay:Time)
    (Traveling and second-pulse and
    Delay=Now-(Now of last time when Speed.Pulse)
    -->
    Display.Ts(2500/Delay))

The G-Train system is now almost completely specified. We just have to add the formal definitions for Weighing and Traveling:

Definition   Traveling is true iff
        PCount = 100 or not (Initial since
                (Now of last time when Depart)) is true

Definition   Weighing is true iff
        PCount < 100 and not (Depart since
                (Now of last time when Initial)) is true

Some transformations use time-dependent postconditions that specify a time interval, which we define as lasting from Now-mindur to Now+maxdur. We also assumed that events such as Speed.Pulse would always be captured by a transformation that is awaiting them. To be quite technical, Speed.Pulse is declared as an asynchronous-transient broadcast; or, in the vernacular, if the support system missed the pulse, it's gone forever.

No train runs without hardware.   To see if our specification works, we must embed it in an environment that roughly simulates the hardware. And, to be executable, such an environment (indeed all of the G-Train model) must be converted into procedural form, from which object code can be compiled. To establish equivalence between declarative and procedural form (identified by [..]), we must add some more constructs to our knowledge base. For example, in

[x := y] and [y := x]

the and indicates that both operations—let's call them P and Q— should be executed in parallel. We leave it up to Refine to figure out exactly how to swap x and y. In general, such a parallel operation can be written in the form

[P||Q]

For a serial operation, we would write

[P;Q]

where ";" has the same sequential meaning as in Pascal, and implies a state change.

We also need means to specify guarded alternate selection constructs, corresponding to the `select` feature in Ada. The operation

```
[G?C]
```

means "wait for the guard G to be true before executing C," or more formally

```
if G then C else [pause;[G?C]]
```

which uses the serial operator in a recursive definition. In addition, we will need

```
[G!C]
```

which says (in sloppy English notation) "make the guard true if you can, then do C." Finally, you'll encounter

```
[A|B]
```

which is defined as

```
if ready(A) then [if ready(B) then A or B
                                else A]
            elsif ready(B) then B
            else [pause; [A|B]]
```

You can work the English translation for this one out as an exercise. If you don't need a pencil, you graduate.

The procedural specification for the environment in which to run G-Train only takes about 10 lines to define in this very-high-level lingo (see Figure 14.3a). G-Train itself (in Figure 14.3b) takes about twice as much (which still represents a concentrate compared with forms we encountered in previous solutions). To simulate the system, Refine will automatically "add water" by translation into executable Lisp or, sometime soon, into Ada.

So, has Refine fulfilled the ambitions of software mathematicians? Only to a limited extent and at a high cost in terms of generality. The main obstacle remains a formal problem definition language. Mathematical symbols don't play well with the cus-

```
Environ::
[Initial ? Display.Init;
   Passenger:: [[Green ? Weight.Weigh(selectarb[lowt..hiwt lb]);
                      [Red ? Passenger]]
                 ! [Depart v PCount=100 ?
                    For i=1 to 38 do
                          [Delay(selectarb[hiavg..lowavg ms]);
                           Speed.Pulse;
                           Delay(selectarb[hidel..lodel ms]);
                           Speed.Pulse];
                      Delay(selectarb[hiavg..lowavg]);
                 ]; Environ]
```

(a)

```
G-Train::
Let PCount: Variable(Integer) = 0
in
[Initial ? Display.Init; Green:=true; Red:=false;
   Weigh-Loop:: Exists(w:lb,start:Time)            -- {Note 1}
      [Weight.Wt>0 ? w=Weight.Wt ∧ start=Now
          ∧ Red:=true ∧ Green:=false] !
                 Display.Weigh(w);
          [[Delay-until(10 sec after start) ? Green:=true
                   ∧ Red:=false; Weigh-Loop]
           ! [Depart v PCount=100 ? Red:=true ∧ Green:=false]];

   Speed-loop:: Exists(start:Time, stop:Time)
       [[Initial ? Display.Init; Green:=true; Red:=false;
                   Pcount := 0]
        ! [[Speed.Pulse ? start=Now] ! Delay-until(Now+4ms);
          [[Speed.Pulse ? stop=Now] !              -- {Note 2}
             (Display.Ts(2500.0/[stop-start])]
           ! Delay(1 sec) ? skip]; Speed-Loop]      -- {Note 3}
       ]
   ]

         -- Note 1: Weight and start time defined by Environ
         -- Note 2: Await the second pulse and display speed
         -- Note 3: Time-out if pulse is lost
```

(b)

Figure 14.3 The Refine solution for G-Train is written in a "broad-spectrum" language. It comprises an environment (*a*) and the executable specification (*b*).

tomers, and English still won't play on computers. Until somebody invents APE (Abstract Pidgin English), Reasoning Systems has to develop a new specification language for each narrow application domain and make sure that every step of its translation into internal Refine representation is indeed provably correct and unambiguous.

Worse yet, a design knowledge base must be compiled for each domain, and the Refine implementors have to understand these design rules sufficiently to translate them into correct assertions. But the system does permit you to make changes at the specification level, and re-refine down to executable code automatically. Therefore, we can conclude that Refine probably comes as close to the undreamable dream as any Shining Knight of type C3P0 (from that Star Wars set, remember?) can.

⯀ Real-life Modeling Poses Tough Challenges

What we didn't ask Refine to do, however, fills a huge solution space compared with what we did ask for. In real engineering applications, it's rarely possible to plug some simple equations into a computer. Usually approximations are needed, which are valid only in a limited range. For example, you can construct an approximate ellipse with a compass if you use three radii: one each for the smallest and the largest curvature and an intermediate one that connects the others smoothly.

That's a very simple case of what Parnas alluded to: "The actual mathematical functions corresponding to pieces of software are simply noncontinuous. And yet, in all the work on proving programs correct, people do manipulations that assume continuity in the arithmetic. A program proven correct using that kind of verification may very well fail." Indeed, we can be fairly sure that it will fail.

Let's examine a real engineering problem taken from the design of traveling-wave tubes (TWTs, to save space). In such a device, a magnetically focused electron beam interacts with an electromagnetic wave traveling along a helix that surrounds the beam (see Figure 14.4). Unlike any other microwave device, a TWT can amplify continuous microwave signals several octaves

Figure 14.4 In a traveling-wave tube, an electron beam (focused by magnets) interacts with the microwave signal traveling along a helix and magnifies it.

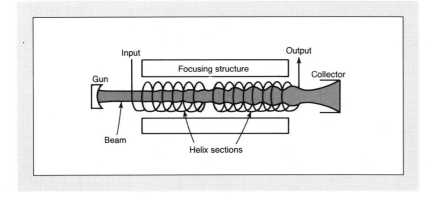

wide (say, 4 to 40 GHz) to levels of 100W or more, approaching a conversion efficiency of 50%. Current solid-state devices can't touch bandwidth or efficiency for a simple reason: electrons travel through a vacuum more easily than through a sliver of silicon or even GaAs.

Such an intricate device can only be designed properly with the help of several computer programs, typically encompassing 10,000 to 100,000 lines of Fortran apiece. A TWT is tough to model although the interaction between the traveling wave and an electron plasma is fairly easily defined by field equations. However, as the electrons bunch together under the influence of both the focusing and microwave fields, an exact mathematical model becomes quite intractable. Approximations must be used that break the beam down into short concentric cylindrical wedges.

When approximated by current filaments, the wedges interact with the fields and with each other. The whole "pudding" of approximations works within narrow but adequate ranges, as proven by comparisons between calculated and measured results. With a price tag of at least $10,000 attached to each device, validation tests must obviously be kept to a minimum or you're out of the TWT business.

If any latent bug surfaces in these design programs, the impact can be devastating. Fortunately, getting 10,000 lines of Fortran reasonably error-free does not pose an insurmountable problem for conventional testing. Proving it correct for each range of constraints, however, seems hopeless. Worse yet, the program makes numerous calls to a scientific subroutine library, mostly for Bessel functions. They, too, are implemented as approximations, and if they fail, so does the TWT.

In fact, this lesson was learned the hard way by designers at RCA's Microwave Operation nearly two decades ago. After about a year of extremely successful computer-aided engineering, the performance of newly designed TWTs began to deviate from the models' predictions. After a desperate search for all conceivable physical causes turned up nothing, it took half a year (and perhaps 30 TWTs at 10 grand a shot) to uncover the culprit.

Several months before disaster struck, the design programs had been moved from an IBM 360 to an RCA Spectra computer for purely political reasons. Naturally, some previous designs were rerun on the new system and were found to produce results identical to at least four digits with the old runs. So why the failures? With time, TWT designs had migrated toward higher frequencies. Thus, the Bessel functions' arguments had changed, and results on the Spectra began to deviate from those on the IBM. Apparently, somebody had truncated one of the Fourier series used to calculate the Bessel function—in the interest of faster performance, or to make the Spectra look superior.

Looking back, it is hard to see how the disaster could have been averted by anybody other than that cost-cutting Fourier-series "hacker." (Did we uncover the etymology of "hacker—one who truncates?") Certainly, none of the advanced programming techniques discussed in this book, whether based on math, AI, or CASE, would have helped in the least. The sheer expense even rules out rewriting the programs in a more modern language. It would seem that practicing engineers and scientists won't benefit much from recent software advances.

⊓ References

1. Carnegie-Mellon University, *Curriculum for Undergraduate Computer Science*, Springer-Verlag, New York, 1985.

2. David Gries, *The Science of Programming*, Springer-Verlag, New York, 1981.

3. C. A. R. Hoare, "An Overview of Some Formal Methods for Program Design," *IEEE Computer*, September 1987, p. 85.

4. Rene Berber, "Formal Methods and Source Code—A Conflict?" *IEEE Computer*, April 1988, p. 8.

5. Robert L. Baber, *The Spine of Software*, Wiley, New York, 1988.

6. Stephen F. Fickas, "Automating the transformational development of software," *IEEE Transactions of Software Engineering*, November 1985, p. 1268.

7. Stephen J. Westfold, "Very-high-level programming of knowledge representation schemes," *Proceedings of the AAAI Conference*, Palo Alto, CA, 1984, p. 344.

Courtesy IBM Archives

A glance at the operator's control panel helps us appreciate the size of IBM's SSEC (see p. 266). Today several minicomputers could easily fit into the console alone.

15

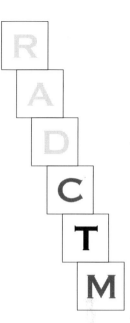

BEAT THE
QUALITY
QUANDARY

Copious methods compete
Some winning test strategies
G-Train goes to a T party

Our beloved waterfall diagram puts testing after detail design and coding. But as we've discussed in Chapter 4, testing must start with requirements analysis and continue throughout all development phases. What we are talking about at this juncture of the software cycle is integration testing, the effort that ensures customers get what they ordered. Sometimes that's harder than it sounds. What Parnas calls passive failures—when software doesn't do the *whole* job—are often not only hard to find, they're even hard to define.[1]

To be more precise, integration testing targets two related but very different goals: (1) to ensure that the software complies with the requirements and (2) to ensure it contains no errors. In other words, we are concerned not only with creating quality software, but also with **validation** and **verification**. Or, as Barry Boehm put it[2]:

"Am I building the right product?" (validation)
"Am I building the product right?" (verification)

Since even old software hands get the two mixed up, let's quote IEEE Standard 729: "*Verification* is the process of determining whether the product of a given phase in the development cycle fulfills the requirements established during the previous phase. *Validation* is the process of evaluating software at the end of the development process to ensure compliance with the requirements." It's the latter activity we are now primarily concerned with.

The two chores are often lumped together under the term "V&V," so it's hard to determine which costs how much. But between the two, estimates range from 25% to 50% of project costs—on critical embedded software as much as the whole design and coding process. But won't the need for expensive tests diminish soon? As you recall, CASE vendors hail automatically generated, error-free code as the trademark of software automation. And the radical CASE wing we encountered in the preceding chapter even talks about provably correct software, obtained by inductive assertion.[3]

Testing pundit William Howden appears more than skeptical: "It can be proved that there is no general purpose, automatable procedure for deciding if a program is correct. This follows directly from the results in the theory of computation."[4] Besides, customers will no more accept "error-free" code on faith than they have accepted parts machined by a numerically controlled lathe. *Que plus ça change que plus c'est la même chose.*

The only difference is that violations of a software requirement are a great deal harder to find than tolerance violations in a gear box. And if a machine shop delivers a clutch assembly instead of a gear box, it will go back by return mail, insides unseen. But you can't tell a word processor from a spreadsheet by its floppy. Indeed, a whole industry has evolved to assist the software customer in his efforts to ascertain that he got the right software, built the right way. You may not find "IV&V" (independent validation and verification) in the Yellow Pages, but the business is booming.

Shake and bake.   Worse still, software quality is even harder to assess than functionality. To test a gearbox, you rattle and shake it, freeze it and bake it, and see if it still shifts properly.

Stress tests on software take different and more varied forms. Unfortunately, few CASE systems interface with any testing tools—which pretty much annihilates the industry's "womb-to-tomb" pretenses.

So we better take a look at testing methodologies as they evolved before the CASE era. Although we concentrate on validation in this chapter, the same techniques prevail in unit tests or module tests as well. Actually, testing is most critical during detail design, where the working code emerges. Writing correct code certainly has become easier than it used to be. Unless you are stuck with obsolete tools, syntax checking should be automatic, and, consequently, cheap. So-called static tests follow, again automatically, during compilation.

Twenty years ago, first compilation of even a 200-line program could be quite a traumatic experience. Half the battle was just to coax the compiler to the finish line, so one could examine its verdict—a long list of (sadistically cryptic) error messages. All too often, extermination of the static bugs uncovered by the compiler still left over 70% of bugs alive; these dynamic bugs surfaced during execution. To unearth them, software designers often wound up tracing possibly faulty control flow on octal *core dumps*. That's no way to spend a weekend.

These bad old days did, however, teach oldtimers the art of "instrumentation." For example, if a nested loop with index variables m and n seemed to go astray, it was fairly easy to insert before each Fortran CONTINUE statement a line to print out the values of m and n. Today some test packages automatically instrument your programs, and not just with "tracer bullets." In fact, such programs can implement the "design rule checking" we advocated via IPs. This is usually done in the form of "assertions," say, ASSERT Speed < 550 in the G-Train example. If an assertion is violated, the test program lets you know. Of course, you can reap similar benefits by liberally inserting lines like

```
IF Speed > 550 PRINT "Speed overflow"
```

except that automatic instrumentation can restore the original code at the flick of a finger.

Yet another soft science.   Needless to say, software testing has evolved into a science in its own right.[5-7] Naturally, as software sage Edsger Dijkstra put it (while promoting correctness proofs): "Testing can only reveal the presence of bugs, not their absence." But then you might remember from Quality Control 101 that you can't even put a confidence value on the quality of any produce until you have found at least one bad apple in the bushel. Fortunately for software testers, the absence of bugs has never posed a problem yet. (Most programs will gratify you with an error every 30 lines of code, give or take 29.)

The most common software test method is still seat-of-the-pants testing, which is about as effective as proof-of-correctness testing. But let's take a brief look at some more dependable methodologies. In segment testing, the goal is to execute each function at least once, while branch testing endeavors to exercise every transfer of control at least once. In practical terms, this amounts to executing each program module (or file in C parlance) at least once, but most programmers are satisfied with 85% test coverage (which is likely to uncover 90% of errors).

Among more ambitious methods, path testing tries to execute every possible path through a given program, but even a single DO loop can render this approach impractical. (Exhaustive testing for the Lunar lander's last 100 bugs, for example, would have taken millennia.) Structured path testing compromises by acquiescing with a single pass through each loop. While branch testing can at best guarantee an error density of less than 1 per 50 lines, path testing can reduce bugs to 1 in 10,000 lines—provided you don't run out of time and money first.

What further complicates the software tester's life is the likelihood that one module's results can impact those of the next one. Therefore, the sequence in which branches are tested can have a major impact. Take a simple program with four branches, and assume that the algorithm requires four loops through any combination of branches (see Figure 15.1a). To test for all these possibilities with just one set of values requires 256 runs. In a large program, the number of runs will quickly get out of hand.

If you can establish, however, that the branches A and B are absolutely independent of branches C and D, you can break the program down into a sequence of two loops, each with only four combinations (see Figure 15.1b). Supposing the subsystems are truly "orthogonal," eight runs per set of values should provide full coverage. This proves the three canons for testability:

1. Modularize your programs.
2. Keep the modules independent.
3. Keep the modules small.

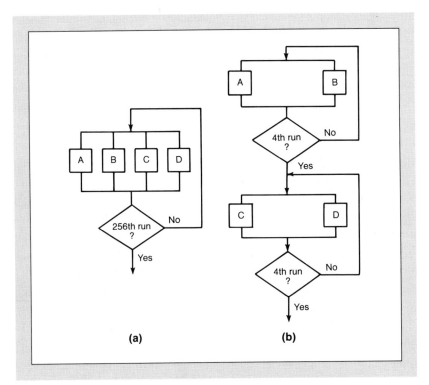

Figure 15.1 It takes 256 test runs to cover all sequential combinations of four modules (*a*). If A and B can be made independent of C and D, the number drops to eight runs (*b*).

Not everybody agrees that path testing is the answer. Parnas calls the process "fundamentally misguided." He points out that the state space occupied by any major program is not only complex, it's huge. Furthermore, all the testing only examines the model of the requirements a designer has developed, not necessarily the proper system. If you recall the speedometer example from Chapter 7, you know whereof he speaks.

⌐ You Need a Winning Strategy

Clearly, without a strategic test plan the battle will be lost before it starts. As we discussed in Chapter 4, such a plan must be laid out at the beginning of a project to cover the whole development cycle. One major component, the integration test plan, could resemble the one displayed in Figure 15.2.

Within such a framework, your best bet in most cases will be to start with requirements-based tests. They can disclose major

Figure 15.2 Each stage in a test plan produces specific reports vital to error estimation. Without such a plan, testing often becomes a haphazard enterprise.

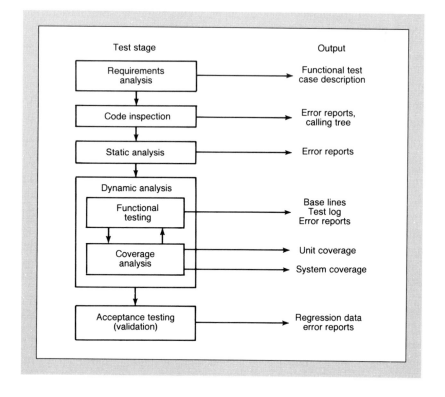

bungles in a hurry, and, as we have seen in earlier chapters, they can most easily be automated. (We'll get back to an example a little later.) Such tests generally belong to the **black-box** category, because you provide inputs and check whether the outputs are correct. Assume your program determines to which class a triangle belongs (equilateral, isosceles, or scalene) from three numbers defining the length of the sides. For a black-box test, you feed the program sets of three numbers and watch the outputs. The tester serves as the "oracle," deciding which answers are correct.

That approach can get tortuous if you validate, say, a word processor. Testing your way through the whole user manual may be tedious, but it certainly can be done. However, on how many different types of files must you run the tests to be sure there are no side effects? Should you perhaps unloose a herd of monkeys to see what happens when key combinations are pressed randomly? You might be better off at this juncture to retreat to the next line of defense—design-based tests that check out your algorithms. They require not only more knowledge of the software, but usually more preparation time.

Implementation-based (or structural) tests should be used to augment the design tests. They serve to check out how well your algorithms match. Obviously, such tests can't be devised without intimate knowledge of the software and, therefore, should be done by the designer—preferably at the unit test stage. This type of test falls in the category of white-box testing, a name that emphasizes how much such tests differ from the black-box variety.

Knowing how the tested program is designed, you can concentrate on those functions you know are most likely to go astray. As the example of Figure 15.1 amply demonstrated, a clean structure in your design (encouraged by CASE tools) can ameliorate the pain for this type of testing a great deal. It also helps if you know what kind of errors to expect. In one sample of 126,000 lines with 2070 mistakes, Beizer[5] reports a preponderance of control bugs (271) and architectural errors (193) over mathematical ones (141). The 404 specification goofs he found shed a dim light on the sample's origin. A much more recent study at Hewlett-Packard, however, confirms the preponderance of logic and design errors, followed by computation bugs. (Different error classifications prohibit a direct comparison.)

One trip is not enough.   Regardless of which test methodology you adopt, running through a given path with one set of data won't suffice. You may assume that your test cases cover all possible paths and still miss such disasters as a division by zero. Guess how many test cases would be needed to check out the simple triangle sorter we mentioned before. Would you believe over 20?

Glenford Meyers[8] begins his book, *The Art of Software Testing*, with this triangle exercise. Some of the less obvious tests follow:

Three test cases each in the three categories (equilateral, isosceles, and scalene) to cover all permutations.

At least one side has zero and negative values.

Three sets like 2, 3, 5 (in all permutations), which render "deflated" triangles.

All sides are of length zero.

At least one case that contains the wrong number of inputs—say, two or four values.

Cases with a mix of integers and real numbers.

In general, you should include test cases that fall inside and outside the solution space. For example, if you know that solutions must fall within a rectangle bounded by $x = 2$, $x = 5$, $y = 3$, and $y = 7$, your test cases should include the following pairs of x and y: (1.9, 4), (5.1, 4), (3, 2.9), and (3, 7.1). In real programs, solution spaces will rarely be two-dimensional, and figuring out their boundaries may well be impossible without computer assistance.

Even worse, bounds can be much more complex than even experts suspect. For example, in Newton's common algorithm for solving higher-order equations, one must be in the ballpark to assure convergence toward a root. But the "fences" between these "attractor" wells turn out to be nearly as complex as Mandelbrot sets.[9] If your software deals with math, you'll be well advised to test in much finer increments along suspected bounds than has been commonly deemed necessary. A technique known as domain testing may be useful in such cases.[6]

As mentioned above, a software tester must also function as an oracle (i.e., know all the correct answers). For the simple triangle sorter, it should be no problem to ascertain them with pencil and paper. But (as you may recall from the Preface) determining correct solutions for all test cases *without* relying on the program under test can be more time consuming than the testing itself. Often programmers must be satisfied with random testing, in which random values that lie within each variable's valid ranges are used.

Enough may not be enough.   While finding 90% of errors may suffice in many cases, it's certainly inadequate for, say, a missile defense system—especially when you don't know how bug-ridden a program was to start with. Top quality certainly requires many test sets. But how much is enough?

One fairly recent method to uncover flaws in test coverage is known as mutation testing. The technique "seeds" software purposely with errors and then watches how many the test programs uncover.[6] These "mutants" try to simulate common errors, from mistyped variable names to erroneous operators to data alterations. Using a mutation testing program, you simply test the software according to your test plan and watch for error reports. A typical set might read like this:

```
25% of mutants executed. 137/160 live
50% of mutants executed. 125/160 live
75% of mutants executed. 103/160 live
100% of mutants executed. 103/160 live
```

In this case, 160 mutants are introduced, 40 at a time. Of the first 40, only 23 actually cause trouble and are removed. Of the second batch, 12 are uncovered. Of the third batch 22 more are found. Executing the remaining 40 yields no further discoveries; obviously they wound up in a section of the code that's left unexamined by the test plan.

Another alternative for quality improvement is quickly gaining acceptance, namely error rate monitoring. Statistically meaningful data for this approach are becoming available, even though few software producers are willing to share data on their own debugging experience. (Either it's too depressing, or their PR agents won't let them.) Prominent among the laudable exceptions are AT&T's Bell Laboratories[10] and Hewlett-Packard.[11,12]

Science + experience = confidence.   Few of us will ever have to face a phone company's software decisions. When, for example, do you stop testing the 40 million lines of the AT&T public network software, knowing that errors remain? This massive software still hatches over 100 bugs a day, but they pose few problems. Scientific methods of quality control (or, as they say in yuppie circles, quality assurance) readily come to the rescue. Drawing on a great deal of experience, workers at AT&T's Bell Labs have collected an impressive body of facts on software failures and have hammered it into statistically significant rules.[7]

Take data from a 10-year-old project—a real-time command and control system comprising 21,700 lines of assembly code. They show that the error rate drops exponentially, when plotted against CPU time (see Figure 15.3*a*). More meaningful is a plot of error rate as a function of cumulative errors (Figure 15.3*b*), because it permits fairly accurate predictions of undiscovered errors—provided the extrapolation is not unduly ambitious. Once 200 errors have been found in the example, the graph predicts that one more bug is likely to surface in the next 10 hours of CPU time. That's not too bad for software that started out with 10

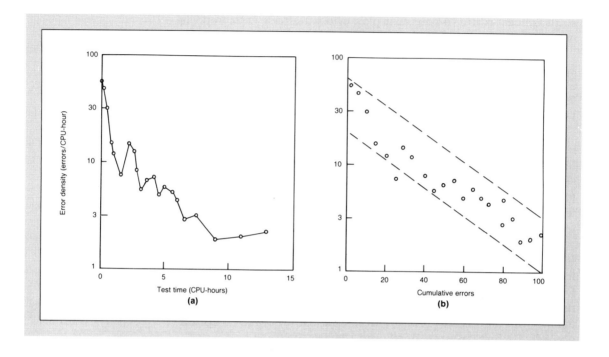

Figure 15.3 Error density in a test at AT&T declined faster than exponentially when plotted against CPU time (*a*). When plotted against cumulative errors, however, estimating the number of remaining errors becomes feasible (*b*).

errors per 1000 assembly instructions. In fact, with an estimated quality of 0.1 errors per 1000 lines, this package could easily be classified as "military strength."

Reliability, defined as the probability of error-free operation over a given period of time, is a function of failure intensity and time. In one typical example, three failures per 1000 hours translated into a reliability of 0.985. Such calculations let the software designer correlate the reliability required for a given application with the rate of error discovery and—once the slope is established—allow the designer to predict the remaining test effort to achieve a given goal.

Another example from Bell Labs demonstrates how the confidence in error projections improves as the number of samples grows.[7] In Figure 15.4, the failure intensity per thousand CPU hours is plotted against calendar time. After some three months of testing, the bug emergence rate has dropped by a factor of 14. Were this a consumer product, an error rate of one every 250 CPU hours should be adequate since at 40 hours per week it translates into a failure every six months or so. A system that works around the clock warrants more testing.

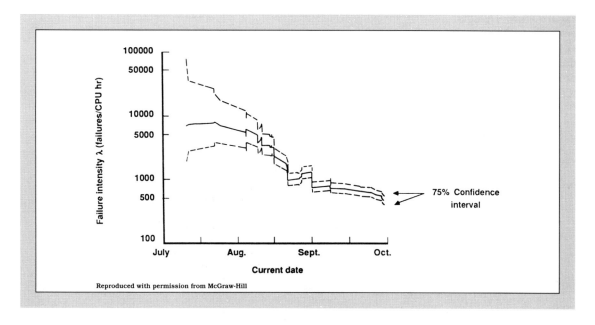

Hardware tested like software. Hewlett-Packard applied the same approach to system utilities for a workstation, even though they were implemented as firmware (programmed read-only memory). The graph in Figure 15.5a represents the error discovery rate as a function of test time. In the beginning, the error discovery rate behaved more capriciously than what passes for normal. This was due not so much to the uneven test effort, but to the implementation in firmware. In standard software, bugs are best exterminated as they surface, but in firmware it makes more sense to collect them for awhile and then issue a revision.

After conversion to a logarithmic scale (see Figure 15.5b), the bug emergence rate of the second 3000 hours stayed close to the average rate established in the first 3000 hours. After drawing in the 90% confidence bounds, it was possible to predict that the release target would be reached after sometime between 5500 and 6000 hours of testing time. Although at release time an estimated 140 errors remained in the firmware, only 3 were reported from the field during the first 18 months. (A 90% confidence level implies that actual remaining errors could be as low as 120 or as high as 250.)

While we may finally have a handle on measuring software quality, the time to relax our efforts remains far off. On occasion we read about claims from overseas that sound unreal—like a

Figure 15.4 The more tests have been run, the more accurately remaining errors can be predicted to a given confidence level (broken lines).

Figure 15.5 Defects per hour in these tests at Hewlett-Packard must decline to a predetermined release level (*a*). Transformation to logarithmic form takes the confidence level into account (*b*).

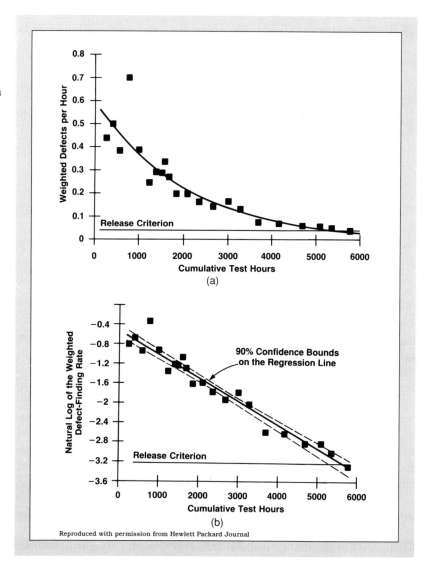

(a)

(b)

Reproduced with permission from Hewlett Packard Journal

Japanese software factory's assertion of 0.01 defects *per year* for a given installation. Whether true or not, Japan does regard software as a strategic growth industry, so **MITI** rides herd on the big computer concerns' software factories plus close to 1000 small software houses. The ministry (as well as its counterpart in Germany) plans to introduce the equivalent of **UL** labels for software.

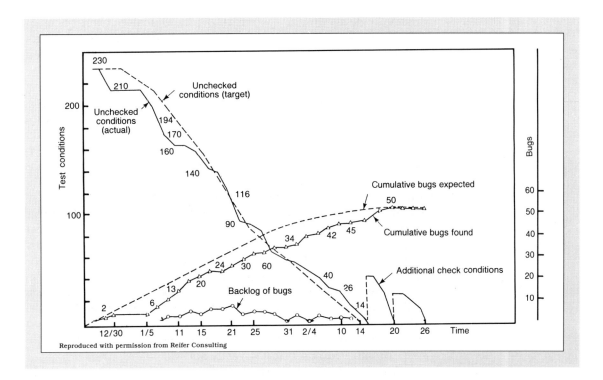

Reproduced with permission from Reifer Consulting

As far as the testing process itself goes, little evidence suggests any foreign breakthroughs. (Even in Europe, only academics occasionally claim success for correctness proofs.) But meticulous planning and record keeping can tell a producer as much as he wants to know about the quality of his code. Figure 15.6, provided by *Reiffer Consultants*, summarizes test results from a major Japanese company, typical of a mid-sized project (50,000 lines of code). In the end, what software quality assurance boils down to is tight monitoring of test data and a great deal of reading. You can probably glean all there is to know about software testing from the referenced books, reports compiled for the Pentagon,[13] and IEEE standards (see Chapter 18).

Figure 15.6 This debugging history, gathered by a Japanese company, shows that discovered bugs (right scale) closely followed predictions when based on predetermined test conditions (left scale).

↳ Checking Out the G-Train

CASE systems have been slow to incorporate test automation in their tool kits, although some progress has been made. For example, Cadre's Teamwork has established a link with a microprocessor development system that provides test coverage, even for multiprocessors. However, none of the G-Train designs was taken to the test, because the few vendors who actually produced code lacked links to testing.

Not to worry, though. As you learned in Chapter 5, tests can be developed directly from G-Train's requirements spec, bypassing mistakes that occur during the design phase. The test tool T, developed by **Programming Environments** (PEI), develops its test cases with little human intervention. "It lets you develop tests from the requirements specification, because T automatically designs, generates, traces and documents test cases from a product description," says the firm's president, Bob Poston.

To generate test data, T must obviously have all the information needed to describe the system under test, its inputs and outputs, and their valid ranges. Because T is not concerned with a program's algorithms, the formal syntax of a system description comes close to plain English. The subject is always a requirement; the verb is in most cases, "is to" (replacing the usual must, shall, or should); and the object is an input. Valid and invalid values are specified in parentheses, and conditions are identified by an IF clause. Of course, T's analysis can be no better than the spec—it can validate but not verify software.

Whether this tool should be your cup of T (served on a PC/AT) depends on the application. However, the 7-Megabyte package turns out to be quite versatile. At a 1988 training seminar (you might call it a T party), programs to be tested ranged from a networking package to a data logger to a C++ compiler. T can be quite effective, with time savings of 70% to 90% documented. More important, quality improvements impress even skeptics. For example, software engineers at Leeds & Northrup in North Wales, Pennsylvania, saw their error rates drop from 1 to 0.07 per 1000 lines, which most likely suited them to a T.[14]

To obtain test cases for our G-Train automatically, the requirements spec from Chapter 7 must be converted to a format that T can understand. In Figure 15.7*a*, the spec has been transformed to six rules. They read like stilted but comprehensible English, provided you know that if refers to a condition in the data, while when refers to an event. All terms created by the user are described in dictionaries that identify names plus group and type definitions where applicable (Figure 15.7*b*).

Missing from Figure 15.7*b* is the Event Dictionary that defines the terms waitclear, scale_reading_okay, and depart_button_pressed. All are of type signal, and no group

```
Requirements Description Table            Verb Dictionary        Testunit:  g-train
                     Testunit: g-train   ------------------------------------------------
                                         block               = aa0014      Group -
------------------------------------------          Type    -
r01                                                 Desc    Prevent entry of passenger
        is to       weigh                                   by displaying a red light
                    person               goto                = aa0011      Group -
        in state    weighing                        Type    -
        using       scale_reading,                  Desc    Make a state transition
                    weight_accumulated_old,  wait            = aa018       Group -
                    count_accumulated_old            Type    -
        producing   weight_accumulated_new,          Desc    Suspend operation after
                    count_accumulated_new                    displaying a green light
        when        scale_reading_okay
                                         weigh               = aa0001      Group -
r02                                                 Type    -
        is to       goto                            Desc    Record weight from scale
                    full
        in state    weighing             Object Dictionary      Testunit: g-train
        using       count_accumulated_old,  ------------------------------------------------
                    count_accumulated_old_max  all_passengers   = aa0021     Group -
        if          last_person_enters is t          Type    -
        when        scale_reading_okay               Desc    All passengers
                                         clear               = aa0019      Group -
r03                                                 Type    -
        is to       block                           Desc    No process
                    next_person
        in state    weighing             next_person         = aa0015      Group -
        producing   red_light                       Type    -
        when        scale_reading_okay              Desc    Passenger waiting behind
        causing     waitclear                               passenger being weighed
                                         person              = aa0002      Group -
r04                                                 Type    -
        is to       wait                            Desc    Passenger being weighed
                    clear
        in state    weighing             State Dictionary       Testunit: g-train
        producing   green_light          ------------------------------------------------
        when        waitclear            full                = aa0012      Group -
                                                    Type    primitive
r05                                                 Desc    No passenger may enter
        is to       block
                    all_passengers       weighing            = aa0003      Group -
        in state    full                            Type    primitive
        producing   red_light                       Desc    Passenger may enter and
                                                            be weighed
r06
        is to       goto
                    full
        in state    weighing
        when        depart_button_pressed

                      (a)                                    (b)
Reproduced with permission from Programming Environments
```

Figure 15.7 The PEI test generator first recasts the G-train requirements as computer-readable rules (*a*). Only those affecting the weighing process are shown. Dictionaries (*b*) define all terms used by the tool, including verbs, objects, and states.

Figure 15.8 The Data item dictionary defines each term's type, unit, range, and test class. Assumed test values are also listed.

```
Dataitem Dictionary     Testunit: g-train
------------------------------------------------
count_accumulated_new
                Type       integer
                Unit       people
                Mn/Mx/Rs  1/100/1
                Tcls       v nm 1    @50
                           v hb      @100

count_accumulated_old
                Type       integer
                Unit       people
                Mn/Mx/Rs  1/99/1
                Tcls       v nm 1    @50
                           v lb      @1
                           v lb +    @2
                           v hb -    @98
                           v hb      @99

count_accumulated_old_max
                Type       integer
                Unit       people
                Mn/Mx/Rs  99/99/0
                Tcls       v nm 1    @99

green_light
                Type       character
                Tcls       v nm 1    @green

red_light
                Type       character
                Tcls       v nm 1    @red

scale_reading
                Type       integer
                Unit       lbm
                Mn/Mx/Rs  0/999/1
                Tcls       v nm 1    @150
                           v lb      @0
                           v lb +    @1
                           v hb -    @998
                           v hb      @999

weight_accumulated_new
                Type       integer
                Unit       lbm
                Mn/Mx/Rs  0/99900/1
                Tcls       v nm 1    @7500

weight_accumulated_old
                Type       integer
                Unit       lbm
                Mn/Mx/Rs  0/99900/1
                Tcls       v nm 1    @7500
                           v lb      @0
                           v lb +    @1
                           v hb -    @99899
                           v hb      @99900
```

Reproduced with permission from Programming Environments

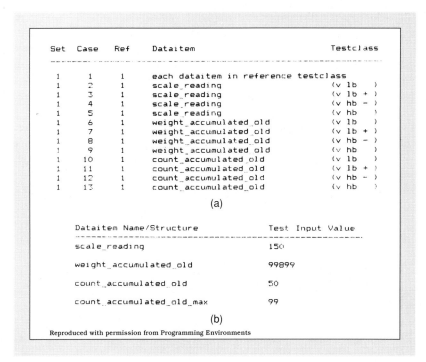

```
Set   Case   Ref   Dataitem                                    Testclass
-------------------------------------------------------------------------
 1     1      1     each dataitem in reference testclass
 1     2      1     scale_reading                              (v lb   )
 1     3      1     scale_reading                              (v lb + )
 1     4      1     scale_reading                              (v hb - )
 1     5      1     scale_reading                              (v hb   )
 1     6      1     weight_accumulated_old                     (v lb   )
 1     7      1     weight_accumulated_old                     (v lb + )
 1     8      1     weight_accumulated_old                     (v hb - )
 1     9      1     weight_accumulated_old                     (v hb   )
 1    10      1     count_accumulated_old                      (v lb   )
 1    11      1     count_accumulated_old                      (v lb + )
 1    12      1     count_accumulated_old                      (v hb - )
 1    13      1     count_accumulated_old                      (v hb   )
```

(a)

```
Dataitem Name/Structure              Test Input Value
-----------------------------------------------------------
scale_reading                        150

weight_accumulated_old               99899

count_accumulated_old                50

count_accumulated_old_max            99
```

(b)

Reproduced with permission from Programming Environments

Figure 15.9 Automatically generated test cases can be viewed in summary form (*a*). In detail reports (*b*), all parameters (here for valid high bounds of case 8) are listed.

designations are needed, because G-Train is so small. Two of the three events were not specifically mentioned in the spec. Like the CASE implementations we discussed in the preceding chapters, a formal T description forces the designer to resolve ambiguities.

Test generation without hassle.   Once the formal description has been entered and any discrepancies resolved, T proceeds to the Dataitem Dictionary (see Figure 15.8). To save space, the internal names and comments have been omitted. Test data are defined by type, unit,* and Mn/Mx/Rs (minimum, maximum, resolution). Test classes (Tcls) usually include nominal values (nm), low bounds (lb), and high bounds (hb). Cases lying inside the low and high bound are identified by "+" and "−", respectively. All of the listed tests are tagged valid (v); tests outside the bounds would be designated as invalid (i).

All test cases, are summarized in Figure 15.9*a*, supplemented with a few "long reports" (Figure 15.9*b*). The long reports

---

*To avoid confusion with "lb" (low bound) the weight unit is called "lbm."

include input values for all involved variables. All 13 tests deal with rule r01, although the last also involves r02. Since we don't have the code to which we could apply the test cases, there's no way to measure their effectiveness (in terms of segments, paths, branches, etc.). As we mentioned in Chapter 4, metrics on software complexity can add valuable information that tests alone can't reveal.

However, PEI has developed its own test *comprehensiveness* measure, TC, for which Figure 15.10 reports partial results. TC is composed of four components, one each for requirements, input,

Figure 15.10 A test comprehensiveness table (*a*) computes all test coverage components as fractions. The results are also available in graph form (*b*).

```
Testing Comprehensiveness                        14:19  Feb 22, 1989
Testunit: g-train    ver 2                                 page   1

-----------------------------------------------------------------------

                   -----INPUT-----    ----OUTPUT-----
           REQT    DATA COND EVENT    DATA COND EVENT    STRUC    TC
weights
            50      20    5    0        0    0    0        25
           ---     ---  ---  ---      ---  ---  ---       ---
           100     100  100  100      100  100  100       100

coverages
            0       1    0    0        0    0    0         0
02/19/89   ---     ----  ---  ---      ---  ---  ,---       ---    = 0.01
            6       16    1    1        3    0    0         1

            0       3    0    0        0    0    0         0
02/20/89   ---     ----  ---  ---      ---  ---  ---       ---    = 0.04
            6       16    1    1        3    0    0         1

            0       5    0    0        0    0    0         0
02/21/89   ---     ----  ---  ---      ---  ---  ---       ---    = 0.06
            6       16    1    1        3    0    0         1

            0       9    0    0        0    0    0         0
02/22/89   ---     ----  ---  ---      ---  ---  ---       ---    = 0.11
            6       16    1    1·       3    0    0         1

            1       10    1    0        0    0    0         0
02/23/89   ---     ----  ---  ---      ---  ---  ---       ---    = 0.26
            6       16    1    1        3    0    0         1

            2       16    1    0        0    0    0         0
02/24/89   ---     ----  ---  ---      ---  ---  ---       ---    = 0.42
            6       16    1    1        3    0    0         1
                                    (a)

    Date       TC
           0                            0.5                     1
           +-------------------------------------- ---------+
           :                                                :
02/19/89   :*                                               :
02/20/89   : *                                              :
02/21/89   :   *                                            :
02/22/89   :        *                                       :
02/23/89   :                    *                           :
02/24/89   :                             *                  :
           :                                                :
           +-------------------------------------- ---------+

                                    (b)
```

output, and structure. Each component consists of a weighting factor and a fraction; the numerator reflects what the tests *have* demonstrated, while the denominator reflects what they *should* demonstrate. In Figure 15.10*a*, 50% (shown as 50/100) of the weight lies on requirements—not because that's all we have to work with, but because it's a typical value for integration tests. The calendar dates merely cluster our test cases, so TC (which is plotted as a function of date) can be printed out (see Figure 15.10*b*). Because only two of six requirements are included in our set, TC only reaches a value of 0.42.

Testing tools catching on.   Readily available—and quite sophisticated—test tools are changing the way software is measured. In the words of Ed Miller, president of **SRI**, "We have finally managed to automate most of the tedium out of software testing. Now we can only hope that software vendors get serious about using the available tools." The tools he is talking about apply dynamic debugging methods that have been known for decades.[15]

Such tools can't design testable software for you, nor will CASE systems relieve you of this burden anytime soon. But software complexity metrics like those developed by **McCabe** can confirm whether you're on the right path.[16] This popular package automatically generates a program graph (see Figure 15.11) from which it calculates complexity.

Once you have built testability (a necessary but not sufficient precondition for quality) into your programs, tools like those from SRI can greatly ease the chore of testing. Not only can you buy tools that analyze test coverage for modules or whole systems, but even one (called CapBak) that captures your keystrokes so that you can repeat tests you improvised—very helpful if you're building a word processor.

CapBak thus helps a great deal with regression testing when combined with SRI's Smarts (Software Maintenance and Regression Test System). Don't let the term confuse you. Regression tests have little to do with polynomial regression algorithms for correlating test data. Rather, regression tests are so named because they are meant to determine whether a change has regressed to other parts of the program. Such tests let you sleep better after distributing a new revision of your software, secure in the knowledge that at least the old code has not been contaminated. Regression tests tend to be especially vital when both a system's software and hardware have been revised.

Figure 15.11
McCabe's complexity
graph automatically
extracts a program's
structure from
the code. Numbers
represent in-line tasks.

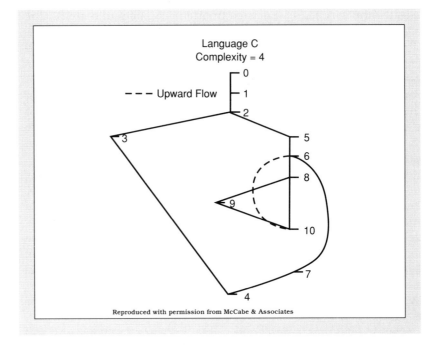

A testbed generator can help you further to set up the right
mix of tests and speed their completion. For example, with its
help, SRI developed a supplemental Unix test suite, consisting
of 471 tests, in a mere four staff-months. And S-Tcat (System
Test Coverage Analysis Tool) tells you whether you've expended
enough effort.

Although this book deals primarily with mainstream software, we have mentioned AI-oriented software repeatedly and will
do so again in the next chapter. It's only fair then to add a few
words about testing AI software, especially in its most common
form—expert systems. They are getting popular because of their
expandability; you just add new rules to the knowledge base. But
because these rules can execute in almost any sequence, testing
an expert system can be a nightmare.

Black-box testing proceeds just about the same way as it does
with conventional software: you feed in the parameters of your
problem and look at the answer. Let's assume you deal with
a diagnostic system for automobiles and after keying in symp-
toms and answering questions the diagnosis appears: "Spark-
plugs (40% probability); Distributor (40% probablity); Battery
(20% probability)." Where is the oracle to confirm or deny the

conclusions? How do expert system builders validate their products? They are still wrestling with the challenge.[17]

As long as the human expert is around, at least obvious blunders will be caught, but that's hardly possible when you apply a method coming in vogue—independent validation and verification (IV&V). And why not? The name gives away the answer: it should be performed neither by the vendor nor the customer. (Remember the New Jersey Motor Vehicle tragedy?) Naturally, in-house tests should precede the formal IV&V procedures and customer tests should follow them. After all, failures go on the record, and no IV&V outfit will refund what you paid your vendor if the software turns out to be flawed.

Still, you can glean the importance of IV&V from data collected by Logicon in San Diego. During V&V contracts on five major packages (over 100,000 lines each), 200 to 500 errors were uncovered. Of those, 40% to 80% stemmed from coding bugs, while mistakes in the requirements still accounted for 20% to 50%. Remember that this sad record applied not to consumer packages but to "industrial-strength" software whose production was closely supervised—supposedly. No wonder DoD insists on IV&V. Perhaps you should, too.

⸗ References

1. William E. Suydam, "Approaches to software testing embroiled in debate," *Computer Design*, November 15, 1986, p. 49.

2. Barry W. Boehm, "Verifying and validating software requirements and design specifications," *IEEE Software*, January 1984, p. 75.

3. Jacques Loeckx and Kurt Sieber, *The Foundations of Program Verification* 2nd Ed., Wiley-Teubner, New York, 1984.

4. William E. Howden, *Functional Program Testing and Analysis*, McGraw-Hill, New York, 1987, p. 86.

5. Boris Beizer, *Software Testing Techniques*, Van Nostrand Reinhold, New York, 1983.

6. Richard DeMillo, et al., *Software Testing and Evaluation*, Benjamin Cummings Publishing, Menlo Park, CA, 1987.

7. John D. Musa, et al., *Software Reliability—Measurement, Prediction, Application*, McGraw-Hill, New York, 1987.

8. Glenford J. Meyers, *The Art of Software Testing*, Wiley Interscience, New York, 1979.

9. James Gleick, *Chaos: Making a New Science*, Viking Penguin, New York, 1987, p. 220

10. John D. Musa, "Tools for measuring software reliability," *IEEE Spectrum*, February 1989, p. 39.

11. Dean Drake and Duane Wolting, "Reliability Theory Applied to Software Testing," *Hewlett-Packard Journal*, April 1987, p. 35.

12. Gregory A. Kruger, "Project management using software reliability growth models," *Hewlett-Packard Journal*, June 1988, p. 30.

13. *Software Test and Evaluation Project Manual, Vol. 3: Good Examples of Software Testing in the Department of Defense*, Report 8606, Georgia Institute of Technology, Atlanta, GA, 1986.

14. Robert M. Poston and Mark W. Bruen, "Counting down to zero software failures," *IEEE Software*, September 1987, p. 54.

15. Michael S. Deutsch, *Software Verification and Validation — Realistic Project Approaches*, Prentice-Hall, Englewood Cliffs, NJ, 1982.

16. William T. Ward, "Software defect prevention using McCabe's complexity metric," *Hewlett-Packard Journal*, April 1989, p. 64.

17. Kamran Parsaye and Mark Chignell, *Expert Systems for Experts*, Wiley, New York, 1988.

16

MAINTENANCE MEANS RECYCLING

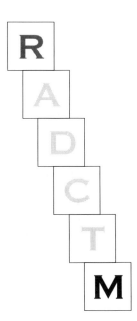

What does "maintenance" mean?
How to recycle software
Still in the laboratory

We have finally reached the waterfall's bottom basin, which bears the label "Maintenance." More than half the funds expended for software in the United States goes into this dubious effort. The *Software Productivity Consortium*—an arm of the aerospace industry—estimates software expenditures at $22 billion. If that number comes close to the mark, at least $10 billion a year could be put to better use in the aerospace industry alone.

According to Figure 16.1, which reflects the cost of nearly $20 million of military avionics software, 60% of the tab wound up in "maintenance." Since software doesn't wear out, where did all that money go? According to the plotted Air Force estimate, only one third had anything to do with correcting mistakes, and—according to the curve—most of that was due to premature release. The bulk (no less than 42% of life cycle costs) wound up in "modification maintenance" over a period of 10 years. Other studies have identified a mere fifth of maintenance as "corrective," a full half as "perfective," and the rest as "adaptive."

Figure 16.1 The huge expense for software "maintenance" can be broken down into a "corrective" and a "modification" component. The latter really represents changes of the original code for reuse in new (albeit similar) applications.

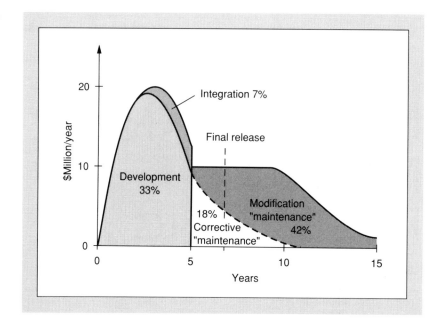

Indeed, numbers seeping out from data processing and management information systems indicate that in the totally different world of Cobol software the cost allocation is nearly identical. Except that DP "maintenance" costs are often pegged even higher—claims of 80% over a program's useful life are not rare. Clearly, the bulk of that also goes into software recycling, primarily the adaptation of dusty decks to new hardware and changed requirements. Yet, this effort has rarely been called reuse or "re-engineering" until the CASE industry popularized the term. That may seem strange since some DP gurus have preached for years that 90% of all new code could be culled from existing software.

Re-engineering is supposed to consist of two phases: reverse engineering and forward engineering. But a closer look at the former proves it to be largely a *Fata Morgana*. Rather than constructing data and control flow diagrams from source code, "reverse" CASE tools can at best produce structure diagrams and flowcharts. Some tools (mostly addressing the Cobol market) analyze the submitted source code and turn it into a cleaner, structured program with documentation.

Even re-engineering's advocates keep expectations at a modest level. For example, database maven (and Turing Award winner) Charlie Bachman, Chairman of **Bachman I S I** admits that automatic re-engineering is an unrealistic goal.[1] The reason appears irrefutable: in the process of CASE-based "forward engineering" the intent of the software designer tends to get lost in implementation detail. Reverse engineering thus resembles unscrambling eggs; entropy torpedoes such attempts.

Whether a human or an intelligent program inspects some source code (and, hopefully, *all* related data structures), they tend to see only the trees planted by a program's architect. The grand design becomes only visible from a more exalted (or abstract) level—especially if that design was contrived by one of Rube Goldberg's numerous disciples in the software trade. Still, the potential savings are so huge that reuse can't be swept under the rug.

Not endorsing code reuse ranks close to deprecating motherhood. Yet few programmers do what they (or their mentors) preach—at least not as advertised. A "reused software designer" is not one who designs reused software, but one who is reused to design the same kind of software again and again. To date, that seems to be the only sure road to software recycling. Trouble is, after a while even the original programmer forgets the original rationale behind his design decisions and data structures. (In due course, most programmers even forget their original employers.)

So what stands behind the discrepancy between words and deeds when it comes to software reuse? The excuses range wide and far. We've already mentioned the technical difficulties, but they are reinforced by shortcomings of the human spirit. There's the bruised ego predicament, the MIS management breakdown, and—between these two—the NIH syndrome. Nor must we forget the high startup cost for module libraries (pigeonholing software is a nightmare) and the training to use them. Besides, recycling smacks of trash in our throwaway culture.

⌐ Reuse Requires Forethought

Still, recycling is the natural way. It would be interesting to know, for example, where the atoms in our bodies spent the last billion years or so. We would soon realize that reuse goes well beyond humdrum intragalactic redistribution. Some molecules, made from these primeval atoms, are coming off our bodies' assembly lines this very moment.

Software reuse has a shorter history, but back in the early baroque days musicians thought nothing of reusing each other's software. Even Bach recycled Vivaldi's—not to mention his own—concerti liberally. But you can't do that with Mozart's Clarinet Quintet, where every note balances every other. The lesson is clear: the more targeted (or call it elegant, skillful, even efficient) a piece of software is, the harder it becomes to reuse.

In other words, if you want to reuse your (or your shop's) software, you better design it with reuse in mind. Thus, the waterfall diagram's linear sequence could be bent into a circle—with reuse replacing maintenance. In this regard, too, software engineering differs little from other disciplines. Any engineer's "waterfall" runs through the same phases:

- Headscratching and doodles
- Tinkertoys and rubberbands
- Sketches and model shops
- Testing and analysis
- Production and (tut, tut) sale

A *good* engineer inserts another phase at the beginning:

- Disassemble the competition's product

This activity, the original "reverse engineering," (and just cleared in court of its sinister connotations) underlies software reuse as well. There is nothing brave or honorable about reinventing the wheel. If you have a mold (and own the rights to it), just make copies. If you like someone else's wheels, reuse the idea, not the implementation "mold."

The only question is: how? Subroutine libraries and Unix filters constitute an established, though not very flexible beginning. We have already explored a better way in Chapters 12 and 13—object-oriented programming (and we'll come back to it shortly). But getting a dozen pages of code from a friend (or from your boss) to adapt for reuse poses a much greater challenge.* Let's see what solutions are emerging.

---

*While designing a self-optimizing circuit analyzer, I once took the global-optimum finder for reverse engineering on a ski vacation. Luckily (for my employer), three days in the Kitzbühel orthopedic ward provided a congenial setting for the task; otherwise, it might have remained undone. I doubt that anybody ever reverse-engineered *my* program—storage limitations forced me to reuse the same array variables over and over. So much for the realities of writing reusable software; cutting corners is a fact of life.

More hype than hope.   Within commercial CASE products, few reverse engineering tools go beyond translation from one procedural language into another. The target language may be a PDL that incorporates some architectural information gleaned from program structure and comments. Or it could just be a modern version of the source language—structured Cobol-85 or Fortran-77—that can untangle the original spaghetti. A translation into Nassi-Shneiderman diagrams and flowcharts merely substitutes a graphic language for a textual one. (Indeed, "flowcharters" preceded the CASE era by decades.)

As far as other graphs are concerned, calling trees and structure charts dominate. Sometimes HIPO and entity relationship diagrams pop up, but rarely outside the Cobol realm. Indeed, few re-engineering tools stray beyond that kingdom. SuperCase from *Advanced Technology International* advertises the probably broadest language spectrum, ranging from Ada to C, from Fortran to PL/M, from Pascal to PDL.

An example from *SPS* (whose Epos you'll remember from Chapter 10) illustrates the function of a reverse engineering tool. Here, a Fortran program will be submitted to the company's Fortran Re-Spec product, which then automatically analyzes the program and translates it into Epos language. The source code, which interpolates values between table entries, comprises five subroutines: initialization, reading inputs, forming intermediate sums, writing outputs, and the actual interpolation routine.

The tool produces a hierarchy diagram showing the modules, and generates a flowchart and structogram (Nassi-Shneiderman chart) for each of the routines. We'll peruse the Fortran routine that does the actual interpolation. It reads:

```
      SUBROUTINE LININP (GA,GF,K,A,F)
      DIMENSION GA(50),GF(50)
      DO 121 I+2,K
      IF (GA(I) .GE. A) GOTO 110
121   CONTINUE
      I = K
110   D = (GF(I)-GF(I-1))/(GA(I)-GA(I-1))
      F = GF(I-1) + D*(A-GA(I-1))
      RETURN
      END
```

In Epos language, the code looks nearly identical, except that it uses the DO/OD construct and adds a listing of input and output variables. From these data, Epos produces the block diagram

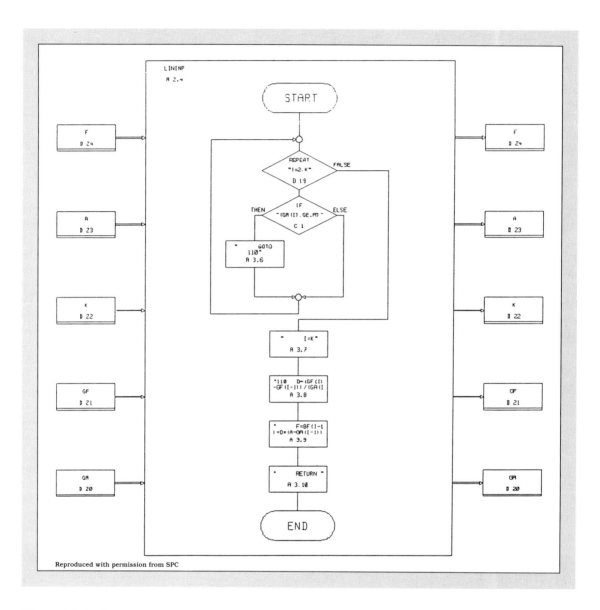

Figure 16.2 Reverse engineering works only across a narrow gap in the abstraction level. Here a flowchart has been generated from existing code.

of Figure 16.2—a flowchart decorated with input and output boxes. This may not seem like much of an accomplishment, but for a somewhat more convoluted program chuckful of GOTOs and nested IFs it can save a lot of time.*

---

*A flowcharter might have kept me away from Kitzbühel altogether, averting three months of left-footed driving.

As you seek, so shall you find. Better add to this sweeping promise the proviso "at best." We have alluded to libraries before, which indeed have been the exclusive vessels for practical software reuse to date. Unix utilities and scientific subroutine libraries come to mind immediately, while the huge *COSMIC* repository for NASA software remains largely unknown.

We have also mentioned applications libraries such as those from *Stepstone* in Chapter 5. Other examples—from the field of embedded systems (and monitored by *Ada Information Clearing House*) include the growing Ada libraries of the STARS repository (currently 230 Mbytes); of *Wizard Software* (over 500 components); and of *EVB* (275 packages). The components in such commercial libraries are designed for reuse, with proper interfaces, and parameterized variables. However, there's a catch; you must first *find* the appropriate library routine. EVB solves the problem with a search tree as in Figure 5.2, but as the scope of the search broadens, hitting a match gets tougher and tougher. If you've ever sweated over a jigsaw puzzle, you'll certainly agree that the effort in matching functions and interfaces grows at least with the square of the available pieces.

We could speed up the search a great deal by sorting the puzzle pieces according to some essential criteria: the number of protrusions and indentations (inputs and outputs); the dominant color (types); and some discernible picture element (function). Because computers excel at searching, such a computer-aided jigsaw puzzle library could cut down a great deal on midnight oil consumption.

Alas, we'll have to wait awhile longer before some current research (to be discussed shortly) gels into products. But the puzzle analogy brings us to the real reason why software reuse seems to languish eternally. If you can implement half of a new program with reused software, you save 50% of the cost, right? Only if your jigsaw puzzle consists merely of two pieces, propped up right on your keyboard. Whenever searching and matching are required, you pay a reuse premium that can more than wipe out reuse savings.

A dubious return on investment. In Figure 16.3, you see a straight, declining line that indicates the ideal cost of a project as a function of the percentage of reused code. Superimposed you find three curves for the interfacing cost, proportional to the product of old and new code fractions—to be precise, $A*x*(1-x)$ if x is the fraction of reused code. (The square function is the

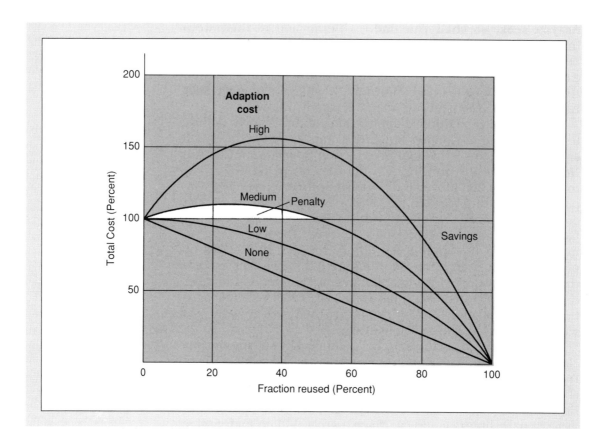

Figure 16.3 Code reuse will make little headway as long as adaptation levies even a moderate penalty (dark area). Only heavy reuse (over 60%) yields substantial savings (white area).

simplest continuous fit for such a graph.) If you can recycle half the code, but the interfacing expense equals the savings, you obviously just break even (curve labeled "moderate").

The surprise comes when you want to replace only one-quarter of the new program with recycled code: it costs you 12.5% more than an all-new implementation (area labeled "penalty"). Even if the interfacing/matching efforts are low, savings remain insignificant unless you can find at least one-third the needed code in a library. That's why *anticipated* savings must exceed 30% of the development cost before software designers are willing to look earnestly for reusable code. Many of us have learned the lesson of retrofitting costs the hard way.

In complex programs (curve labeled "high"), you must be able to substitute recycled code for 75% of a program before you realize any savings at all. And, unless you are working on a very simple problem, the only way to get off the "high" curve is to use a well-designed library or some form of object-oriented programming. Should we just throw in the towel on reuse? No, but we may have to cool our heels until the computer industry's efforts bear fruit. We have already mentioned the SPC. In addition, the ***Microelectronics and Computer Technology Corp.*** (better known as MCC), supports a number of research projects that address the reuse problem.[2] Cataloging program modules stands high on the consortium's agenda, even though it has not yet zeroed in on a specific direction.

Tough as the challenge is, once a system for code reuse is set up, savings are quite real. NASA (Langley) reports a 4:1 return on investment for its reusable software, and that's after the cost of newsletters and recycled recycling seminars. (If you pay any taxes, you'll be happy to hear this.) Without an appropriate environment, the cost of retrofitting the space shuttle software could have been astronomical. In the three years since the Challenger disaster, no fewer than 3800 requirements were changed, resulting in 900 software releases and 3 major upgrades. (Included is a port to new hardware for mission control.)

⌐ Waiting in the (Laboratory) Wings

While the jigsaw puzzle analogy may be a bit naïve, it highlights the difficulties in cataloging software components. Some promising research at the Naval Postgraduate School addresses the problem. For example, Luqi[3] has established an automated ***alias*** list that would direct all searches for Fetch, Obtain, Input, Get, or Retrieve to the keyword Read. Thus, the search for the proper function becomes much easier.

Furthermore, a prototype system description language (PSDL) assists in the description of algorithms. To convey its flavor, the notation

Reply = @[x] @b @[y] @c => x <= y

defines that an output sequence (inferred by the keyword Reply) must be sorted in increasing order. The arrows indicate logical implications, while @ serves as a concatenation operator.

At MIT's AI labs in Cambridge, a more ambitious effort known as Programmer's Apprentice has been underway since the early 1970s.[4,5] The most recent version is known as KBEmacs (Knowledge-based editor in Emacs) and has demonstrated productivity gains by a factor of 3 to 10 on some small Ada programs.[6,7]

Ideally, the most efficient way to fix old programs or generate new ones would be to recycle algorithms. Coupled with an "algorithm compiler," an algorithm library could do for general programming what Unix filters accomplish in a narrower domain.[8,9] However, recognizing algorithms automatically must wait for HAL (although even 2001 seems an optimistic date). Still, AI holds out some hope for automatic recognition of "programming clichés."

Even though the Programmer's Apprentice lingers at MIT's AI incubator, it's instructive to examine what nearly two decades of research have yielded. A cliché is an algorithmic fragment that can't be readily expressed as a subroutine—say, the code to read records in a file. KBEmacs examines both the control and data structures of a submitted program module and reduces the structures to a "plan"—conceptually similar to an IP decomposition.

Search of a cliché library by plan attributes lets the user browse among alternatives and then string suitable segments together via simple commands. Some of the AI and cliché concepts have been applied to data structures by Bachman (whose company we mentioned earlier). Eventually, *procedural* clichés will find their way into the company's products as well. **Netron's** "frames" represent a different solution to the cliché concept—one that has already proven its viability.

Whether the MIT approach can be dubbed re-engineering remains open to argument. To modify an existing program, the user would let the Apprentice look for clichés that resemble those in the program and then *replace* them with suitable ones from the library. Its components are not only known to be correct, but also to be **context free**. (Unexpected interactions between components remain the *enfants terribles* of high-level programming against which even the gods of software have battled in vain. In software Valhalla functional elements can simply be strung together like algebraic formulas.)

Work at MIT continues. The next system will add a reasoning module that can detect contradictions. Traditionally, software science has tried to verify programs against their specification—an ambitious goal. Finding contradictions between code and a partial specification should be much easier to accomplish, especially in the debugging phase. Furthermore, limitations in the plan concept (e.g., recognizing data structures) must still be overcome. The Sorcerer's Apprentice still has a lot to learn—and knowing when to quit will be part of its curriculum.

Software under the MicroScope.   Naturally, MIT is not alone in its quest to ease the programmer's lot. With MicroScope, *Hewlett-Packard*'s AI lab takes a less ambitious approach that should bear fruit much sooner. While presently limited to the analysis of Common Lisp programs, the MicroScope tool set should eventually broaden its horizon.[10]

MicroScope provides both static and dynamic information about programs. Cross-references for functions and variables, including function call graphs, exploit the system's static database. Queries like "Who calls?" or "Who binds?" let the user access the desired code sections quickly.

On the dynamic side, the MicroScope user can specify source level events to be monitored. An execution history browser assists the user in tracking a program's behavior, by watching for either event combinations or event sequences. The user can specify his wishes in declarative fashion, and MicroScope translates them into the procedural form that's needed for looking over a compiler's shoulder.

Being rule-based, MicroScope can easily expand its knowledge base. The tool set's common user interface further breaks down resistance to learning yet another CASE system. The user also benefits from the object-oriented package's expandability. Although MicroScope's approach differs radically from that of KBEmacs, the two are not mutually exclusive. In fact, in many ways they complement each other and point the way to closer man-machine cooperation. And that, after all, is the final goal of the whole CASE game.

⅃ References

1. Charlie Bachman, "A CASE for reverse engineering," *Datamation*, July 1, 1988, p. 49.

2. Ted Biggerstaff and Charles Richter, "Reusability framework, assessment, and directions," *IEEE Software*, March 1987, p. 41.

3. Luqi, "A computer-aided prototyping system," *IEEE Software*, March 1988, p. 66 (special CASE issue).

4. C. Hewitt and B. Smith, "Toward a programming apprentice," *IEEE Transactions on Software Engineering*, March 1975, p. 26.

5. Richard C. Waters, "The Programmer's Apprentice: A session with KBEmacs," *IEEE Transactions on Software Engineering*, November 1985, p. 1296.

6. Richard C. Waters, "KBEmacs: Where's the AI?" *AI Magazine*, Spring 1986, p. 47.

7. Charles Rich, "The layered architecture of a system for reasoning about programs," in *Proc. IJCAI-81*, August 1981, p. 1044.

8. Kaare Christian, *The Unix Operating System*, 2nd ed., Wiley, New York, 1988.

9. Keith Haviland and Ben Salama, *Unix System Programming*, Addison-Wesley, Reading, MA, 1987.

10. J. Amras and V. O'Day, "MicroScope: A program analysis system," *IEEE Software*, May 1988, p. 50.

17

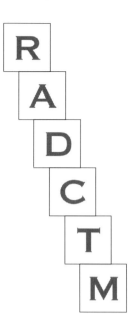

Buyers' Guide to CASE Systems

Technical integrity reigns supreme
The tool must suit your needs
Management concerns do count

As far as the discussion of CASE systems is concerned, we have reached the end of the line. In preceding chapters you had a chance to get acquainted with a broad spectrum of CASE tools, but even so we have only scratched the surface. Before you take the big leap forward into software automation make sure to CASE the joint. Opportunities to watch demos abound, and seminars on the subject sprout like dandelions (pretty to look at, but rarely useful). CASE books are also flourishing, though computer magazines and newsletters can better keep you abreast of the latest wrinkles.[1-3]

Nevertheless, it makes sense to ponder each CASE's fortes and foibles while a demo (or article) still sticks to your mind. Naturally, not all features of a CASE tool are equally important. In a recent survey of CASE users, technical issues topped the wish list[4] ("Checks logic," 96%; "Supports full life cycle," 78%; and "Fully integrated," 74%). Management capabilities followed

(54%), with interface issues bringing up the rear. We'll broach these three main topics in the same sequence.

The first group of questions you should ask yourself (and designated vendors) must deal with your intended use. After all, if a CASE system can't do your job, nothing else matters in the least:

- Can the system handle real-time problems?
- Does it flag deadlocks and races?
- Can it hack large programs (how many modules)?
- Will it interface with your databases?
- Will it accommodate existing programs (or libraries)?
- Does the system speak the proper languages?
- Does it support parallelism or concurrency?
- For embedded software, can it handle hardware modeling?

Don't regard this list as complete. A transaction system, for example, may demand local optimization for speed, which could require hardware simulation. Or, if you want to include an expert system, can the offered CASE tools handle declarative programming? Will they at least accept prefabricated code segments, so you can embed a small inference system?

Integration and completeness vital.   When you analyze a CASE system's technical capabilities, nothing even approaches tight integration in importance. We are not concerned here with a closely coupled report or even code generator, but with the coupling between graphical and internal representation of your evolving program. While modern CASE tools present the user primarily with graphic software views of a program, the system's database must capture more than arcs and geometric shapes.

Unless the database contains the meaning of a function bubble or control arc it can't guarantee consistency or correctness of an emerging program. Behind the pretty pictures a rigorous "language" must be sequestered that captures every click of your mouse and distills the impact of every change. Asking the right questions can be vital:

- Do you have access to the system's database?
- Can the database be consulted by other tools?
- Is the database expandable (e.g. object-oriented)?

- Can you edit the formal description?
- Will the result appear in the graphics?
- Is graphic editing reflected in the formal text?
- Are all graphic views consistent with each other?
- Does the design language afford process visibility?

Next ranks the CASE system's completeness—which phases of the software life cycle are covered by the tool. All too often the front and back ends of the waterfall are served by different tools which may not by fully integrated (as defined earlier). Here are some assertive questions:

- Is a requirements language included?
- Who supports this language?
- Does the system include a code generator?
- Can you verify the final code against this spec?
- Does the system generate test cases?
- Will it inform you of test coverage?
- Can you seed the code with assertions?
- How does the system support maintenance?
- Does it implement reverse engineering?
- Can you move freely within the life cycle phases?

To elaborate on the last question, some CASE systems are so rigid that you can only move in the direction of further decomposition. As we've noted more than once during the G-Train implementations, real life is no one-way street. If you must return to square one every time an implementation detail needs to be changed, your productivity goes down the (G-Train) tube. Moving backward in the life cycle, as you'll recall from the previous chapter, can destroy higher-level design information. Furthermore, a retroactive change's consequences must be carried forward by the CASE system into all the affected descendants. So don't be surprised if this last question produces more waffling than answers.

The CASE for finding fault.   While it would be nice to just feed a requirements spec into a CASE system and then press the "Implement" button, such is not yet in the cards. CASE can help us in the process of decomposing and transforming requirements into algorithms and code. But, more importantly, it can stop us when we wander off the straight and narrow along the way.

Two groups of CASE tools cooperate in this endeavor: static and dynamic analyzers. The former check types and variables against dictionary entries; the latter execute the design.

Let's first look at the static analysis and what a CASE vendor should tell you about it:

- What cross-reference reports are available?
- Can you display calling trees?
- Does the system statically check typing?
- Does it work even for dynamic binding?

Static analysis tools have been around for decades, so you shouldn't run into much trouble with them. Dynamic analysis, however, lets you execute your program and observe the code's behavior. The feature is better known as simulation, and by their simulators you shall recognize the winners:

- Can you simulate during all design stages?
- Can you simulate even from requirements?
- Are real-time descriptions (graphs) executable?
- What functions are predefined?
- Is hardware simulation possible?
- Is the simulation animated—e.g., via tokens?
- Are time-domain views available?
- Can state diagrams be executed?
- Can you simulate concurrent processes?
- Can the simulation be stopped—e.g., via breakpoints?
- Can it be reversed?
- After corrections, can it be resumed?

Clearly, if real-time is your game, a simulator that passes this interrogation can boost your productivity immensely. It alone should pay for the whole CASE system in less than a year—especially if you work with embedded systems. One question, whether the system can simulate concurrent processes, needs a follow-up query: "How many?" As you'll see in Chapter 19, simulating massively parallel systems is still an art practiced primarily in university laboratories. We can only hope that moderate parallelism can be handled by standard CASE systems before the multiprocessor machines inundate us.

⸲ Get Tools that Suit Your Temperament

Once you're confident that a CASE system has the technical moxie you need, it's time to explore less critical issues—for example, whether the tool supports your favorite methodology. While correct solutions certainly outweigh comfort, it's also true that a system that accepts your working habits will get you past deadlines more easily.

Most modern CASE tools are anchored in the Yourdon-DeMarco data flow diagram, and most supply Chen's entity relationship graphs. When it comes to data structures à la Jackson or real-time control and state diagrams, however, the pickings get slimmer. You should also insist on a modicum of creature comforts—naturally, only if they boost productivity. Make sure to ask:

- Does the system support your favored methodology?
- For data flow, is it Gane-Sarson, Yourdon-DeMarco, or both?
- For control flow, Ward-Mellor, Hatley-Pirbhai, or both?
- In what form can you specify time delays?
- Are state transitions depicted in a way you like?
- Can you work both top-down and bottom-up?
- How does the system display error messages?
- Are they adequately integrated with the graphs?
- Can you apply object-oriented techniques?

The last question is meant more in the spirit of Ada than Smalltalk. It's unlikely that you'll find a CASE system that is equally proficient in procedure-oriented data flow and message-oriented object-ivity. Beyond this sort of schism you should, however, insist on maximum flexibility:

- Does the system proffer an open architecture?
- Can it be modified (reasonably) by the user?
- How easily can you customize interface graphics?
- Will it permit cohabitation with existing tools?
- Does it produce the kind of reports you need?
- Or can you interface with existing documentors?
- In how many languages is the system proficient?
- Does that include any fourth-generation languages (4-GLs)?

- Can you expand and modify graphics to suit you?
- Can communications be synchronous and asynchronous?
- Can you choose between black-box and white-box tests?
- Are your favorite metrics available?
- Does the system measure complexity? Completeness?
- On what types of computers will it run?

No softworker is an island.   Except for the sovereign programmers of the old school (who'd spurn CASE tools anyway), most of today's software designers toil in groups. That imposes a number of additional stipulations on CASE systems, dealing with data security and teamwork. For example:

- Are needs for shared access and protection balanced?
- How are read and read-write access controlled?
- Can the data dictionary be subdivided and recombined?
- How does the system enforce version control?
- Does its configuration management satisfy you?
- How are changes propagated to other team members?
- How does the tool implement traceability?

Teamwork also brings with it the need for integration and project management. Even automatic event triggering and linkage with tool functions are emerging. Some CASE systems emphasize these "Upper CASE" needs, while others lack management tools altogether. Finding the right balance may not be easy, and you may have to resort to separate tools.[5] Access of management tools to the project database can speed administrative chores substantially. For example:

- Does the system incorporate cost estimation?
- Can it be easily updated via code metrics?
- How can metrics be collected for reports?
- What project tracking mechanisms are available?
- How can standards and procedures be enforced?
- Does the system support electronic mail?
- Does it facilitate design and status reviews?
- Does it implement critical path scheduling?
- Can you implement user-defined high-level tasks?
- How good is the fit with the present organization?

- For example, can multiple projects be monitored?
- Can you implement priorities among projects?
- Can you play what-if games on proposed designs?
- Are you satisfied with audit trails and tracking?

   Don't regard the questions in this chapter as a checklist to be verified before takeoff. Rather, look at it as a wish list, and count the blessings that materialize under the tree. If the CASE industry can agree on standards (to be discussed in the next chapter), you may someday be able to put together a system that satisfies all your needs. In the meantime, all you can do is field your queries.

   When all the answers are in, you'll have to ask yourself the ultimate question: "Are the features worth the price?" Many factors will influence the buying decision but perhaps none as much as your image of the selected vendor(s). How long has he been in business? How good are his user training and field support? (Training and support often devour several times the tool cost!) Most importantly, how strong is the vendor technically?

   Some copycat outfits know how to market their grab bags of features. Their demo may look great, but what good is that if they don't know what they're doing? Let your "short list" candidates solve a problem of *your* choice. That is the only valid demo, and it soon separates the wheat from the chaff. Of course, it also helps if *you* know what *they* are doing. By now you probably will.

⸙ References

1. Michael Gibson, "A guide to selecting CASE tools," *Datamation*, July 1, 1988, p. 65.

2. Dallas E. Webster, "Mapping the design information representation terrain," *Computer*, December 1988, p. 8.

3. CASE Outlook (see CASE Consulting Group, Appendix D).

4. Harvey A. Levine, "Two separate worlds moving slowly closer," *Software Magazine*, March 1989, p. 32.

5. Ken Orr, et al., "Methodology: The experts speak," *Byte*, April 1989 (special CASE issue).

⌐ Reader's Wish List:

18

A PLEA
FOR CASE
STANDARDS

The trouble with standards
Computers can talk and listen
CASE tools are still islands

Without standards, a technological civilization like ours could never emerge. We speak a standard language (more or less), use a standard character set (give or take), and plug standard connectors into standard sockets. Unless we stray too far in time or space, that is—which brings us to a charming aphorism: "The beauty of standards is that there are so many to choose from."

Though we may curse when the last three-prong adapter has disappeared (or we can't find a nail file to depolarize the latest gizmo), 3 types of connectors are better than 20. When it comes to software, however, even 20 would be a relief. Granted software is harder to standardize than power outlets, where four adapters and a transformer can get us through the "civilized" world, but we could do better than we are doing.*

---

*For example, take the calendar date. ISO Standard 2014 approved by many countries (including the U.S.) in 1976, lets you write April 1, 1989 as 19890401, or 89-04-01, or 89 04 01. Just wait a few years and interpret the meaning of 01-02-03. In Europe it's February 1, 2003, in the United States January 2, 2003, and in Computerland (hopefully) February 3, 2001. But never mind; on 01-01-01 (or even earlier) all older systems will crash anyway due to "clock overflow," since 12-31-99 is their "doomsday."

Of course, there are standards and standards. We can't do much about those imposed by customers, except shun their business—which may be hard to do if your specialty includes flight controllers and rocket simulators. So we put up with the 250 requirements of DOD STD 2167A, like it or not. In the unruly software world, we can't even blame a big customer for trying to instigate a modicum of conformity. But we can lament the impact that 2167A and its predecessors had on the fledgling CASE industry: tying up scarce talent to devise software for cranking out "reports" instead of programs.

At least 2167A—unlike its predecessors—no longer crams every kind of software into the same mold. Indeed, the standard has become so flexible you need support software to manage it, such as Tailor from *Logicon* to, well, tailor your statement of work so it forms a coherent (and legal!) subset of 2167A. It might even be a good idea for software managers outside the Pentagon's orbit to extract a suitable subset for internal use, especially when large software systems are involved.

A second type of standards could be classified as self-imposed, which takes in most of the IEEE standards, such as IEEE 1042, *Guide to Software Configuration Management.*[1] Literally dozens of similar standards exist (or are in the making), covering the whole software life cycle. But, as one reader of *IEEE Software* put it: "they come closer to the least common multiple than the greatest common divider."

True enough, many IEEE standards are unenforceable guidelines and thus help the software manager more than the software designer. But then the IEEE is inherently an educational brotherhood, and guidelines are better than chaos. Furthermore, some IEEE standards get promoted to higher levels, such as FIPS (Federal Information Processing Standards) or ANSI (American National Standards Institute). Some might even make it to the top of the ladder, the ISO (International Standards Organization).

However, exalted status is no guarantee for adoption in practice. Languages standardized by ANSI and even ISO still are plagued by dialects, except for the lucky few that started life as proprietary tongue like Fortran or C. The latter just achieved standard status—in the nick of time, before popularity shattered it. In fact, if the standard flies, C might gain by the standard's additions, which carefully plug some of the language's voids, so to speak.[2] A standard for parallel Fortran might also come in before the flood of parallelism inundates us (as discussed in the next chapter).

Standards of the third kind.   Even more important than languages for the well-being of computing are operating systems. Imagine our quandary if PC-DOS and Unix had not dammed a flood of some 120 OS contenders a decade ago.[3] Remember that PC-DOS is a *binary* standard (providing software in *object code* for direct hardware access), while Unix was meant to mate *source code* (written in C) to the hardware. Unfortunately, Unix dialects have recently developed at an alarming rate. But a number of trade organizations throughout the world have managed to brush aside myopic greed and come to terms with AT&T, which after all holds the copyright.[4]

By now all major players have elected the IEEE Posix Standard 1003.1,[5] which standardizes system calls. By the end of 1989, Standard 1003.2 should bring agreement at the shell level as well and a real-time Posix standard (1003.4) should also be in place, ending the uncertainties on such semistandards as Carnegie-Mellon University's Mach (see Figure 18.1). However,

Figure 18.1 Without standards, CASE tools will remain ineffective. Fortunately, the Posix standard for operating systems inspires hope for progress.

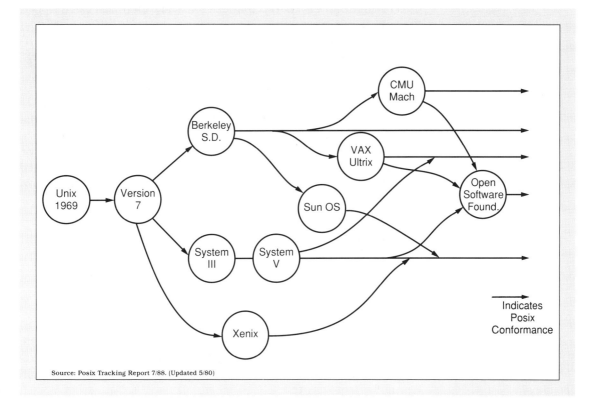

Source: Posix Tracking Report 7/88. (Updated 5/80)

even though Posix helps Unix users, not all systems houses will be happy. Internally, not all Posix implementations will play the same way, because some will be based on AT&T's System V and others on IBM's AIX-3. The former's kernel includes interface drivers that work with interrupts, while the latter interposes a "virtual resource manager" (VRM). For example, an attempt to port the ISO transport-level protocol together with an Ethernet driver from System V to AIX requires an extra VRM interface that not only slows the system down but consumes precious system programmer time. Furthermore, Posix permits options that can make Posix-compatible systems incompatible with each other. X/Open's "common application environment" will iron out any snags at the user end, but not for the system builder.

Still, we do have a standard, thanks to user pressure. Most influential was the **Open Software Foundation** (OSF) whose membership count approaches the 100 level (from over a dozen countries), followed by international impetus via X/Open, which is strongest in Europe and Japan, and from Unix International Inc.[6] The much-debated Japanese software factories have upped the standards ante with their Sigma project[7] (Software Industrialized Generator and Maintenance Aids—ouch!) which anticipated Posix by combining System V and Berkeley 4.2 BSD features in its workstation specs.

How much difference pressure from "superusers" (like OSF and X/Open) can make becomes apparent when you compare Posix's success with the fate of a previous OS effort by the IEEE called "Mosis" (Microcomputer operating system interface standard). It mosied along for years in committees, only to be ignored after adoption. Rightly so, because where standardized system calls were desperately needed, a dissertation emerged on "how to implement on OS."

⤷ CASE Systems are Still Deaf and Dumb

With all this standardization, why can today's CASE tools still only talk to themselves? After all, NFS (Network File System) ties not only Berkeley's 4.2 BSD and System V together, it even interfaces with MS-DOS. So, CASE tools that run under DOS and Unix have access to most of the market.[8] Portability at the network level is therefore no longer an issue. But CASE depends on graphics, and when it comes to graphics the software world is still far from united.

True, efforts to unify systems at the windowing level are underway. The best of Microsoft's Windows, Sun Microsystems' NeWS (Network Extensible Window System), and MIT-developed X-Windows[9] are available via OSF-sponsored UECs (user environment components), even though widespread windowing may overburden NSF links. But even with a windowing standard in place, at a lower level several graphics standards still vie for the lead. And graphics are as essential a part to software design by now as they have been to hardware design by means of CAE (computer-aided engineering) all along.

Emphasizing the similarity between hardware CAE and software CASE, EDIF (Electronic Design Interchange Format, developed for IC design) can serve as the linkage medium between tools.[10] CASE vendors have already demonstrated the transfer of such fare as data flow diagrams between competing systems, but a CASE standard aspires to more than moving bubbles from one screen to another. Suppose one of the systems uses rectangles to depict processes and dotted curves or even tables for data. Within the host computers, all this information is represented as bits, which need not have any meaning to humans at all but must permit expansion into displays with the desired format. Indeed, the EDIF code in the mentioned demo contained not only bubble and arrow descriptions, but all the functional information as well. From it, a suitable compiler could compose any desired graph or even a textual definition.

Now imagine a joint software design effort between companies X and Y, using CASE systems from vendors A and B. They want to combine data flow diagrams of different subsystems into a hierarchy tree of the whole system. Let's assume that vendor A's CASE can perform the transformation from his Ward-Mellor data structure to his (relational) HIPO database, but vendor B uses IDEF-0 representations, stored in a network *schema*. It will take some pretty smart translation programs to move the data from Y's B to X's A tool. Needless to say, no such program exists yet.

Three ways to bridge the gap. Basically, the two different databases could be made to communicate in three ways: (1) translate A's format into B's or vice versa; (2) translate both into a common intermediate form; or (3) fashion a database that both A and B can access. The first approach is being used by CASE vendors who incorporate specific tools in their products in joint marketing agreements. Such "bridges" are efficient and invisible to the user, but obviously won't let you put together your own customized CASE tool kit.

The second approach has originally been embraced by EDIF, and now by its CASE sibling, CDIF. It succeeded in the CAE game (albeit slowly), because it forced no successful player to recognize anybody else's format as a standard. It's winning again in the CASE field, but there's one big difference: in CAE the symbols for schematics were well established and so was the concept of "netlists"—the wiring that interconnects the symbols. (That's where the IP comes from.) CASE has no such bedrock to build upon; every vendor devised his own (all too often adobe) foundation. We can't build cathedrals on any of them.

We must remember that CDIF, like EDIF, merely imposes a standard *format* for data interchange, leaving implementation details up to individual CASE vendors. The effort is supported by the **Electronic Industries Association**, to which most CASE vendors belong. This sponsorship adds credibility to CDIF as a future standard. EDIF was also sponsored by EIA and still had to struggle for acceptance. However, since the CDIF team has learned from EDIF's mistakes, it's already approaching standard status. Still, CDIF cannot tackle the questions related to each CASE system's underlying data repository. Indeed, while a dozen CASE standards are in the works, not one of them has cracked this formidable barrier.

Deeper down, two solutions.   This brings us to the third alternative, for which one solution consists of a "backplane" (analogous to the motherboard of a computer) introduced by **Atherton Technology**. This company, supported by Digital Equipment and other hardware platform vendors—as well as major CASE players and aerospace users—are exploring an integration standard called CIS (Common Integration Service, previously also dubbed CATIS). It wants to evolve a nonproprietary standard that addresses primarily the issues that were not resolved by CDIF.

These deeper levels include version control, access control, file naming, a common user interface, and portability—the issues addressed by an IPSE (Integrated Project Support Environment). In addition, CIS naturally needs to tackle problems more directly related to CASE, such as source code management and the relationships between data from different tools and different vendors. These tools should address the whole life cycle, from project management to testing and reverse engineering. Tools and the database must be shareable, yet prevent mutual interference. Software development often proceeds along several "twigs"— offshoots from major branches—but the underlying database must also permit these twigs to be reunited with the mother branch, if not the root.

As if these demands were not arduous enough, a CASE standard also must be open ended to accommodate future tools as well as present ones. The only feasible approach appears to be an object-oriented system with limited inheritance. In this regard, it would differ from Europe's PCTE +, the second phase of the Portable Common Tool Environment. Funded under the Common Market's Esprit project, PCTE has already spawned some European CASE products, foremost Emeraude, developed by the French conglomerate Groupe Bull.

In essence, PCTE + will combine PCTE with an IPSE, tying together integration and portability. This approach demands deeper standardization than many American vendors seem willing to accept. Especially the communications and I/O models incorporated in PCTE + go beyond the goals of the CIS group. While Europe's CASE vendors and ECMA (European Computer Manufacturer's Association) members will have to adhere to PCTE +, their American counterparts may have to comply with CAIS-A, the DoD-imposed Common Ada Interface Standard. More precisely, some of their biggest customers—including the members of SPC—will require CAIS, which thus dangles a juicy carrot before CIS. However, CAIS and PCTE aren't that far apart; PCTE's sponsors are bidding for DoD's CAIS funding, and both pay little more than lip service to the object-oriented creed.

Another alternative for an integration standard has been advanced by **NIST** (National Institute for Standards and Technology—formerly the National Bureau of Standards) and was recently elevated to ANSI Standard X3.138.[11] NIST, too, embraces a limited object-oriented approach. Because this paradigm couples data with the procedures (or "methods") that can operate on them, it should be flexible enough to accommodate even future CASE tools. Only in this roundabout way, believe some, can the required flexibility be ensured.

IRDS (Information Resource Dictionary System) specifies four layers, only two of which are mandatory parts of the standard. As Figure 18.2 shows, the bottom layer represents the data themselves—bit strings in computer memory. The metadata layer defines what those data mean; the layer thus defines entities, relationships, and attributes (called ERA for short). You could

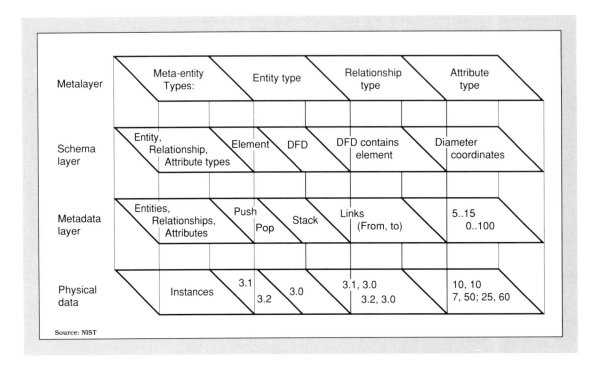

	Meta-entity Types:	Entity type	Relationship type	Attribute type
Metalayer				
Schema layer	Entity, Relationship, Attribute types	Element / DFD	DFD contains element	Diameter coordinates
Metadata layer	Entities, Relationships, Attributes	Push / Pop / Stack	Links (From, to)	5..15 / 0..100
Physical data	Instances	3.1 / 3.2 / 3.0	3.1, 3.0 / 3.2, 3.0	10, 10 / 7, 50; 25, 60

Source: NIST

Figure 18.2 The IRDS standard devised by the National Bureau of Standards should facilitate the transfer of CASE information between different tools. The bottom layer contains actual data; the next one identifies entities, relationships, and attributes; the third defines their type; and the fourth (optional) permits broader definitions.

regard this layer as the formal variables, bound to the bottom layer's actual variables. Above the ERA layer, a schema layer defines the types of entities, relationships, and attributes—a kind of class structure that's tied together in an optional schema description or metaentity layer.

The standards discussed in this chapter, both evolving and established ones,[12] are not mutually exclusive. For example, CDIF could choose IRDS as its database model and PCTE+ as its integration model. Whatever the eventual outcome of the standardizing work, there can be no doubt that the future of the CASE revolution will be tightly linked to its success. An improper database organization, for example, can derail the CASE express and undo a decade's work. More than the CASE vendors' future hangs in the balance.

ʟ **References**

1. IEEE Standards Bearer (for access see Appendix D).

2. Thomas Plum, *Notes on the Draft C Standard*, Plum Hall, Cardiff, NJ, 1988.

3. Max Schindler, "Microcomputer operating systems branch into mainframe territory," *Electronic Design*, March 19, 1981, p. 179.

4. Tom Manuel, "A single standard emerges from the Unix tug-of-war," *Electronics*, January 1989, p. 141.

5. Bruce Hunter, "Standards and the IEEE P1003.7 Committee," *root* January 1989, p. 24 (see InfoPro Systems in Appendix D).

6. David Fiedler, "Unix International Inc.," *Unique*, vol. 5, February 1989, p. 3 (see Infopro Systems in Appendix D).

7. Noburu Akima and Fusatake Ooi, "Industrializing software development: A Japanese approach," *IEEE Software*, March 1989, p. 13 (Special Issue, "Far East").

8. Tim Chase, "Comparing Unix with other systems," *TC Interface*, September 1988, p. 64.

9. Frank E. Hall and James B. Byers, "X: A window system standard for distributed computing environments," *Hewlett-Packard Journal*, October 1988, p. 46.

10. Harvey Clawson, "Understanding EDIF conventions to transfer circuit data," *Electronic Design*, December 1987, p. 49.

11. Alan Goldfine and Patricia Konig, *A Technical Overview of the Information Resource Dictionary System*, 2nd ed., NBSSIR 88-3700, distributed by NTIS, Springfield, VA.

12. Gene Forte (Ed.), *1988 CASE Industry Directory*, Case Consulting Group, Portland, OR, 1988 (see Appendix D).

Courtesy IBM Archives

When Gottfried Wilhelm von Leibniz first cranked up his five-function calculator in 1694 (shown on p. 32), he ushered in the number crunching era. Does his pensive look betray some misgivings?

19

THE MEGAMACHINES ARE COMING

The lure of multiprocessing
Next-generation software
A new tower of Babel
The debugging debacle

Nearly half a century ago IBM watched the evolution of "electronic brains" with a good deal of skepticism. A blue-ribbon management panel—so the story goes—assessed the market potential of computers that could perform thousands of additions a second. The verdict was announced by Thomas Watson himself: seven of them could meet all the world's computational needs.

We know better now. Any old PC can run rings around Eniac and its 50 floating-point operations per second (FLOPS, for short). In fact, MFLOPS (megaflops—millions of FLOPS) in desktop machines barely raise eyebrows today. And as Parkinson predicted, appetite keeps outrunning available means. If recent trends persist we'll reach desktop GFLOPS (billion FLOPS) well before the millenium turns (see Figure 19.1).[1]

Then progress will suddenly stop, because even at the speed of light only a billion "signals" can pass through a 1-foot box—unless, that is, we learn to process more than one data packet at a

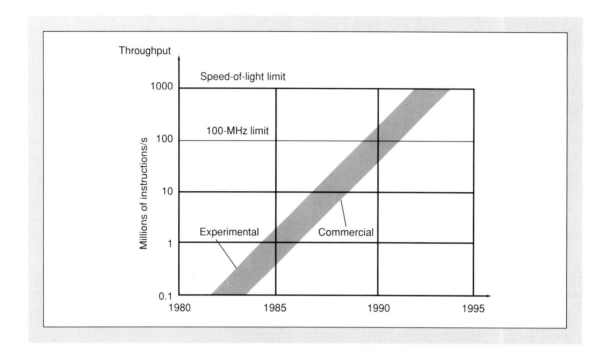

Figure 19.1 As processor throughput increases, the speed of light begins to play a role. In those lofty regions, only parallelism can increase throughput further.

time. No wonder parallel processing has been a hot research topic for years. Thanks to cheap microprocessors, you can already buy workstations with a dozen CPUs for the price of a fancy car.[2]

Alas, such a computer may complete your chores only two to six times faster than one with an equivalent single CPU. It all depends on the degree of parallelism inherent in your job. You have no problem if you want your computer to pick the phone numbers of all women named Florence from the New York directory (the CD-ROM version, naturally). You can assign each processor two letters of the alphabet and off they go. At the end, the partial lists must still be merged, but any word processor can collect a dozen files in a jiffy.

Life gets tougher if you want your computer to manipulate vectors. To add $A(i)+B(i)$ poses no problem, because the sum vector $C(i)$ consists of all the elements' sums ($A(1)+B(1)$, $A(2)+B(2)$, etc.). For simplicity's sake let's assume both vectors have the value (1, 2, 3, 4). All of these additions—which yield the result (2, 4, 6, 8)—can be done in parallel, as we noted back in Chapter 8. But with more complex transformations, we'll soon run into trouble. Take the "inner" product of the vectors, which

consists of the sum of all partial products A(i)*B(i). One way
to calculate it would be

```
10    DO 40 i=1,4
20    P(i) = A(i)*B(i)
30    IF i=1 S(i)=P(i)
         ELSE S(i)=P(i)+S(i-1)
40    CONTINUE
```

This Fortran code looks contrived, but it will serve to demonstrate some multiprocessing idiosyncrasies. We'll only monitor
the statements that do useful work—20 and 30. You may ask
"Why **Fortran**?" That's still the dominant language in the land of
Megamachines.[3]

We assume that both arrays again have the values (1, 2, 3,
4). By plugging in the four values for i, we obtain for the partial-
products vector P = (1, 4, 9, 16); so the final result, S(4),
must be 30. Let's see what happens if we run the problem on
three processing elements (PEs). As Figure 19.2 demonstrates,
all PEs get off to a running start on line 20. The first processor
has no problem executing line 30 either, but the second one gets
stuck when it starts looking for P(1). This product isn't available

Figure 19.2 In this
simple matrix product,
repeated waits for
intermediate results
reduce hardware
utilization (shaded
area) drastically.

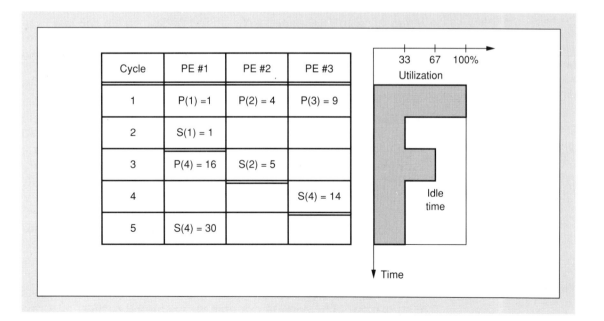

Cycle	PE #1	PE #2	PE #3
1	P(1) =1	P(2) = 4	P(3) = 9
2	S(1) = 1		
3	P(4) = 16	S(2) = 5	
4			S(4) = 14
5	S(4) = 30		

33   67   100%
Utilization

Idle
time

Time

until one execution cycle later, and for P(2) the third processor has to wait yet another cycle. When the fourth calculation runs (on PE #1 again), it too falls victim to synchronization overhead.

All told, of the 15 execution cycles available on the three processors, only 8 were able to do some work. This amounts to a PE efficiency of 53% —not much to brag about. Another way of looking at it is that on a single PE it would have taken 80 cycles to run the above program 10 times. On three PEs it should have taken one-third of that, or 27 cycles. In fact, it took 50 cycles, which amounts to a speedup of 1.85 instead of the hoped-for 3.0.

If you go through the same exercise with different vector sizes, you'll readily see that efficiency and speedup vary all over the lot, depending on how well the problem fits the hardware. In our example, the poor performance can be traced to the need for communications between S(i) and S(i-1) (called index inter-dependency).

In the vector example, we assumed that all PEs shared the same memory. No matter which PE calculated a variable's value, it was stored in the same location. Had each processor stored its own vectors (including copies of A and B), only PE #1 would ever have accomplished anything. The other two would have looked for S(i-1) in vain. We also assumed that some guardian angel would prevent the PEs from reading in a vector element that was not yet computed. Without such serendipity, PE #2 would have grabbed whatever value happened to be stored in S(1) from the last run. In fact, some computers wake up with all ones (hex FFFF) in memory, which would have produced errors in the billions and billions of percent for the first run.

Multiprocessing 101.   Young and intractable though the field of parallel processing may be, some knowledge (and affiliated jargon) has accumulated from which we can benefit. In the above example we dealt with vectors, because they are the simplest data structures in multiprocessing. Arrays (which we might classify as vectors of vectors) dominate in the "hard" sciences, where most of the demand for parallel number-crunching originates. Consequently, vector and array processors have been around for decades, as have vectorizing compilers that hunt for Fortran DO loops. This simple type of parallelism is known as "synchronous multiprocessing."

Recent megamachines aim higher—ideally for universal employment. The sorting example we examined earlier, or a ray-tracing graphics program, typify one major branch on the multi-processor tree: all the PEs (except perhaps for a "master") do the same job. Such systems, which handle only a single instruction stream but multiple data streams (hence called SIMD machines), pose few problems and can easily be improvised even from net-worked PCs.

Much more desirable are MIMD (multiple instruction, mul-tiple data) systems because (theoretically) they can tackle any job efficiently. Needless to say, they also pose a much greater technical challenge, even in their SPMD (single program, multi-ple data) incarnation, which parallelizes a single large program. MIMD computers have sprouted a whole jumble of architectures to best satisfy the needed communications between the execut-ing processes. Simplest among them is the common-memory kind, which we assumed in the tiny vector example. Typically, such machines combine a dozen or so PEs in a single box and run under Unix-like operating systems. Because the bus often becomes a communications bottleneck, these machines tend to saturate as the number of processors reaches double digits.

No wonder academic laboratories have pursued more challenging architectures—known as ensemble machines—where each PE owns at least *some* memory. Configurations range from tree structures (e.g., Dado from erstwhile Fifth Generation Computers) to computing surfaces (where PEs form lattices as in the ill-fated Illiac) to hypercubes (cubes of four or more dimensions, first proposed back in 1965). A glance at Figure 19.3 conveys not only the richness of configurations, but also the range of connectivity. None of them can be classified as fully connected; for that, each PE would have to be linked to every other one in the network.

In a tree, for example, nodes at the leaf level may have to send messages all the way down (rather, up—we are talking software here) to the root. In a 4-cube, a message can get from any node to any other in no more than four hops. In an 8-cube, which boasts 2^8, or 256 nodes, messages may have to be routed through as many as seven PEs before they reach their destination. It is clear that programs have to be spread in such a way over this structure that those with the most data traffic reside close to each other—topologically speaking. Hypercubes can usually be reconfigured dynamically into a range of topologies from rings to trees. Even so, some parts of such programs as finite-element modeling (for structural design) or circuit simulation (for digital design) may execute faster in serial than in parallel form.

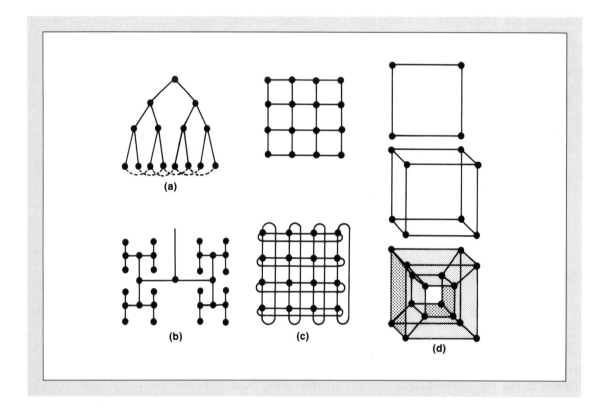

Figure 19.3 Processing elements can be linked in many ways. Binary trees (*a*) make for good chip utilization (*b*), and grids can be looped into surfaces (*c*). N-cubes (*d*) range from two-dimensional (top) to well beyond four-dimensional (bottom).

Although hypercubes with up to 65,536 (i.e., 2^{16}) elements have been built, these behemoths tend to be too rigid for general use. Once PEs grow into the hundreds, flexibility can be restored with a different routing mechanism—crossbar switches. They work more or less like telephone exchanges, which, as we all know, can accommodate millions of talkative participants. Although expensive and a bit sluggish, crossbar-connected multiprocessors (like Cogent's desktop unit) can easily be reconfigured into whatever architecture suits the program best at every moment during execution.[4]

⌐ Software for the Next Generation

As we have stressed throughout this book, software and hardware mirror each other in many ways. Nowhere is that more obvious than in multiprocessor applications. You recall from the vector product that the efficiency of such machines depends on a match between the parallelism of the problem and that of the hardware. Running six comparable tasks on five PEs practically guarantees poor speedup. So do processes whose execution time can vary widely, but which require periodic synchronization— for example, if they must set a conditional jump by comparing intermediate results.

Things are more complicated than that, however. If we wanted to build a monitoring package for the Chicago hub of a nationwide G-Train system, we'd have several choices. Assume that six lines are converging in Chicago. We could just link six computers, each running a copy of the whole G-Train package. Whenever fewer than six trains are active (which would likely be most of the time), some computers would remain idle. Chances are we'd get by with three PEs, but if even four trains became active, such a coarse-grain solution would produce some unhappy travelers.

It makes more sense to break the monitor system down into smaller tasks—say, to the level used in Figure 7.2. The boarding and speed monitoring functions never occur simultaneously and are of different duration. Boarding might require 15 minutes, while the trip to Seattle (direct, of course) would take over 7 hours. While one PE takes care of the Seattle train, another PE can handle up to 28 boarding operations. Such a medium-grain operation would save us some hardware.

The PE that monitors the Seattle train would still spin its abstract wheels most of the time. You may recall that each speed measurement takes just milliseconds, while the intervals between them can run several minutes. Why not treat each speed calculation as a distinct task that can be performed by any available processor? Now we have a fine-grain solution that needs even fewer PEs. Should we break the calculations down even further? The ultimate fine-grain solution would fragment programs into elementary operations (addition, division, comparison). In data flow machines these operations are indeed performed by herds of specialized small PEs.

Not quite as extreme, the "sawdust" school advocates breaking tasks down into such small elements that every PE's every idle moment can be put to good use. But there's a catch. For one thing, each context switch between tasks produces a fixed overhead—saving the old calculation's values, reading in the new ones, making sure there'll be no deadlock between processors, and so forth. More importantly, processes can't be broken down arbitrarily. Critical sections—DO loops, CASE constructs, and the like—must be executed without interruption.

The smallest reasonable code segments are usually called "threads," and they just happen to coincide with the smallest reasonable IPs. As we found in Chapter 8, decomposing procedures beyond in-line code segments that can run without any interference from control signals makes little sense. You may recall that we don't consider array or vector operations as true DO loops; many of them can now be simply offloaded to vector coprocessors.

To conclude the multiprocessing appraisal of the G-Train hub, we'd probably be served best with a mix of medium-grain processes (for boarding) and fine-grain processes (for speed calculation). To make sure the hardware fits this mix like a glove, we'd have to examine the PEs' technical specs in detail. But we already know that we'll need fewer than a dozen PEs, so a common-memory architecture should serve the Chicago hub superbly.

Let us recapitulate and generalize what we have discovered so far. We must watch out for these multiprocessing foibles:

- Match architecture and application
- Match architecture and data structures
- Optimize the size of program chunks
- Decide *how* best to carve up the program
- Monitor speedup versus array dimensions
- Check and recheck overheads due to:
    Synchronization
    Message passing
    Deadlock resolution
    Garbage removal
    Livelock*

Unlike serial programs, the multiprocessing variety may catch you off balance with every new run. Algorithm, problem size, and computer size tend to be interrelated in unfathomable ways—at least without the benefit of hindsight. In fact, even purely sequential bugs may suddenly appear during parallel execution. For example, one of the processes can inadvertently pass some variable to an obscure subroutine and get picked up by another process.

---

*That's when communications overhead consumes all available resources. (Remember the endless refrain "Yes I can"; "No you can't". . . ?)

Nor does a parallelized program necessarily outrun its serial elder. Benchmarks, run by Ametek on its hypercube (see Figure 19.4) demonstrate these anomalies. In some ratios of problem size to computer size, a *serial* version of the program may run faster than a parallel one. In fact, under some conditions the parallel algorithms lagged as much as 400% ! The tests examined which of several algorithms worked best for solving differential equations—a very common application of multiprocessors in scientific computing. The scattering method ran fastest on up to 32 PEs, while two Gaussian-elimination and standard serial cyclic reduction method split first prize for larger hypercubes.

Figure 19.4 The fastest algorithm for a given application depends not only on the number of processors (horizontal axis), but also on the size of the problem (vertical axis). Often the serial algorithm is fastest (dark areas).

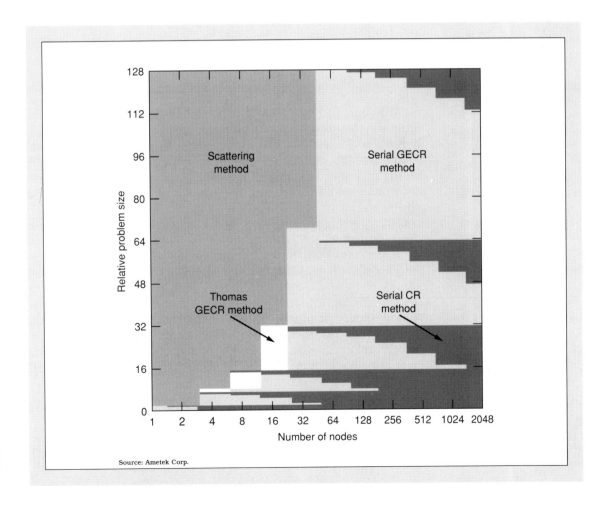

Source: Ametek Corp.

To P or not to P.   Parallel processes must somehow be "packaged" to preserve their integrity. Theoreticians have tackled the problem for decades, but Dijkstra's 1968 introduction of semaphores has impacted developments to this day.[5] In his work, Dijkstra conceived the P and V operations, which still crop up in technical papers.

Based on the Dutch words *proberen* (to try) and *verhogen* (to increase), these operations describe the attempted decrease and increase of the semaphore's value, respectively.[6] In other words, "to P a semaphore" means to decrement its value, unless it is already zero. Or, you can V a binary flag, mutex, for mutual exclusion in a queue by stipulating

```
V(mutex): IF  queue not empty THEN
             -- remove a process from the queue
             ELSE mutex := 1
```

Although you can ensure process integrity with semaphores alone, the resulting code can get quite opaque. When shared variables are scattered through a whole program, the monitor (or secretary) concept simplifies matters. A monitor becomes a domicile for "critical sections" (say a loop that must never be interrupted), which are removed from their native processes. Whenever a process wants to enter a critical section, it calls the appropriate monitor procedure. Only after one process exits can the monitor enter another.

The monitor concept has been used to turn serial languages like Pascal into parallel ones; Concurrent Pascal provides an example. (It is not to be confused with Simultaneous Pascal.) In a concurrent language, multiple processes normally share the same address space; in others, they can communicate by exchanging messages, or via the rendezvous method. Both monitors and semaphore locks can safeguard critical code sections, but we must remember that code integrity is only one prerequisite for multiprocessing.

Program modularity plays just as important a role, and, with Modula-2 and Ada firmly established in softwareland, most recent (and hopefully all future) software can now be considered intrinsically parallelizable.[7] However, parallel languages also need specific directives to convey the software designer's multiprocessing wishes to a compiler. These have often taken the form of extensions to such popular languages as Fortran, C, or Lisp, although special parallel languages have also evolved—to wit Occam or DGL (data graph language).[8]

One other trait divides parallel languages. Some (like Occam) require that the programmer define which PE tackles which assignment, while the majority (including Ada) leaves the matching of processors and processes to the computer. It goes without saying that in most cases automatic assignment takes the prize because it greatly facilitates load leveling. That's doubly true if the assignment can be dynamic (i.e., change during execution). Occam, unfortunately, is a static language that doesn't condone such freewheeling behavior.

↳ Babylonian Tower of the Second Kind

Historians like to point out that those unwilling to learn from past mistakes are condemned to repeat them. Indeed, the multiprocessing language jungle must strike us as "*déjà vu* all over again." Just like 25 years ago, every new computer struts into the marketplace trailed by a retinue of proprietary languages.[9,10]

First came the Fortran dialects, aimed at parallelizing dusty decks. These venerable programs, ranging from weather forecasting to mechanical stress simulations, often represent huge investments in precious scientific manpower. Hence, they remain just as entrenched in the technical world as Cobol is in data processing and commerce. Worse yet, these Fortran programs don't just tie up plentiful IBM mainframes, but scarce Cray supercomputers with their gluttonous appetite for double-precision numbers. (Crays are, however, gaining favor in DP circles. When fully burdened, they can be 20 times cheaper than time-shared mainframes.)

You can't just plunk a Fortran deck into a parallel system. A benchmark series run at **IBM**'s Palo Alto lab revealed that among the tested systems only Alliant's FX/8 came close to accepting original code. The test used in Babb[8] and Karp[10] (an approximation of π known as the n-point rectangular quadrature rule) required only one compiler directive. Inserted just before the DO loop, this directive relaxes accuracy somewhat and permits loop vectorization. Sequent's Balance takes a different tack. Its directive spreads the summation loop over several processors—efficient even for small jobs thanks to the Balance's hardware locks. The processes are started with the command

```
ISTAT = M_SET_PROCS(NPROCS)
```

and terminated with a library subroutine:

```
CALL M_KILL_PROCS
```

IBM's Parallel Fortran for the 3090/ VF series works similarly but requires a little more rewriting:

```
PARALLEL LOOP 10 i=1, intervl
      PRIVATE (SUML)
   DO FIRST
      SUML = 0.0
   DO EVERY
      suml = suml + f((i-0.5)*w)
   DO FINAL LOCK
      SUM = SUM + SUML
10 continue
```

In these lines, the original code is identified by lower case and Parallel Fortran by upper case.

A worker's paradise. As an alternative, the IBM machine resorted to the master-worker model, as did a number of other implementations.[10] Although very effective for "assembly line" jobs, the approach offends a growing number of computer egalitarians. (HAL is watching. Someday the American Computer Liberties Alliance may get this role model outlawed.) Users of the master-worker model included the Cray X-MP, the Elxsi 6400, the BBN Butterfly, and Flexible Computer's Flex/ 32. This approach requires a subroutine (invoked on the Flex/ 32 from a COEND block) that synchronizes the workers.

Return of results from the worker processes can also be tricky. Flex/ 32 applies a WHEN construct:

```
WHEN (SUM .EQ. SUM .AND. INIT)
   THEN SUM = SUM + SUML * W
   ELSE SUM = SUML * W
   ACTIVATE (INMIT)
END WHEN
```

The strange construct SUM .EQ. SUM constitutes a flag that tells the preprocessor to treat what follows as a critical section.

One hypercube participated in the test: *Intel*'s iPSC.[11] Since the *n*-cube is controlled by a cube manager, programs must comprise a host and a cube part. The former calls SENDMSG (CID, TYPE, INTRVL, 4,I,PID) from a DO loop which sends messages with the required parameters to the PEs. Outside the loop, a similar function call, RECVMSG(..), collects the results. Since each node owns its private memory, synchronization poses no problem. Still, the code comprises 14 lines for the host and 26 lines for the PEs, compared to the serial program's 14-line total. In part, the additional code is needed to collect output in COMMON blocks for shipment as a single message—a ruse to keep the communications overhead in check.

Although Fortranesque dialects can be used to define individual processes on a hypercube, such languages obviously don't feel at home there. Fortran fits much better into the synchronous world of array processors than into asynchronous message-passing architectures. Theoretically, synchronous (blocking) and asynchronous (nonblocking) message passing may be equivalent; however, in practice users tend to pick one of the camps, and settle there for good.

This fact became obvious after the development of Concurrent C at Bell Laboratories.[12] Synchronous message passing was chosen because it's easier to implement, especially for a rendezvous mechanism. This method for data exchanges between processes has been popularized by Ada for embedded systems. (In modern aircraft, for example, 5 to 30 computers have to cooperate.) Unfortunately, some Ada implementations treat concurrent tasking like function calls—the calling process must wait for a result before it's permitted to continue. Obviously that's no way to attain massive parallelism, and Alliant avoids it in its FX/Ada, as do other emerging parallel Ada versions based on the *Verdix* development system. You'll also do well to keep in touch with still maturing Ada 9x by calling her bulletin board from time to time (800-ADA-9X25).

A rendezvous in C? Si! Concurrent C has chosen the extended rendezvous as its model, though it's called a transaction (keyword trans). A simple example conveys the flavor of the language; it manages a buffer that can hold max characters and employs two processes, put and get:

```
process spec buffer(int max)
{
    trans void put(char x);
    trans char get();
};
```

Here, the first transaction puts *x* into a buffer unless it's already full. The second one returns the next character or waits if the buffer is empty.

To let the buffer manager choose which process to honor, depending on available space, you'd write:

```
select {
    (n < max):
        accept put (x)
            {buf[in] = x;}
        n++;
    or (n > 0):
        accept get()
            {treturn buf[out];}
        n--
        out = (out + 1) % max;
}
```

Selection depends on the guards checking n; the client process remains suspended while the block following accept executes. The new keyword treturn returns a value while also exiting from the block.

To start a new buffer process of size 256, you can write

```
create buffer(256)
```

To constrain acceptance in the rendezvous, the construct

```
accept put suchthat (boolean)
```

is available, where the Boolean term must evaluate to True. A timed transaction permits the client process to quit if it gets bored, by means of a within clause. Or it can take a short nap via the delay statement. Altogether Concurrent C adds 17 keywords to its mother tongue.

Often acceptance of a process depends on its priority. For this purpose Concurrent C offers the parameterized keyword

```
            process spec service()
            {
                trans result get(int prior_level, data d);
            };
            process body service()
            {
                for (;;)
                {
                    accept get(prior_level, d) by (-prior_level)
                        {....perform service...}
                }
            }
```

(a)

```
        task Service is
            entry Register(Urgent:in Integer; I:out ID);
            entry Get_Service(ID)(D:Data; R:out Result);
        end Service

        task body Service is
        begin
            loop
                for J in I..Register'Count loop
                    accept Register(Prior_Level: Integer; I: out ID) do
                        -- return service ticket in I
                    end Register;
                end loop;
                if (true xxx) then -- xxx: a job is waiting for service
                        -- assign J as ticket for next service
                    accept Get_Service(J)(D:Data; R: out Result) do
                        -- perform service
                    end Get_Service;
                end if;
            end loop;
        end Service;
```

(b)

Reproduced with permission from Silicon Press

by (-prior_level). An example (see Figure 19.5a) shows that a single call suffices to pull rank in a service routine, while the equivalent Ada task (see Figure 19.5b) needs two such calls. In case you wonder, the two programs' byte score is 357:144. Ada "wins" by a landslide.[12]

Figure 19.5 A service routine in Concurrent C (a) requires only a fraction of the code needed for the equivalent Ada routine (b).

Enter data flow. So far we've dealt with parallel languages that looked very much like their serial cousins. Where then are all the languages that will truly cater to massive parallelism?[13] Actually, the book from which we took the Fortran examples provides a clue—it examines the Loral Dataflow LFD 100, which sports a rather unusual architecture.[8]

This machine employs a form of data flow programming[14] that might better be called "process flow programming." Loral's data flow graphs resemble data flow diagrams (see Figure 19.6a). Internally the graph elements are described by their imports and exports, as the example for the first worker shows:

```
G10: worker_1 = "worker" <C0> <P10>
G11:    import {word[6] d01_intrvl_me_nprocs}
G12:    export {word[2] d03_sum}
```

The word[n] clause defines the length of inputs and outputs for each process, and <C0> specifies where the process runs. (Each of the three process types in the figure employs between 8 and 13 lines of fairly normal Fortran.)

For the fun of it, we've included an IP version of the Loral setup in Figure 19.6b. The problem consists of the approximation of an integral by slicing the area under the curve into thin rectangles and then adding up their heights—the classical $\Sigma f \Delta t$ method. The Manager splits the function into big chunks, which it passes to the Workers. Each of them integrates its chunk and passes the result to Summing, which adds up the partial results. The "signal" flow is the same as in Figure 19.6a; control flow turns on the worker processes first and then, when they are finished, the summing process.

We could decompose the IPs further, to the point where we could distinguish between the processes responsible for communications and those assigned to number crunching. Then we'd have to decide which of them we want to realize in software and which in hardware. Since the communications machinery would be needed no matter what problem we want to solve, let's put that part into hardware; we'll need at least one input channel and one output channel for each of the processes.

Aren't we lucky. A few bright people in England had precisely the same idea nearly a decade ago. Today we can buy the fruits of their labors from **Inmos** under the enigmatic name of Transputer. (It reflects the inventors' hope that someday their product will be as ubiquitous as transistors are today.) Each Transputer contains, on one chip, a powerful microprocessor, a large cache memory, and four fast (hardware-controlled) communications links, of which we can use as many as we wish. It's obvious that most of the topologies in Figure 19.2 can readily be implemented with Transputers.

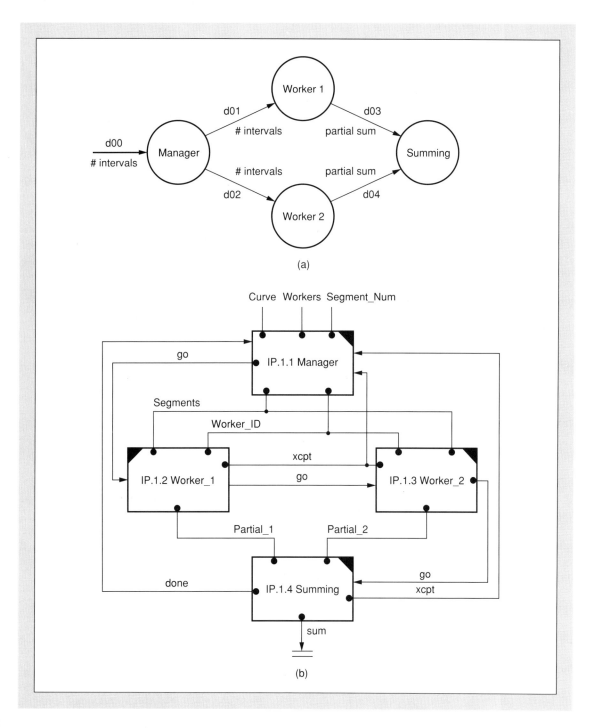

Figure 19.6 The Loral computer employs a form of data flow programming (*a*). In IP form, the sequence of events becomes more explicit (*b*).

From Oxford, with elegance.   So where has this nifty machine been hiding? Funded originally by public research grants, Inmos underwent a series of painful metamorphoses in its brief life. (Getting off the dole is never easy. As of last year, Inmos belongs to SGS Thompson Microelectronics.) To make matters worse, the transputer was originally touted as a high-level language machine with (naturally) its very own language called Occam.* Outside the philosophers' den, however, the computer world yawned and kept on tinkering with assembly code.

Now that Inmos has published the Transputer's native instruction set, the company is reaping a flourishing crop of potential customers. This detour is somewhat of a pity because Occam demonstrates at least the requirements, if not the best solution for parallel languages.[15-17] For sequential code, Occam closely resembles Pascal, except that it permits multiple assignments such as:

```
x, y, z := a, b+3, 10
```

"Tables" construct arrays, for example:

```
['a', 'b', 'c']    [x * y, x + 4]
```

Because it was originally meant to serve as the native language of the Transputer, Occam's operators include many needed only for "bit diddling," like left and right shift as well as bitwise AND, OR, XOR, and NOT. Lacking are nonnumeric operations and constructions (e.g., concatenation, records).

More important, however, are Occam's concurrency features—the ways in which sequential threads can be combined into a multidimensional fabric. To assign jobs to two workers under the direction of a boss, we would write

```
PAR boss()
    PAR i = 0 FOR 3
        worker (i)
```

PAR is the parallel replicator and spawns four equal processes. This, however, does not mean that there will necessarily be par-

---

*By not so sheer coincidence, much of the Transputer brainstorming took place in Occam's old haunt, Oxford University. The thirteenth-century philosopher William of Occam became famous for his "razor," which stipulates that among several solutions to a problem the simplest one is best. Amen.

allel communications channels from boss to worker as in Figure 19.6. Rather, an *ukase* can be passed from boss to worker (0), from there to worker (1) and so on down the chain, with answers returning on a similar channel in the reverse direction.

To accomplish this, a sequential process inside the workers' program could accept an order from the in channel and pass it to the out channel with this routine:

```
WHILE i <= n
    SEQ
        in ? order
        out ! order
```

The question mark means "read from the named channel," while the exclamation point identifies the corresponding write operation for a given channel.

In addition to the parallel and sequential replicators, Occam offers the "alternation," which corresponds to a logical OR. As an example, consider the merger of two communications channels into one:

```
ALT
    left ? packet
        joint ! packet
    right ? packet
        joint ! packet
```

Depending on whether the left or the right channel carries data packets, this construct routes them to the joint channel.

You can find a nice example of the Transputer's ability to map an algorithm into hardware in Perrott.[6] A matrix multiplication (as in Chapter 8) can be implemented with a square lattice of Transputers whose communications links are defined as follows:

```
CHAN north,south,east,west:
VAR a,b,x
SEQ
    PAR
        north ? a
        west ? b
    x := x = (a * b)
    PAR
        south ! a
        east ! b
```

This code segment is embedded in a procedure that also contains row and column definitions.

⌐ But Does This Program Work?

Now that you have tasted the flavor of parallel languages, you might ask yourself which one is best. Unfortunately, the question is irrelevant because even the most expressive or reliable language is of little use if you can't debug its programs. The literature bristles with tales of irreproducible results.[18] In fact, some stories reveal such eccentricities that parallel computers appear nearly human. (Clarke's HAL may not make it by 2001, but he's *en route*).

In Chapter 15 we discussed the "instrumentation" of programs for debugging purposes. On a parallel system, however, such tricks as inserting PRINT statements won't work because I/O disrupts the normal time relationship between processes. This is known as the "probe effect," which must be avoided at any cost. Indeed, sometimes the only solution is to just leave the probes inserted during normal execution.

To make life even more interesting, the "oracle" paradigm with its omniscient user does not work well for parallel programs either. In other words, getting correct answers does not prove a program correct—it proves only that no erroneous segments were executed in this particular run. So, before you decide on a parallel language, you better make sure what debugging support comes with it.

Inmos demonstrated an Occam programming environment as far back as 1982.[19] By now the Transputer Development System has grown into an impressive instrument. Combined with other tools from *CSA*—including a parallel C—it makes software design for the Transputer easier than for almost any other multiprocessing system. In no small measure, the development system's might stems from the "folding" feature that creates a *de facto* PDL (program development language) for Occam.

The folding paradigm demonstrates information hiding at its best. With a single keystroke, the user makes the details of a program segment disappear, level by level, until only the "outline" of the software package under construction remains on the screen. Occam's replicators simplify the process, since program detail largely resides within their local scope. A folded screen handler procedure might look like this during development:[20]

```
{{{body
WHILE going.in OR going.data
    SEQ
        clock ? waketime
        waketime := waketime PLUS millisecond
            ALT
                going.in & in ? char
                    ... print to screen
                monitoring & clock ? AFTER waketime
}}}
```

The triple braces mark top and bottom "creases" (beyond which the text can't be viewed), and the three dots mark the fold, where detail is hidden. (This fragment exhibits one of Occam's oddities: the variable going.in would usually be written as going_in.)

This example could easily be transformed into a data flow diagram. In fact, Inmos has at times considered implementing a visual representation, but neither the company nor its Oxford mentors abode by Occam's razor in this case. That's a pity, because in debugging parallel programs the amount of information to be conveyed to the programmer can be staggering. A vendor who doesn't employ every means of boosting the communications bandwidth will eventually regret it.

To read a screenful of code text (2000 characters) takes well over 60 seconds. In the same time, the eye can absorb at least two full-screen pictures of 300,000 pixels each, which could convey 40 times as much information as the text. (The theoretical bandwidth ratio is much higher.) Color can improve the throughput even further—much more for pictures than for text. Alas, even the CASE industry is still feeling its way through the interface dilemma for *sequential* programming. Efficient verification of *parallel* programs remains largely an academic exercise.

Mastering the hypercube.   Compare, for example, two methods for debugging hypercube programs: Inmos's textual one and visual Tuple Scope, which is, for example, used by **Cogent**. Instead of using Occam and its development system, the company—one of several startups implementing a hypercube with Transputers—has opted for Linda as the system language.[21,22] Linda avoids some of the problems we encountered with other parallel languages and offers a visual debugger to boot.

Developed at Yale University and commercially available from *Scientific Computing Associates*, Linda is more a multiprocessing paradigm than a language.[23,24] Linda gets around the problems of synchronization, locking, and message passing by taking these functions away from processes or processors and turning them over to a "bulletin board." Messages are posted in tuple space, a content-addressable (or associative) memory region. Available resources search tuple space for appropriate messages. Thus, Linda sidesteps the tough problem of process interactions; if one "worker" process functions correctly, all will.

To see how Linda acts in an operating system (where, for example, Cogent's Linda resides), consider the screen handler PIX (parallel interactive executive), a PostScript-based window server compatible with Sun's NeWS. To increment a value `val` in dictionary `dict`, PIX uses this statement:

```
dict/val in 1 add out
```

The Linda operator `in` removes the tuple containing `val` from tuple space `dict`, and while it's being updated in one process, no other process can get hold of it—until the Linda process `out` puts the tuple back in circulation. Thus, `in` corresponds to Occam's `?` or to `P(semaphore)`, and `out` to `!` and `V(semaphore)`. (The two commands must be interpreted from the *process's* viewpoint: "bring `in`" or "send `out`.")

Tuples are simply collections of related symbols and data—say, `<"day", 5, "Friday">`—and tuple lookup corresponds to the `select` operation in a relational database. If a process contains the Linda command

```
in ("day", ? &day_num, ? day_str)
```

it will try to withdraw a matching tuple from tuple space. The first tuple in this paragraph indeed matches the request's "wildcard" fields (identified by ?). The first such field is a pointer to a storage location—a formal variable that is now bound to 5. The second contains no `&`, because in C the name of a character array is already its address; the formal variable `day_str` is now bound to the actual variable `Friday`.

A tiny language for a change. In addition to the `in` and `out` procedures, Linda comprises `rd` and `eval` commands. The former works like in, except that it does not remove the matched tuple. The latter's function is more complex; eval emulates out while also spawning a new process known as an active process tuple—Linda's mechanism for creating parallel processes. When all of an active tuple's variables are bound, it becomes inactive and ready to be incorporated in a Linda program's solution.

These four commands (plus two variants) make up the whole Linda language. Well, not quite. If you buy C-Linda or Fortran-Linda you also get a number of tools and, above all, the Linda kernel. It contains (sometimes machine-dependent) code for setting up and searching tuple space. Until associative memory becomes a standard processor feature, the pattern-matching algorithm can make or break the whole tuple method.

Although Linda has by now been installed on about a dozen parallel computers, data on its performance are still sketchy. Tuple exchanges take from a fraction of a millisecond on the Encore or Sequent machine to several milliseconds on the *Intel* hypercube. In the latter case, however, nearly 4 ms were exacted at the time by the machine's message-passing overhead, which has since been reduced to 0.4 ms.

Performance in actual applications would be more important but remains even sketchier. On a matrix multiplication problem, speedup was about 78% of ideal on an iPSC with 8 nodes, but reached only 64% with 16 nodes. Matching of DNA sequences (which requires little communications) came in at 94% on 16 nodes but fell to 71% on 32 nodes. Performance on the Encore with 16 PEs was close to the hypercube with the same number of nodes. A search for prime numbers on the Encore computer with 10 PEs came in at a speedup of 8.3—83% of ideal.

To see how Linda's debugging aid Tuple Scope functions, let's inspect Figure 19.7, which illustrates a run of the DNA search on a common-memory machine. The purpose of the search is to find matches between short strings of the integers 1 to 4 (each standing for one of the basic amino acids) and longer strings that could, for example, represent "designer genes." The left small window holds the target tuple of the current search. By clicking the mouse on that (or any other) sphere, the user can open it up and view its content.

The top large window displays some hundred tuples from the sequences in the database, waiting for workers to match them. Each tuple appears on the screen in the order in which it has been spawned. In the lower window, result tuples are waiting for the master (still busy adding new worker tuples) to collect them.

Each sphere retains its individuality, so that irregular patterns form as work progresses. The job is done when all tuples in both windows have vanished.

In addition to the tuples, Tuple Scope displays processes numbered in sequence of appearance. An inactive process shows as a black rectangle; if its most recent activity was an out, it appears as a down arrow in the window where it has just "tupled." Logically enough, a process shows as a white up arrow after an in, like the ones numbered 3 to 6 in the figure. A blocked (waiting) process would appear as a diamond. Command buttons at the screen top let the user choose single-step, slow, or unmonitored execution. The Run button starts execution and the Break button interrupts it.

Linda has proven its mettle on a number of concurrent computers but not yet on massively parallel systems. Although hypercube versions are underway, it remains to be seen how they stand up in practical use. (Past tests on the iPSC may not be too meaningful.) If debugging hundreds of parallel processes seems tough, the prospect of debugging *thousands* at once may appear impossible. Yet, hypercubes of order 10 and up (over 1000 PEs) are on the market—even disregarding the Connection machine. They will need debuggers custom-tailored to match both the topology and the programs.

Seeing is believing. Computer scientists at *Tufts University* have pursued the hypercube debugging problem for years, both on Intel's and *NCube*'s machines. One solution, called Seecube, has been available since 1987 at a nominal license fee, and the more powerful Seeplex approaches release. While Seecube primarily relies on stored data that are played back postmortem fashion, Seeplex aims at real-time performance.[25] The following discussion will focus on the latter.

Since extant hypercubes primarily rely on message passing for communications, both of the Tufts systems attach themselves to the message streams. And, to broaden the information bandwidth, both rely on color as a third dimension (with time providing a fourth). Just by observing traffic volume at the global level, the user can judge which nodes are too "hot" (showing up as yellow) and which are too "cold" (blue). Gross errors, such as load imbalances, thus become readily apparent. But that's just the beginning.

In fact, Seeplex can display no fewer than 256 parameters of 94 distinct types on each node. And the user can access each

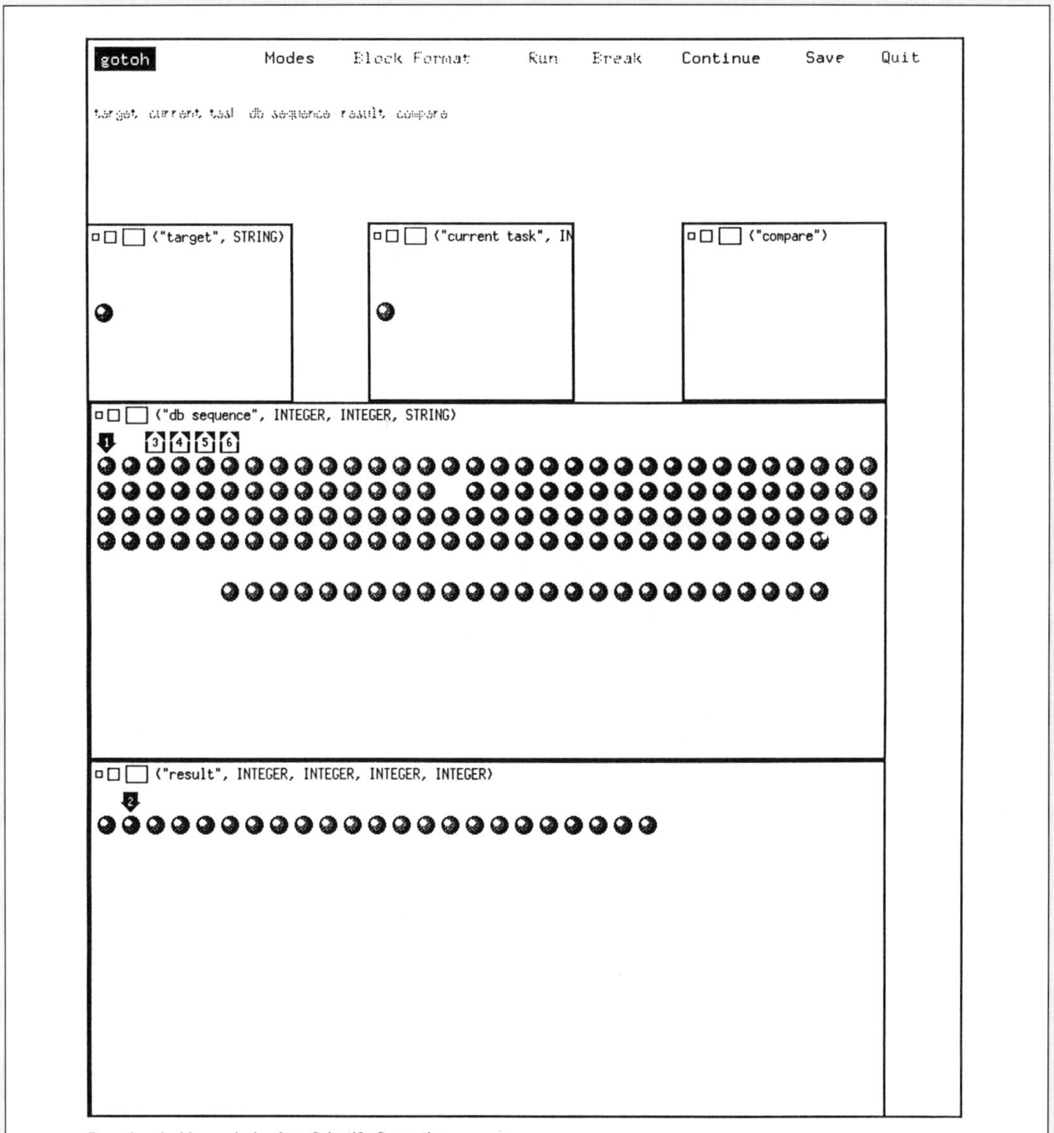

Reproduced with permission from Scientific Computing

Figure 19.7 Tuple Scope supports the Linda paradigm of parallelism. Each of the spheres in the upper large window depicts one search tuple; solution tuples aggregate in the lower window.

parameter in five ways: current value, last change, average value, the difference between current and average value, and the difference between current value and an average over all nodes. That amounts to 1,356,800 parameter values on a 1024-node system—clearly much more information than any user can readily absorb. The Seeplex designers' main challenge has therefore been to devise displays that convey as much of these data as possible in the most meaningful manner.

Seeplex derives this monitoring power by tapping the custom-built Simplex operating system for the NCube, which is completely compatible with NCube's Vertex operating system. Although collecting all this data takes at most 10 machine cycles (a 10% overhead), it makes sense to collect only what will be used. That way the multiprocessing bogyman, the probe effect, can be kept at bay. Even so, data remain in local memory only to be "synchronously frozen" for shipment to the host (normally a Sun workstation).

Seeplex uses windows into parameters of a given type, displaying their values and positions. Thus, similar measurements for different parts of the system can easily be compared. Viewing such snapshots in sequence conveys the system's dynamic behavior. Data are collected by a library of subroutines, which are used like communications primitives except that they store diagnostics event traces in a node's memory. A second set of routines cross-references the time-stamped traces and sorts them into a global trace. In addition, "ghost" processes can accompany the working processes in each processor to help with data collection.

How to draw in 10 dimensions.   Hypercubes can be visualized in a number of ways. Seecube's "3-cubes in space" format (see Figure 19.8a) may be easiest to comprehend, but it can't readily be expanded beyond a 5-cube. Links between the nodes are split; each half is dedicated to one direction of transmission. Unfortunately, actual links between nodes can only be shown *within* 3-cubes; the user must mentally find the target node for channels *between* 3-cubes (e.g., node 12 connects to its equivalent in the top-left cube, node 4). Displays in the form of a binary Pascal triangle (see Figure 19.8b) avoid this problem and serve as a natural representation for embedded binary trees. From top to bottom, each "layer" differs from the next one by one bit of the numbering scheme. In a butterfly diagram like that of Figure 19.8c, messages always appear as diagonals in the same direc-

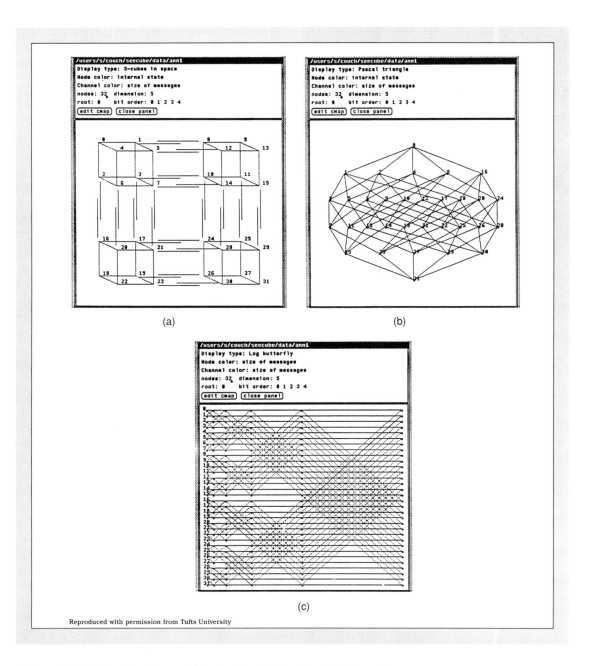

(a)

(b)

(c)

Figure 19.8 Seeplex offers a wide range of views for events in a hypercube: "3-cubes in space" (*a*) is most easily understood; the Pascal triangle (*b*) represents binary trees; and the butterfly diagram (*c*) clarifies message traffic.

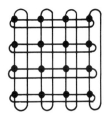

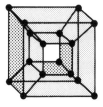

tion, perhaps offset along the vertical dot rows, which in this graph represent nodes.

Above 5-cubes, the best model is the n-torus grid of Figure 19.3c, which shows nodes as intersections on a square lattice. That illustration represents the same 4-cube shown in Figure 19.3d as a squared-off torus. The grid can be turned into a doughnut by first wrapping it around a horizontal axis until the top meets the bottom; then the resulting tube has to be bent until the left side mates with the right side. At first glance the grid and the cube don't appear topologically identical. But if you regard the latter as hollow and made of putty, it's easily kneaded into a bagel.

Color greatly helps the user to visualize an n-cube's complex inner "life." In Figure 19.9a (see the color insert next to p. 215) colors from the palette (bottom right) are assigned to a number of parameters, shown in the horizontal rows on the right. Starting at the bottom, you see how node numbers are identified (as "Text"). Next, the bottom half and then the top half of the double squares, which appear next to the node numbers, are tagged, and in the top row (partly obscured) the color scheme for the nodes themselves is set up. For simplicity's sake a 4-cube (at the left) demonstrates the message links, split in half to separate traffic in the two directions.

An intriguing alternate display is the "Gray code circle" (see Figure 19.9b) whose links (diagonals and sides) are again bisected to distinguish between incoming and outgoing traffic. Especially for larger hypercubes, this representation is quite viable (see Figure 19.9c). An interesting quality makes it even more useful: links between subcubes appear as parallel lines. Although the number of nodes (located on the circumference) is not limited in theory, Figure 19.9c approaches the practical limit.

In larger hypercubes, clustering messages by subcubes may become more revealing. The user can display the length of message queues (a giveaway for load imbalance) at each node in the form of a bar chart, or he can view the state of all processors as a function of time. The latter format has proven most lucid to discover processes waiting for the arrival of messages. Often summary displays, which extract node status from the time display, may reveal a problem most clearly. Figure 19.9d shows the activities of all nodes in three lines apiece, as a function of time. The first line gives the node's state, with a color code that uses red for idle, green for computing, yellow for writing, and blue for reading (which also blocks the node). The second line color codes the message intensity from blue for "no traffic" to white for "rush hour," while the third line uses a similar scale for the worst-case number of bytes in the messages.

This graph contains a great deal of information—in fact, too much. Once you suspect some irregularity you'll probably want to avail yourself of yet another Seeplex feature—sorting by color. In Figure 19.9e you can readily see which nodes get bogged down reading inputs and which carry the heaviest computing load. Since color selection remains under user control for summary graphs, your display choices are nearly unlimited.

Even more than Tuple Scope, Seeplex facilitates debugging by making visible the behind-the-scenes activities of process management. However, well-balanced execution of a program on a multiprocessor does not ensure the correctness of results. If you are solving a number-crunching problem, you may have to examine reams of numerical results—a tedious way to debug your application code. That's where general-purpose visualization tools come into play. They are already common in fields like fluid dynamics.[26] However, they tend to be pricey like the supercomputers they serve.

Caution—vectors crossing.   Recently more affordable tools have begun to emerge. One developed at the University of Washington for MIMD systems with nonshared memory—aptly named Voyeur—serves as an example. To be effective, a debugging system must control execution (e.g., by single stepping), gather data during the run (via embedded probes), and then transform the data into a meaningful display. Voyeur concentrates on the last two steps.

As an example, consider a program that simulates fluid dynamics. To simplify matters, let's assume the system under scrutiny has cylindrical symmetry—in a top view, all the flow proceeds along radii. Any other flow direction indicates an error in the model or in the operating system. A sequence of Voyeur views, displayed in Figure 19.10, illustrates what happens during several successive "generations" of execution.

The first view, taken after generation 4, implies that all is in order; vectors at the innermost grid circle point radially outward. After generation 6, however, it's clear that the bottom row of the grid is in trouble. One generation later, the deviation from radial flow still seems to be limited to one vector, but after generation 8 the calculation shows evidence of having blown up altogether.

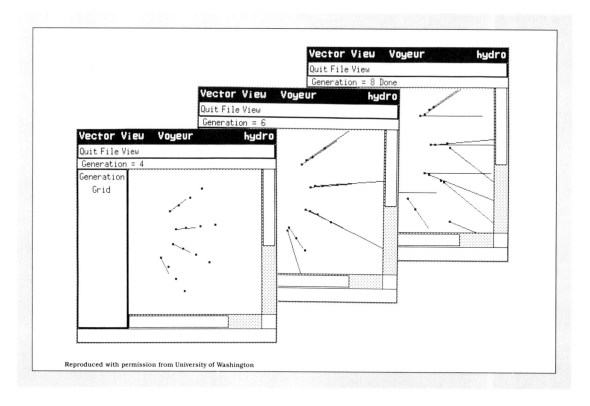

Reproduced with permission from University of Washington

Figure 19.10 Visualization of results will be just as important for debugging parallel programs as visualization of internal operations. Here Voyeur shows how a problem in fluid dynamics goes out of control after a few iterations.

The user can now look at some variables' values during this last generation and narrow down the error in the algorithm.

That's where another Voyeur option comes in—the trace view. The user displays the code in a selected subset of PEs with current values of the variables inserted. Each of the node windows can be opened up to show more detail. For nonnumeric programs—say, a game of "Sharks and Fishes"—the user can view the movement of icons before zeroing in on tables of messages in the form

z p 1 12 3 4 s

The first half of this line identifies it as a Voyeur message from PE #1 at time 12; the remainder puts the location of a shark at coordinates 3,4.

While Voyeur's two formats for displaying results—vectors and icons—can indeed accommodate two large classes of applications, it's also clear that different applications will require additional preparation. But at least the nitty-gritty of accessing and collecting variables, creating icons, and displaying simultaneous windows need not be repeated. For example, creating the radial display in the general vector class took a few hours. Tools of this type are nice to have for traditional serial computers; for multiprocessors they will prove indispensable. We'll explore the general trend toward visualization further in the next chapter.

⸗ References

1. Jack Dongarra, "Computer benchmarking: Paths and Pitfalls," *IEEE Spectrum*, July 1987, p. 38.

2. Tom Manuel, "Supercomputers: The proliferation begins," *Electronics*, March 3, 1988, p. 51, (special issue).

3. John M. Levesque and Joel W. Williamson, *A Guidebook to Fortran on Supercomputers*, Academic Press, San Diego, CA, 1988.

4. *Computer*, January 1989, (special issue on supercomputer design).

5. Edsger W. Dijkstra, "Cooperating sequential processes," in F. Genuys (ed.), *Programming Languages*, Academic Press, London, 1968.

6. R. H. Perrott, *Parallel Programming*, Addison-Wesley, Reading, MA, 1987.

7. David A. Mundie and David Fisher, "Parallel processing in Ada," *Computer*, August 1986, p. 20.

8. Robert G. Babb, *Programming Parallel Processors*, Addison-Wesley, Reading, MA, 1988.

9. Alan H. Karp, "Programming for parallelism," *Computer*, May 1987, p. 43.

10. Alan H. Karp and Robert G. Babb, "A comparison of 12 parallel Fortran dialects," *IEEE Software*, September 1988, p. 52.

11. David Scott et al., *The Art and Science of Programming Concurrent Supercomputers*, Intel Scientific Computers, 1988.

12. Narain Gehani and William D. Roome, *The Concurrent C Programming Language*, Silicon Press, Summit, NJ, 1989.

13. Bob Cushman, "Matrix crunching with massive parallelism," *VLSI Systems Design*, December 1988, p. 18.

14. John A. Sharp, *Data Flow Computing*, Wiley-Horwood, New York, 1985.

15. C. A. R. Hoare and A. W. Roscoe, *The Laws of Occam Programming*, Technical Monograph PRG-53, Oxford University, 1986.

16. Inmos Ltd., *Occam 2 Reference Manual*, Prentice-Hall, Hempstead, UK, 1988.

17. Dick Pountain, *A Tutorial Introduction to Occam Programming*, Inmos, Bristol, England, 1986.

18. *IEEE Software*, January 1988, (special issue on parallel programming).

19. Pete Wilson, "Programming system builds multiprocessor software," *Electronic Design*, July 1983, p. 129.

20. Inmos, *Transputer Development System*, Prentice-Hall, Hemstead, UK, 1988.

21. Tom Merrow and Noel Henson, "System design for parallel computing," *High Performance Systems*, January 1989, p. 36.

22. Tom Williams, "Software machine model blazes trail for parallel processing," *Computer Design*, October 1, 1988, p. 20.

23. Sudhir Ahuja et al., "Linda and friends," *Computer*, August 1986, p. 26.

24. David Gelernter, "Getting the job done," *Byte*, November 1988, p. 301.

25. Alva L. Couch, "Graphical representations of program performance on hypercube message-passing multiprocessors," dissertation, Tufts University, Medford, MA, April 1988.

26. Lawrence Rosenblum, "Visualization of experimental data at the Naval Research Lab," *Computer*, August 1989, p. 95 (special issue on scientific visualization).

20

MAKING A CASE FOR THE FUTURE

Graphics in—graphics out
Parsing a visual language
Database bedrock basics

In the preceding chapter we discussed one type of future CASE systems—those dealing with multiprocessors. But traditional von Neumann machines will be with us for decades and so will CASE tools designed for them. How will such systems change in years to come? We have already noted several trends.

In Chapter 16 we observed that libraries of reusable software will help to increase programmer productivity as well as code quality. In Chapter 18 we looked into standardizing issues, coming away with the hope that someday we'll be able to assemble CASE systems to suit our tastes and needs more closely. And in Chapter 19 we explored the impact of parallel processing. All these trends will fuse with others already incubating at research labs across the world. Most spring from artificial intelligence and its stepchild, object-oriented-programming.

Back in Chapter 14 we observed how an expert system combines with software algebra to generate programs semiautomatically. In this chapter we'll concentrate on a more

"What's the use of a book without pictures?"

Alice in Wonderland

pervasive contribution of AI to programming—graphics. Ever since **glass teletypes** (CRT monitors) began to replace the metal variety, AI researchers have been fascinated with the possibilities of a two-dimensional man-machine interface. Even though Apple Computers lays claim to the Macintosh icons and menus, these are just two of the tools AI researchers developed.

In fact, icons represent a graphical command language, which in turn inspired more general visual languages. Graphical output, too, owes a debt to AI workers, propelled by such efforts as the Smalltalk language (discussed in Chapter 12) and direct manipulation. To give a simple example for the latter, let's perform a *Gedankenexperiment*. Turn on your faithful Mac and put a spring object on the screen. Now connect a mass object to its bottom hook and apply a vertical force. When you hit the Return key, the screen picture starts to oscillate, and if you use a suitable program, output data (say, amplitude and oscillation frequency) appear in screen windows. You can then add friction, and the amplitude will die down.

Direct manipulation represents the epitome of graphic programming and animation. Developed originally at the University of Illinois for the Plato learning system, it is now a commercial product of Control Data's Training and Education Group in Minneapolis. Of more practical interest to technical users, however, is a program called LabView from **National Instruments**.[1] With it, an engineer can, for example "wire up" a test circuit on the screen to represent his bench setup, and then "design" his dream instrument's front panel on the screen. He can specify a frequency range, and the connected signal generator on the bench will begin a frequency sweep, while the results appear on the screen.

In Figure 20.1 a very simple test circuit appears in the bottom part, with the mock panel above it. Low and high frequency have been set at 1 and 10 kHz, respectively, with an increment of 100 Hz and an amplitude of 1 volt. The displayed transfer function (output voltage versus input voltage) reveals that the circuit under test exhibits a cutoff frequency around 7 kHz. LabView improves on direct execution by inserting real test equipment in the loop, thus transforming the *Gedankenexperiment* into a real one. (The simplistic example, chosen deliberately to concentrate on the essentials, hardly conveys LabView's versatility.)

While academic work on the concept of direct manipulation also continues (for example, with ThingLab at the University of Washington[2]), graphic computer *input* also remains a cherished

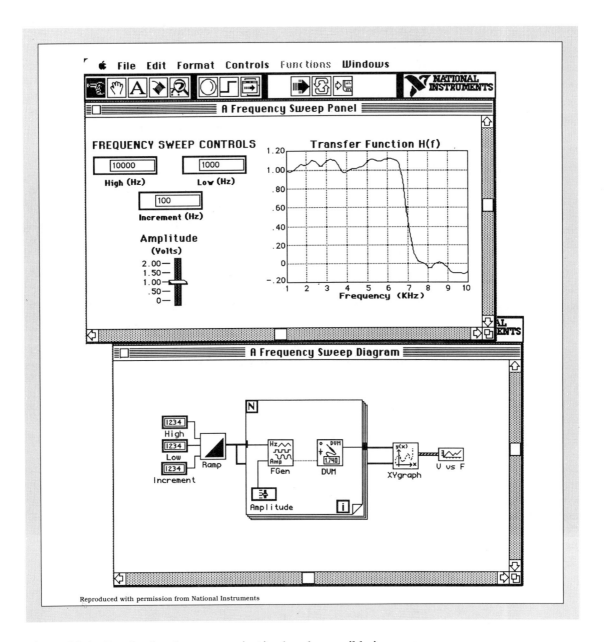

Figure 20.1 Purely visual programming is already possible in some domains. The test circuit in the bottom screen produces the display at the top, given the shown control settings.

research topic. Actually, visual programming—though in very limited scope—arrived on the commercial scene years ago in the guise of "screen painters" (or form generators) and spreadsheets. Even though this form of "programming" is restricted to the ASCII character set, it extends the conventional character-string languages into two dimensions. Consequently, the inputs must be parsed in the context of their location on the screen—an essential characteristic of visual programs.

In fact, by this standard, programming in a query language like QBE (query by example) is more visual than programming with icons. Even though an icon can be moved all over the screen, it stands for the same action, no matter where you click your mouse on it. Pointing to icons accomplishes no more than pointing to one choice in a menu of system commands. (An interesting question arises here—does "mousing" by itself constitute a visual procedure?) Indeed, icons are often shunned because you can't readily compose "sentences" with them. Unless, that is, you combine the graphic symbols with command words, as in Blox[3] where the graphics primarily serve to prevent syntax errors in otherwise conventional languages (see Figure 20.2).

Closer to executable graphics are systems that let you interconnect shapes, as does LabView. Aside from its application as a laboratory instrument driver, it can indeed be used to "compose" purely abstract programs. But, you might ask, where are the verbs? Simple: they hide in the connecting arcs, just as in

Figure 20.2 Blox ensures correct syntax in a Pascal-like language by excluding improper configurations. Coding, reduced to a jigsaw puzzle!

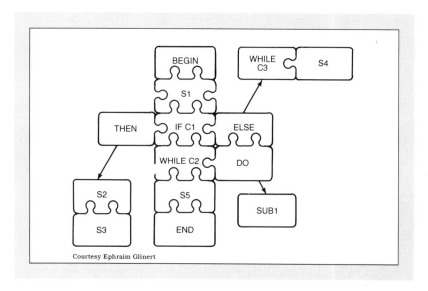

Courtesy Ephraim Glinert

a state diagram or a flowchart. An arrow pointing from A to B says "B gets A" (or B := A). To parse a data flow diagram, a system usually need only look at the arrow roots and tips; to parse a flowchart (as in Figure 8.2*a*), it also needs to recognize a few shapes.

⌐ How to Parse Executable Graphics

One special form of flowchart, the Nassi-Shneiderman diagram (like the one back in Figure 8.4) simplifies parsing. All the parser has to do is find the top left corner of a given box to determine the program sequence and then read its content (be it text or just a diagonal line). Consequently, converting such charts to program text poses no big problems, as **Scandura's** Prodoc proves. Long ago all kinds of flowcharts and syntax trees migrated to academic CASE tools that accommodate a slew of graphics languages, or, as some workers in the field prefer, executable graphics.

The challenge grows with a purely visual editor like vmacs (a takeoff on emacs, naturally) for the PAM (pattern matching) and VennLisp languages.[4] VennLisp can be regarded as a visual form of Lisp, because internally its graphic elements are linked like Lisp atoms. Little wonder then that it can be parsed like Lisp, by looking at the visual equivalent of parentheses in Figure 20.3—nested rectanglular spaces. The illustration represents the following expression:

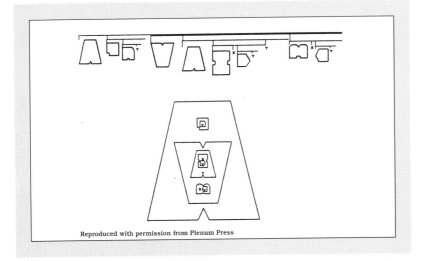

Reproduced with permission from Plenum Press

Figure 20.3 When parsing a VennLisp "statement," the compiler treats nested space like nested parentheses in normal Lisp. The symbols at the top represent (from the left) And, Not, Null, Or, And, Equal, First, Member, Last.

$$\wedge \neg \, h \, ^y$$
$$\vee \, \wedge = \, ^x \rightarrow ^y \, ^y$$
$$m \, ^x \, \leftarrow \, ^y$$

```
(AND (NOT (NULL? Y)
    (OR (AND EQUAL? X (FIRST Y)) Y)
        (MEMBER? X (REST Y))))
```

Don't be misled by VennLisp's divine serenity; behind the facade lurk *demons*—background routines that watch out for such transgressions as unusual dragging behavior.

In the preceding chapter we scrutinized some CASE tools that employ very customized outputs. As we noted, they can greatly facilitate the formulation and debugging of many types of algorithms[5]—say, activities in a buffer or stack manager. For the more general user, a program like Balsa (Brown University algorithm-simulator and animator) simplifies the process of visualization even more by providing such standard representations as bars, trees, or dot graphs.[6,7]

Take, for example, the Manhattan algorithm, which finds intersections of lines (important in circuit board design) as in Figure 20.4a. The view at the left, a Y-tree, contains a node for each end point, keyed to the y coordinate of the point in question. The corresponding X-tree (top) contains nodes only for those vertical lines that intersect the scan line (near the bottom of the main window) at its current position. When the search line reaches the bottom of a vertical line, a node is added to the X-tree; when it reaches a horizontal line, the X-tree is traversed to determine intersections. Being able to watch the actual execution of the algorithm like a movie (note the Rewind and Fast-Forward "buttons" at the bottom of the screen) should help a lot in locating any false steps.

Another example deals with the package-wrapping algorithm for finding the envelope of objects in a plane (see Figure 20.4b). As the row of insets on the screen shows, the algorithm first finds the southern-most point and then "wraps a string" around the points in a counterclockwise direction. Again it's obvious that watching the screen during execution will reveal errors much faster than burrowing through reams of code, even with a very efficient textual debugger.

Built upon clay?   Wonderful as graphic representations for software are, we still must worry about the "cement" that will hold a complex software system together. This cement is the infrastructure that correlates the graphics with their meaning—

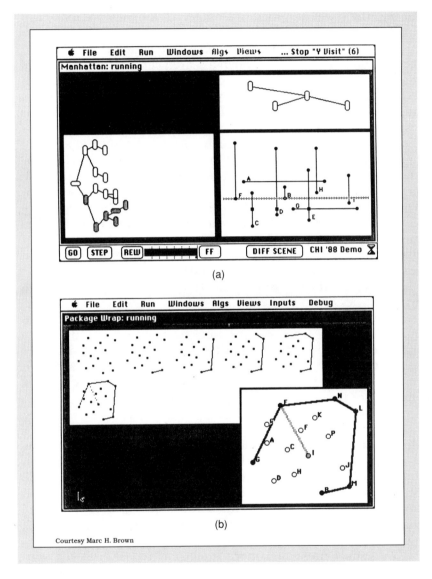

(a)

(b)

Courtesy Marc H. Brown

Figure 20.4 Animation of a range of problems is easy with the Balsa II tool kit. The Manhattan algorithm (*a*) finds intersections of lines; the package-wrapping algorithm (*b*) constructs the envelope for a set of objects.

the database. We have barely mastered the organization of textual data with (often conflicting) data storage methods, from simple file structures to relational schemas to network schemas and so on. With graphics thrown in, life in the data stores will get even tougher. This is compounded by the fact that our collections of code modules (including tools and graphics) continue to grow.

The solutions we examined in Chapter 16 for software reuse will not suffice for long.

If you ever tried to find books on a specific subject matter in a library, you know how hard such a search can be. It is not always possible to categorize subjects neatly in a class tree. Even though computers simplify the chore by letting you look for keywords, finding a package to monitor magnetically levitated trains, for instance, will drive you up the proverbial search tree. Collections of software artifacts will very much resemble an encyclopedia.

Exact and detailed descriptions are obviously important for such a work, but often the most valuable feature lies in the quality of cross-indexing. Hypertext shows the way toward a solution. When you come to a reference like "see levitation," hitting a single key will get you to the entry *levitation* and to further references. Hypertext networks have started to grow in a number of disciplines, and once they mature they will impact the way you design software as much as CASE does.

No wonder the computer industry consortium **MCC** relies on hypertext heavily in its Leonardo software design environment.[8] To get a taste of hypertext power, try a PC version like Houdini from **MaxThink**. Once you are hooked, you may well decide to organize your own design knowledge base that way, and never again will you waste exasperating hours in a fruitless search for that *one* program which—you think—would exactly fit your present need.

Mene, mene, tekel. While hypertext may solve the problems of maintaining a software library, it won't be powerful enough to link CASE systems. Indeed, the handwriting is on the wall. Grandiose schemes for software automation that have been advanced in recent years (and in this book) will stand or fall with the infrastructure that coordinates program objects with the information they represent.

We simply must find more intelligent repositories for both our programs and CASE tools.[9] In the long run, knowledge bases like those in expert systems may prove most powerful—especially when coupled with graphical user interfaces.[10] But for now, object-oriented databases represent the next evolutionary step beyond relational ones, by adding "methods" (say, retrieval or processing routines) to the structure definitions. Thus, different users can utilize the same data in totally different ways without the need for complicated programs. Furthermore, the objects are never duplicated (only pointed to), so maintenance loses much of its terror.

The versatility of a commercial version, GemStone from *Servio Logic* (with over 50 predefined classes and 600 methods) is mirrored in its applications. They range from data processing in banks to managing the thousands of charts administered by the National Oceanic and Atmospheric Administration (NOAA). Land contours, structures, and lake depths can all change with time, thanks to man-made and natural alterations. Keeping the whole collection consistent poses an untenable management problem without an appropriate "live" database.

Soon software and its CASE tools will dwarf the NOAA's problems. Indeed, some vendors maintain that *no* extant database can tackle the challenge. In your search for the ideal CASE system, make sure to scrutinize the underlying repository. It will not star in any glitzy demo—indeed, it could easily slow execution down. In the long run, however, it's the bedrock of the database that supports the superstructure—especially one that promises to grow into the (Babylonian) clouds. CASE vendors better heed the handwriting on the wall, lest they share the fate of *Belshazzar*.

⅃ **References**

1. Jeff Kodasky and Robert Dye, "Programming with pictures," *Computer Language*, January 1989, p. 61.

2. Alan Borning, "Defining constraints graphically," *CHI Proceedings of the ACM*, April 1986, p. 137.

3. Ephraim P. Glinert, "Out of flatland towards 3-D visual programming," in *Proceedings of Fall Joint Computer Conference*, Dallas, 1987, p. 292.

4. Shi-Kuo Chang, et al., *Visual Languages*, Plenum Press, New York, 1986.

5. Edward R. Tufte, *The Visual Display of Quantitative Information*, Graphics Press, Cheshire, CT, 1983.

6. Marc H. Brown, "Exploring algorithms using Balsa-II," *IEEE Computer*, May 1988, p. 14.

7. Marc H. Brown, *Algorithm Animation*, MIT Press, Cambridge, MA, 1988.

8. Max Schindler, "Coding languages to change little as libraries offer reusable code," *Electronic Design*, January 7, 1988, p. 96 (interview).

9. Kamran Parsaye, et al., *Intelligent Databases*, Wiley, New York, 1989.

10. James Foley, et al., "Defining interfaces at a high level of abstraction," *IEEE Software*, January 1989, p. 15 (special issue "User Interfaces").

A

A STEREOSCOPIC VIEW OF COMPUTER HISTORY

⌐ Calculators from the Middle Ages to the Electronic Brain

Computer historians as well as popular writers in the field tend to see progress in computer hardware as dominated by a few men of supreme stature—Babbage, Boole, and Turing, for example. In reality, the technology of computers, like almost any other, evolved slowly over the centuries. To make matters worse, historians overlook the fact that the modern computer serves in two distinct functions: (1), as a powerful calculator, and (2), as a controller, embedded in other machinery from toaster to airplane. These two branches evolved separately, except for a few joint ventures in the fairly recent past. By keeping this duality in mind, you'll gain a much deeper understanding of today's trends.

Automating numerical computation has been the goal of mathematicians for centuries. In fact, Leonardo da Vinci had already sketched out a 13-digit decimal calculator in the 1400s. So clear were his drawings that the machine was finally constructed some years ago and can be admired in the IBM museum. The first to actually build a calculator was probably Blaise Pascal,

DaVinci: Plans for
13-digit calculator

1500

Regiomontanus'
Eagle

1600

Napier's Bones

Pascal: Adder

Morland: Multiplier

1700 Leibniz: Calculator
Leibniz dies

Writing automaton

Mahon-Stanhope's
Demonstrator

1800 Jacquard: Pattern
loom

1820 Thomas: Calculator
Babbage: Difference
engine

1840
Ada Lovelace dies
Boole: Formal logic
Scheutz: Printing
calculator
1860 Babbage: Analytical
engine (partial)

1880 Telephone exchange

Hollerith: Tabulator

1900 Dial telephone

Teletypewriter

1920 Great Brass Brain

Television broadcast

who conceived his *machine à calculer* in 1642 at age 19 (see p. 34). Blaise's father was a tax collector, and he had his son help him with *l'addition* during tax season. This was too boring for the bright youngster, and he decided to solve that problem once and for all. (Who says that nothing good ever came from taxes?)

When completed in 1645, Pascal's Arithmetic Engine was the size of a cigar box. It was operated with a stylus and functioned pretty much like an odometer. Each of its eight wheels advanced the one to its left by one digit for every complete revolution. Although Pascal built 50 of his gizmos, and each could do the work of six men, they failed to make him rich for a simple reason—six men were cheaper than one Arithmetic Engine.

In fact, young Pascal had anticipated a modern phenomenon: the scientific breakthrough that turned into a marketing disaster because of poor quality control. (The art of gear cutting turned out to lag far behind Pascal's ingenuity.) That was fortunate for us, because it forced Pascal to pursue worthier goals than selling calculators.

In spite of his precarious health, Pascal went on to invent the hypodermic needle, the hydraulic press, and—inspired by Parisian traffic jams—public transportation. Thanks to his knowledge of gear cutting, he was able to build (and actually wear) a wristwatch two centuries before the Swiss caught on to them. (Pocket watches known as Nuremberg Eggs, however, had been around for nearly a century.) Pascal's probability theory and other mathematical advances paved the way for Newton and Leibniz, and Pascal's writings have shaped the character of French literature to this day.

Tax accounting also motivated an Englishman, Samuel Morland, to build a calculator in 1666. It was similar to Pascal's, except that it added and subtracted pounds, shillings, pence, and farthings. But for survival in unsettled times, Morland had to rely on other resources. He became a diplomat, spying both for Cromwell and Charles II. Nevertheless, Morland was an outstanding engineer who designed and commercially produced pumps 1000 times more cost efficient than competing models. In 1673 Morland added a pocket-sized multiplying calculator to his bag of tricks. However, this first pocket calculator succumbed to competition from a more powerful foreign design from an even greater innovator—an ill omen for later times.

The inventor was Gottfried Wilhelm von Leibniz. He was born in Leipzig (now East Germany) just one year after Pascal built his calculator. Like Blaise, Gottfried was something of a

Wunderkind. Young Gottfried largely educated himself in his father's library, and by age 8 he had taught himself Latin. But Leibniz did not pursue mathematics until he was 26 and an established law professor. He jumped the gun on Boole by publishing a symbolic language applicable to "all reasoning processes." Starting from scratch, Leibniz invented calculus and the notation we still learn today (like the integration symbol that immortalizes the long forgotten "long S," standing for *summa*).

In 1694 Leibniz built a mechanical calculator that could add, subtract, multiply, divide, and even crank out (literally) square roots (see p. 32). No wonder Morland stood no chance against such a superior design. In fact, the Calculation Machine eventually begat the hand-cranked Swiss calculators still in vogue in the 1950s. Leibniz (shown on p. 366) had also ferreted out a way to enter all the multiplicand's digits simultaneously and pass numbers into an accumulator (call it a "register") via a movable carriage. In fact, he left little for his epigones in the field to discover, except ways to actually build his marvels.

Lagging technology largely accounts for the slumber that befell mechanized arithmetic for nearly a century. Historians record several variations on the theme of Leibniz, scattered all over Europe. None seem to have engendered much interest either with the courts or the public. The spirit of the baroque and rococo cared more for amusement and music than for analysis and calculus. Artisans were too busy making fabulous toys to bother with calculators.

The other parent. And that brings us to the second lineage of the modern computer, made up not of philosophers and mathematicians, but of engineers and craftsmen. Automata were all the rage at European courts in the eighteenth century, but they can be traced to ancient times. As far back as 400 B.C., Archytas of Tarentum is said to have made a wooden pigeon that could fly. Such a feat was not claimed again until 19 centuries later when Regiomontanus (whose prosaic real name was Johann Müller) supposedly built an eagle that flew before Emperor Maximilian I through the gates of Nuremberg.

Singing, fluttering birds, a writing boy (1760), and even a chess player (made in Switzerland) amused courtiers and later a science-stricken public at numerous exhibitions. These automata employed control mechanisms that survive to this day: analog ones like cams, and digital ones like pins (as in music

1500	DaVinci: Plans for 13-digit calculator
	Regiomontanus' Eagle
1600	Napier's Bones
	Pascal: Adder
	Morland: Multiplier
1700	Leibniz: Calculator
	Leibniz dies
	Writing automaton
	Mahon-Stanhope's Demonstrator
1800	Jacquard: Pattern loom
1820	Thomas: Calculator
	Babbage: Difference engine
1840	Ada Lovelace dies
	Boole: Formal logic
	Scheutz: Printing calculator
1860	Babbage: Analytical engine (partial)
1880	Telephone exchange
	Hollerith: Tabulator
1900	Dial telephone
	Teletypewriter
1920	Great Brass Brain
	Television broadcast

boxes), and punched cylinders or cards (as in player pianos). The analog mechanisms eventually spawned the nearly forgotten analog computer*; the cards, as some more seasoned readers may remember, found widespread use in our own days as well.

The first computer.   In fact, punched cards stem from the first practical *ordinateur* (as the **Académie Française** has christened computers). It was of the "embedded" variety—what today would be called a numerical controller—and went on line in 1799 to automate looms. This did not happen by chance. Watt's steam engine had recently fathered the industrial age, and factories were springing up all over Europe. Mechanical looms brought affordable fabrics to the masses—and a few problems as well. History books tell of the machine-smashing Luddites, but are silent about the lot of the "shedding boys."

On a hand loom, the weaver could control individual groups of "warp" threads to create the "shed," through which the shuttle passes. The raised threads are seen in the finished cloth, while the rest remains hidden beneath the shuttle's "woof" threads. Weaving complex patterns (including brocades and tapestries) by hand was not only cumbersome, it was expensive as well, because few weavers commanded the necessary skills. Here was definitely an opportunity to make handsome profits.

So why did mechanical looms pose new problems? They were too fast for proper shedding by a single weaver. Cheap help was used to pull the thread groups on command—primarily young boys. One of them was Joseph Marie Jacquard, and he soon decided what he would do when he grew up: he would find a better way to control the shed. By 1799 he had reached his goal. Jacquard controlled the loom with a loop of punched cards, connected with glued-on fabric strips, folded in harmonica fashion as shown in Figure A.1.

---

*Analog computers may not fit into this discussion, but at least one must be mentioned. Called "The Great Brass Brain," it computed the tides in the world's harbors for the U.S. Coast and Geodetic Survey. In operation from 1910 until 1966, the machine never lost data in a brownout, because stopping the crank just interrupted the ongoing calculation. The 2500-pound monster accommodated up to 37 input terms to simulate both heavenly bodies and harbor features, and it produced graphs as well as printouts. Graphs are very handy in a place like Seattle, where the two daily tides can differ from each other by as much as 10 feet one day and not at all a week later.

Courtesy IBM Archives

Figure A.1 The Jacquard loom was the first control "computer"; it still dominates the textile industry around the world.

The rows of holes in the cards were a form of microcode, programmed to raise the proper sets of warp threads, as the design demanded. Complex patterns could now be produced inexpensively—most famous among them was Jacquard's portrait, which required no fewer than 24,000 punched cards. Little wonder that within just 30 years over 10,000 high-tech Jacquard looms were clattering away in France. Today, their descendants throughout the world number in the millions.

First to apply punched cards to calculation was an English mathematician whose name has become the linchpin of modern computer lore—Charles Babbage (p. 210). For Britannia to rule the waves, her ships needed accurate astronomical and nautical

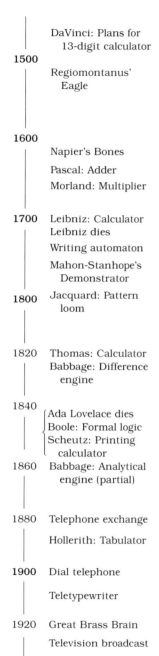

DaVinci: Plans for
  13-digit calculator

1500

Regiomontanus'
  Eagle

1600

Napier's Bones

Pascal: Adder

Morland: Multiplier

1700 Leibniz: Calculator
Leibniz dies

Writing automaton

Mahon-Stanhope's
  Demonstrator

1800 Jacquard: Pattern
  loom

1820 Thomas: Calculator
Babbage: Difference
  engine

1840

Ada Lovelace dies
Boole: Formal logic
Scheutz: Printing
  calculator

1860 Babbage: Analytical
  engine (partial)

1880 Telephone exchange

Hollerith: Tabulator

1900 Dial telephone

Teletypewriter

1920 Great Brass Brain

Television broadcast

tables. Once the Fourier series facilitated exact calculation of transcendental functions, tables of logarithms and trigonometric functions could be compiled. In France teams of up to a hundred "computers" (members of an honorable trade until renamed "operators" in 1941) toiled over the laborious calculations. Then careless typesetters often obliterated the mathematicians' laborious tallies.

Babbage, who knew everybody of consequence (including Darwin, Laplace, Poisson, Wheatstone, and Fourier himself) persuaded the Chancellor of the Exchequer in 1829 to fund development of a mechanical printing calculator that would sidestep all the errors. For a feasibility model, he received the grand sum of 1500 Pound Sterling. To be fair, 1500 pounds back then was a lot of silver and would have paid Professor Babbage's salary for three years.[1]

Babbage called his device a Difference Engine (see p. 152). That name goes back to Leibniz's difference calculus, which was now to be applied to the Fourier series. Increments were called first, second, third (and so on) differences, with increasing powers of the variable. (Constant factors were calculated by hand.) The Engine was to cover five such levels, yielding 19 decimal places; the Engine, to be driven by steam, would just add up the values and set the results into type automatically. Though money was still a Sterling commodity in Babbage's day, it did not last long enough. The inventor had to return to the trough time and again. In 1832 the Engine was "near completion" once more, although it hadn't yet performed even one of the promised 19-digit calculations. By then, Babbage had gone through 17,000 of the crown's (and about 20,000 of his own) Pounds, and work stopped for good. Whether or not Babbage conceived the computer, he definitely discovered the cost overrun.

Calculators galore. Impressive as the Difference Engine's specifications were, similar efforts proliferated throughout Europe and even in the New World. For example, in 1854 Swedes George and Edward Scheutz built a calculator with 15-place accuracy that cast up to 120 lead strips each hour for printing (see Figure A.2). Babbage may not have been too happy that the brothers succeeded where he had failed, but he nevertheless promoted their work in France until it was honored with a prestigious gold medal.

Courtesy IBM Archives

Anyway, Babbage primarily made history with his later, also uncompleted work—the general-purpose Analytical Engine. Its gears and levers were to be programmed with punched cards, borrowed from Jacquard's loom, which Babbage greatly admired. (He managed to obtain two woven Jacquard portraits—much coveted because they were not for sale.[2,3]) The Analytical Engine was to use separate cards for the input of variables, constants, and operator sequences—what we would call programs today. In fact, Babbage's claim to fame rests primarily on the concept of separate storage, calculation, and I/O sections.[4]

With the application of Jacquard's cards in Babbage's Analytical Engine, the control and computation branches of automation joined briefly for the first time. To be exact, it was a virtual union, because the Engine fizzled when Babbage's allotted time ran out at age 79. A committee was appointed in 1879—three years after the pundit's death—to contemplate the Engine's

Figure A.2 Babbage may have been the first to think of a printing calculator, but the first to work (shown here) came from the Scheutz brothers' shop.

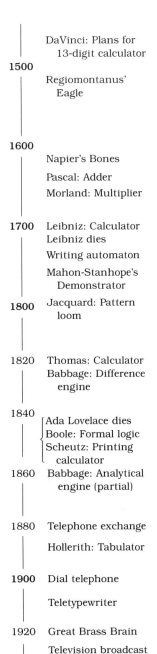

DaVinci: Plans for
13-digit calculator

1500

Regiomontanus'
Eagle

1600

Napier's Bones

Pascal: Adder

Morland: Multiplier

1700 Leibniz: Calculator
Leibniz dies

Writing automaton

Mahon-Stanhope's
Demonstrator

1800 Jacquard: Pattern
loom

1820 Thomas: Calculator
Babbage: Difference
engine

1840
Ada Lovelace dies
Boole: Formal logic
Scheutz: Printing
calculator
1860 Babbage: Analytical
engine (partial)

1880 Telephone exchange

Hollerith: Tabulator

1900 Dial telephone

Teletypewriter

1920 Great Brass Brain

Television broadcast

future. Only one person would possibly have been able to take up Babbage's legacy—his oldest son Herschel, who had tinkered with the "mill" (the processing section) when Babbage was still wrestling with implementation details. But Herschel had followed the lure of India, and after extensive deliberations the committee praised Babbage's ingenuity and concluded that no estimate of the completion costs could be made.

Although the Analytical Engine died with its inventor (so what else is new?), it is nevertheless firmly established in computer lore as the world's first programmable computer. Sadly, Babbage was known in his country for 70 years only as the instigator of the "Babbage law." Annoyed in his reflections by street musicians and organ grinders, he persevered in his fight to ban them and so became, as one of his many detractors put it, "a public benefactor after all." That's not much to show for the life of a genius.

Babbage proposed several application examples for his Engine, including the tough three-body problem (important to space travel nowadays). Whether the Analytical Engine could have tackled such an ambitious project or not will remain an enigma. We can be sure, though, that no such thing was ever programmed by Ada, Countess of Lovelace. But that's a whole different story, which is discussed in Chapter 2.

From the New World.   Had Babbage been able to finish his work, perhaps the computational branch of our computers' ancestry would not have forgotten punched cards, until Herman Hollerith rediscovered them. But the second time around, cards were here to stay for several generations. Borrowing Jacquard's punched cards and wedding them to relays turned out to be a stroke of genius. The marriage begat—after repeated metamorphoses—an offspring that matured into something truly terrific: IBM. (Perhaps a fairy had whispered "Something borrowed, something blue.")

An important distinction can be made between Jacquard's and Hollerith's cards, though; the former carried instructions, while the latter carried data. Hollerith applied his cards to tally the 1890 U.S. Census; no programmers were needed. (Some believe IBM's ancestral link to number shuffling has kept the company out of the controller lineage of computers to this day.) Nevertheless, Hollerith deserves the credit for bringing electricity to computing. The holes in his cards closed the circuit for relays that ratcheted the counter gears that tallied the census figures that allowed politicians to gerrymander their districts.

However, the tabulators' big challenges were to come much later. In World War I the machines (shown on p. 126) kept track of production from pocket knives to airplanes. Perhaps even more importantly, tabulators ushered in the Welfare State in 1935, when they began to sort 500,000 Social Security records a day. No wonder Hollerith's outfit prospered and added ever bigger electromechanical calculators to its product line. We'll get back to those in a little while, because they contributed very few genes to modern-day computers.

Rather, the seed that eventually grew into microprocessors (e.g., the 8088) or supercomputers (e.g., the Cray) developed in the relay-packed telegraph and telephone exchanges of the early twentieth century. The relay, as its name implies, first served to relay telegraph pulses when the distance was too great for direct transmission. Thus, relays started their careers as amplifiers, but telegraph designers soon found other uses for them. For instance, take multiplexing circuits, which permit several telegraph signals to be transmitted over just one pair of wires. These circuits—control computers at heart—grew complex enough to benefit from George Boole's binary calculus. Few computer science students ever learn that binary logic had nearly a century of experience under its belt before computer designers rediscovered it.

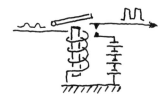

ꙫ Great Leaps Forward in the Past 50 Years

Around the time when relays began to tabulate data for Hollerith, they also came into their own for automatic telephone switching. Their puberty years in local exchanges (the LANs of their day) gave way to adulthood when nationwide networks emerged. By the time Europe slid into World War II, mass-produced, fast relays stood ready to go on to better things than merely routing phone calls. Inventive engineers on both sides of the Atlantic took up the challenge.

In 1938, while the Wehrmacht overran Austria, George Stibitz at Bell Labs tinkered with his Model K (for kitchen table) complex-number computer.[5] These numbers, which consist of a real and an imaginary part, play a big role in communications engineering. While Stibitz was doing research on the phone company's relays, the idea struck him to harness them for the cumbersome multiplication and division of complex numbers. He hard-wired the two algorithms (additions were done as multiplications with 1) and was able to put the Model K in service by October 1939.

All Stibitz machines were based on decimal arithmetic, but individual digits were encoded in binary form (**BCD** or binary-coded decimal). Such encoding was quite common in the phone business, because it saved wires. For example, a switchboard for 7-digit numbers would need 70 wires in decimal form, but only 28 (4 per digit) in BCD. The unused 6 bits per digit were handy for toting telephone control information or, in the Model K, carries and the like. All numbers were of the format $0.x + j\, 0.x$, where x represents 7 digits. Consequently, a great deal of intermediate storage became necessary, which was implemented with standard telephone crossbar switches rather than stepper relays (see p. 224).

In later models, Stibitz returned to relays because they were much faster. The Model V, which was in service from 1946 to 1958 had more than 9000 of them and weighed 10 tons. It also incorporated floating-point arithmetic. One interesting sidelight must be mentioned, namely AT&T's early demonstration of remote computer access. In October 1940, a few months after the Model I entered service, its use could be demonstrated during a conference at Dartmouth College. The phone company had rigged up modems (then called coder-decoder) and an 8-line trunk, and the demo proceeded without a hitch.

Unknown Pioneer.   With World War II in full swing, outside the United States the momentous computer advances at AT&T never registered. Consequently, relay computers evolved quite on their own in Germany at about the same time. Konrad Zuse (phonetically unrelated to Dr. Seuss), a civil and mechanical engineer, had started tinkering with mechanical binary computers in his Berlin home as early as 1936. The first working model was finished in 1938; it consisted of a 16-word, 32-bit storage unit (*Speicherwerk*) and a floating-point processing unit (*Rechenwerk*).[6]

Needless to say, Zuse had never heard of Babbage, even though he arrived at the same system architecture for his machine. He even used home-brew punched tape (made from old movie films) for programming, close enough to Babbage's punched card concept. All of which goes to show that a given problem often brings about almost identical solutions, no matter how far separated in space and time.

By 1937 Zuse had graduated to relays, at least for the processor. His Z2, built to try out the basic logic, employed 200 relays. Slowed down by the war, the fully electromechanical Z3 wasn't completed until 1941, by which time the German Aeronautical Laboratory (*Deutsche Versuchsanstalt fuer Luftfahrt*) had taken a mild interest in Zuse's work. The Z3 functioned with 600 relays in the processor and 1800 in memory (64 words of 22 bits). Like the Leibniz calculator, it performed the four arithmetic functions plus square roots.

Although largely unknown to the American computer science establishment, the Z3 was the first programmable digital computer, and it was actually used to solve practical problems like systems of linear equations and their determinants, quadratic equations, and Eigenvalues (for resonances in airplane wings).* It was destroyed in air raids but reconstructed after the war. The copy shown in Figure A.3 can be admired in the *Deutsches Museum* in Munich.

Zuse's next computer, the Z4 (also known as V4 for *Versuchsgerät*) expanded the memory to 1024 words, although at first only 64 were implemented. The machine's architecture anticipated such recent innovations as pipelining, instruction look-ahead, and, of course—like its predecessor—floating-point arithmetic. A keyboard provided input for data and instructions, while a *Fernschreiber* (teletypewriter) served as the output device. Had Zuse found as powerful a sponsor as Wernher von Braun, the machine could have been implemented with electron tubes (under consideration as far back as 1933!) and advanced the state of the computer arts by a decade or two.

As things turned out, the Allied invasion of Germany put a hold on Zuse's work by forcing his four-year-old company (*Zuse Apparatebau Berlin*) to take refuge in an Alpine village. There, word of the "V4" spread to Allied intelligence officers, who took a (rather disappointed) look at it in its tool shed and declared it harmless. (The rockets' red glare has always impressed people more than the progeny of the abacus.) Unable to resume work

1930	Zuse: Mechanical binary logic
	Turing Machine
	Zuse: Z1
	Stibitz: Model K
	Aiken: Mark 1
1940	Zuse: Z3
	Atanasoff: ABC
	Hopper finds bug
	Zuse: Z4
	Zuse: Plankalkül
	E & M: Eniac
	IBM 603
	V-Neumann's report
1950	Turing: ACE plans
	MIT: Whirlwind
	E & M: Edvac
	E & M: Univac
	Zemanek: Mailüfterl
	Backus: Fortran
	Integrated circuit
	AN/FSQ
	Cobol design
1960	Algol-60
	PDP-1 Mini
	Fortran IV release
	Kurtz: Basic
	IBM: PL/1
	Moore: Forth
	Brass Brain retired
	Colmerauer: Prolog
1970	Intel 4004 micro
	Ritchie: C
	Xerox: Smalltalk
	Wirth: Pascal
	AT&T: Unix
	Intel 8086
1980	Ada released
	Microsoft: DOS

---

*A specialized version ran in my Bohemian hometown, a few blocks from where my father designed relay-controlled milling machines. "Now they want yet another cabinet for their relays," he complained when the logic circuitry didn't pan out. Control and calculating computers were practically neighbors, yet remained total strangers.

Courtesy Konrad Zuse

Figure A.3 Konrad Zuse built the first general-purpose relay computer in 1937. A later production model, destroyed in World War II, was rebuilt as shown here.

on the Z4, Zuse passed the time by designing the first general-purpose computer language in 1945, which he called *Plankalkül*; you'll find more about it in Chapter 2.

On the home front. On this side of the Atlantic, war pushed computer progress into high gear. Artillery and bombers needed better trajectory calculations, and electromechanical machines were pressed into service. Best known of these is Howard Aiken's Mark I, begun in 1939 as a joint effort of Harvard University and IBM. The "Automatic Sequence Controlled Calculator," as it was formally known (shown on p. 244), traces its ancestry directly to Babbage's Analytical Engine, which was known to Aiken. The main difference lay in the number wheels and coupling between the shafts that ran the length of the calculator section. Electromagnetic clutches and stepper relays performed their tasks reliably where Babbage's levers and notches had failed.

Thus, Mark I was more closely related to mechanical calculators than to a digital computer like Zuse's. When completed in 1944, the machine contained 760,000 components, including 1400 rotating switches, 72 rotating mechanical registers (used in IBM's tabulators), and 4 paper tape readers. It cost $500,000 (which amounts to 100 "kilobucks per ton"), one-third of which was contributed by the Navy and the balance by IBM, which planned to take the ASCC commercial.

The computer's first major assignment was the calculation of Bessel functions, so it was nicknamed "Bessie." A lucky coincidence, because when Bessie ran it sounded like a roomful of ladies, busily knitting sweaters. Computer lore has it that the first "software bug" surfaced in Cambridge shortly thereafter, when a fresh-baked Navy lieutenant named Grace Hopper retrieved a moth, squashed in a relay. (Hopper figures prominently in software history—see Chapter 2.) Another computer guru cut his teeth on the Mark—Fred Brooks, famous for his "Mythical Man-Month."[7] Aiken was not an easy taskmaster, unmoved by such newfangled jargon as "bugs" and "Booleans." "I'm a simple man," he was fond of saying, "and I want simple answers." Listen up, Harvard!

Word of the Mark I project had reached German intelligence during the war, and through a friend of a relative the story had seeped down to Zuse. Naturally he was anxious to find out more about the American undertaking, but he failed. We can only wonder whether word of Zuse's work ever reached Allied intelligence. If so, it never influenced Aiken, because his machine merely extended the art of the decimal calculator. IBM chairman Watson thought that Aiken grabbed too much credit for the Mark I and left the development of the successor models to Aiken and the Navy. With the Mark III, finished in 1951, the evolution of mechanical calculators came to its end. It had begun with Pascal's *machine à calculer* over three centuries before.

Meanwhile, IBM combined Aiken's concepts with those of the Model 603 electronic calculating machine to produce the Model 604 in 1948, of which 5600 were manufactured. The emerging giant really got into the swing of the times with its SSEC (selective sequence electronic calculator), which could boast of 12,500 tubes in the processor (for speed) and 21,400 relays that stored 150 numbers of 20 digits each. For years the SSEC remained the only computer accessible to the public, even though at $300 per hour (over 2000 of today's anemic bucks) the machine's public remained somewhat limited (see pp. 266 and 314).

1930	Zuse: Mechanical binary logic
	Turing Machine
	Zuse: Z1
	Stibitz: Model K
	Aiken: Mark 1
1940	Zuse: Z3
	Atanasoff: ABC
	Hopper finds bug
	Zuse: Z4
	Zuse: Plankalkül
	E & M: Eniac
	IBM 603
	V-Neumann's report
1950	Turing: ACE plans
	MIT: Whirlwind
	E & M: Edvac
	E & M: Univac
	Zemanek: Mailüfterl
	Backus: Fortran
	Integrated circuit
	AN/FSQ
	Cobol design
1960	Algol-60
	PDP-1 Mini
	Fortran IV release
	Kurtz: Basic
	IBM: PL/1
	Moore: Forth
	Brass Brain retired
	Colmerauer: Prolog
1970	Intel 4004 micro
	Ritchie: C
	Xerox: Smalltalk
	Wirth: Pascal
	AT&T: Unix
	Intel 8086
1980	Ada released
	Microsoft: DOS

Blood, sweat, and tears. In England, of course, the war also gave mechanical calculation a lift. Not only was it needed for the development of radar, but (perhaps even more) for efforts to break enemy codes. A bright young mathematician by the name of Alan Turing distinguished himself by cracking the German Enigma code.* While this was a software triumph, Turing also advanced the hardware end of the electronic computer. The first code crackers were known as "bombes," because they deciphered code by brute force. The later Colossus machines worked with 2400 tubes but lacked storage. When the war ended, Turing helped design the ACE (automatic computing engine) but then left the project. When information was released to the press in 1950, ACE was hailed as the most advanced computer in the world, but only a scaled-down version ever saw the light of day.

In Chapter 1 we had discussed the Turing machine, a conceptual model of computing—whether by man or machine. After leaving the ACE project, Turing returned to more theoretical work, hounded by the question "Can computers think?" He had not reached a conclusion by the time he ended his life in 1954, distressed by his infatuation for a young boy. Or did he accidentally create and ingest cyanide, as his mother claimed? Her view can't be dismissed out of hand, because at times Turing's mind worked in curious ways. At the height of the London bombings, he converted all his savings to silver bars, which he buried in Bletchley Park—never to be found again. Much in Turing's life remains an enigma.

⌐ Birth of the Electronic Brain

In America, meanwhile, Presper Eckert's and John Mauchly's Eniac made history, as did John von Neumann's common-storage architecture. But here, too, quick-draw "historians" have painted a muddled picture. The facts about the true evolution of America's "electronic brains" might never have surfaced had Eckert's later employer, Sperry Rand, not gotten greedy and tried to stick Honeywell with a $250 million royalty bill.

---

*Actually, Turing had some help. In fact, the Nazis had shot themselves in the foot when they fired a Polish engineer, Richard Lewinski, from an Enigma plant because he was a Jew. Lewinski was smuggled to Paris, where Turing met him in 1939. Lewinski was able to reconstruct much of the Enigma mechanism from memory, which greatly reduced the scope of the cipher search.

As Federal District Judge Earl Larson put it on March 13, 1972: "Eckert and Mauchley did not themselves first invent the automatic electronic digital computer, but instead derived that subject matter from one Dr. John Vincent Atanasoff." Now an American court had joined ancestral Bulgaria in honoring this obscure scientist as the true father of the digital computer. (In 1970 he had been awarded the order of Cyril and Methodius, named after the inventors of the Cyrillian alphabet.)

So, is established computer history a lie from A(tanasoff) to Z(use)? Not quite; life just isn't as "clean" as abstract thinkers (which sometimes includes judges) would like it. Atanasoff, a physics professor at Iowa State College in Ames from 1930 to 1942, needed a way to solve partial differential and integral equations. He found analog machines, widely used for this purpose at the time, too inaccurate and slow. By the fall of 1939, he had built a breadboard machine using tubes and his own logic circuitry. Tube-driven flip-flops were too expensive for storage, so Atanasoff used capacitors and "jogging" circuitry—in other words, dynamic RAM. In fact, 30 of the finished computer's 300 tubes served to recharge the capacitors, arranged on a bakelite drum.[8-10]

With the aid of a student, Clifford Berry, Atanasoff was able to finish his Atanasoff-Berry Computer (or ABC machine) in 1942—then promptly left it behind to work at the Naval Ordnance Laboratory in Washington, D.C. But we are getting ahead of the story. In 1940 Atanasoff had met John Mauchley at a conference, and the following year Mauchley wrote to Atanasoff asking how he was doing with his "computing device."

A year later Mauchley visited Atanasoff and stayed at his house for several days. They tinkered with the computer and talked into the night. Mauchley even read a manuscript that described the principles and implementation of the ABC machine. Although impressed with it, Mauchley later voiced one major disappointment: the ABC needed an operator to reload it during calculations—he had hoped it would be automatic. While in Ames, Mauchley received word that he had been accepted at the Moore School of Engineering at the University of Pennsylvania. His instructor was to be John Eckert.

In 1943 Eckert and Mauchley submitted their proposal for the Eniac (Electronic Numerical Integrator and Calculator) to the Army Ordnance Corps. The Corps was in a hurry to revise its trajectory tables when it found that big guns tended to fire long on the sands of Africa. The project was directed by John Brainerd, and in February 1946 the result was formally unveiled (just as

1930	Zuse: Mechanical binary logic
	Turing Machine
	Zuse: Z1
	Stibitz: Model K
	Aiken: Mark 1
1940	Zuse: Z3
	Atanasoff: ABC
	Hopper finds bug
	Zuse: Z4
	Zuse: Plankalkül
	E & M: Eniac
	IBM 603
	V-Neumann's report
1950	Turing: ACE plans
	MIT: Whirlwind
	E & M: Edvac
	E & M: Univac
	Zemanek: Mailüfterl
	Backus: Fortran
	Integrated circuit
	AN/FSQ
	Cobol design
1960	Algol-60
	PDP-1 Mini
	Fortran IV release
	Kurtz: Basic
	IBM: PL/1
	Moore: Forth
	Brass Brain retired
	Colmerauer: Prolog
1970	Intel 4004 micro
	Ritchie: C
	Xerox: Smalltalk
	Wirth: Pascal
	AT&T: Unix
	Intel 8086
1980	Ada released
	Microsoft: DOS

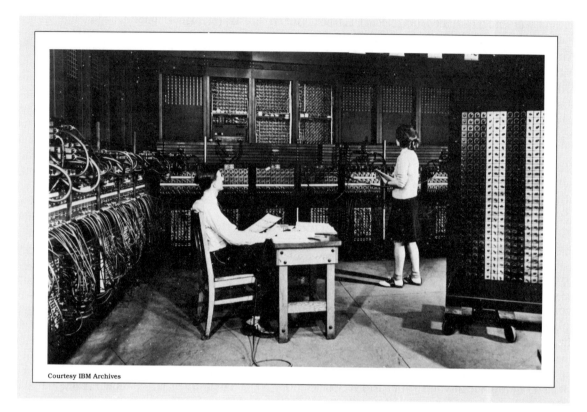

Courtesy IBM Archives

Figure A.4 The era of electronic computers began in earnest with Eniac. A small computer factory could fit in the space needed for this first "electronic brain."

its creators left the university in a huff over patent rights). The world's largest electronic device, shown in Figure A.4, nearly filled a 30-by-50-foot room and Eniac's 17,468 tubes heated it quickly even in the cold of February. The Corp's demands were easily met with an execution time for division of 24 milliseconds. The rest, as they say, is history; even with a paltry storage of 20 words, Eniac had fired the opening shot for the computer era.

Word of the electronic brain spread fast among scientists, including Hungarian-born mathematician John von Neumann. While most of his colleagues at Princeton University's Institute for Advanced Study took pride that their work was unrelated to the world of concrete science, von Neumann did not regard lowly engineering problems with disdain. He said: "The sciences don't try to explain, or even to interpret. They mainly make mathematical models which . . . describe observed phenomena. The justification of such a construct is solely and precisely that it is expected to work."[11] In fewer words: Never mind the theory—it's results that count.

Good designs need good models. To help scientists, von Neumann was even willing to tolerate approximations, the true mathematician's satan. At the time, Edward Teller was modeling the hydrogen bomb—not a product to be developed by trial and error. Only exact and complex models could avert disaster. (A decade later crude modeling of the Electra turboprop brought the lesson home when metal fatigue yanked the planes out of the sky). Von Neumann was determined to have a computer in his own ivory tower and demonstrate its value to science. He took a deep interest in the Moore School of Engineering's next project, the Edvac.

In fact, von Neumann contributed to the theory of the machine's logic, based on Eckert's description of a stored-program architecture made possible by hundreds of mercury memory cells. Why then are we calling such computers "von Neumann machines"? In June 1945 the mathematician prepared a "First Draft of a Report on Edvac," which included his thoughts on the stored-program computer in its 101 pages, and distributed it to members of the Moore School.[12,13] Because it was to be a draft, only von Neumann's name appeared on the document; thus, another myth was born. Edvac proved its mettle with the very first job—simulation of the hydrogen bomb.

Unlike Papa Eniac, the offspring was no monster. Eniac designers had collared a new corollary to Murphy's law—computer failures grow with the fourth power of the tube count. So, Edvac made do with 4000 tubes, supplemented with 10,000 crystal diodes. The machine ran from 1952 to 1962 and convinced every major university that it, too, needed its "electronic brain." That went especially for MIT, which couldn't very well tag along behind Harvard forever. MIT leapfrogged the whole relay epoch with Whirlwind, a 16-bit racehorse that could zip through half a million additions in a second—even if it was a 150-kilowatt drain on the campus power supply. Jay Forrester had invented magnetic storage for this machine, a giant leap for computerkind even though the idea first came to New Jersey enterpreneur Oberlin Smith in 1878.

One MIT student, who did his master's thesis on Whirlwind, was to have an impact on the machine's not so distant future: Kenneth Olson. When Whirlwind's electric bill provoked its shutdown in 1959, by-then president Olson of Digital Equip-

1930	Zuse: Mechanical binary logic
	Turing Machine
	Zuse: Z1
	Stibitz: Model K
	Aiken: Mark 1
1940	Zuse: Z3
	Atanasoff: ABC
	Hopper finds bug
	Zuse: Z4
	Zuse: Plankalkül
	E & M: Eniac
	IBM 603
	V-Neumann's report
1950	Turing: ACE plans
	MIT: Whirlwind
	E & M: Edvac
	E & M: Univac
	Zemanek: Mailüfterl
	Backus: Fortran
	Integrated circuit
	AN/FSQ
	Cobol design
1960	Algol-60
	PDP-1 Mini
	Fortran IV release
	Kurtz: Basic
	IBM: PL/1
	Moore: Forth
	Brass Brain retired
	Colmerauer: Prolog
1970	Intel 4004 micro
	Ritchie: C
	Xerox: Smalltalk
	Wirth: Pascal
	AT&T: Unix
	Intel 8086
1980	Ada released
	Microsoft: DOS

ment led the old chum to pasture in the computer museum. For company, Olson invited MIT's next breakthrough as well—the first transistorized computer dubbed TX-0. One of its designers was Gordon Bell, later to become the architect of the VAX. At the time, transistors weren't more reliable than tubes (though certainly easier on the fuse box). To facilitate repairs, the solid-state heirs to the throne mimicked their electron-tube forefathers by hiding inside plug-in plastic tubes.

Another Whirlwind descendant chose a different path. The AN/FSQ-7 grew into the world's biggest computer ever, weighing in at 175 tons. This behemoth settled at McGuire Air Force Base in New Jersey to power the SAGE (semiautomatic ground environment) system for aerospace defense. Although the mammoth computer was eventually replaced, the 13 SAGE centers continue to guard the nation.

Computers go commercial.   Let us backtrack a bit to the time when Eckert and Mauchley traded the security of an ivy-clad laboratory for the rough winds of enterprise. In the fall of 1947, they contracted with Northrop to build the Binac (binary automatic computer) for the Air Force's Snark missile control system. Binac broke new ground as the first redundant computer with two CPUs, each with 700 tubes, that were to check each other's operation. Although delivered in 1949, it went 178% over budget and cast a shadow over the two pioneers' real ambition, which was to design a marketable computer.

In 1950 they nevertheless began to design the world's first commercial general-purpose machine—the Univac (Universal Automatic Computer). But soon the money ran out, and they had to accept a buyout offer from Remington-Rand. The struggle was worth it, though. With 5000 tubes Univac I ran at 2.5 MHz—25 times faster than Eniac. The machine was delivered to the U.S. Census Bureau, beating Hollerith's successor IBM to the punch. It also made the public aware of the new technology when it finished tabulating the 1952 presidential election returns within 45 minutes after the polls closed. ("Ike" Eisenhower had beaten Adlai Stevenson handily.) Remington-Rand next made history with its Project 13—the world's first real-time computer. It was christened Univac 1101 (13 in binary form) and became the progenitor of many communications systems.

We already made the acquaintance of TX-0, which ushered in the solid-state era of computing. But the transistor, too, has a much longer history than most expect. In fact, Shockley attempted to make a copper-oxide field-effect transistor back in 1939, but success did not come until 1947, when a point-contact transistor actually amplified the human voice. (Perhaps it was the sentence "Come here, Bardeen and Brattain, I need you!") The junction transistor emerged in 1951, and two years later it showed up in hearing aids—royalty free, in honor of Alexander Graham Bell.

Just seven years later, the integrated circuit emerged and sparked the revolution that would bring about the PC era. In the 20 years since Jack Kilby of Texas Instruments turned on the first IC, no fewer than 150 billion have been produced world-wide—almost 30 for everyone alive today. By early 1971, this new technology led to the first microprocessor—Intel's 4004, whose 2300 transistors provided the same computing power as Eniac's 17,500 tubes.

Lost and found: control computers. For quite a few pages now, we have been talking only about number-crunching computers of the calculator breed. Whatever became of the controllers, the second ancestral line we emphasized earlier? Because control applications rarely crave arithmetic, the lowly relay satisfied controller needs for half a century—until commercial ICs changed the world forever. When users caught on to Intel's 4004 and its offspring, both computing branches united for a while, as the same chips powered calculators as well as controllers. By now, specialization has separated their paths again. A still undiscovered law of nature decrees that specialized gizmos always produce more bang per buck, regardless of the application.

In Europe, relays also stayed in the calculator branch of computing until the continent had dug out from under the war's rubble. Zuse managed to sell or lease some machines (the Swiss Federal Technical University—better known as *ETH*—was his first customer), but by the time Europe became competitive once more, IBM had pretty much cornered the computer market. Academic research, hampered by lack of funds, tinkered with relay machines a little longer. But by and large, Europe's academics concentrated on theory and software, as reviewd at some length in Chapter 2. Not until the mid-1950s did small systems, modeled after the American pattern, sprout at Europe's universities. The one at the

1930	Zuse: Mechanical binary logic
	Turing Machine
	Zuse: Z1
	Stibitz: Model K
	Aiken: Mark 1
1940	Zuse: Z3
	Atanasoff: ABC
	Hopper finds bug
	Zuse: Z4
	Zuse: Plankalkül
	E & M: Eniac
	IBM 603
	V-Neumann's report
1950	Turing: ACE plans
	MIT: Whirlwind
	E & M: Edvac
	E & M: Univac
	Zemanek: Mailüfterl
	Backus: Fortran
	Integrated circuit
	AN/FSQ
	Cobol design
1960	Algol-60
	PDP-1 Mini
	Fortran IV release
	Kurtz: Basic
	IBM: PL/1
	Moore: Forth
	Brass Brain retired
	Colmerauer: Prolog
1970	Intel 4004 micro
	Ritchie: C
	Xerox: Smalltalk
	Wirth: Pascal
	AT&T: Unix
	Intel 8086
1980	Ada released
	Microsoft: DOS

Courtesy IBM Austria

Figure A.5 Mailüfterl, built at the Technical University of Vienna, Austria, was the first fully transistorized digital computer.

Technical University of Vienna was given the name *Mailüfterl* (spring breeze, to distance it from Forrester's Whirlwind) by its designer, Heinz Zemanek (see Figure A.5).

Zemanek, now an IBM fellow and 1986 recipient of the ACM's Computer Pioneer award, reminisces: "Although I was part of a large company [IBM] for many years, I always remained a member of the University as well. I believe that this linkage between academia and industry is the *sine qua non* for healthy technical development." He points to the fact that many early computers sprang from the fertile soil of academe. But he also admits that he built *Mailüfterl* (the first fully transistorized computer in Europe) against the advice of some more-established colleagues, who questioned its scientific significance.[14]

Zemanek, who considers himself both an engineer and a mathematician, comments on the software crisis: "Mathematicians are used to working with unreality. When they claimed computer programming for their own, they staked out more terrain than they could cultivate."* Zemanek, by the way, founded the "Vienna method" of formal language definition when he formally defined IBM's PL/I. Luckily for him, he had nothing to do with the design of the languishing language itself. (Read all about it in Chapter 2.)

⸗ References

1. Maboth Moseley, *Irascible Genius: The Life of Charles Babbage*, Henry Regnery Co., Chicago, 1970.

2. Jerry M. Rosenberg, *The Computer Prophets*, Macmillan, London, 1967.

3. Anthony Hyman, *Charles Babbage*, Princeton University Press, Princeton, NJ, 1982.

4. Philip Morrison and Emily Morrison, *Charles Babbage and His Calculating Engines*, Dover, New York, 1961.

5. Paul E. Ceruzzi, *Reckoners*, Greenwood Press, Westport, CT, 1983.

6. Konrad Zuse, *Der Computer, Mein Lebenswerk*, Springer-Verlag, Heidelberg, 1984.

7. Frederick Brooks, *The Mythical Man-Month*, Addison-Wesley, Reading, MA, 1975.

8. David Gardner, "Will the inventor of the first digital computer please stand up?" *Datamation*, February 1974, p. 84.

9. Robert Slater, *Portraits in Silicon*, MIT Press, Cambridge, MA, 1987.

10. Clark R. Mollenhoff, *Atanasoff, Forgotten Father of the Computer*, Iowa State University Press, Ames, 1988.

---

*Some of Professor Zemanek's ideas may have rubbed off when he taught me the basics of logic circuitry, which, of course, meant relays at that time and place. When he showed off his first relay machine, Zemanek was faced with many questions about the contest between electronic brains and human ones. In one lecture he quipped: "Well, the latter are a lot more fun to make."

11. James Gleick, *Chaos: Making a New Science*, Viking Penguin, New York, 1987.

12. Herman Goldstine, *The Computer from Pascal to von Neumann*, Princeton University Press, Princeton, NJ, 1972.

13. Nancy Stern, *From Eniac to Univac*, Digital Press, Bedford, MA, 1981.

14. Gerhard Chroust, *Heinz Zemanek—Ein Computerpionier*, R. Oldenbourg, Vienna & Munich, 1986.

B

Excuse Me, But How Do Computers Work?

ꙮ Primer on Computer Hardware and Software for the Neophyte

This book does not presume computer expertise on the reader's part. Although a technical background will help, most professionals and students should be able to follow as well. The only prerequisite is that new basic skill labeled "computer literacy." However, even a college education does not yet guarantee much intimacy with our era's most universal tool, nor are introductory texts for the intelligent layman easy to find. The following pages will attempt to bridge the gap.

Perhaps the biggest obstacle to computer literacy is the binary number system, which all modern computers use. We have learned in school where the decimal system comes from: *homo sapiens* has 10 fingers on which to count. If this is so, then the binary system must have been invented by *equus circensis*. Perhaps an ancient Babylonian mathematician observed how a circus horse scraped the sand with his hoof, and so discovered the binary system. That would explain why it has been known for some time—long before the digital computer.

Not that other number systems weren't popular as well. Most of Europe was hooked on base 12 until the Middle Ages, and the ancient Mayans worked with a radix (or base) of 20. (It seems they were nimble enough to count their toes as well as their fingers.) The Mayans used the symbol ○ for the One, and — for the Five, so that ○○ would mean 7 in the lowest position, 7×20 in the next one, and 7×20^2 or 2800 in the third position. Compared with the decimal system, where the same positions identify Ones, Tens, and Hundreds, the Mayans certainly had a leg up when it came to big numbers—in fact, they used it to good advantage for quite sophisticated astronomical computations.

To bridge the gap between decimal and binary systems, let's create a unit called a Hand and say that 2 Hands = 1 Guy and that 2 Guys = 1 Pair. In this system 101 means 1 Pair + 0 Guys + 1 Hand. Now we can add Hands: 1 + 1 = 10, because 1 + 1 Hands give 0 Hands and a carry, which equals 1 Guy and 0 Hands. Using more scientific terminology, in the decimal (base 10) system the digits represent powers of 10, and in the binary (base 2) system powers of 2. Or, to spell it out in detail:

decimal	*binary*
$10^0 = 1$ One	$2^0 = 1$ Hand
$10^1 = 1$ Ten	$2^1 = 1$ Guy
$10^2 = 1$ Hundred	$2^2 = 1$ Pair

Now we are ready to perform some arithmetic. We'll do it in small steps, first in decimal notation:

A = 2345	first addend
B = 6759	second addend
I = 8094	first intermediate sum
C = 1010	first carry value
I = 9004	second intermediate sum
C = 0100	second carry value
T = 9104	the total sum
C = 0000	the empty carry

This addition may look strange at first because we put on paper what we normally do in our heads. Looking at the first addition, we had in the first column $2 + 6 = 8$, which goes into the first column of I. In the last column we get $9 + 5 = 14$, which is 4 Ones and 1 Ten. The Ones go into the I line, and the Ten goes into the proper column of the carry (C) line. We add the Tens and Hundreds the same way, in any sequence as long as we keep the different units in their proper columns.

To get the total, we just add the intermediate sum and the carry, which in one case (for the Tens) gives us another carry, so we have to repeat the process once more. No matter what the addends' values, we wind up with the correct total, as long as we keep adding until there are no more carries.

For a binary addition we'll assume:

A = 0011	first addend: $2^1 + 2^0 = 3$
B = 0110	second addend: $2^2 + 2^1 = 6$
I = 0101	intermediate sum
C = 0100	first carry
I = 0001	intermediate sum
C = 1000	second carry
T = 1001	sum: $2^3 + 2^0 = 9$
C = 0000	empty carry

We performed the binary addition with exactly the same steps as its decimal counterpart, starting out with 1 Guy and 1 Hand plus 1 Pair and 1 Guy. The result is 1 "Quad" (2 Pairs as in a quadrille) and 1 Hand, which fortunately adds up to 9 Hands. *Quod erat demonstrandum.*

Computers have to perform this kind of operation for all their arithmetic. Of course, we assume that we deal with binary computers, whose unit of calculation isn't called a Hand, but a bit (short for binary digit). A Quad (2^3) is the only other unit that has a special name—a byte. Multiplication is performed by repeated addition, which altogether seems rather tedious for two numbers in the billions. But no matter, binary logic is fast enough. This is not to say that digital computers will always work with a binary system. In fact, ternary (base 3) adders have been built, and they are much faster because the extra bit can take over the carry function.

The truth will out.   One reason why all the early digital computer research was done with binary systems (see discussion in Appendix A) was because their ancestors were built with relays, and relay switches have only two states—on and off. But when magnetic memory appeared on the scene, a switch to ternary arithmetic gained some (but obviously not enough) support. A magnet has three states: + (or north), − (or south), and 0 (unmagnetized). What probably tipped the balance in favor of the binary approach was the close correspondence with Boolean logic. It too knows only two states: True (usually equivalent to "on" or "1") and False ("off" or "0"). Thanks to Boole, a whole computer can thus be "calculated" much as a mechanical engineer calculates a bridge.

Binary circuits can be implemented with "gates," which perform the primitive logic operations of AND, OR, and NOT. The operations are normally represented in truth tables like this one for AND:

A＼B	T	F
T	T	F
F	F	F

The two operands' values are identified as row and column headings, while the results form the table's body. For example, you can see that True AND True yields True, True AND False yields False, and so on.

The OR function looks like the complement of the AND function. We know from the preceding table that only T AND T = T (with all other combinations F). The equivalent definition for OR says that F OR F = F, while all other combinations yield True. Assume you invite Jack AND Jill to your party. Only if they both come has your wish come True. But if you invite Jack OR Jill, only one of them need show to make you happy.

English is a bit vague here—did you mean that only one of the pair was invited? That case is technically known as an exclusive or (XOR), which yields False for T XOR T. The normal OR corresponds to that wonderful new expression "and/or." (What did lawyers do before Andor arrived?) We still have to define NOT, but that's almost too obvious to talk about. NOT True is False, and vice versa.

⌐ From Snowflakes to Avalanches

Now that we understand what bits can do to each other, we can go on and build a supercomputer. How all those little bits must be arranged to crank a billion 10-digit divisions out every second is, however, a bit more complicated. Just as nature's atoms form molecules and molecules are arranged in certain shapes to make an automobile, so a computer's switches form gates, which are combined into integrated circuits, which must be wired properly to crank out MFLOPS.

You may remember FLOPS (floating-point operations per second) from other chapters, but we assumed there that you know what a floating-point operation is. It's fairly easy to understand how integers (or natural numbers) of any size can be assembled from powers of 2, but what about fractions? We could decree that every number stored in a hypothetical computer represents not a One, but a Thousandth. So, the binary value 1001 would not stand for 9 but for 0.009. In such a machine, what happens if you multiply 1×1? The result would come out as 1 Thousandth when, in reality, it should be 0.000001—which can't even be expressed in our hypothetical machine.

The solution is to devise a gliding scale—a number system where the decimal point can be moved about. In such a floating-point number—say, 1111001—the starting string of 1s might be the value (or mantissa), while the last three digits (the exponent) determine where the decimal point should be. Since 1111 means 15 and the exponent is 1 (meaning "shift left one decimal"), we—and our hypothetical computer—know that the string stands for 1.5. If we also want to use negative numbers, another bit (the sign bit) would be needed to flag a minus sign.

We are now up to a total of 8 bits, which not so long ago was all we could expect in a desktop machine. By now even 32-bit systems are common, and writing all those strings of zeroes and ones could get rather tiresome. So computer engineers have devised an abbreviation called hexadecimal (or just hex) notation. It's nothing more than numbers with radix 16—which poses a problem because we have no numerals higher than 9. New numerals had to be created, for which the beginning of the alphabet was chosen. Thus, A means 10, B is 11, and so on, up to F for 15.

Going back two paragraphs, let's expand 1111001 with a sign bit added at the end, which yields 11110010. In hex the number would read "F2" because F is short for 1111, and 2 for 0010. In some computers all bits are set to all ones rather than zeroes when the machine wakes up. If you display four registers (intermediate storage), you'll obtain FFFF, FFFF, FFFF, FFFF for a 32-bit system. In the bad old days it was often necessary to use core dumps (which display all of a computer's memory), amounting to many pages of Fs intermingled with other numerals. That was the only way to trace the goings-on inside a computer, and it probably turned many a user into a nut. (In the even worse days before hex became popular, an octal—base 8—system was used; it obviously yielded printout bundles twice as thick.)

From a gate to a metropolis.   Now we know how computers crunch numbers and what these numbers look like in memory. But among the multitudes of today's computers only a minority uses its ALU (arithmetic-logic unit) primarily for doing arithmetic. Far more monitor inventories or write books (albeit with some human help), where the logic far outweighs the arithmetic. A simple PC can look through a whole book like this one for a single word in a matter of seconds. When we type text (be it a program or a novel) into a PC, each keystroke sends 1 byte to memory. The letter A, for example, has the "value" 01000001, which corresponds to the integer 65.

To see whether an unknown character X is an A, we need only perform XOR(A, NOT X). Let's say X = 01000011. Its negation is NOT X = 10111100. Remember that an XOR only returns True if the two operands are *not* equal. XORing the two bytes A and NOT X bitwise (bit by bit) tells us that they are nearly complements, but no cigar. The seventh bit does not match, and the search consequently fails—X is in fact a C. The same kind of comparison takes place during execution of an IF; we could formulate the preceding comparison as

IF (X = A) THEN Search = True

Such a search can naturally only work if all PCs use the same translation standard between a letter and its byte value. Fortunately they do, and the conversion is known as ASCII code. Actually, normal ASCII defines only 7 bits (or 128 characters). If the first bit is 1 rather than 0, we talk about extended ASCII; the additional 128 combinations are used for foreign characters and graphics components from which you can compose window frames, borders, and tables. The extended set, regrettably, isn't all that standard, but let's count our blessings, not our curses.

The ALU normally constitutes the most essential part of the central processing unit or CPU, which also contains registers and control logic that puts the ALU through its paces (see Figure B.1). How else would the number cruncher know whether to multiply two values as integers or as floating-point (also called real) numbers? Sometimes the CPU also contains algorithms for such primitive operations as an integer multiplication A × B:

1. Set Counter to 0.
2. Set Sum to 0.
3. Add A to Sum.
4. Add 1 to Counter.
5. Compare Counter with B.
6. IF False go to 3.
7. ELSE enter Sum in Accumulator.

(The accumulator is the register in which results are kept.)

The wizards of OS.   But what if the routine does not reside in the CPU? And how do A and B get from a keyboard or floppy disk into the CPU? All these housekeeping functions are performed by relatively small programs called "utilities", usually merged into an operating system (OS). Any or all of these utilities can be

Figure B.1 In a small computer the ALU (arithmetic-logic unit) dominates the processor hardware. The system bus ties all the components together.

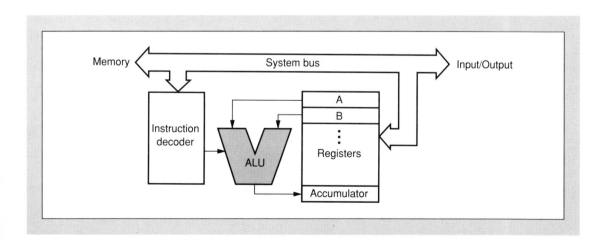

implemented either as software or as hardware. In the latter case, we call it "firmware" and store it in read-only memory (ROM).*

Whichever way it's implemented, a subroutine library contains algorithms for all kinds of math and logic operations. It would translate the mnemonic MULT X,Y into machine-language command sequences (e.g., the seven lines above), each consisting of zeroes and ones. Inside the CPU a decoder converts the machine-language code (called object code) into the control logic (on/off switches) that activates the ALU.

As a user you'll probably tell the computer to multiply X and Y in a high-level language, not via assembly language mnemonics as in the preceding paragraph. In Fortran (or Basic) you'd simply write Z = X * Y—called a source code statement. But now we need another utility, a translator, to produce object code. For Basic you'd most likely use an interpreter that translates the source code into object code one line at a time. This approach permits you to change your mind as you go along, because the interpreter need only redo the changed code. If, for example, you find a few lines later that X should be multiplied with the constant A rather than the variable Y, you just rewrite the line as Z = X * A and restart the calculation from this point.

Alas, there's a price to be paid for the interpreter's flexibility; it won't execute your program very fast since it must create new object code during every run. When it comes to speed, a compiler beats the interpreter almost anytime. A compiler translates the whole program at once and produces on object-code "piano roll" that will play the same piece, be it a Fourier transform or the "Toccata and Fugue in d" (Bach forbid) *ad nauseam* faster than an interpreter ever could.

If Z = X * A is part of a major program (written in Fortran, perhaps), it will likely be compiled. Compilers also tend to look for shortcuts. Let's say your program reads:

```
Z = X * A
U = X * A + Y
```

Any respectable compiler will recognize that it can substitute Z for the product in the second line and save a lot of time. The catch

---

*Too bad we are saddled with the software/hardware dichotomy. When the *Académie Française*, guardian of the French language, had to find a native term for *le software* it chose *logiciel*. This term—loosely translated as "logicware"—catches the spirit of firmware as well as software. Perhaps we should set aside *le chauvinism* and adopt the French term.

with compilers is that you won't find out whether anything went awry until the whole program has been compiled and executed. Therefore, it pays to keep your program modules short and use a language that permits them to be compiled separately. Or you can use an incremental compiler, which lets you debug in an interpretive mode.

Numbers in, pictures out.   We know now—in crude terms—what's going on inside our faithful PC, but not how to get information in and out. To feed programs and data into memory, we need a keyboard handler or a disk driver; to make the result visible a screen handler is needed. All such peripheral drivers naturally must match the computer hardware at one interface and the specific model of a peripheral at the other. It's customary to split up this matching function between the operating system proper and the handler utilities.

Figure B.2 conveys how an OS—or DOS (disk operating system), if it's loaded from a disk—handles the traffic between the CPU and its peripherals. You could say that the function of an OS resembles that of the *cerebellum*, our ancient "little brain," which coordinates muscle functions, vision, and other parts of the human hardware. Without it, the firmware (or, as some call it, wetware) of our gray matter—where the "applications" run—wouldn't be of much use.

But the OS fulfills another vital function. Each PC manufacturer must adapt an OS like PC-DOS for his hardware, so that

Figure B.2 To run a user program, a PC needs quite an array of system software in addition to the operating system proper.

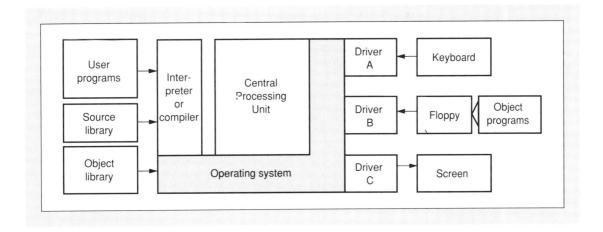

it presents a standard interface (also called a virtual machine) to the outside world. Peripheral makers can then provide the specialized software that lets their peripherals communicate with this interface by means of standardized commands (system calls).

The IBM PC represented such a turning point in computer usage, because it established a de facto standard for the virtual PC-machine with standardized system calls. It was in the interest of both peripheral and clone makers to adhere to the standard. On the flip side, IBM lost control over its creation—an "error" it doesn't intend to repeat. Hence, OS/2 was developed and billed as the next-generation OS for PCs; it's been slow to catch on precisely because IBM means to keep it under its wing.

Most input for PCs comes in one of two forms: (1) binary program files from a floppy (usually obtained from a software vendor) or (2) ASCII text from a keyboard or a disk file (usually containing data). For output, the traditional ASCII streams sent to the screen and printer are beginning to give way to graphics. If the crude graphics from the extended ASCII set are adequate for your purpose, you can indeed put pictures on the screen (and on paper via dot-matrix printers) without any extra hardware.

What you see on today's CASE workstations, however, are called "bit-mapped" graphics. While ASCII permits you to put your choice of a character or graphic element into (typically) 1760 small rectangular boxes on the screen, bit mapping provides much more control. With a 9-by-6 character matrix, you gain access to 54 times as many spots on the screen—roughly 100,000 points called pixels (short for "picture elements"). To use bit-mapped graphics, you need an extra card that converts bit strings into screen locations. As resolution improves, the number of pixels per screen grows, and so does the memory you need to store a screenful of dots. By now a million pixels, each with three colors and several intensities are no longer unusual. As Mbit memory chips become more common, so will high-resolution graphics.

This brings us to the end of the 50-cent tour through the realm of computering, as some like to call it. Since many professionals spend half a lifetime understanding computer science in all its aspects, we have obviously only scratched the surface. Or, to use a more dynamic metaphor, this little excursion should bring you up to speed so you can glide effortlessly through the rest of the book's pages.

C

THE JARGONAUT'S CATECHISM

⌐ An Irreverent Glossary of Software Engineering Terms

Ever since Latin fell into disuse among scholars, they had to create specialized argots to take its place. After all, *any* self-respecting "effete elite" (courtesy Spiro Who) must have a way to tell Ins from Outs. Nobility and showbiz, of course, still bestow instant recognition at the drop of a name, but how do the rest of us crash the gates to elysium? Physicists can name an effect after themselves, and physicians an illness. If a chemist concocts a dynamite compound, he can institute a noble prize. We soft-workers have to achieve immortality the old-fashioned way—as jargonauts.

So, if you have any ambitions to be recognized as a CS[†] maven you must know how to advance the state-of-the-jargon in the most obfuscating fashion. With all the competition from PR agents and other hype mongers, that's getting to be a science all by itself. But even if you merely want to follow the scholars' technobabble, a jargon primer is vital. Furthermore, appreciation

---

[†]CS: Computer Science

of jargon's finer points will greatly enhance the entertainment value of this volume. Behold, then, the laws of CS Newspeak:

Jargon's highest honors (★★★★★) go to the wordnapper, who, by perverting a perfectly good word, removes it from usage by the Outs. No computer scientist has attained this exalted state, but just to convey the concept, ponder this: nobody is likely to coin the term "Gay Nineties" for *this* century's last decade.

At the ★★★★ level, neologisms (like "wordnapping") share honors with deceptions. For example, Ada's *short-circuit* concept will derail any Out's train of thought, sending it to a fusebox instead of a Boolean expression. Verily, a work of genius. Outside the CS realm, *tax simplification* readily comes to mind—a truly demonic deed from the fecund fields of Washington.

If you lack the imagination for such creative trickery, obfuscation at the ★★★ level permits you to unearth archaic terms or meanings. *Engine*, when applied to a piece of software, should send at least the (computerwise) semiliterate mind on a fruitless errand. Similarly, talk about *strong typing* and evoke images of grandma pounding away on her old Underwood, when you really mean rigorous type-checking.

Oxymorons like *artificial intelligence* rate only ★★. So do redundant tautologies and plain-vanilla syntax variations in the pursuit of semantic mutation, as in *floppy disk* (where the "k" is now firmly entrenched). Don't overlook the subjugation of a foreign word (say, *glasnost*); it permits you to impart the meaning of your choice. Beware, though; this approach may be misconstrued by clever Ins as a naïve attempt to distance yourself from Podunk, *n'est-ce pas?*

Lone-star status at best goes to nouns used as verbs or vice versa, no matter how well architected. Even if you concense your every define with a revered teach, not even ignoraming plebes will blink an eye. Especially once a semantic give-back or grammatical don't has conquested *The New York Times*, consider it useless for jargonauting. Remember, "Before long, the truth outs," as a magazine headline recently put it. (Honest, cross my heart!)

And now, *aux barricades, citoyens*! Paradigm your way to fame and fortune.

Abstraction ★★★ The ability to detach a concept from its implementation, which separates scientists from engineers. Use this test to tell them apart. Put the subject at one end of a room and an object of great attraction (no sexist comments, please) at the other. Explain that the subject can advance half the remaining distance whenever you sound a chime. When you ring, the scientist will stand still, knowing that simple math precludes reaching the object. An engineer will move forward, sure to come close enough for all practical purposes.

Abstract data type ★★ Objects that are known by what you can do with them, not what they are—that is, properties and operations are defined, regardless of implementation. Sounds more like "concrete data type," no?

Académie Française ★★ Panel of some 40 academics entrusted with the purity of *la belle langue*. Mandates use of *bureautique* (office automation), *calculette* (pocket calculator), *didacticiel* (courseware), *informatique* (information science), *logiciel* (software), *ordinateur* (computer), *tableur* (spreadsheet), *tirage* (hardcopy), and 2000 more. Maliciously accused of coining the terms *l'hot-dog* and *laissez faire*.[1]

Algol ★★ "Algorithmic Language," meant to put IBM's "Formula Translator" (Fortran) in its place. As a transnational as well as academic effort, Algol was naturally a breech baby. At one point, a European participant banged the table, shouting "No, I will never use a period instead of a comma as the decimal delimiter!!"

Algorithm ★★ More properly, algorism, from the Latin *algorismus*; derives its name from the mathematician Abu Jafar Mohammed ibn-Musa al-Khuwarizmi (native of Khuwarizmi, now Khiva). Although forgotten by all but his latter-day colleagues, Abu Jafar's writings still affect us all; they first introduced Arabic numerals to European scholars. In CS: (1) Whimsical syn. for recipe. (2) Whimsical syn. for solution. Alleged kinship with "Al got rhythm" is patently false.[2]

Alias ★★★ When two or more variables denote the same data object. Practically the inverse of **overloading** and even more prone to producing **side effects**.

Artificial intelligence ★★ (1) A branch of computer science that elicits the intelligence of an ant from megabuck computers; (2) a branch of cognitive psychology that finds happiness in stunning graphics.

Assembly ★★ Short for assembly code (aka native code), a forgettable mnemonic version of machine language.

Backtracking ★ An **expert system** working its **inference engine** in reverse, taking the user from the desired goal back to the point of departure.

BCD coding ★ In "binary-coded decimal" each decimal digit is treated as a separate number. Sensible approach for data such as phone numbers, where each digit represents the root of a subtree (with 10 neatly arranged branches apiece).

Binding ★★ Associating a name with a value. "Early" b.: plugging the value in at *first* opportunity (compilation). "Late" b.: ditto, at *last* chance, usually via "Dynamic" b.: different values are used during execution (e.g., by using **pointers**). Typical of **object-oriented** programming. Ada does it with mirrors (i.e., *you* rig the pointers).

Black-box test ★★★ Treats a software package as if it were a hi-fi component. (Actually, "black box" not only predates the color switch from silver to black, but even predates the term "hi-fi." Some conjecture a relation to black magic, others to the Ford Model T.)

CASE ★★★ (1) Computer-Aided Sales Expert; (2) Cute Antonym for Software Engineering; (3) Bubble chart generators.

Circuitous ★ See circular.

Circular ★★ See circuitous.

Computer Science ★★★ (Abbrev. Compsci or CS) In all but hard-core engineering colleges, a soft science. Called "The costly enumeration of the obvious,"[2] compsci should more graciously be regarded as sci-fi for mathematicians. Stumped by human stupidity in its attempts to prove transitory states of human synapses logically correct, the discipline retreats into the rigor (mortis) of automata. (See also **Artificial intelligence**).

Context free ★★ Another CS term for "independent," when **orthogonal** won't do—for example, transformations that don't depend on their sequence of execution.

Construct ★★ A feeble attempt to convert "construction" into CS slang. Generally an atomic software module larger than a single line of code. Examples: CASE, IF/ THEN/ ELSE.

Control $^{1/2}$★ A hardware or software system's logic, which determines what happens to **data**.

Core ★★★ (e.g., core dump) Still applied to main memory, even though magnetic cores have not been used in most computers for decades. *Never* was meant for apple parts.

Data ★ Just an ungrammatical plural, by now treated among all CS literates as singular. Some diehards contrived the dodge "data object," a bona-fide singular. Example: a datum is a data object.

Demon ★★ (also "daemon") A routine that lurks in the background and (1) pounces on unwary users with unexpected pyrotechnics (e.g., pop-out windows) or (2) catches a hacker's blunders and quietly puts them right. (Just goes to show that only *some* demons are fallen angels.)

Dialect ★★$^{1/2}$ An underhanded attempt by straight hackers to rub it in to the AI crowd. While *people* can span quite a dialectic gap, *computers* invariably stumble (and usually perish) when addressed in the argot of the adjacent valley.

Directed graph ★★★ Bubbles connected by arrows. Examples: data flow diagram and state graph. Vulgar mutants employ polygons, in which case "flowchart" must be used (but never in CS).

Dynamic ★★ (1) Anything that happens during or after compilation. (2) In industry, a product feature competitors still lack.

Edge ★★★ Hi-falutin' syn. for "arc" in a graph. While an arc is usually understood to subsist in a two-dimensional world, an "edge" implies (at least) three-dimensional superiority.

Elegance ★★★ Desirable, but *je ne sais quoi* property of software written in **Algol**, Pascal, or Lisp.

Entropy ★★ The third law of thermodynamics mandates that any closed system drifts into chaos—and computer systems bear out the rule. The fact that living things can violate this law has been used to prove the existence of a Creator.

ETH ★ *Eidgenössische Technische Hoschschule* (Zurich), where Algol and Pascal incubated. Switzerland is legally not a federation, but an *Eidgenossenschaft*. (On August 1, 1291 at Rütli the founders swore an oath to stick together against all comers. What other contracts have held for 700 years?)

Expert system ★★ Supposed to capture human experts' knowledge in a "knowledge base" and process it via an **inference engine**. To date, the only practical reward for 40 years of AI research.

FOO ★★★★ Favored function name, especially in Lisp. A quaint reminder of computing's World War II origins and Turing's time. It's a bowdlerized abbreviation of FUBAR (also written, phonetically, as Foobar). As the scuttlebutt has it, the British Navy favored this term to describe the usual *faux pas* of military intelligence: F%@#*d Up Beyond All Recognition.

Fortran ★ IBM's 1956 "Formula Translator." Old languages never die, they just metamorphose away. Currently, a Parallel Fortran draft standard known as Fortran 8x (or soon 9x) is in the works. It primarily supports the fork-join model of parallelism via PARALLEL DO, SPREAD DO, and PARALLEL REGION.

Glasnost ★★ (Russian) Usually translated as "openness," but that hardly squares with Lenin's definition: "The word which itself heals the wounds it inflicts." Did we miss something?

Glass teletype ⋆ Term used for the first CRT monitors, when the "teletypewriter" was the standard I/O device. By giving the user a second dimension, it encouraged interactive computer operation. Never accepted by CS's serial thinkers.

Grammatik ⋆⋆⋆ (1) German for "grammar". (2) A style analyzer for third-grade teachers.

HLL ⋆ Simplistic abbreviation for high-level languages. Fools nobody anymore.

Heuristic ⋆⋆⋆ Euphemism for poorly understood dependencies, for example, between inputs and outputs of the living brain. Sounds more scientific than empirical or alogical.

Hex, hexadecimal ⋆⋆ Although "hex" is said to be short for "hexadecimal" (base-16), all visitors to Lancaster, Pennsylvania know that Hexes came from witches and predate CS by millennia.

Icon ⋆ Misspelled Russian religious idols, now degraded to visual labels on computer screen. Nevertheless, they have preserved their religious fire, kindling legal warfare.

Inference engine ⋆⋆⋆ A program conisting mostly of IF/THEN decision tables in C (after conversion from Lisp).

Informatics ⋆ European term for CS, but slanted toward software. Good term, since few CS folk dig hardware anyway.

Information hiding ⋆⋆⋆⋆ Absence of **glasnost**. In software, attributed to Professor Parnas. However, the concept can be traced to Felix Dzerzhinski, founder of the Cheka in 1919.

Inheritance ⋆ Like parent, like child. Except *you* decide who inherits what.

Instantiation ⋆⋆ Creating a more concrete instance of something more abstract. (Taken in CS as manifestation of entropy.)

Interrupt ⋆⋆ A system crash, caused on purpose. Software interrupt: a voltage blip originating from a transistor in the decoder. Hardware interrupt: a voltage blip from an external transistor.

IP ⋆⋆⋆ Integrated Procedure—software equivalent to IC (integrated circuit). See pp. 135–140 for details.

Jargon ⋆ Specialized idioms used by tight-knit groups. In CS all computer languages (including math and graphics) are really machine-readable forms of professional jargons.

Logic language ⋆⋆⋆ (e.g., Prolog) Used to prove programs correct. (Example: Bach is mortal; Everyman is mortal; => Everyman is Bach.)

Management ⋆⋆ Euphemism for running after programmers with time sheets. Will never work because managers don't get to the office until hours after the programmers go home.

Memory dump ★ (Also core dump) Sadistic printout of object code for debugging purposes, aimed at filling vacancies in the cuckoo's nest with programmers.

Message ★★★ Procedure call for a **method**.

Meta ★★★ Very useful prefix in the software trade because it means both "between" and "beyond." Hence, a metaglossary could be a glossary of glossaries or a glossary that didn't make it.

Method ★★★★ Object orientors' Newspeak for procedures.

Methodology ★★★ CS Newspeak for **method**, which is no longer usable except as a replacement for "procedure."

MITI ★★★ Thanks to its similarity to "MIT" (Massachusetts Institute of Technology), the acronym for Japan's Ministry of International Trade and Industry entered our jargon with a noble aura. By now many believe it stands for "Ministry for Imposition of Tilted Infield."

Murphy's law ¹ᐟ²★ Professor Murphy discovered that the concept of entropy applies to mental as well as physical energy. Engineers (who sometimes understand entropy) swear by Murphy—except when they swear at him. You just can't win.

Neologism ★ Words liable to precipitate SIC-ness. ("Yes, truly, that's what this turkey calls it!")

NIST ★★★★¹ᐟ² National Institute for Standards and Technology—a fancy title Congress giveth to the National Bureau of Standards (NBS) as it taketh away the funding.

Object code ★★★ Also called "binary code," this is code after translation from human-readable (sic) into machine-readable form. Since the former is called source code, the logical term would be "sink code."

Object-oriented ★★ Programming method providing procedure inheritance via "classes." (Caution: just adding a superclass "alphanumeric" to Fortran-77 will *not* turn it into Obtran.)

Orthogonal ★★★★ CS term for "independent." (Origin: the *x*-axis and *y*-axis projections of a vector (or wave), which are not independent at all but are just different views of the same thing.)

Overloading ★★★★ CS for "homonymous"—same word with different meanings. Like **short circuit**, "overloading" now has a second meaning. Time to blow a fuse, teach.

Paperless office ★★★★ (1) A mirage created by Madison Avenue to help Wall Street sell Weyerhauser stock. (2) Syn. for the oxymoron "office automation."

Paradigm ★★★ High-faluting CS substitute for "model" or "example"; recently assuming the meaning of "method" or "approach."

Parse ¹/²★ "To break down, giving the form and function of each part" says the dictionary, and that's exactly what a parser does to source code. As jargon, a real flop.

PERT chart ★★ A bubble chart for the "Project Evaluation and Review Technique." Yet another ruse to hide the horrible fact that time is a one-way street.

Platform ★★★ A metal box on which programs can be piled up. (The box usually contains a mighty micro called workstation.)

Petri net ★ (1) Named after its inventor, this expanded state transition diagram supports timing, making it ideal for use with embedded systems. (2) A net for catching Petri dishes.

Place and route ★ Just a descriptive term applied to the stage in hardware design where software places components on a screen and interconnects them under observation of "design rules." Modified P&R programs could be applied to software if represented as **IPs** or equivalent, but that would make life too easy for CS students.

Pointer ★★ Sometimes called "reference," this is actually the storage location of a data object that's known by a symbolic name. Pointer programming restores to HLLs like C the sharpshooter's accuracy that machine-language programmers once mastered.

Predicate ★★★ CS syn. for "assertion." The word was washed ashore after the decomposition of English grammar.

Prototyping ★★ Simulated execution of nonexisting software. If done with hot air and mirrors see **vaporware**.

Quality control ★★ Euphemism for random testing. A growing number of vendors admits to lack of control by renaming the activity "Quality Assurance."

Reverse engineering (also re-engineering) ★★ Attempt to reconstruct a programmer's thinking. Analogous to "unsolving", for example $1 + 1 = 2$, yielding the equation

$$\ln\left[\lim_{z \to \infty}\left(1 + \frac{1}{z}\right)^z\right] + (\sin^2 x + \cos^2 x) = \sum_{n=0}^{\infty} \frac{\cosh y \sqrt{1 - \tanh^2 y}}{2^n}$$

Robustness ★★★ A program that doesn't crash the system when fed anti-data. "Extremely robust": a program that can only be stopped by dynamiting the computer.

Schema ★★ Originally a printer's error in a paper about database schemes. The term was adopted as its flag by DBMS (database management system) activists.

Short-circuit form (in Ada) ★★★★ If the first operand in an `and then` expression evaluates to False, the whole is False. Related to `or else`. (Origin: mistranslation of "shortcut.")

Side effect ★★★ When **aliased** variables cause the modification of a data object bound to a nonlocal variable. Often abused for interprocess communications or to crash a computer.

Simulation ★ Just what it says: a computer pretending to be something else.

Software ★ (1) Computer-readable expression of thoughts. (2) Whatever it takes to make hardware do something useful. Introduced in 1946 by one Merrill Flood to replace "nonhardware" (over objections of General Eisenhower.)

Software engineer ★★★★ (1) DP: A system analyst washed ashore amongst embedded systems. (2) CS: A computer science graduate. (3) A hardware designer fed up with transistor diddling. Only the last bears any semblance to reality.

Software factory ★★★ (1) A PC-AT used for copying floppies; or (2) a Japanese ruse for doubling the number of programmers per square meter of costly floor space.

Softworker ★★★ From German "Softwerker"—Soft: abbreviation of software; Werker: workman. Comprises programmers, analysts, coders, and software engineers under the motto "Softworkers of the world, unite".

Spaghetti code ★★ Created by Cobolites or Dining Philosophers fighting over shared forks. Too descriptive for jargonautics.

State machine ★★★ Originally, "finite state machine" (FSM). The term thus includes a CD or DAT player before the analog filter creates ∞ states. CS: syn. for automaton, which is a syn. for digital computer. If quantum mechanic perseveres, all the world is a FSM—and we are all automata.

Structured ★★★ Data processing version of **elegance**. Originally called GOTO-less programming—good guys fighting **spaghetti code**. COMEFROM was tried without success.

Structogram ★★ European second-order abstraction of a flowchart. Step 1: Remove the flow, leaving a Nassi-Shneiderman chart. Step 2: Remove visual clues (e.g., diagonals) for IFs or CASE, leaving a purely orthogonal table. Thus the structogram easily camouflages as a movie schedule.

Task ★ A software module big enough to perform useful work. Often implies parallelism as in "multitasking." Syn: shtick.

Terminal ★★ (adj.) Final stages of a fatal disease. (noun) A terminal TV set, whose tuner has already expired.

Third normal form ★★★ A relational database from which all redundancies have been expunged. Good jargon because the term means absolutely nothing to an Out.

Typing ★★★★ This short form for "type checking" was an excellent jargon until word processing made "strong typing" (5 carbons) or "weak typing" (unreadable) totally meaningless.

UL label ★ With it, the (insurance) Underwriters Laboratories certify that a gadget will not readily execute its user. Although a software equivalent has been adopted in far-out lands, U.S. hackers are too honest for such a bluff.

Validation ★★★ Process of verifying that a program does what your lawyer thinks it should.

Vaporware ★ Too true to be good as jargon. Industry: announced programs written only after sufficient inquiries. CS: underpinning for theses. Syn: WORN (written once, ran never).

Verification ★★★ To ascertain that all shortcuts in a program's development have been **validated**.

VHDL ★★★ Extract of alphabet soup; stands for VHSIC Hardware Description Language, where VHSIC stands for Very High Speed Integrated Circuits. Needless to say, all the terminology bears the imprint of the Pentagon.

VHLL ★★ Very-HLL; a notch more abstract than an **HLL**. (Apply only to your own group's latest idiom.)

Waterfall diagram ★★ The obvious sequence of events in building something. CS: ultimate curse.

Write-only code ★ (WOC) The software equivalent for write-only memory (WOM). WOC turns into a tame black hole as soon as the originator departs. (Black holes are massive aggregates of [black] IBM cards from which the paper has been removed, leaving only the code. [Source: CS synopsis of *2010: Odyssey two*].)

⸫ References

1. *Abacus*, no. 2, 1987, p. 30.

2. Stan Kelly-Bootle, *The Devil's DP Dictionary*, McGraw-Hill, New York, 1981.

ADDRESS LIST

CSA, see Computer Systems Architects

DACS, see Data & Analysis Center for Software

IDE, see Interactive Development Environment

SES, see Scientific and Engineering Software

SRI, see Software Research Inc.

SPS, see Software Products & Services, Inc.

ACT Corp., 417 Fifth Avenue, 5th Floor, New York, NY 10016 (212-696-3700)

Ada Information Clearinghouse, Room 3D139 (1211 Fem St./C-107), The Pentagon, Washington, DC 20301 (703-685-1477)

Advanced Technology International, 1501 Broadway, Suite 1314, New York, NY 10036 (212-354-8280)

Athena Systems Inc., 139 Kifer Court, Suite 200, Sunnyvale, CA 94086 (408-730-2100)

Atherton Technology, 1333 Bordeaux Drive, Sunnyvale, CA 94089 (408-734-9822)

Bachman Information Systems Inc., 4 Cambridge Center, Cambridge, MA 02142 (617-354-1414)

Borland International, 1800 Green Hills Road, P.O. Box 660001, Scotts Valley, CA 95066-0001 (408-438-8400)

Cadre Technologies Inc., 222 Richmond Street, Providence, RI 02903 (401-351-5950)

Case Consulting Group, 11830 SW Kerr Parkway, Suite 315, Lake Oswego, OR 97035 (503-245-6880)

Cogent Research, 1100 NW Compton Drive, Suite 309, Beaverton, OR 97006 (503-690-1450)

Complete Logic Systems, 741 Blueridge Avenue, North Vancouver, B.C., Canada V7R 2J5 (604-986-3234)

Computer Systems Architects, 950 N. University Avenue, Provo, UT 84604 (801-374-2300)

Context Div., Mentor Graphics Corp., 8285 SW Nimbus Avenue, Beaverton, OR 97005 (503-646-2600)

COSMIC Software Information Services, University of Georgia, Athens, GA 30602 (404-542-3265)

DACS (Data & Analysis Center for Software), Kaman Sciences Corp., P.O. Box 120, Utica, NY 13503 (315-336-0937)

Digital Equipment Corp., CASE Product Marketing, 110 Spit Brook Road, Nashua, NH 03062 (603-881-2505)

Digitalk Inc., 9841 Airport Boulevard, Los Angeles, CA 90045 (213-645-1082)

Electronic Industries Association, 2001 Eye Street NW, Washington, DC 20006 (202-457-4981)

EVB Software Engineering Inc., 5320 Spectrum Drive, Frederick, MD 21701 (301-695-6960)

Expertware Inc., 3235 Kifer Road, Suite 220. Santa Clara, CA 95051 (408-746-0706)

Government Printing Office, Superintendent of Documents, Washington, DC 20402 (202-783-3238)

HALT Americans for Legal Reform, 1319 F Street NW, Washinton, DC 20004

Hamilton Technologies, Inc., 17 Inman Street, Cambridge, MA 02139 (617-492-0058)

IBM Scientific Center, 1530 Page Mill Road, Palo Alto, CA 94303 (415-855-3261)

IEEE Service Center, 445 Hoes Lane, Piscataway, NJ 08855-1331 (201-562-3800)

i-Logix Inc., 22 Third Avenue, Burlington, MA 01803 (617-272-8090)

Imperial Software Technology, 60 Albert Court, Prince Consort Road, London SW7 2BH, England (01-581-8155)

Index Technology Inc., 1 Main Street, Cambridge, MA 02142 (617-494-8200)

InfoPro, Systems, P.O. Box 220, Rescue, CA 95672 (916-677-5870)

Inmos Corp., P.O. Box 16000, Colorado Springs, CO 80935 (719-630-4000)

Intel Scientific Computers, 15201 NW Greenbrier Parkway, Beaverton, OR 97006 (503-629-7777)

Interactive Development Environments, 595 Market Street, 10th Floor, San Francisco, CA 94105 (415-543-0900)

Interactive Software Engineering, Inc., 270 Storke Road, Suite 7, Goleta, CA 93117 (805-685-1006)

Intermetrics Inc., 733 Concord Avenue, Cambridge, MA 02138 (617-661-1840)

Knowledge Systems Corp., 114 MacKenan Drive, Suite 100, Cary, NC 27511 (919-481-4000)

Logicon Strategic and Information Systems, P.O. Box 85158, San Diego, CA 92138-5158 (619-455-1330, Ext. 715)

Mark V Business Systems, 16400 Ventura Boulevard #303, Encino, CA 91436 (818-995-7671)

MaxThink, 44 Rincon Road, Kensington, CA 94707 (415-540-5508)

McCabe & Associates, 5501 Twin Knolls Road, Suite 111, Columbia, MD 21045 (800-638-6316)

Mentor Graphics Corp., 8500 SW Creekside Place, Beaverton, OR 97005-7191 (503-526-4750)

Meta Software Corp., 150 Cambridge Park Drive, Cambridge, MA 02140 (617-576-6920)

MetaSystems, 315 E. Eisenhower Parkway, Suite 200, Ann Arbor, MI 48108 (313-663-6027)

Microelectronics and Computer Technology Corp. (MCC), 3500 West Balcones Center Drive, Austin, TX 78759 (512-343-0978)

Nastec Corp., 24681 Northwestern Highway, Southfield, MI 48075 (313-353-3300)

National Instruments, 12109 Technology Boulevard, Austin, TX 78727-6204 (512-250-9119)

NCube Corp., 1825 NW 167th Place, Beaverton, OR 97006 (503-629-5088)

Netron Inc., 99 St. Regis Crescent North, Downsview, Ontario M3J 1Y9 Canada (416-636-8333)

Ontologic Inc., 3 Burlington Woods, Burlington, MA 01803 (617-272-7110)

Open Software Foundation, 11 Cambridge Center, Cambridge, MA 02142 (617-621-8700)

ParcPlace Systems, 1550 Plymouth Street, Mountain View, CA 94043 (415-691-6700)

Polytron Corp., 1700 NW 167th Place, Beaverton, OR 97006 (800-547-4000)

Production Systems Technologies Inc., 5001 Baum Boulevard, Pittsburgh, PA 15213 (412-362-3117)

Programmer's Shop, 5 Pond Park Road, Hingham, MA 02043 (800-421-8006)

Programming Environments, Inc. (PEI), 4043 State Highway 33, Tinton Falls, NJ 07753 (201-918-0110)

Project Technology, Inc., 2560 Ninth Street, Suite 214, Berkeley, CA 94710 (415-845-1484)

Quintus Computer Systems, Inc., 1310 Villa Street, Mountain View, CA 94041, (415-965-7700)

Rapitech Systems Inc., Montebello Corporate Park, Suffern, NY 10901 (914-368-3000 or 800-FORTRIX)

Rational, 3320 Scott Boulevard, Santa Clara, CA 95054 (408-496-3600)

Ready Systems, 470 Patrero Avenue, Sunnyvale, CA 94086 (408-736-2600)

Reasoning Systems Inc., 3260 Hillview Avenue, Palo Alto, CA 94304 (415-494-6201)

Reifer Consultants Inc., 25550 Hawthorne Boulevard, Suite 208, Torrance, CA 90505 (213-373-8728)

Scandura Intelligent Systems, 1249 Greentree Lane, Narberth, PA 19072 (215-664-1207)

Scientific and Engineering Software, Inc. (SES), 1301 West 25th Street, Suite 300, Austin, TX 78705 (512-474-4526)

Scientific Computing Associates, 246 Church Street, Suite 307, New Haven, CT 06510 (203-777-7442)

Servio Logic Corp., 1420 Harbor Bay Parkway, Suite 100, Alameda, CA 94501 (415-748-6200)

SET Laboratories Inc., P.O. Box 83627, Portland, OR 97283 (503-289-4758)

SofTech Inc., 460 Totten Pond Road, Waltham, MA 02154 (617-890-6900)

Softool Corp., 340 South Kellog Avenue, Goleta, CA 93117 (805-683-5777)

Softstar Systems, 28 Ponemah Road, Amherst, NH 03031 (603-672-0987)

Software Productivity Consortium (SPC), 2214 Rock Hill Road, Herndon, VA 22070 (703-742-7157)

Software Products & Services, Inc., 14 East 38th Street, New York, NY 10016 (212-686-3790)

Software Research Inc. (SRI), 625 Third Street, 4th Floor, San Francisco, CA 94107 (415-957-1441)

Software Systems Design, Inc., 3627 Padua Avenue, Claremont, CA 91711 (714-625-6147)

STARS Repository (of Ada Software) c/o Lavinia Maddox, Naval Research Labs, 4555 Overlook Avenue, Washington, DC 20375 (202-404-7335)

Stepstone Corp., 75 Glen Road, Sandy Hook, CT 06482 (203-426-1875)

Technology Research Group, 2 Park Plaza, Suite 510, Boston, MA 02116 (617-482-4200)

Teledyne Brown Engineering, Systems Analysis and Technology Division, 300 Sparkman Drive, Huntsville, AL 35807 (800-633-4675)

Tuft's University, Computer Science Department, c/o D. Krumme, Medford, MA 02155 (617-381-3652)

Verdix Corp., 14130-A Sullyfield Circle, Chantilly, VA 22021 (703-378-7600)

Wizard Software, 2171 Parfet Court, Lakewood, CO 80227 (303-986-2405)

X/Open Co., 1750 Montgomery Street, San Francisco, CA 94111 (415-773-5383)

Zoo Vaporware Ass., 999 Terminal Street, Nowhere, YZ (800-888-9999)

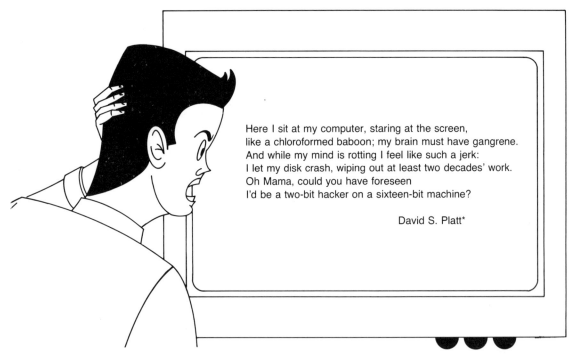

Here I sit at my computer, staring at the screen,
like a chloroformed baboon; my brain must have gangrene.
And while my mind is rotting I feel like such a jerk:
I let my disk crash, wiping out at least two decades' work.
Oh Mama, could you have foreseen
I'd be a two-bit hacker on a sixteen-bit machine?

David S. Platt*

*Reprinted with permission from *Journal of Irreproducible Results*

E

AUTHORS' CROSS-REFERENCE

Italics indicates periodicals. A,C: Appendix A,C.

Author	Chapters	Author	Chapters
Abramowitz, Milton	8	Boehm, Barry	*1*
Ahuja, Sudhir	*19*	Booch, Grady	3, 13
Akima, Noburu	*18*	Borning, Alan	*20*
Amras, J.	*16*	Breton, Thierry	1
Anderson, Gordon	*11*	Brodie, Leo	3
Arthur, Lowell	4	Brooks, Frederick	4, A
Babb, Robert	19	Brown, Judith	5
Babb, Robert	*19*	Brown, Marc	20
Baber, Robert	14	Brown, Marc	*20*
Bachman, Charlie	*16*	Bruen, Mark	*15*
Bailey, Stephen	*12*	Budd, Timothy	12
Baldwin, Roger	*4*	Buhr, R. J. A.	13
Beizer, Boris	15	Byers, James	*18*
Beneich, Denis	1	Carnegie-Mellon	14
Bentley, John	8	Case, Albert	1
Bentley, John	*8*	Ceruzzi, Paul	A
Biggerstaff, Ted	*16*	Chase, Tim	*18*
Birnes, William	3	Chignell, Mark	15
Boar, Bernhard	5	Chikofsky, E. J.	1
Boehm, Barry	4, 15	Christian, Kaare	16

Author	Chapters	Author	Chapters
Chroust, Gerhard	A	Greenberg, Ross	4
Clark, K. L.	12	Grogono, Peter	*12*
Clarke, Arthur	6	Haley, Paul	*12*
Clawson, Harvey	*18*	Hall, Frank E.	*18*
Clocksin, W. F.	12	Hamilton, M.	*13*
Coats, R. B.	8	Harel, David	8
Cole, J. W. P.	3	Harris, Thomas	*4*
Comeau, Greg	*3*	Hart, John	8
Couch, Alva	19	Hatley, Derek	9
Cox, Brad	12	Haviland, Keith	16
Cunningham, Steve	5	Hawking, Stephen	9
Cushman, Bob	*19*	Henson, Noel	*19*
DeMarco, Tom	4, 6	Hersh, Sanford	*8*
DeMillo, Richard	15	Hewitt, C.	*16*
Department of Defense	3	Hinder, Victoria	*1*
Deutsch, Michael	5	Hoare, C. A. R.	19
Deutsch, Michael	*9*	Hoare, C. A. R.	*14*
Dijkstra, Edsger	19	Horn, Berthold	12
Dongarra, Jack	*19*	Howard, Willis	*5*
Drake, Dean	*15*	Howden, William	15
Edwards, H. K.	*7*	Hyman, Anthony	A
Fairley, Richard	4	Inmos Ltd.	19
Fickas, Stephen	*14*	Jazayeri, Mehdi	3
Fiedler, David	*18*	Jensen, Kathleen	3
Fisher, Alan	1, 4	Jones, Capers	4
Fisher, David	*19*	Joyce, Edward	*4*
Foley, James	*20*	Kant, Elaine	*8*
Forgy, Charles	12	Kantowitz, Barry	5
Forte, Gene	1, 4, *9*	Karp, Alan H.	*19*
Friedman, Frank	3	Kelly-Bootle, Stan	C
Gardner, David	*A*	Kernighan, Brian	3
Gehani, Narain	19	Khoushy, Dan	*8*
Gelernter, David	*19*	Knuth, D. E.	8
General Electric	4	Koffman, Elliot	3
Ghezzi, Carlo	3	Konig, Patricia	18
Gibson, Michael	*17*	Kowalski, R. A.	12
Gilman, Leonard	2	Kruger, Gregory	*15*
Gleick, James	15, A	Kull, David	*4*
Glinert, Ephraim	20	Lammers, Susan	4
Goldberg, Adele	12	Landreth, Bill	4
Goldfine, Alan	18	Larmey, Christopher	3
Goldstine, Herman	A	Larson, Harry T.	*4*

Author	Chapters
Law, Averill M.	3
Ledgard, Henry	3
Levesque, John	19
Levine, Harvey	*17*
Liswood, Woody	*4*
Loeckx, Jacques	15
Maibaum, Thomas	5
Manuel, Tom	*4, 18, 19*
Martin, James	6
McAfee, John	*4*
McClure, Carma	6
McLaughlin, Larry	5
Mellish, C. S.	12
Mellor, Stephen	6, 9
Mellor, Stephen	9, 13
Merrow, Tom	*19*
Meyer, Bertrand	12
Meyer, Bertrand	*12*
Meyers, Glenford	15
Mollenhoff, Clark	A
Morrison, Philip	A
Morrison, Ron	4
Moseley, Maboth	A
Mundie, David	*19*
Musa, John	15
Musa, John	*15*
Nabkel, Jafar	*4*
Nelson, Dale	3
Newell, Allen	*8*
Noparstak, Barbara	*12*
O'Day, V.	*16*
O'Toole, K.	*8*
Ooi, Fusatake	*18*
Pagan, Frank	2
Page-Jones, Meilir	6
Parsaye, Kamran	15, 20
Payne, W. H.	*3*
Perrott, R. H.	19
Peters, Tom	4
Pirbhai, Imtiaz	9
Plauger, P. J.	3
Poston, Robert	*15*

Author	Chapters
Pountain, Dick	19
Pressman, Roger	4, 6
Pyle, I. C.	3
Ramamoorthy, C. V.	1
Rich, Charles	16
Rich, Charles	*5*
Richter, Charles	*16*
Ritchie, Dennis	3
Robson, David	12
Roland, Jon	*4*
Roome, William	19
Roscoe, A. W.	19
Rose, Allen	2
Rose, Allen	2
Rosenberg, Jerry	A
Rosenblum, Lawrence	*19*
Ross, D. T.	*6*
Russell, Edward	3
Salama, Ben	16
Schick, Barbara	2
Schindler, Max	*3, 10, 12, 18, 20*
Scott, David	19
Sedgewick, Robert	8
Sharp, John A.	19
Shi-Kuo, Chang	20
Shlaer, Sally	9, 13
Shneiderman, Ben	5
Shriver, Bruce	12
Sieber, Kurt	15
Simonyi, Charles	3
Slater, Robert	1, A
Smith, Anne	*4*
Smith, B.	*16*
Smith, Jim	*4*
Somerville, Ian	4
Sorkin, Robert	5
Stankovic, John	*9*
Stegun, Irene	8
Sterbenz, Pat	8
Stern, Nancy	A
Stroustrup, Bjarne	12
Stroustrup, Bjarne	*12*

INDEX

Terms in italics can also be found in Appendixes C or D.

About the Author

Max J. Schindler graduated as Diplomingenieur (Master's) in Electronics from the Technische Hochschule Wien, Austria (Vienna Technical University) and stayed on as a teaching assistant. He was awarded a Doctor of Technical Sciences Summa Cum Laude in Solid State Physics in 1953. In the course of his thesis work he also obtained three patents. He then served as Department Engineer in the Tungsram tube plant in Vienna and after three years joined the Aeronautical Research Lab in Dayton, Ohio as a Research Scientist.

Schindler transferred to RCA in 1958 and worked both at the Harrison, New Jersey Microwave Division and the David Sarnoff Research Center in Princeton. He led design groups for several advanced devices which required computer modeling. Schindler wrote software for modeling magnetic focusing fields for microwave tubes, followed by programs for the design of traveling-wave tubes and of solid-state circuits. The self-optimizing version of the latter, called COSMIC, is still in use and gained Schindler an RCA Engineering Award.

After the Microwave Operation closed in 1975, Schindler founded Prime Technology Inc., serving as a computer consultant and as software editor for Electronic Design. The latter activity led to two Jesse Neal awards for excellence in technical writing.

Schindler is a Senior Member of the IEEE and served as North Jersey Section Chairman in 1974/75, for which he obtained the IEEE Centennial medal. He is listed in American Men and Women of Science and Who's Who in the Computer Industry.